D1570253

THE EUROPEAN UNION AND THE CULTURE
INDUSTRIES

The European Union and the Culture Industries
Regulation and the Public Interest

Edited by

DAVID WARD

ASHGATE

Published by
Ashgate Publishing Limited
Gower House
Croft Road
Aldershot
Hampshire GU11 3HR
England

Ashgate Publishing Company
Suite 420
101 Cherry Street
Burlington, VT 05401-4405
USA

Ashgate website: http://www.ashgate.com

British Library Cataloguing in Publication Data
The European Union and the culture industries : regulation
    and the public interest
    1. Mass media - Law and legislation - European Union
    countries 2. Mass media policy - European Union countries
    3. Information society - European Union countries 4. Public
    policy (Law) - European Union countries 5. Public
    broadcasting - Law and legislation - European Union
    countries
    I. Ward, David, 1966-
    343.2'4099

Library of Congress Cataloging-in-Publication Data
The European Union and the culture industries : regulation and the public interest / edited
by David Ward.
    p. cm.
    Includes index.
    ISBN 978-0-7546-7018-6
    1. Mass media--Law and legislation--European Union countries. 2. Mass media policy--
European Union countries. 3. Information society--European Union countries. 4. Public
policy (Law)--European Union countries. 5. Public broadcasting--Law and legislation--
European Union countries. I. Ward, David, 1966-

    KJE6946.E97 2008
    343.2409'9--dc22

                                                                    2007037050

ISBN 978-0-7546-7018-6

Printed and bound in Great Britain by MPG Books Ltd, Bodmin, Cornwall.

Contents

List of Cases and Council Decisions

List of Directives and Regulations

Notes on Contributors

Monica Ariño is a Policy Advisor for Ofcom's international team. She graduated in law at the Autonoma University (Madrid) and in 2005 obtained a PhD from the European University Institute (Florence). Monica has specialized in communications regulation, competition law and convergence policies, with a focus on the audiovisual sector. She is particularly interested in how regulators are responding to regulatory challenges associated with new media platforms such as the Internet and mobile technologies. She has published widely and has been a visiting scholar at the Universities of Oxford and Columbia (New York). Prior to joining Ofcom, Monica was a lecturer at Central European University (Budapest).

Maurizio Borghi holds degrees in social sciences and in philosophy as well as a PhD in economic history. He is a Research Fellow at Bocconi University of Milan, where he teaches intellectual property law and philosophy. Maurizio has been a visiting scholar at the Center for the Study of Law and Society, University of California, Berkeley and has published a book on the history of copyright and the book trade in Italy and articles on intellectual property, access to knowledge and legal theory.

Oliver Carsten Füg is a Research Fellow and PhD candidate at the Centre for Regulatory Governance in the Department of Politics at the University of Exeter. He holds degrees in political science and European studies from the Universities of Copenhagen and Bonn and specializes in communications law and policy of the European Union. His main interests are in content regulation and media concentration in the context of convergence and the relationship between competition law and sector-specific regulation in the audiovisual industry. He has been involved in media and telecommunications related studies and consulting projects for the European Commission, the European Parliament, the Commissariaat voor de Media (together with David Ward) and several industry actors.

Alison Harcourt is Senior Lecturer in Politics at the University of Exeter. Before joining the University of Exeter in 2004, she held research positions at the European University Institute, University of Oxford, the University of Manchester and the University of Warwick, and was Visiting Fellow at the Max Planck Institute for Common Goods in Bonn. She holds a PhD from the University of Manchester, Department of Government. Alison has acted as media expert for the European institutions and national governments. She has published widely on the subject of European Union media policy including her recent book *European Union Institutions and the Regulation of Media Markets* (2006, Manchester: Manchester University Press).

Anna Herold holds a PhD from the Law Department of the European University Institute in Florence. She is currently a policy officer at the European Commission (Directorate General for Information Society and Media, Audiovisual and Media Policies Unit), where she is dealing with the implementation and development of European Union audiovisual policy. She worked previously as a case-handler in the Directorate General for Competition in the media anti-trust division. She has published on issues relating to European Union audiovisual law and policy, competition and WTO law and their impact on cultural diversity.

Beata Klimkiewicz is Assistant Professor at the Institute of Journalism and Social Communication, the Jagiellonian University, Cracow, Poland. She received her PhD from the Institute of Political Sciences, Jagiellonian University and studied at the Oxford University and the Columbia University. Since 2000, she has been a member of the Advisory Panel of Experts on Freedom of Religion and Belief for OSCE. She has co-operated with Open Society Institute in Budapest, Media Diversity Institute in London, Peace Institute in Ljubljana and provided an expertise for the European Parliament and Council of Europe. Since 2006, she has been a member of the Steering Committee of COST Action A30 *East of West: Setting a New Central and Eastern European Media Research Agenda*. Recent research interests include media pluralism and diversity, media policy in Europe, media reform in Central Europe, media representations of minorities and minority media.

Carles Llorens is a Lecturer on Media Policy and Economics at the Communications Faculty at Autonomous University of Barcelona. He was an academic visitor at the Centre for Socio-Legal Studies and PCMLP (University of Oxford) from March 2006 to January 2007. He obtained a PhD in audiovisual communications at the Autonomous University of Barcelona in 2001. He won a Marie Curie Fellowship from the European Union's 4th Framework Programme for Research and Development. He was assigned as a pre-doctoral researcher to CRID (Centre de Recherches Informatique et Droit), University of Namur (Belgium) from 1996 to 1998, where his research topic was media and telecommunications regulatory convergence. His current interests include a focus on European media policy, and competition media policy and public service television in particular.

Tarlach McGonagle holds an LLM degree in International Human Rights Law (University of Essex, 2001). He joined the Institute for Information Law (IViR) of the University of Amsterdam in 2001 and has worked there since in editorial and research capacities. He is currently completing his PhD thesis on the interface between freedom of expression and minority rights under international law. He regularly advises and provides reports for the Council of Europe and was one of the independent experts involved in the drafting – at the invitation of the OSCE High Commissioner on National Minorities – of a set of international Guidelines on the use of Minority Languages in the Broadcast Media (2003). He has published widely on international media law, freedom of expression and minority rights and is a regular contributor to publications issued by the European Audiovisual Observatory in Strasbourg, including on such topics as political debate and the media; co-regulation of the media; jurisdiction over broadcasters; existing regulatory frameworks and the new media.

Maria Lillà Montagnani holds a degree in Law and PhD in Competition Law and is Assistant Professor for Commercial Law at Bocconi University of Milan, where she teaches intellectual property law and marketing and the law. Her recent research focuses on the intersection between intellectual property law and competition law in the digital environment and the software market, subjects on which she has published articles in Italian and European reviews.

Rostam J. Neuwirth is Assistant Professor at the Faculty of Law of the University of Macau. Previously he was a visiting Professor at the West Bengal National University of Juridical Sciences in Kolkata (India) and a former Professor at Hidayatullah National Law University in Raipur (India) where he taught European Union Law and the Law of the World Trade Organization (WTO). Rostam has also worked for the International Law Bureau/Dept. I.4 (European Law) of the Federal Ministry for Foreign Affairs in Austria. Following his studies in Austria and France, Rostam gained an LLM from the Institute of Comparative Law at McGill University and a PhD in Law from the European University Institute in Florence. He has published a number of monographs and articles in international journals on various aspects related to the issue of trade and culture focusing particularly on NAFTA, WTO and the European Union's approach to the culture industries.

Seamus Simpson is a Principal Lecturer at the Department of Information and Communications, Faculty of Humanities, Law and Social Science, Manchester Metropolitan University, UK. His research interests lie in European and global communications policy and regulation, areas in which he has published widely. He is author of two books: *Globalisation, Convergence and European Telecommunications Regulation* (2005, Edward Elgar) (with Peter Humphreys, University of Manchester) and *The New Electronic Marketplace: European Governance Strategies in a Globalising Economy* (2007, Edward Elgar) (with George Christou, University of Warwick).

David Ward has a wide range of interests in media policy, law and development and has been an advisor on a range of media issues for numerous government and non-governmental organizations. David has published three books on various aspects of communications policy (2002, 2004 and 2007) and most recently completed an edited book entitled *Television and Public Policy: Change and Continuity in an Era of Global Liberalization* (Lawrence Erlbaum, 2007).

Lorna Woods is Professor of Law at the School of Law, City University. Her research is focused in two main areas: the law of the European Union, especially the internal market; and broadcasting regulation, particularly at the European level – that is, both European Union and Council of Europe. These areas are linked, as much of the EC broadcasting law is based on the rules relating to provision of services; there are clear parallels between the two European systems as regards broadcasting, as well as the impact of human rights considerations in this area. She has published in leading interdisciplinary journals and those relating to communications as well as law journals in these fields such as Entertainment Law Review, as well as in highly respected, peer reviewed academic publications (International and Comparative Law Quarterly; British Year Book of International Law). She has also published a number of books including *EU Law* (9th Ed) (2006, Oxford University Press) (with Jo Steiner, Christian Twigg-Flesner); *Free Movement of Goods & Services within the European Community* (Ashgate European Business Law Series) and *European Broadcasting Law and Policy* (2006, Cambridge University Press).

Acknowledgement

I would like to thank Emily Gibson for all of her enthusiasm, comments and ideas whilst copy editing the manuscript.

Introduction

David Ward

The evolution of the European Union (EU) as both an economic and political project aiming to combine the resources of a group of nation states has had some profound consequences on certain aspects of the legal and regulatory systems of its member states. Important industrial and social regulatory issues that represent core functions of the traditional nation state have to a degree been transferred to combine the political, economic and social resources of a group of nation states to provide for a coherent regional bloc that is seen to generally bring about greater benefits for business, consumers and citizens. Today the EU's mandate covers a huge array of areas including important aspects of the culture industries that is the focus of this volume. The growth of the EU's mandate into new areas such as the audiovisual sector has not been unproblematic, as historically these industries have been the sole regulatory responsibility of the member states. Aligning the audiovisual and telecommunications industries to the principles of the common market, given the inherent contradictions in the culture industries and their role in cultural, social and economic spheres of life, has not been without its difficulties. Nevertheless the growth of regulatory mechanisms at the EU level and the nature of these instruments have, to some extent, brought about a partial re-configuration of regulatory parameters and the distribution of regulatory responsibilities as member states comply with the obligations established in the EC Treaty and the principles of the internal market framework and the European Commission (EC), as the guardian of the Treaty, seeks to ensure compliance across a range of industries to its principles and rules.

The culture industries are also an important reference point for gauging broader policy initiatives of the EU and assessing the success or failure of the policy instruments that have been developed by the European institutions and is a key litmus test for EU policy as the communications sector represents one of the most challenging policy domains that the EU has entered. Not only are the audiovisual and telecommunications industries undergoing significant changes in a dynamic sector brought about by innovation in technical delivery capacity, but also the culture industry is an area that has been central to a range of debate about national cultures and the impact of the growth of the EU on the sovereignty of the member states. This is especially so concerning the liberalization of the television and telecommunications industries over the last 20 years that has seen significant structural changes in both sectors. The EU is seen as a central agent of change in these developments and its influence on the regulatory structures of the communications sectors has been much debated, but rarely put in context of the full range of activities that today the institutions of the EU policy framework covers.

These legal and regulatory instruments that have developed at an EU level have been shaped by a range of factors which leads to a complex process of policy development (Nugent 1999; Wallace 1990). These challenging policy dynamics are compounded in an increasingly complicated sector like the communications one that appears to be continuously developing challenges for regulators as mediums such as the Internet proliferate across the region testing traditional regulatory instruments and forcing legislators to rethink modes of regulation.

This should not detract from the increasing importance of the EU sphere for the communications sector. Areas that were strictly off limits to the EU have become important policy domains and the range of activities it undertakes in the sphere of the culture industry has increased to cover copyright, media concentration, the protection of minors, international trade, and content stimulation in the television and film sectors and even the funding of public service broadcasters. Underpinning many of the themes in the following chapters is a sense that the EU has developed a wide range of regulatory capacity in the audiovisual and telecommunications sectors as the EC's regulatory mandate has been increasingly justified by the European Court of Justice in numerous judgments that recognize that the culture industry is not only part of the social and cultural landscape of the member states but also a key economic activity carried out for remuneration. On the other hand, there is also a sense of how fragile and restricted the EU regulatory framework is as it pushes the limits of its institutional mandate and consensus between the member states.

Imperfect regulatory measures that have been employed at EU level or at least an incomplete framework that lacks important tools for accounting for public policy objectives in the culture industries appears to characterize EC policy in this field. Furthermore, the EU is increasingly relying on a policy development framework that falls short of traditional methods for developing policy in this field as the EU turns to soft law (see Harcourt, Chapter 1) to resolve the possibility of sclerosis in its policy development as it approaches areas that the member states show little enthusiasm in ceding to the EU policy framework.

The uniqueness of the audiovisual industry and its dual nature as an economic and cultural phenomenon means that policy development must strike a balance between contrasting priorities and, at times, conflicts between trade and culture (see Neuwirth, Chapter 11). The EC has not been unsuccessful in achieving this balance to some degree in certain areas and although it has employed essentially economic instruments to balance the economic and cultural nature of the sector a level of protection has been introduced. Essentially economic and liberalizing concepts designed to ensure the functioning of an internal market, as a key pillar of integration established in the Treaty, are not always easily aligned to the historical policy framework that has evolved in individual member states and they are not in themselves sufficient to ensure public interest objectives are achieved in this vital sector for European societies and economies (see Herold, Chapter 2). This is particularly the case for the audiovisual sector where institutions such as public service broadcasters and public support mechanisms such as those enjoyed by the film sector receive large sums of public finance usually dressed up in arguments about national culture and the role of the media in democracy. The complexities are further increased by the architecture of the EU itself as it is composed of policy making processes whose design, all things being equal, is inextricably stamped with a trade off between the terms of the EC Treaty and national interests. Policies at EU level are characterized by different conceptual models of media policy that produce potentially negative and productive results. This is no more evident than in the EC's initial approach to the question of media pluralism on a Community level. The stakes have increased with the challenges of enlargement of the EU to provide a framework for new members to align their legal frameworks to the *acquis*, a theme explored by Klimkiewicz in Chapter 4.

Simpson (Chapter 5) provides an analysis of the evolution of the telecommunications framework in the EU in an industry that he argues is the most Europeanized and developed of all the sectors covered by this edited volume. Although Simpson acknowledges a degree of success in policy initiatives in this area, he also concludes with a key point made in all of the following chapters: that EU policy is incomplete and faced with a series of challenges in future years to provide an adequate framework for the legal and regulatory environment in a highly dynamic and increasingly complex industry. These challenges are no more so in the area of convergence as outlined in Chapter 6 by Ariño and Llorens in their analysis of the questions posed for EU regulation in regulating and establishing a legal framework in an increasingly converged multi-media experience. The speed of convergence and the revolutionary changes to the communications industry identified in the Bangemann Report into the so-called global information society in the 1990s (EC 1994) may not have matched its authors' expectations, but it is nevertheless, a powerful force for change in the sector as data compression technologies and more flexible consumption patterns emerge from traditional models of one to many communications.

A key argument put forward by Ariño and Llorens in this respect, is that new modes of regulation offer more attuned instruments to solve regulatory problems in an increasingly converged industry particularly in the area of content. These regulatory solutions, however, can not in themselves provide solutions to the problems that justify state regulation in the sector and chapter seven by Lorna Woods takes up the issue of jurisdiction – one of the most contentious areas of EC policy where grey areas abound between both what constitutes a service and therefore falls within the provisions of the Television without Frontiers Directive and its long awaited revision in the Audiovisual Media Services Directive[1] as well as a clear definition as to which jurisdiction is responsible for applying regulation in the audiovisual field.

The question of EU content regulation is taken up in Chapters 8, 9 and 10 as the authors provide an analysis of three different areas of content regulation. In chapter 8, Füg describes the development of EU policy in the area of the protection of minors and specifically the EC's response to cross-border and cross-platform content ratings and labelling systems. McGonagle in chapter 9 outlines the development of the highly debated quota issue established in the Television without Frontiers Directive and concludes that despite the quota now enjoying a largely unquestioned position in the Directive's revision, the regulatory rationale underlying the quota

---

1   Directive 2007/65/EC of the European Parliament and of the Council of 11 December 2007 amending Council Directive 89/552/EEC on the coordination of certain provisions laid down by law, regulation or administrative action in member states concerning the pursuit of television broadcasting activities, OJ L332/27 of 18 December 2007.

lacks imagination and rather than approach the key issues of promoting European works tends to be tied to political arguments about cultural policy and the protection of the media sector against a perceived threat from US industry. The final chapter dealing with content issues is Chapter 10 by Montagnani and Borghi on copyright protection. Copyright is in many respects central to all of the issues discussed in this book and the question as to how best establish an adequate legal framework both for creative work that enables a space to be guaranteed between exploiting creativity economically, but at the same time maintaining a climate whereby society has access to a broad range of resources and creativity and this is not stifled by either purely market imperatives and mechanisms or over regulation by member states and the EU. The final chapter by Neuwirth (Chapter 11) sums such a dilemma up when discussing the conflict between trade and culture, a dilemma inherent in the contemporary market economies of the EU and made increasingly difficult due to the dual nature of the audiovisual industries and their perceived role as serving both the social and cultural needs of member states but also playing a key part in their economies: a contradiction that will only prove more difficult with the diffusion of new technologies and the increasing growth of global capitalism.

The EU's policy bodies, as are the institutions responsible for policy development in the member states, are faced with major regulatory questions in the next few years. The magnitude of these issues is reflected in the development of the revised Television without Frontiers Directive, the flagship of EU instruments in the audiovisual sector. In the recent revision of the Directive, parts of the original provisions that have been carried through to the new Audiovisual Media Services Directive look redundant, whilst other parts apparently proposed to take on board questions of convergence in the industry have met with resistance from the member states. In a similar vein, the EU's approach to copyright protection is incomplete and lacks a comprehensive approach to the legal foundations to protect copyright and will need to be overhauled to provide a satisfactory framework. The Directives are the most visible of instruments in the media sector, however, there are other key areas where the role of the EC will be crucial in the forthcoming years. The EC have engaged in a wide range of activities related to the audiovisual sector and the Treaty encompasses broader issues such as state aid and market behaviour and these areas are becoming increasingly complex as the traditional boundaries that have characterized the audiovisual and telecommunications industries blur.

In this respect, the EC has clearly experienced difficulties in developing a satisfactory framework for the regulation of the communications industry beyond competition policy issues, or as Scharpf has argued a capacity for negative integration and lack of positive measures (Scharpf 1996). The EU's complex structure of policy development and its institutions, together with a restricted mandate based on the EC Treaty have proved burdensome in a highly dynamic industry. The trade offs between member states and their role in shaping EU policy instruments and the architecture of the EU itself together with the EU's overarching objectives established in the Treaty are not perhaps the most suitable foundations for the regulation of the communications industry. Nevertheless, the EC has found novel ways to push through policy instruments and where there has been a failure to develop satisfactory regulatory tools taking account of a broad number of issues the EC relies upon member states to ensure public interest objectives are met, or more precisely under the principle of subsidiarity the member states retain the right to impose measures that go beyond those established in the Treaty. The key question is how effective is such a regime and to what extent it is able to provide for a satisfactory regulatory framework that allows commercial interests and market functionality and the public interest to be balanced in a sustainable manner at both member state and EU levels. As the following chapters demonstrate, the EC is faced with huge challenges in the next years to both retain its position as a policy initiator and ensure the provisions of the Treaty are respected in a sector that poses profound regulatory challenges.

References

European Commission (1992), *Pluralism and Media Concentration in the Internal Market: An Assessment of the Need for Community Action, Commission Green Paper*, COM(92) 480 final, Brussels.

European Commission (1994), *Europe and the Global Information Society. The Bangemann Report.*

European Commission (2007), Commission Staff Working Document: Media Pluralism in the Member States of the European Union, SEC(2007) 32, Brussels.

European Parliament (2000), *Report on the Communication from the Commission to the Council, the European Parliament, the Economic and Social Committee and the Committee of the Regions Principles and guidelines for the Community's audiovisual policy in the digital age*, COM(1999) 657 – C5-0144/2000 – 2000/2087(COS), Final A5-0209/2000, of 18 July 2000.

Nugent, N. (1999), *The Government and Politics of the European Union*. Basingstoke: Macmillan Press.

Scharpf, F. (1996), 'Negative and Positive Integration in the Political Economy of European Welfare States', Marks, G., et al. (eds), *Governance in the European Union*, London: Sage, 15–39.

Wallace, W. (ed.) (1990), *The Dynamics of European Integration*. London: Pinter, for The Royal Institute for International Affairs.

Chapter 1

Institutionalizing Soft Governance in the European Information Society

Alison Harcourt

The use of 'new' or 'soft' governance by European Union (EU) institutions has expanded dramatically in recent years. Soft governance is seen as a way to bypass political stagnation to further European integration presented by the traditional Community method. The traditional Community method refers to legislation initiated by the European Commission (EC), for example, directives, regulations, recommendations and decisions, and ratified by the Council of Ministers and the European Parliament (EP). The policies covered by the traditional method have been mapped out by, and expanded through subsequent EU Treaties (namely the 1957 Rome Treaty, the 1987 Single European Act, 1992 Maastricht Treaty, 1997 Amsterdam Treaty and 2001 Nice Treaty).

By contrast, 'soft governance' refers to non-binding agreements made between participating actors established outside the Community method. Policy is agreed upon in 'soft' policy fora, for example, EU committees, national regulatory authorities (NRAs) and industrial fora. In what is termed 'committee governance', market rules are agreed within committees of the EU usually in consultation with national experts and/or industry representatives. Similar agreements are made within NRA platforms through best practice and policy coordination. Self-regulation is agreed within fora representing industry.

The present trend is towards the institutionalization of soft governance by the European institutions. In this way, the EU has been able to overcome impasses at more formal levels and make progress in key policy areas such as the information society. Since Lisbon, the Council of Ministers has established open method of coordination (OMC) committees, which govern the eEurope initiative. In parallel, there has been a proliferation in EC committee governance in information society policy. The Directorate General for Information Society (DG Info Soc) operated 72 committees in 2006 alone. In addition, the EU has embedded financial provision for the establishment of European-level NRA platforms into legislative packages such as the Regulatory Framework for Communications, which agree on sector rules in coordination with the EC. In line with this, 'co-regulation' has been introduced at the European level wherein rules agreed upon by self-regulatory bodies are formalized through (soft or hard) legal instruments and overseen by co-regulatory fora. This chapter investigates soft governance in information society policy. It argues that the use of soft initiatives has further anchored a technocratic style of governance within this particular policy sector.

Institutionalizing Soft Governance

In the mid-1990s, European integration hit a lull. Following a regulatory surge in the 1980s, by 1992 the production of legislation by European institutions had slowed considerably due to resistance from member states concerned with red tape, implementation costs and resistance to increased political integration. At the 1992 European Council in Edinburgh, member states formally agreed to slow the growth in policy by limiting the number of initiatives per year. The political emphasis turned to subsidiarity and flexibility as was formalized later that year by the Maastricht Treaty. By 1997, only seven new directives were passed by the EU in a single year. The move was towards move effective and better regulation. A programme to monitor and accelerate policy implementation based upon the Sutherland reports was produced during the mid-1990s. This was followed by a series of action plans initiated at the 1997 European Council in Amsterdam. In preparation for the Lisbon Council, the Mandelkern Group (consisting of ministers for public administration) introduced the 'better regulation' agenda at the EU level, which became a core component of the Lisbon agenda. This was followed by the 'better lawmaking' Action Plan, which undertook to 'legislate less but better' (European Commission 2002a). The European Convention on Institutional reform, following the Laeken Declaration, established a working group on the simplification of instruments and procedures. The working group recommended to the European Convention that the EU concentrate on implementation and simplification of existing EU law rather than the production of new legislation. The aim of 'better regulation' is to slim down existing rules and remove administrative burdens through cost effective regulation. At this time, 'regulatory impact assessments' were introduced at the European level.

Faced with this political mandate, the European institutions turned to 'new' or 'soft' governance to overcome impasses to regulatory expansion.[1] At the 2000 Lisbon Summit, the European Council proposed the use of soft governance in application to policy areas not covered by the *acquis communitaire*. It introduced the OMC method in an explanatory memorandum following the Lisbon meeting. The OMC method was to be utilized in six policy areas that include information society policy.[2] The Council identified EU information society policy as covering broadband, e-business, e-government, e-health, e-inclusion, e-learning and security policies. The OMC was designed to coordinate member states' policies through benchmarking, setting guidelines, targets and timetables, peer review monitoring and information exchange. Specifically, the explanatory memorandum stated that the OMC was responsible for:

- Fixing guidelines for the EU combined with specific timetables for achieving the goals which they set in the short, medium and long term

---

1　　This has been discussed extensively in the academic literature (Heritier 2001; De La Porte 2002; Scott and Trubeck 2002).

2　　The six policy areas are: the information society, research and development (R&D), enterprises, economic reforms, education, employment and social inclusion.

- Establishing, where appropriate, quantitative and qualitative indicators and benchmarks against the best in the world and tailored to the needs of different member states and sectors as a means of comparing good practices
- Translating these European guidelines into national and regional policies by setting specific targets and adopting measures, taking into account national and regional differences
- Periodic monitoring, evaluation and peer review organized as mutual learning processes; and
- A fully decentralized approach to be applied in line with the principle of subsidiarity in which the EU, the member states, the regional and local levels, as well as the social partners and civil society, will be actively involved, using varied forms of partnership. A method of benchmarking good practices on managing change will be devised by the EC networking with different providers and users, namely the social partners, companies and NGOs.[3]

Significantly, the Lisbon meeting set up the Information Society Project, which aims to create a dynamic 'knowledge-based economy with more and better employment and social cohesion' by 2010 (i2010 initiative). It named key issues such as e-government, e-democracy, e-voting, e-learning, e-culture, e-health, e-banking, e-education, e-media, e-security, e-business, e-commerce and so on.[4] The idea for the e-initiatives had actually come from the EC, which was preparing the ground for the launch of its eEurope initiative.[5] The following year, the Council published its 2005 eEurope Action Plan (2002b) under the OMC method.

The EC interpreted the OMC as a political move by the Council to encroach upon its own policy-making powers. This is because the OMC method is executed within the European Council, thereby bypassing the EC and EP.[6] This interpretation is more than evident in the EC's 2001 White Paper on European Governance, which responded to the Lisbon Summit. The Paper recognizes the difficulties with traditional EC policy-making methods but insists on the continued use of the Community method, which has proved essential for European integration. If alternative methods are developed, it argued, it should be chiefly the EC, not the Council of Ministers, which should advance new approaches to governance. In particular, it objected to the use of OMC in areas already covered by the *acquis communitaire*, which would include information society policy.

3　European Council, Lisbon European Council Presidency Conclusions (23–24 March 2000), http://www.consilium.europa.eu/ueDocs/cms_Data/docs/pressData/en/ec/00100-r1.en0. htm, para. 37.

4　On e-voting see Kies 2002. For e-learning see Noam 1998.

5　The Lisbon European Council Presidency Conclusions gave recognition to the eEurope proposal.

6　In the traditional 'Community method', the Commission has a monopoly over the right of initiative, the Council of Ministers and EP adopt proposals, member states implement under observation of the EC that may refer a state to the ECJ. Under the OMC method, the European Council initiates, the national strategies of each member state are implemented by the state, and the EC can only coordinate and make recommendation to the member state.

But the 2001 White Paper is both reactive and opportunistic. The Lisbon agenda presented the EC a window of opportunity to enlarge its own regulatory sphere through the use of soft governance. DG Info Soc has long engaged in soft approaches to governance. The Lisbon agenda and the OMC greatly provided political *legitimacy* and *expansion* of these types of initiatives. With its White Paper, the EC embraced the i2010 initiative and commenced upon its eEurope programme. Since Lisbon, a growing number of committees have been operating within and around the European institutions dealing with information society policy.

Committee Governance

Research into committee governance is challenging. EU committees have for a long time operated invisibly. Within the EC, the names of experts and their nationalities are not publicized due to privacy laws. Their identity is unknown and there is no public information as to who is represented. In addition, procedures for their consultation are complex. Authors have argued that the system of committee governance and comitology is opaque and undemocratic and is undermining the role of the legislature (the EP) and distorting representation in the EU (Kohler-Koch 1998; Maurer and Larsson 2002). Empirical studies however have pointed to the high level of consensus found in committee governance, which has led to a greater capacity for harmonization and ultimately closer European Union (Dehousse 2003).

Parallels between committee governance and technocratic governance can be drawn. Technocratic governance is recognized as a process taking place in relative isolation from public debate (Rhodes 1988; Jordan and Richardson 1979). A technocratic policy process is best administered by a closely knit policy community which is hampered by the active involvement of MEPs, the media, national political parties, regions, and/or citizens. Politicization of a policy initiative and democratic processes are seen as inefficient and could lead to the loss of support of industry as well. Technocratic policy-making is seen to lead to an increase in efficiency, but accountability may be lost in the process. Hence, the embrace of committee governance represents an easy transition from existing technocratic procedures.

The EC categorizes committees as: 'comitology committees', 'policy-making committees', 'social dialogue committees' and 'joint committees'. Comitology committees are committees responsible for the implementation of EU legislation. Policy-making committees are committees that operate within the EC. Social dialogue committees are fora for dialogue between industry and civil society representatives and joint committees are committees established by the EC through international and bilateral treaty negotiation.[7]

Comitology Committees

Comitology committees are used for overseeing EC implementation of directives. Once adopted, EU legislation is implemented by the EC. However, the Council

---

7   There were 170 such 'joint' committees in 2004.

retains control through so-named 'comitology committees', which consist of Council-appointed experts from the member states which approve the EC's proposals for implementation. The committees must follow procedures, referred to as 'comitology', as outlined in the Comitology Decision (1999/468/EC) of 28 June 1999. There are three types of comitology committees: advisory, management and regulatory committees, which operate according to the 'Standard Rules of Procedure' laid out by the EC in January 2001.[8]

The EP has long argued that comitology undermines the role of the EP and thereby deepens the democratic deficit in the EU (Hix 2000; Dehousse 2003). The Parliament has lobbied for greater representation of the EP in committee decision making. Some changes have been made particularly following the *Rothmans* Court of First Instance ruling[9] (Dehousse 2003, 808). This promoted the 1999 Comitology Decision, which introduced greater transparency by making documents publicly available and providing an annual report on committee meetings. However, it only publishes documents which are approved for the 'public repository' (that is, COM, C and SEC documents). These are also the only papers that the EP is permitted to view. The 1999 Decision allows the EP to a 'right of scrutiny' on draft implementation papers and can express 'disapproval' by any changes to legislation made by the EC and Council in the comitology (implementation) stage. (However, the EP often argues that this role is so minor as to be negligible). Agendas are only made available to the public at the end of the year. Committee membership and opinions remain anonymous. Subsequent pressure for transparency (see below) led to the establishment of an online 'comitology register' in 2005.[10] The comitology register does not list comitology committees as such but provides information on agendas of comitology committee meetings, draft implementing measures, committee minutes and voting results.

In its 2001 White Paper on European Governance, the EC requested amendments to the comitology procedure and questioned the need for 'management' and 'regulatory' committees. However, the 2004 draft of the Constitutional Treaty declares in Article I 35 that it is 'the Commission's intention to continue to consult experts appointed by the Member States …, in accordance with its established practice'. Hence, the comitology procedure is well ingrained and there is little impetus for institutional change.[11] The EP gained further ground with the last comitology revision in July 2006 with the EP being given the right to veto an adoption of legislation with a majority of members.[12]

---

8   OJ C38/3 of 6 February 2001, p. 3.

9   Rothmans International BV v. Commission of the European Communities T-188/97 [1999] ECR II-02463 (CFI). Commission Decision 94/90/ECSC, EC, Euratom on public access to Commission documents – Decision refusing access to documents – 'Rule on authorship' – 'Comitology' committees.

10   EUROPA, http://europa.eu.int/comm/secretariat_general/regcomito/.

11   The EP did however gain an advisory role in OMC committees from 2001.

12   Council Decision of 17 July 2006 amending Decision 1999/468/EC laying down the procedures for the exercise of implementing powers conferred on the Commission (2006/512/ EC).

Policy-Making Committees

Only recently did the EC take some steps towards greater transparency of committee governance. Lobbying by members of the Parliament have been flanked by European-level lobbying groups such as Alter-EU (Alliance for Lobbying Transparency and Ethics Regulation),[13] EPACA (European Public Affairs Consultancies Association),[14] SEAP (the Society of European Affairs Professionals)[15] and AALEP (Association of Accredited Lobbyists to the EP). Other interested parties, particularly from the UK, such as the UK Consumers' Association and UK House of Lord's European Communities Committee, have long stressed the overwhelming need for committee visibility. A significant push came post-2003 from the new accession states, which have greatly been influenced by American thinking on transparency. Interestingly, some leading German academic lawyers, such as Neyer, Jörges, Sand, Voss and Teubner, have argued against this, stating that the introduction of an 'American style Administrative Act' is faulted as it would hinder quality and efficiency in committee decision making (Jörges and Neyer 1997, 247; Jörges, Sand and Teubner 2005; Jörges and Voss 1999). Academic debate aside, steps were finally taken to make the process at least more visible.

In 2004, pressure from the EP resulted in a commitment from the EC president, Barroso, to make public a database of expert committees. In September 2005, the EC made public its list of formal and informal expert groups, which is available through a searchable database online.[16] The database lists the 'policy making committees' which advise the EC according to the rules on expert groups.[17] The list gives details of the committees and their role and classifies members according to categories (for example competent national authorities, national administrations, scientists, academics, partitions, NGOs, industry representatives, and so on). Some documents and meeting minutes are published online. However, names of those on committees are not published and the database excludes independent experts. The list is divided into 'formal groups', which are set up by EU legislation (for example in a decision or a directive); 'informal groups', which are set up by the EC DGs; 'permanent groups', which have existed for more than five years and 'temporary groups' which are set up *ad hoc* for a specific task (lasting less than five years).

---

13   ALTER-EU is a 'coalition of over 140 civil society groups, trade unions, academics and public affairs firms, calling for EU lobbying disclosure legislation, an improved code of conduct for European Commission Officials, the EC to terminate cases of privileged access and undue influence granted to corporate lobbyists'.

14   An association of 30 established in 2005.

15   SEAP defines itself as 'the professional organization for European Affairs Professionals' set up in 1997.

16   EUROPA, Register of expert groups, http://europa.eu.int/comm/secretariat_general/regexp/.

17   Official procedure was established in C(2005)2817 and SEC(2005)1004.

Social Dialogue Committees

The 2000 White Paper Reforming the Commission[18] obliged the EC to provide lists of interest groups involved in formal consultation. The 2001 White Paper on European Governance[19] recommended publication of these lists. In March 2005, Commissioner Siim Kallas announced a European Transparency initiative. As part of this, the European institutions are to clarify the rules for consultation of interest groups and make the process more transparent. As a result, in 2005, the CONNECS database of 'civil society' organizations was published online.[20] The database provided two things: a list of committees that are set up for formal consultation by the EC, labelled 'consultative bodies' (including social dialogue committees) and a list of independent interest groups, labelled 'civil society organizations'. The EC states that formal consultation is made with 'trade unions, employers' federations, NGOs and CBOs (community based organizations) and religious organizations'. Informal consultation groups are defined as 'non profit making civil society organizations'. Although the database claims to list 'civil society' groups, upon examination, both lists (formal and informal) reveal a sizeable representation of industry and industrial associations perhaps reflecting the groups that the EC has chiefly consulted to date. However, the registration of civil society groups (non industry) is growing. This move towards transparency was welcomed by industry as well as civil society groups. Following the adoption of a Commission Green Paper entitled the European Transparency initiative,[21] the CONNECS database will be replaced by a voluntary register for interest representatives in 2008. The database is presently unavailable.

Committee Governance in Information Society Policy: Between the Technical and Political

DG Info Soc regulates telecommunications, audiovisual (broadcast and radio) and 'eEurope' policies under one roof. Expert groups have been operating within DG Telecommunications since the early 1980s, but the policy was not defined as the information society until the 1994 Europe and the Global Information Society report.[22] Until 1994, information society policy primarily comprised solely of telecommunications and e-commerce policies, but today encompasses a wider range of policy areas, including audiovisual policy, Internet, broadband, privacy, copyright and eEurope policies. In 1999, DG Info Soc was established (formally DG Telecommunications) which, over time, annexed other DGs' units. In 2005, DG Info Soc absorbed the 'media' unit of DGs Education and Culture, which deals with the Television without Frontiers revision.

---

18   COM(2000) 200 of 1 March 2000.
19   COM(2001) 428 of 25 July 2001.
20   CONECCS Database, http://europa.eu.int/comm/civil_society/coneccs/index_en.htm.
21   COM(2007) 127.
22   The Bangemann Report (1994d) was a report of the (Bangemann chaired) Council of Ministers Higher Level Group, entitled Europe and the Global Information Society, as submitted to the European Council for its meeting in Corfu on 24–25 June 1994.

DG Info Soc is a large Directorate General spread out between Brussels and Luxembourg which consumes one-fifth of the EC's annual budget. Under the Barroso Commission, DG Info Soc was re-organized into eight units.[23] A 'Media Task Force' was set up to gauge the impact of initiatives upon the public interest. The DG overseas audiovisual and communications policies, the i2010 initiative and the Lisbon strategy. The newer policies arose from the 'eEurope' initiative, which claims to aspire to goals of social inclusion and defeating the 'digital divide' as well as economic growth. As such, it has taken on boarder social and public interest policy goals. However, the legacy of DG Telecommunications which long engaged in technocratic approaches to policy making and promotion of large industry is more than evident. DG InfoSoc operates 72 committees dealing with the information society. Examination of many of these committees shows a substantial input from European industry.

This DG has practiced soft regulation since the mid-1990s. Examples of this are the 1995 Data Protection Directive[24] and the 2000 Electronic Commerce Directive,[25] which outline 'codes of conduct' for national governments. Another example is found in the Annex of the 1998 Council Recommendation on the Protection of Minors and Human Dignity,[26] which stipulates 'Indicative guidelines for the implementation, at national level, of a self regulation framework for the protection of minors and human dignity in online audiovisual and information services'.[27] The guidelines contain legal recommendations and codes of conduct and monitoring mechanisms. Another example is the EC Action Plan on Safer Use of the Internet (1999).[28] The EC advanced these and other initiatives through regular reviews and progress reports.

---

23 Audiovisual, Media and Internet, Electronic Communications Policy, Lisbon Strategy and Policies for the Information Society, Converged Networks and Services, Digital Content and Cognitive Systems, Emerging Technologies and Infrastructures, Components and Systems, and ICT Addressing Societal Challenges.

24 Directive 95/46/EC of the European Parliament and of the Council of 24 October 1995 on the protection of individuals with regard to the processing of personal data and on the free movement of such data, OJ L281, p. 31, of 23 November 1995; updating Directive 2002/58/EC concerning the processing of personal data and the protection of privacy in the electronic communications sector (Data Protection Directive), OJ L201 of 31 July 2002.

25 Directive 2000/31/EC on certain legal aspects of information society services, in particular electronic commerce in the Internal Market (Electronic Commerce Directive), OJ L178 of 17 July 2000.

26 Recommendation 98/560/EC on the development of the competitiveness of the European audio-visual and information services industry by promoting national frameworks aimed at achieving a comparable and effective level of protection of minors and human dignity, OJ L270 of 7 October 1998.

27 Council Recommendation 98/560/EC of 24 September 1998 on the development of the competitiveness of the European audiovisual and information services industry by promoting national frameworks aimed at achieving a comparable and effective level of protection of minors and human dignity (OJ L270 of 7 October 1998).

28 (1999) Annex to Council Decision No. 276/1999/EC adopting a multiannual Community Action Plan on promoting safer use of the Internet by combating illegal and harmful content on global networks, OJ C33 of 6 February 1999.

2002 Regulatory Framework for Communications

Following the Lisbon agenda, DG Info Soc was able to greatly expand its use of soft governance particularly under its Regulatory Framework for Communications. Recognizing that committees can make great strides in forwarding EU-level policy consensus, the EC wrote provisions for the establishment of a number of committees and co-regulatory fora into the directives. The 2002 Regulatory Framework for Electronic Communications and Services consisted of five directives and one decision (the Framework Directive, Authorisation Directive,[29] the Access Directive,[30] the Universal Service Directive,[31] the Data Protection Directive[32] and the Radio Spectrum Decision[33]). In order to guide implementation, DG Info Soc set up the 'Communications Committee' and planned a 'High Level Communications Group'.[34] A number of other committees were provided for within the individual directives to implement the new regulatory framework.

The Communications Committee (COCOM) began operation on 24 April 2002 and was meant to replace (but has not yet replaced) the pre-existing ONP Committee and Licensing Committees which were operating under the 1998 regulatory package for telecommunications. The Communications Committee 'assists the Commission in carrying out its executive powers under the new regulatory framework and the Regulation on the .eu Top Level Domain'. It is a comitology committee concerned with the implementation of the regulatory framework for communications and operates in accordance with the Council Comitology Decision. The committee also acts as a platform for the exchange of best practice between regulatory agencies. The Communications Broadcast Issues Subgroup (CBISS) is a subgroup of the Communications Committee (COCOM). The subgroup deals specifically with broadcasting policy issues which fall under the new regulatory framework prior to discussion in COCOM.

The regulatory framework provided for a High Level Communications Group (HLCG). Meant to be made up of EC functionaries, NRA representatives, telecoms operators, user organizations and standardization bodies, it was to function as an advisory group at the European level. It was meant to replace the existing High Level Regulators Group (HLCG). The High Level Regulators Group was originally

---

29   Directive 2002/20/EC on the authorisation of electronic communications networks and services (Authorisation Directive), OJ L108 of 24 April 2002.

30   Directive 2002/19/EC on access to, and interconnection of, electronic communications networks and associated facilities (Access Directive), OJ L108 of 24 April 2002.

31   Decision 2003/548/EC on the minimum set of leased lines with harmonised characteristics and associated standards referred to in Article 18 of the Universal Service Directive, OJ L186, 25 July 2003.

32   Directive 2002/58/EC concerning the processing of personal data and the protection of privacy in the electronic communications sector (Data Protection Directive), OJ L201 of 31 July 02.

33   Decision 2002/622/EC on a regulatory framework for radio spectrum policy in the European Community (Radio Spectrum Decision), OJ L108 of 24 April 2002.

34   These were to replace the pre-existing Open Network Provision (ONP) Committee and Licensing Committee.

established in 1992 as a forum for ministerial representatives, but evolved into a meeting of NRAs. Under telecommunications policy, it advised the ONP and licensing committees of the EC. The NRAs were opposed to the institutionalization of the HLCG and instead preferred to rely on the existing Independent Regulators Group (IRG) and European Committee for Telecommunications Regulatory Affairs of the European Conference of Posts and Telecommunications (ECPT/ECTRA).

The European Regulators Group (ERG) was established by a 2002 EC decision[35] under the regulatory framework.[36] The ERG acts as a forum for NRAs which oversee telecommunications and media markets. The ERG was designed to replace the Independent Regulators Group (IRG), which was the pre-existing voluntary group comprised of representatives from NRAs. However, since this time, the NRAs continue informal meetings within the IRG in addition to meeting formally within the ERG. Usually both groups meet back to back usually with the same delegates attending. The IRG is concerned with the implementation of the Regulatory Framework for Electronic Communications and Services and meets four times a year.[37]

A number of technical standards have been agreed under the Regulatory Framework, which are formalized in a 2006 decision.[38] These are organized under the following categories: transparent transmission capacity; publicly offered user interfaces; interconnection and access; services and features; numbering and addressing; quality of service and broadcasting services. Examples of technical standards agreed under 'broadcasting services' are the DVB-MHP standard[39] for interoperability in interactive television; and the WTVML standard for a lightweight Microbrowser for interactive television applications.

Radio spectrum is considered to be an 'electronic communications service' which is covered under the 2002 regulatory framework. Radio spectrum policy does not just cover radio but all modes of wireless transmission, from cellular phones, CB radio, terrestrial television broadcasts, ADSL modems, telephones, to satellite positioning systems. The framework builds upon pre-existing regulation, namely the 1999 Radio

---

35   Decision 627/2002/EC establishing the European Regulators Group for Electronic Communications Networks and Services (European Regulators Group Decision), OJ L200 of 30 July 2002.

36   The ERG runs in parallel to the European Council's Communications Committee set out in Articles 22 of the Framework Directive. The Communications Committee is composed of national ministries or NRAs of the member states.

37   The IRG and ERG operate in parallel to the pre-existing NRA platforms in the communications sector which operate *externally* to the Commission: the European Platform of Regulatory Authorities (EPRA) (broadcasting), the European Radiocommunications Committee (ERC) (radio), and the European Committee for Telecommunications Regulatory Affairs (ECTRA) (telecommunications).

38   Commission Decision of 11 December 2006, Amendment of the List of standards and/or specifications for electronic communications networks, services and associated facilities and services (2006/C 71/04) OJ C71/9, March 23, 2006.

39   This standard is Multimedia Home Platform (MHP) developed by the Digital Video Broadcasting (DVB), which is a consortium of industry.

and Telecommunications Terminal Equipment (R&TTE) Directive.[40] The EC set up a number of committees to deal with radio spectrum under the 2002 framework. These were the Radio Frequency Identification (RFID) Impact assessment and recommendations group (dissolved January 2006), the Radio Spectrum Committee and the Radio Spectrum Policy Group.

The Radio Spectrum Committee (RSC) was established under the Radio Spectrum Decision. The RSC is a comitology committee operating through the through advisory and regulatory procedures in accordance with the Council Comitology Decision. The Radio Spectrum Committee interacts with the Radio Spectrum Policy Group. The Radio Spectrum Policy Group (RSPG) was also created under the Radio Spectrum Decision. It operates internationally to the EC and is comprised of member state representatives, EC and EP functionaries, the European Conference of Postal and Telecommunications Administrations (CEPT)[41] and the European Telecommunications Standardisation Institute (ETSI). The RSPG advises the EC on radio spectrum policy.

The RSC is very active. Thus far, it has agreed upon spectrum harmonization for radio local area networks (RLANs), which provide wireless broadband access for computers and portable devices and on spectrum harmonization for short range radars in cars. The committee is now working to develop common standards for GSM and third generation mobile communications; the use of spectrum for hearing aids under the European Radio Messaging System (ERMES); harmonizing national regulation on high speed short range communications and imaging applications using Ultra Wide Band (UWB); and technology, harmonization of frequency bands for Short Range Devices (low power, low cost equipment); harmonizing the use of spectrum for Terrestrial Flight Telecommunications System (TFTS), and providing additional spectrum for third generation mobile communications (by 2008). The Committee also represents the EU in international fora such as the International Telecommunication Union (ITU) and the World Radio Conference.

In all of these initiatives, the RSC has adopted a 'market-based approach'. The EC is proposing that spectrum should be subject to market tradability (the buying or selling of frequency bandwidth) through the EU. For example, in 2006, the EC proposed that one-third of spectrum below 3GHz (that suited for terrestrial communication) should be privatized and managed by the market. Operators would be given the right to trade frequency rights in a given spectrum band for terrestrial services and to use those frequencies in a flexible manner. This policy initiative provides a stark contrast in the ways in which committee governance operates to democratic governance. The EU's policy proposal agreed upon within a committee is based upon the developing UK policy model of a spectrum trading system. By comparison, the UK policy was

---

40   This replaced the 1998 Directive and national approval regulations. Infrastructure is covered separately by the 1989 Electromagnetic Compatibility (EMC) Directive 89/336/EEC and the 1972 Low Voltage Directive (LVD) 73/23/EEC.

41   CEPT holds the Electronic Communications Committee (ECC) comprised of radio- and telecommunications regulatory authorities of the 45 CEPT member countries.

enacted in Parliament, namely, under the 2003 Communications Act,[42] following extensive public consultation built upon an independent review.

The 2002 Regulatory Framework also set up the e-Communications Consultation Task Force (eCCTF). The first key task was to agree upon relevant market definition.[43] The Committee now exists to monitor member state conformity to European regulation. Under Article 7 of the Directive on Electronic Commerce Directive,[44] it requires a notification procedure for new regulatory initiatives at the national level which affect incumbent telecommunications operators.[45] A number of decisions have been made under Article 7. For example, in 2004, the eCCTF disagreed with Ofcom's proposal to impose differential regulatory obligations on 2G and 3G mobile operators. By contrast, it did not dispute the notification made by the German regulatory authority, BNetzA, in another decision; thereby allowing wholesale access to Deutsche Telecom's VDSL-based access network.

Audiovisual Policy

DG Info Soc is presently revising its Television without Frontiers Directive resulting in the Audiovisual Media Services Directive (AVMS).[46] The AVMS Directive and the regulatory framework for communications are inexplicitly linked. The EC pursued two streams of liberalization: networks on the one hand and content on the other. Beginning in the late 1980s, two landmark Directives, the Television without Frontiers and Open Network Provision, established the backbone of the EU communications policy framework. The 1990 Open Network Provision (ONP) Directive provided open access to telecommunications services and networks based upon the principle of non discrimination and the elimination of exclusive rights. The 1989 Television without Frontiers Directive provided for capital mobility within Europe for services previously confined to national markets – television and radio signals. The 'regulatory framework for communications' is presently expanding the scope of network liberalization in Europe whereas the AVMS Directive loosens requirements for content carried on those networks. Hence, the AVMS Directive can be seen as a part of a general framework of market liberalization in operation by DG Info Soc.

---

42   Communications Act 2003 (UK), c. 21.

43   Commission Recommendation 2003/311/EC of 11 February 2003 on relevant product and services markets within the electronic communications sector susceptible for *ex ante* regulation in accordance with the Framework Directive ('the Recommendation'), OJ L114 of 8 May 2003, 45.

44   Directive 2000/31/EC on certain legal aspects of information society services, in particular electronic commerce in the Internal Market (Electronic Commerce Directive), OJ L178 of 17 July 2000.

45   Institut belge des services postaux etdes télécommunications (IBPT).

46   Directive 89/552/EEC on the coordination of certain provisions laid down by law, regulation or administrative action in Member States concerning the pursuit of television broadcasting activities [1989] OJ L298/23, as amended by Directive 97/36/EC [1997] L202/60.

The AVMS Directive was proposed on 13 December 2005 and was approved at the end of 2007.[47] The most significant modification of the new directive is the liberalization of cross-border broadcasts of on demand services (such as the downloading of films and programming via satellite, cable and the Internet). The AVMS Directive extends the country of origin principle to on demand services (labelled as non linear services). At the same time, it extends the existing Television without Frontiers requirements on content and advertising to new service providers. These requirements have been loosened. The Directive allows for more advertising breaks within: films made for television (excluding series, serials, light entertainment programmes and documentaries), cinematographic works, children's programmes and news programmes (every 35 minutes); it liberalizes new forms of advertising (allowing for split screen, virtual and interactive advertising and product placement); abolishes the daily limit on television advertising; and drops all restrictions on teleshopping. Hence, new service providers will be subject to stricter regulation than before, but a service provider need only apply for authorization in one member state in order to gain access to the whole of the EU market. The EP proposed a further loosening of the advertising limit to 30 minutes (for films made for television; cinematographic works, children's programmes and news programmes) rather than every 35 minutes proposed by the EC. The EC's proposed directive has been revised to include this.

The AVMS Directive has a strong soft governance component. Even though the Directive aspires to the EC's Communication on Better Regulation for Growth and Jobs in the EU,[48] which calls for 'less' regulation, it is clear from the statement below that the EC views self and co-regulation as a realm for expansion of European policy. The proposal text of the Directive states that:

> Both, co- and self-regulation instruments, implemented in accordance with different legal traditions of member states can play an important role in delivering a high level of consumer protection. Measures aimed at achieving public interest objectives in the emerging audiovisual media services sector will be more effective if they are taken with the active support of the service providers themselves. Thus self regulation constitutes a type of voluntary initiative, which enables the economic operators, social partners, non-governmental organizations or associations to adopt common guidelines amongst themselves and for themselves. Member states should, in accordance with their different legal traditions, recognize the role which effective self-regulation can play as a complement to the legislation and judicial and/or administrative mechanisms in place and its useful contribution to the achievement of the objectives of this Directive. However, while self-regulation might be a complementary method of implementing certain provisions of this Directive, it cannot constitute a substitute for the obligation of the national legislator. Co-regulation gives, in its minimal form, a 'legal link' between self-regulation and the national legislator. Co-regulation gives, in its minimal form, a 'legal link' between self-

---

47 Audiovisual Media Services Directive 2007/65/EC, OJ L332 of 18 December 2007.

48 Commission of the European Communities Brussels, COM(2005) 97 final, Brussels, 16 March 2005. Communication from the Commission to the Council and the European Parliament. Better Regulation for Growth and Jobs in the European Union, SEC(2005) 175.

regulation and the national legislator in accordance with the legal traditions of the member states.[49]

Similar to the 2002 package of directives, the AVMS will set up a Contact Committee under Article 23a which will be 'composed of representatives of the competent authorities of the member states. It shall be chaired by a representative of the EC and meet either on his initiative or at the request of the delegation of a member state'. Committee function will be (a) to facilitate implementation 'through regular consultation on any practical problems arising from its application, and particularly from the application of Article 2' (b) 'to deliver Opinions on member state implementation' (c) to act as a 'forum for an exchange of views ... pursuant to Article 4 (3)' (d) 'discuss the outcome of regular consultations which the Commission holds with representatives of broadcasting organizations, producers, consumers, manufacturers, service providers and trade unions and the creative community'; (e) to 'facilitate the exchange of information between the member states and the Commission on ... the development of regulatory activities ... as well as relevant developments in the technical field' and (f) 'to examine any development arising in the sector on which an exchange of views appears useful'.

Along with other amendments, the EP injected another instrument of self-regulation, namely a code of conduct for children's advertising. Under Chapter II, 'member states and the Commission should encourage audiovisual service provider to develop a code of conduct regarding children's programming containing or being interrupted by advertising, sponsorship or any marketing of unhealthy and inappropriate foods and drinks such as those high in fat, sugar and salt and of alcoholic beverages'.[50]

To complement AVSM revision, in December 2006, the EP and the Council adopted a Recommendation on the Protection of Minors and Human Dignity and on the Right of Reply[51] in December 2006 building on an earlier 1998 Council Recommendation. A notable addition to the 1998 version is the recommendation that 'industry should develop positive measures, such as harmonization through cooperation and the exchange of best practices between the regulatory, self regulatory and co-regulatory bodies of the member states'. The EC's role is outlined in the Recommendation as 'facilitat(ing) and support(ing) the formation of networks by

---

49   Amendment 36 (Recital 25) of the Amended proposal for a Directive of the European Parliament and of the Council amending Council Directive 89/552/EEC on the coordination of certain provisions laid down by law, regulation or administrative action in member states concerning the pursuit of television broadcasting activities (Audiovisual Media Services without Frontiers) COM/2007/0170 final, COD 2005/0260.

50   Amendment 108 subject to the following rewording Article 3f from Amended proposal for a Directive of the European Parliament and of the Council amending Council Directive 89/552/EEC on the coordination of certain provisions laid down by law, regulation or administrative action in Member States concerning the pursuit of television broadcasting activities (Audiovisual Media Services without Frontiers) COM/2007/0170 final, COD 2005/0260.

51   Protection of Minors and Human Dignity Recommendation, http://ec.europa.eu/comm/avpolicy/reg/minors/index_en.htm.

self regulatory bodies and the experience exchange between them so as to assess the effectiveness of codes of conduct and approaches based on self regulation in order to ensure the best possible standards for the protection of minors'. Under this Recommendation, the EC is now considering the introduction of a 'European free phone number and generic second level internet domain name reserved for monitored sites committed to respecting minors and their rights'. This initiative was preceded by the Safer Internet Action Plan which prepared the way for the EC's 2005 Safer Internet Decision.[52]

Another parallel initiative was agreed in 2006. The European Charter for the Development and the Take-up of Film Online was agreed upon by industry in May 2006 at the Europe Day of the 59th Cannes Film Festival. The EC used the Cannes event to seek approval of key stakeholders from the film, content, telecommunications and Internet service industries. The Charter was initiated and strongly promoted by Commissioner Viviane Reding. The EC followed this up with a proposal for a Charter on Content Online, a public consultation of which was held in the latter part of 2006 and with a Communication on Creative Content Online, which was adopted on January 3, 2008.[53]

In addition to these measures, the EC has used soft measures to accomplish other goals in audiovisual policy. For example, the EC has been attempting to harmonize 'digital rights management' (DRM) for the legal distribution of digital content building up on its 2001 Directive on the Harmonization of Copyright and Related Rights in the Information Society.[54] This is discussed in a formal 'contact committee' (the Copyright in the Information Society Committee) created by Article 12 of the 2001 Directive. Digital content is no different to any other kind of content and subject to the existing European and national agreements on copyright. The EC's aim with this policy was twofold: firstly it wished to agree upon on a common European identification standard for digital content.[55] For example, the International Standardisation Organisation (ISO) has identified standards for existing content (for example ISBN for books, ISWC for music, ISRC for sound recordings and ISAN for films). Secondly, the EC wished member states to agree on common technology which will manage the copying of digital. The argument is that digitalization has greatly increased the risk of privacy as data (both personal and copyrighted) can be reproduced so quickly and easily.

Through its committee, the EC attempted to have member states agree on software that can instantly levy fees on users at the moment of copying onto, for example,

---

52   Safer Internet Decision of the EP and of the Council of 11 May 2005 establishing a multi-annual Community Programme on promoting safer use of the Internet and new online technologies, Decision 854/2005/EC.

53   Commission of the European Communities Brussels, COM(2007) 836 final; Communication from the Commission to the European Parliament, the Council, the European Economic and Social Committee and the Committee of the Regions on Creative Content Online in the Single Market, http://ec.europa.eu/avpolicy/docs/other_actions/col_en.pdf.

54   Directive 2001/29 of 22 May 2001.

55   For example, the UK-based International DOI Foundation has developed a Digital Object Identifier (DOI), which identifies and classifies digital content (for example under author, date, country of origin and so on).

personal computers, CD-ROM or DVD burners, or mobile phones. This software would be able to identify the activity, refer to the regulations under which it could be used and enforce them. The content would have a 'digital signature' that could be scrambled, encrypted, 'watermarked' or 'digitally wrapped' with rule requirements. The EC identified a number of companies and industry consortia that provide such software.[56] The idea, most likely, was to guarantee that a European company was chosen over a foreign competitor. Despite having established a High Level Group on Spectrum Management comprised of key industry players who would be using this software,[57] industry did not agree that standards should be established by the European institutions. Following lobbying, particularly by the music industry, the EP attempted to put an end to the EC's initiative in December 2006 with its report Towards a European Policy on the Radio Spectrum, in which it argues that the EC should let the market decide on this issue and not adopt a specific standard.[58] The market is choosing other options for example key players, such as Murdoch's BSkyB, have adopted Mircrosoft software for DRM management for downloading football games in the UK. In January 2007, however, the US Senate proposed a bill[59] making digital rights management software mandatory in podcasts and Internet radio broadcasts. The bill does not specify a standard but those lobbying for the bill support the use of Samsung and Pioneer software.

i2010

Lisbon legitimized the EC's 'e-Europe' initiative, which was renamed 'i2010'. Following the Lisbon Summit, DG Info Soc published its eEurope Action Plan[60] as established in an EC Communication.[61] The EC's High Level Group, chaired by Wim Kok, produced the November 2004 paper 'Facing the Challenge – The Lisbon strategy for growth and employment'. Then on June 2005, the EC announced its i2010 – A European Information Society for Growth and Employment initiative

56   The Commission listed them back in 2002 in a staff working paper as Secure Digital Music Initiative, Microsoft Digital Asset Server (DAS), IBM Electronic Media Management System, InterTrust, Liquid Audio, ContentGuard, Info2Clear, TV Anytime, Digital Video Broadcasting Group.

57   GESAC, IFPI, Vivendi, Eurocinema, FEF (Federation of European Publishers), the BBC, France Telecom, Vodafone, FastWeb, Philips, Nokia, Alcatel, Siemens, HP, the New Media Council and BEUC.

58   Towards a European Policy on the Radio Spectrum, 18 December 2006, A6-0467/2006, Committee on Industry, Research and Energy. Rapporteur: Fiona Hall.

59   Platform Equality and Remedies for Rights Holders in Music Act of 2007, (Perform Act), s. 256, introduced on January 11, 2007 at the 110th Congress 1st Session, http://www.govtrack.us/congress/bill.xpd?bill=s110-256.

60   eEurope Action Plan, http://europa.eu.int/information_society/eeurope/index_en.htm. This includes a number of e-initiatives such as the eEBO (eContent Exposure and Business Opportunities) and eContent initiatives.

61   European Council and European Commission (2000), *eEurope 2002: An Information Society for All*, action plan prepared for the European Council of Feira, 19–20 June 2000, http://europa.eu.int/information_society/eeurope/action_plan/actionplantext/index_en.htm.

which is to run for five years.[62] The aim is to create a 'market-oriented regulatory framework for the digital economy'. Closer reading of the description of programme reveals an old style 'European champion' strategy to implementation, the goal of which is to (1) promote 'European champions' (both private sector and state) to compete with the 'US and Japan' and (2) to provide services through public sector funding. i2010 created a number of initiatives to be executed through committee governance. Committees operating under i2010 including the: eEurope Advisory Group, the e-Accessibility Expert Group, e-Communications Consultation Task Force (eCCTF), eEurope+ Statistical Working Group, e-Government Research and Development, e-Health Working Group, e-Safety Forum, and eTen.[63] All of these committees' fora have produced and are forwarding soft initiatives.

The eEurope Advisory Group established by the Modinis Rules Decision[64] which overviews e-initiatives and information exchange across policy areas. It further monitors the progress of the eEurope 2005 Action Plan. The e-Advisory Group established a number of subcommittees: the e-Health Committee, the Benchmarking Committee, e-Accessibility, Broadband, and e-Government.

The e-Accessibility Committee works alongside the e-Accessibility Expert Committee set up by the High Level Group on the Employment and Social Dimension of the Information Society. It coordinates standardization with a number of European standardization bodies such as CEN, CENELEC, ETSI, the Joint Technical Committee Broadcasting (CENELEC/ETSI/EBU) and other coordination groups ICTSB and DATSCG. A number of pan European-wide standards have been agreed through this expert group. In consultation with CENELEC, the Expert Group agreed standards on the usability of IT-based electrical products for people with special needs including design and technology. CENELEC is now working on technical standards for digital TV and interactive services and on 'access for all to broadcast and video applications'. With ETSI, the following standards were agreed: requirements of assistive technology devices in ICT, speech recognition voice user interfaces, generic user command, control and editing vocabulary for ICT products and services; the multimodality of icons, symbols and pictograms; guidelines on design for ICT products and services; European alphanumeric characters; assignment for 12-key telephone pads and multi-modal interaction, communication and navigation. Together with the ICT Standards Board (ICTSB), a federation of European standards organizations, DG Info Soc set up coordination for standardizing 'Design for All' assistive technology together with industry and the European Disability Forum (EDF) and the Association for the Advancement of Assistive Technology in Europe

---

62   Communication 'i2010 – A European Information Society for Growth and Employment' COM(2005) 229 Final Issue Paper.

63   E-Ten (Trans-European Telecommunications Networks) is a funding programme which runs from 2004–2009. It funds 'trans-European e-services in the public interest'. These administered through the Trans-European Telecommunications Networks Financial and Guidelines Committee.

64   Modinis Rules Decision 2256/2003/EC of 17 November 2003 (OJ L336, 1–5, 23 December 2003).

(AAATE). Under its 2006–2007 work plan, the EC identified possible co-regulatory measures based upon standards agreed.

The e-Government Committee was also named in the Modinis Rules Decision. Operating within DG Info Soc, the Group set up an e-government observatory, established codes of good e-government practices; and benchmarking including an 'e-government index'. The group also produced a number of documents such as the preparation work for: a 2005 Ministerial Declaration made by EU Ministers on e-government in Manchester;[65] a directors general of public administrations meeting on the accessibility of public sector websites;[66] drafted the Council of the EU conclusions on e-government for all Europeans,[67] and the declaration made by EU Ministers on e-inclusion[68] to ensure the 'accessibility of all public websites by 2010 through compliance with the relevant W3C common web accessibility standards and guidelines'. Most recently, the group published its i2010 e-Government Action Plan: Accelerating e-Government in Europe for the Benefit of All in April 2006. Along with the European Public Administration Network (EPAN), the OMC group is to draft 'specifications for multi platform service delivery strategies allowing access to e-Government services via a variety of channels, e.g. digital TV, mobile and fixed telephone and other interactive devices' in 2008. It has recommended the funding of research projects and support from Structural Funds. Two other committees operate within DG Info Soc relating to e-government: the Legal Barriers in e-Government Group, which exchanges information on e-government legal and organizational barriers in support of the corresponding Modinis study; and the Identity Management in e-Government Group, which facilitates 'the exchange of information, experience and good practice in the area of e-Government services and enablers e.g. identity management and other related issues such as interoperability and the economics of government'.

Related to this, the Public Sector Information Group (PSI Group) coordinates implementation of the 2003 PSI Directive on the re-use of public sector information which deals with the way public sector bodies should advance and re-use their information resources.[69] The PSI Group set up with the MEPSIR project which has defined a methodology to measure the re-use of public sector information (PSI) in the EU and compare this to its use in the USA. In 2004, it also drafted a proposal for a directive establishing an infrastructure for spatial information in the Community (INSPIRE).

The e-Health Committee was set up in June 2005 and was replaced by the i2010 subgroup on e-health in 2006. Meetings are held circa three times a year back to back with DG SANCO's Health Systems Committee. Core members are drawn from national telecommunications ministries which consult interest groups and industrial associations who are organized under the e-Health Stakeholders' Group. The

---

65 http://www.egov2005conference.gov.uk/documents/proceedings/pdf/051124declaration. pdf.

66 5–6 December 2005, Newcastle.

67 Luxembourg, 8–9 June 2006.

68 11 June 2006, Riga.

69 Directive 2003/98/EC of 17 November 2003, OJ L345/90 on 31 December 2003.

committee agreed upon the e-Health Action Plan, which is being implemented by DG Info Soc by means of the MODINIS budget. Actions include the documenting of best practice and benchmarking, and the development of integration and interoperability of health information systems and electronic health records and professional mobility. Another committee deals with advanced broadband e-health applications and services.

The e-Safety Forum was established by the 2003 e-Safety Communication.[70] The Forum is a formal, temporary group operating within the EC. The forum in turn operates 13 working groups.[71] Each of the groups is led by key representatives from European industry. For example, the Digital Map Working Group is led by representatives from Teleatlas and Navteq and are creating a 'digital map database'.

In 2005, the EC also published its Communication on Digital Libraries[72] under i2010. The Communication set up a High Level Group, which agreed upon a number of initiatives, the most salient of which is the funding of a 'European digital library'. Following Google's Library project,[73] the EC is funding the digital scanning of books. In doing so, it is, in essence, matching private sector with public finance. The High Level Group has also released a communication on digital libraries of scientific and scholarly information; a recommendation on digitalization and digital preservation; and initiated funding of the digitalization of European literary and audiovisual cultural heritage.

Also related to i2010, under the Directive on Privacy and Electronic Communications,[74] a 'contact network of spam enforcement authorities' (CNSA) was set up comprising of national authority representatives to facilitate the exchange of information, experiences and good practices in the fight against spam in accordance with ITU recommendations in this area. The network concluded a voluntary agreement for a common procedure for dealing with cross-border complaints on spam.

70   COM(2003)542 final of 15 September 2003.

71   Accident Causation Data Working Group (WG) led by Michael Hollingsworth, ACEA; Communications WG led by Uwe Daniels, Bosch; Digital Maps WG led by Ad Bastiaansen, Teleatlas Yannis Moissidis, Navteq; eCall Driving Group led by Michael Nielsen, ERTICO led by Dr. Wolfgang Reinhardt, ACEA; Heavy Vehicles led by Dr. Jürgen Trost, DaimlerChrysler; Human-Machine Interaction led by Annie Pauzie, INRETS, Alan Stevens, TRL and Christhard Gelau, BAST; International Co-operation led by Jacob Bangsgaard, ERTICO; Real-Time Traffic and Travel Information led by Dr Heinz Friedrichs, Bosch; Research and Development led by Ulf Palmquist, EUCAR; Road Maps led by Risto Kulmala, VTT and Hans-Jürgen Mäurer, DEKRA; User Outreach led by Johann Grill, FIA; ICT for Clean Mobility; and Service Oriented Architecture.

72   Communication on Digital Libraries COM(2005) 465.

73   Google's ambition is to scan every book ever published and make it available and searchable online.

74   Directive 2002/58/EC concerning the processing of personal data and the protection of privacy in the electronic communications sector, 12 July 2002.

Consultation with Industry and Civil Society Groups

EC initiatives in the information society field have relied heavily on agreement between key private actors. The EC established a number of High Level Groups comprised of industrial leaders to steer the European agenda. The first High Level Group was the Bangemann Group that was composed of 20 European industry leaders and set up in 1994 and the second Group was established in 1995. It was the Bangemann Group II that attained industry consensus on the 2002 regulatory framework for communications. This was succeeded by the High Level Group chaired by Wim Kok in 2003. The EC has also encouraged the establishment of European federations with which it could hold dialogue with industry. Examples of these in the 1990s were the Digital Video Broadcasting (DVB) group, the European Telecommunications Platform (ETP) and the European Telecommunications Network Operators' Association.[75] The EC liaised with these groups informally to agree on standard setting.[76] The EC still has such relationships with a number of industry groups today. With this, the EC is encouraging self-regulation and co-regulation. Indeed, the EC is seeking to legitimize existing self-regulatory bodies, to cement them at the European level, and to establish new bodies perhaps based upon national models.

The MHP Implementation Group (MHP Multimedia Home Platform) was set up to implement the MHP standard in conjunction with EC committees. In 2006 it had 82 members from industry. Under its 2002 regulatory Framework Directive,[77] the EC recommends, but does not impose, the DVB-MHP API standard for interoperability in interactive television. In 2006, the EC decided not to mandate a compulsory standard for API but encourage the use of MHP. The MHP standard is in use by European Broadcasters Union (EBU) and its members (the European association of public service broadcasters) and the Nordig Consortium (of Nordic broadcasters and communications operators in Denmark, Finland, Sweden, Norway and Iceland). However, other API standards are more commonly used by private industry. The Open TV API standard (developed by the US group Liberty Media) is used by the following European operators: Télévision Par Satellite (TPS) and Noos interactive services in France, BSkyB and British Interactive Broadcasting's (BIB) in the UK, Sweden's Telia, Denmark's Tele Danmark Kabel, Italy's Stream, Spain's Via Digital and the PrimaCom cable network in Germany. Canal+ uses MediaHighway (which

---

75   Industry group for European electronic communications network operators established in May 1992 'to establish a constructive dialogue between its member companies and decision-makers'.

76   For example, the DVB agreed a number of standards on: the transmission of satellite services (DVB-S), cable (DVB-C), terrestrial (DVB-T), service information (DVB-SI), and videotext (DVB-TXT) for European markets. It in turn established the DAB (Digital Audio Broadcasting) standard for radio broadcasting, the compression standard for digital television (DVB -MPEG 2), the DVB – CSA (Common Scrambling Algorithm) for scrambling and two standards for decoders (used in set-top boxes,) multicrypt and simultcrypt.

77   Directive 2002/21/EC on a common regulatory framework for electronic communications networks and services (Framework Directive), OJ L108 of 24 April 2002.

was developed by Canal Plus). Betanova was developed by BetaResearch and is used by Premiere in Germany and Austria.

The Embedded Systems European Technology Platform coordinates a 'European industrial strategy for the area of embedded systems' and 'better coordination between member states'.[78] It liaises with DG Info Soc's European Technology Platform in Embedded Systems Committee. The Networked Electronic Media (NEM) group, funded by Eurescom, was set up in 2005 to 'focus on an innovative mix of various media forms, delivered seamlessly over technologically transparent networks, to improve the quality, enjoyment and value of life'. It deals with convergence of broadband, mobile and new media services. Essentially, it lobbies for European funding to be put into the high tech field. On the steering committee sit 24 European telecoms companies, the EBU and the BBC. Recipients of funding, however, are mainly universities.

The expansion into cultural and social policy by DG Info Soc under the i2010 agenda has meant that a wider number of groups are consulted on a regular basis. There are three 'formal' consultation committees listed in the CONNECS database for 'information society policy', namely: the Comité de dialogue sectoriel 'Télécommunications', the Radio Spectrum Policy Group (RSPG), and the Satellite Action Plan Regulatory Working Group (SAP-REG). The Comité de dialogue sectoriel 'Télécommunications' has two members: ETNO, the European Telecommunications Network Operators' Association representing industry, and UNI-Telecom representing unions. The Radio Spectrum Policy Group is a NRA association. The Satellite Action Plan Regulatory Working Group has many members, including ETNO (again), the European Association of Satellite Operators, the Mobile Satellite Users Association and other groups representing industry.[79] Hence, of the 'formal' 'civil society' groups consulted in the Comité, most of them are made up of representatives from industry. For information society policy, the database lists 54 'informal' 'civil society' groups. Even though they are meant to represent civil society, a great number of these groups actually represent industry.

---

78   It has three working groups: Application Drivers for Embedded System Design Research (headed by Hugo De Man, IMEC); Technology Challenges for Future Intelligent Embedded Systems (led by Andrea Cuomo, Corporate Vice President, General Manager Advanced System Technology STMicroelectronics); and Governance (represented by Jan van den Biesen, VP Philips Research). Governance: Debriefing from the Working Group.

79   European Telecommunications Office, Telia, Eutelsat, Debitel, Hughes Spaceway, Alenia Aerospazio, Alcatel Space Industries, Euroconsult, Telecom Italia, Telespazio Spa, Elsacom Spa, Astrium-Space, New Skies Satellites NV, MCS Europe, Telenor Satellite Services, Eutelsat, Pegasus Development Corporation, Global VSAT Forum, Telia AB, Ellipso Inc, DASA, Covington and Burling, ERO, Telenor, Inmarsat, DETECON GmbH, LE GOUEFF Avocats, Alcatel Space, Skybridge LP, France Telecom, Squire Sanders and Dempsey LLP, GE International, BT, Compagnie des Signaux, Hogan and Hartson LLP, Tele Danmark A/S, Alcatel/Skybridge, GE Americom, Telespazio Spa, BT Global, Comsys, Hispasat SA, DeTeSat, Swedish Space Corporation, Radiocommunications Agency, Teledesic Communications SPAIN SL, Teledesic Belgium, ECTEL, EUROSPACE, KPN Satcom, Inmarsat, CISI.

This is unsurprising in itself but one has to wonder why the EC defines private sector groups as 'non profit making civil society organizations'.

A number of other industry groups are consulted regularly under i2010. The EC established the 'Produits et ingénierie des services à l'horizon 2010' committee to collaborate on technology and methodology for product development in manufacturing. It collaborates with IMS (Intelligent Manufacturing Systems), which is a private platform on which industry, governments and academia to cooperate internationally. The Single European Electronic Market (SEEM) discussion group was set up in 2002 following a workshop on the Single European Electronic Market organized by DG Info Soc's Electronic Commerce Unit. It exists to promote ICT research in Europe. The National IST Directors for RTD forum also advises the EC on research in the ICT sector. The EC also set up the New Working Environments Group established to provide advice on the policies affecting new working environments. This group is comprised of EC functionaries and industry representatives. It has two subgroups: the Aspects Stratégiques (national administration representatives) and the Aspects Techniques (practitioners). DG Development set up the 'member states' experts on Information Society and Development' to coordinate, with member states, European policy on the growth of the information society in developing countries and WSIS policy.

Dialogue with industrial groups is flanked by the creation and decentralization of European-level agencies that have long been in operation and cooperation with the European institutions. The European Radiocommunications Office (ERO) was established in Copenhagen in 1991. The ERO houses the Electronic Communications Committee (ECC) of CEPT. As mentioned earlier, CEPT organizes the Electronic Communications Committee (ECC), which is in dialogue with the EC and comprised of radio and telecommunications regulatory authorities of the 45 CEPT member countries. The ECC replaced the European Committee for Telecommunications Regulatory Affairs (ECTRA) and the European Radio Communications Committee (ERC) in 2001. Other agencies include the European Union Satellite Centre,[80] which was established by a 'joint action' of the European Council in 2001[81] in Madrid; the European Telecommunications Standards Institution (ETSI); CENELEC;[82] CEN;[83] EICTA[84] and the European Space Research and Technology Centre (ESTEC).

To complement policy advice provided by industry groups and civil society organizations, DG Info Soc has established a number of European research

---

80   European Union Satellite Centre, http://www.eusc.org/.

81   Council Joint Action of 20 July 2001 on the establishment of a European Union Satellite Centre (2001/555/CFSP).

82   European Committee for Electro-technical Standardization (CENELEC) was created in 1973 as a result of the merger of CENELCOM and CENEL.

83   The European Committee for Standardization (CEN) was founded in 1961 by the national standards bodies in Europe.

84   The European Information and Communications Technology Industry Association was formed in 1999 and merged with EACEM (European Association of Consumer Electronics Manufacturers) 2001 to form the European Information, Communications and Consumer Electronics Technology Industry Associations. The group consists of 36 national digital technology associations.

institutes. The Joint Research Centre (JRC) seeks to provide policy support to the EC 'to provide autonomous and Europe wide expertise to improve understanding of the links between technology, the economy and society. It comprises eight research institutes located in five different EU member states.[85]

Conclusion

Europe's path towards soft governance in 'information society' policy seems to be set. This is disconcerting, particularly in a policy area which claims to work towards the promotion of European integration and building of civil society in Europe. Key variables missing from the soft governance model are transparency, legitimacy and democratic input to policy-making processes. Since the 2005 European Transparency initiative, the EC has taken some steps towards greater transparency of committee governance, however processes remain opaque and lack consultation requirements. Although this lack of transparency may be resulting in greater efficiency, it essentially lacks legitimacy and accountability. Transparency is particularly important considering that the EU is already suffering from a democratic deficit. In addition, soft governance and self-regulation are essentially weak instruments of control as they are neither binding nor legally legitimate and do not hold up in court.

Although highly technical, the choice of a standard usually favours one company over another. Closer examination of the standards chosen pinpoint to the promotion of key European industries over foreign competitors. This result reflects the style of decision making, that is, the consultation of European industry and European associations only, which closes the door to non-European actors in the process. This interest in supporting European champions can compromise effective market regulation. The difficulty in earmarking standards is of course that by the time standards have been agreed upon, the market will have chosen different standards or moved on to newer technology.

A related argument can be made about supporting European industry. As companies operate in global markets, it is difficult to identify a company as 'European'. Although a company may be employing and paying tax in Europe today, it does not necessarily mean that it will be doing so tomorrow. Ownership should count as less of a factor in regulation, as the idea of regulation is to hold companies accountable to the public interest through efficient regulatory requirements, rather than to favour one company over another based upon investment decision making. The 'European champion' policy of the EC is outdated. It should move towards transparency and effective market regulation in a globalized digital economy. However, political factors seem to hold weight.

---

85 The Institute for Reference Materials and Measurements (IRMM), the Institute for Transuranium Elements (ITU), the Institute for the Protection and the Security of the Citizen, the Institute for Environment and Sustainability, the Institute for Health and Consumer Protection (IHCP), the Institute for Energy (IE) and the Institute for Prospective Technological Studies (IPTS).

References

Dehousse, R. (2003), 'Comitology: Who Watches the Watchmen?', *Journal of European Public Policy* 10(5) October, 798–813.

De La Porte, Caroline (2002), "Is the Open Method of Coordination Appropriate for Organising Activities at European Level in Sensitive Policy Areas?" *European Law Journal* 8(1), 38–58.

European Commission (1994), *Europe and the Global Information Society, Recommendations to the European Council*. Report by the High Level Group on the Information Society ('Bangemann Report'). Brussels, May 1994.

European Commission (2002a), *European Governance: Better Lawmaking*, Communication from the Commission to the Council, the European Parliament, the European Economic and Social Committee and the Committee of the Regions, COM(2002) 275, Brussels, 5 June 2002.

European Commission (2002b), *eEurope 2005: An Information Society for All*. Presented to the Seville European Council of 21–22 June 2002, COM 263, Brussels, 28 May 2002.

Heritier, Adrienne (2001), 'Overt and Cover Institutionalization', in A. Stone Sweet, W. Sandholts and N. Fligstein (eds) *The Institutionalization of Europe*. Oxford: Oxford University Press.

Hix, S. and Follesdal, A. (2006), 'Why There is a Democratic Deficit in the EU: A Response to Majone and Moravcsik', *Journal of Common Market Studies* 44(3), 533–562.

Jordan, G. and Richardson, J. (1979), *Governing Under Pressure: The Policy Process in a Post-Parliamentary Democracy*. Oxford: Blackwell.

Jörges, C. and Voss, E. (1999), *EU Committees: Social Regulation, Law and Politics*. Oxford: Hart Publishing.

Jörges, C. and Neyer, J. (1997), 'Transforming Strategic Interaction into Deliberative Problem-Solving: European Comitology in the Foodstuffs Section', *Journal of European Public Policy* 4, 609–625.

Jörges, C. et al. (eds) (2004), *Transnational Governance and Constitutionalism: International Studies in the Theory of Private Law*. Oxford: Hart Publishing.

Kies, Raphael (2002), 'E-voting and opinion formation: le potentiel democratique et la regulation de l'espace', Paper presented to the EUI Working Group on Media Law and Policy. European University Institute, Badia Fiesolana. 6 November 2002.

Kohler-Koch, B. (1998), 'Die Europäisierung nationaler Demokratien. Verschleiss eines europäischen Kulturerbes?' M. Treven (ed.), *Demokratie – eine Kultur des Westens? Opladen*, 263–288.

Maurer, A. and Larsson, T. (2002), 'Democratic Legitimacy in EU Politics – No Way Out for Committees', in G.F. Schaefer (ed.), *Governance by Committee, the Role of Committees in European Policy-Making and Policy Implementation*.

Maastricht: EIPA.

Noam, Eli (1998), 'Will Books Become the Dumb Medium?', *Educom Reivew* 33(2).

Rhodes, R. (1988), *Beyond Westminster and Whitehall*. Routledge: London.

Scott, J. and Trubek, D.M. (2002), 'Mind the Gap: Law and New Approaches to Governance in the European Union', *European Law Journal* 8(1), 1–18.

Chapter 2

European Film Policies and Competition Law: Hostility or Symbiosis?

Anna Herold[1]

Competition law intervenes in almost every field of economic activity within the contemporary world. The concept of antitrust law was hardly known across Europe half a century ago and today it has become a phenomenal legal tool to deal with unfair behaviour of market players and is seen as a correction mechanism for nearly all the anomalies in the European Union (EU) marketplace. The practical omnipotence of the European Commission (EC) in the competition policy field serves as a symbol of the success of the European integration process.

However, not all sectors of economic activity lend themselves easily to the intervention of competition authorities. It has long been recognized that some economic sectors make non-commercial contributions that go beyond their ability to generate profit. As some of these sectors, especially the film industry, are gradually becoming integrated into the economic integration regimes, states find it increasingly difficult to draw upon them to fulfil both economic commitments and sometimes conflicting social, cultural and political ones. Indeed, there is an inherent tension between the 'protectionist' measures that might allow governments to cultivate the non-commercial aspects of certain sectors (for example, cinema) and the principles of liberal trade or – even more significantly – laws of the internal market. The conflict between 'market and culture' in the context of cinema also provides a window on the larger debate surrounding the apparent threat that globalization poses to cultural diversity.

It is therefore legitimate to ask whether economic law can effectively cope with the challenges of the cultural industries, as exemplified by the film industry, in the context of global competition. At issue is the degree to which cultural goals can be accommodated by – rather than surrendered to – commercial ones in the legal frameworks of the economic integration organisms. Leaving aside the implications of cinema policies at the international level, the focus of this chapter is on the relevance of EU competition law, as an important part of European economic constitution, for European film policies, inherently wedged between cultural and market considerations.

The European audiovisual sector, suffering from deep structural weaknesses and a huge trade deficit in relation to the United States (Puttnam 1997), causes problems

---

1   The views that are expressed are those of the author alone and do not represent the views of the European Commission.

in light of competition law, the solutions to which have provoked many headaches and have been subject to vivid controversies. The case of cinema is emblematic in this context, due to a specific political and legal context in which the European cinema industry operates, characterized by significant public financial intervention and a strong regulatory framework. This, in turn, results from the specific, double nature of film – cultural and economic – which explains the strategic importance of cinema industry both in terms of its cultural impact and economic profitability. In fact, European policies in this field are always hybrid fusions of cultural and industrial objectives, even if the latter tend to be camouflaged in some countries.

The relevance of EU competition law for the cinema sector results precisely from its economic dimension: since there is an economic activity, competition rules apply automatically. The EC (and the national courts and competition authorities after the May 2004 decentralization of EU competition law enforcement[2]) apply competition law to the cinema industry actors operating at the EU level, as to the other economic players in the internal market. However, the European cinema sector represents, arguably, a specific field of economic activity, abiding by its own rules in the competition law context. This is especially visible in the application of one of the three pillars of EU competition law, namely state aid rules, which pose limits to public intervention in the economy, with an explicit flexibility, though, as far as cultural aid is concerned. This might be less evident in the two remaining branches of competition law, ensuring respect of the market discipline by operators (antitrust) and exercising control of market structures (mergers). Nonetheless, it is argued in this chapter that there has been a special relationship developed between film and competition policies, in all aspects of the latter, even if to a different degree. This chapter is an attempt to outline some features and nuances of this relationship, which, contrary to the common and often only theoretical juxtaposition of culture and free market, might be much more harmonious and complementary in practice.

The real issue with regard to maintaining cultural diversity in the film sector when framing economic policy in the liberalization and integration context is not whether it is a legitimate goal[3] but rather how it can be achieved. This is where EU competition law may have a positive role to play.

EU Competition Law and Film Markets

There are three main areas where EU competition law potentially gains its relevance for the film sector. Firstly, state aid to the cinema sector enjoys a particular exemption possibility from the EU rules; its effects are, however, controlled so as to ensure that it does not run contrary to the common market objectives. Secondly, antitrust laws aiming at eliminating anticompetitive agreements and abuses of dominant position of market players in the EU media industry are intended to ensure diversity of outputs, including audiovisual content. Thirdly, merger control is supposed to

---

2   Council Regulation 1/2003/EC on the implementation of the rules on competition laid down in Articles 81 and 82 of the Treaty, [2003] OJ L1/1.

3   Article 151(4) of the EC Treaty obliges the EU to take cultural aspects into account in its action under other provisions of the Treaty.

guarantee that no excessive concentrations in the media sector are created which could be detrimental to effective competition, while taking into account the need to have European companies of a sufficient size to compete at the global level.

State Aid and Public Film Support

The first and possibly the most important angle from which to analyze the interaction of competition and film policies is that of EU state aid law. In view of the financial and political significance of the support that the European cinema receives from the public purse, it appears obvious that the state aid granted to the cinema industry receives particular attention from the EU competition authority, sanctioned by a specific approach towards cultural aid introduced into the EC Treaty. However, this 'tolerance' of public intervention in the cinema sector within the framework of EU competition law is not to be taken for granted; on the contrary, it is a source of continued tensions and intense discussions and thus deserves careful examination.

In general, state aid is incompatible with the EU common market, insofar as it affects trade between member states and by favouring certain undertakings or productions, distorts or threatens to distort the competition. Therefore, state aid to any sector of the economy is, in principle, prohibited by European law, namely by Article 87(1) of the EC Treaty. However, in view of the fact that culture remains a matter of competence of the member states,[4] some authors have argued that subsidies in the cultural sector should not be governed by the EU state aid rules (Schaefer, Kreile and Gerlach 2002, 184).

Yet, given the fundamental significance of the preservation of undistorted competition within the EU constitutional landscape, denying the EC competence to check the compatibility of film support schemes with state aid law would run against the aims and legal order of the EU. Certain cultural activities did develop into important industrial sectors in their own right, which are clearly subject to the EU common market regime. Therefore, cultural activities cannot be *a priori* excluded from the scope of application of Article 87(1) of the EC Treaty (Slot 1994). As acknowledged by the European Court of Justice (ECJ), the competition provisions apply without exception to all gainful activities whether of economic, cultural or social nature (Hancher et al. 1999, 78). Furthermore, the introduction of a special exception clause on cultural aid in Article 87(3) of the EC Treaty after Maastricht would not have been logical if this type of aid was not within the scope of the Treaty. This has been confirmed by a number of ECJ judgments concerning cultural aid.[5]

---

4   Article 151 of the EC Treaty. The substance of this Article 151 of the EC Treaty was not changed by the Treaty of Lisbon of 13 December 2007 (which replaces the Draft Treaty establishing a Constitution for Europe, http://european-convention.eu.int/docs/Treaty/cv00850.en03.pdf), see Article 2(12) (adding new Article 2E) and 2(126) (introducing procedural amendments to Article 151(5)) of the Treaty of Lisbon amending the Treaty on European Union and the Treaty establishing the European Community, [2007] OJ C 306/1.

5   *SIDE* v. *Commission*, [1995] ECR II-2501; *SIDE* v. *Commission*, [2002] ECR II-1179.

The inclusion of a separate title on culture (Article 151) into the EC Treaty in 1992 has important repercussions on the cultural sovereignty of the member states: since Maastricht the EC has two, somehow contradictory, tasks: apart from the responsibility of preserving undistorted competition, it is obliged, according to Article 151(4) of the EC Treaty, to take into account the cultural diversity of the member states in all its actions. As a consequence, the relationship between national cultural sovereignty and EU competition competence may seem, at least at first sight, controversial within the EU constitutional order.

A solution to this apparent conflict has been provided by the same Maastricht Treaty, which added the (above mentioned) further discretionary exemption to Article 87(3) in the form of a separate subparagraph (d), concerning 'aid to promote culture, and heritage conservation, where such aid does not affect trading conditions and competition in the Community to an extent that is contrary to the common interest'. The significance of this cultural derogation is reinforced by the fact that although the Maastricht Treaty introduced new provisions in other policy areas, for example, education, culture is the only one in which a separate provision was made to state aid.

Despite this clear cultural derogation from the EU state aid regime, which may also certainly benefit the cinema sector, and although the EC had been favourable towards state aid to European film industries,[6] application of Article 87(3)(d) of the EC Treaty is not free from controversies. The topicality of the tension between cultural and competition rationale in the field has been shown recently in the debate evolving around the criteria on control of state aid granted to the cinema sector, established by the EC and officially announced in the 2001 Cinema Communication.[7]

The criteria established laid down a guidelines framework under which all national aid schemes since notified have been approved. In substance, however, the criteria also formalized the EC's practice of gradually putting in place a *de facto* cap on admissible public support to European film production (Klevjer Aas 2001). The heated discussion on the potential limitative effect of the guidelines shows how policy considerations related to competition do affect the priorities and measures of national cultural policy. Among the fiercest critics of the EC's criteria were not only the directly concerned, that is, the EU cinema industry chiefs, but also the European Parliament. Both insisted that any reexamination of the EC's position on film state aid control (imminent as the guidelines' validity was to expire in June 2004), should lead to an increased flexibility rather than a stricter application of EU rules, and a genuine consideration of the cultural and industrial needs of the European audiovisual (mainly cinematographic) sector. Whereas the cinema professionals tend to invoke

---

6   Provided that the aid scheme was brought in line with the internal market provisions, see European Commission Decision 89/441/EEC of 21 December 1988 on aid granted by the Greek Government to the film industry for the production of Greek films, [1989] OJ L 208/38.

7   European Commission (2001), Communication from the Commission to the Council, the European Parliament, the Economic and Social Committee and the Committee of the Regions on certain legal aspects relating to cinematographic and other audiovisual works, COM(2001) 534 final.

cultural arguments when criticizing the EC's approach, the Parliament, on its part, considered that the EC was ignoring the industrial dimension of the EU audiovisual sector, in particular the fact that it is far from being competitive internally and externally.[8]

For the EC, as the EU competition authority, the main problem in the context of national aid to cinema is not its volume[9] but certain territoriality requirements, that is, so called 'territorialization' clauses of some aid schemes, on the basis of which aid is made conditional upon a certain amount of the film's budget being spent in a particular member state. Territorialization clauses, by privileging national investment, may constitute a barrier to the free circulation of workers, goods and services across the EU. They may therefore fragment the internal market and hinder its development, which creates obvious problems from a competition point of view.[10]

As a result, the 2001 guidelines prescribe that member states may not require producers to spend more than 80 per cent of the film or television work budget on their territory, which means that at least 20 per cent of the budget should be left free for the expenditure in other member states. Still, this rather limited 20 per cent margin remains problematic from the internal market perspective since, as hinted at above, territorialization may create exclusionary and therefore anticompetitive effects. In addition, by preventing recourse to goods and services originating in other member states, territorialization may run contrary to the Treaty provisions of free movement of goods and services. Therefore, having regard to the development of the single market for film production, the EC reserved itself a possibility of further changes to increase the 20 per cent rate of untied expenditure, in order to ensure coherence of the different national support schemes with the internal market.[11] Yet, as a result of a huge consultation exercise with the member states and EU cinema professionals conducted by the EC, it clearly emerged that the 2001 guidelines were widely considered a good – and indispensable – basis for the development of the sector. Given such unanimous support for the existing rules by both EU countries and the film industry, the EC adopted a decision to renew the 2001 communication

---

8   European Parliament (2002), Report on the Commission communication on certain legal aspects relating to cinematographic and other audiovisual works, A5-0222/2002 final.

9   European Commission (2004), Communication on the follow-up to the Commission communication on certain legal aspects relating to cinematographic and other audiovisual works (Cinema communication) of 26 September 2001 (OJ C43 on 16 February 2002) and proposal for a recommendation on film heritage and the competitiveness of related industrial activities, COM(2004)171 final.

10   On the other hand, the EC considered that such clauses might be justified, under certain circumstances and within certain limits, in order to ensure the continued presence of human skills and technical expertise required for cultural creation.

11   See European Commission Decision in cases Nos NN 49/97 and N 357/99 – Ireland, 'Section 35/481' tax-based film investment incentive, available at http://ec.europa.eu/community_law/state_aids/comp-1997-95/nn049-97.pdf. In the context of the revision of the guidelines, possibilities of reducing the territorialization permissible to a lower percentage or linking territorialization with aid intensity in order to free supported film production to take place outside national borders were discussed, see Eupolitix 2004; La Tribune 2004.

until June 2007, extending thus the validity of the guidelines criteria for a further three years.[12]

In view of the pressure under which the European audiovisual sector operates, the EC further accepted the 'territorialization' clauses within the minimal 20 per cent limits set by the previous criteria. Simultaneously, it pronounced itself willing to accept higher amounts of aid in the future provided however that they comply with the general legality criteria and, in particular, that barriers to the free circulation of workers, goods and services across the EU are reduced.[13] During the period in which the existing criteria will continue to apply, the EC planned to carry out a study on the cultural and economic impact of the existing aid schemes, which has been tendered in 2006.[14] With this study, the EC wishes to examine in particular the effects of the territorialization clauses, analysing for instance their impact on co-productions. This assessment of the impact of the territoriality conditions is aimed at continued legal security for the fundamental pillar of audiovisual policies across Europe represented by national aid schemes. At the same time, it shows that the EC's approach towards national aid schemes to film industries might well be revised, particularly with respect to their effect on the functioning of the common market.

In sum, it would seem that a workable *modus vivendi* has been found within the EU as far as state aid to cinema is concerned. Nevertheless, it might be an evolving *modus*, as the EC's position may well be revised one day, particularly as regards the 'territorialization' clauses. More generally and in the long term, different options have been hypothesized for the future EU control of state aid to the film industry. It may be that the calls of EU leaders for the state aid control to be 'properly targeted at the key market failure that inhibits enterprises' and for competition policy to 'take more account of necessary industrial developments'[15] are also taken seriously in the cinema sector. It was suggested that another forthcoming intergovernmental conference might be asked by the industry to revise the provisions of Article 87(3)(d) of the EC Treaty, and recognize explicitly the legitimacy of public aid systems to film and audiovisual works in order to guarantee that these support aids continue to exist unimpeded (Agence Europe 2004). In this unlikely scenario, it might even happen that more member states would endorse the French proposal to include cultural aids in the category of automatic exemptions of Article 87(2) of the EC Treaty, creating a legal presumption of their general legality (France 2002). A less

---

12   European Commission (2004), Communication on the follow-up to the Commission communication on certain legal aspects relating to cinematographic and other audiovisual works (Cinema communication) of 26 September 2001 (OJ C43 on 16 February 2002) and proposal for a recommendation on film heritage and the competitiveness of related industrial activities, COM(2004) 171 final.

13   This may prove impossible if territoriality requirements persist.

14   On 24 August 2006, see OJ S173, 12 September 2006, reference 2006/S173-183874. The preliminary findings of the study results of July 2007 are available at www.eufilmstudy. eu.

15   Letter of Tony Blair, Gerhard Schröder and Jacques Chirac to Romano Prodi, February 2004.

utopian medium term solution would be to adopt a group exemption[16] regulation for the category of film and television production aid. Such a block exemption would give legal certainty to the sector by enabling states to grant aid without notification (CNC 2003). However, this would require a previous amendment of the so-called enabling regulation that confers powers to the EC to adopt such exemptions.[17]

In any case, the EC can be expected to revise its position on territorialization at some point,[18] given its potential restrictive internal market and anticompetitive repercussions, in view of the evolution in the internal market and the study which is being conducted. This demonstrates that the EC's tolerance of government intervention in the film sector is not unconditional, but is integrated into the larger vision of the internal market, encompassing also film goods and services. In this respect, the vigilance over the negative consequences of cinema state aid on this market might be seen as better serving the goals of cultural diversity than uncritical acceptance of any type of support.

On the whole, however, and in view of the particular plight of the European audiovisual sector, subject to constant external pressures, one could hardly ever imagine the EC fundamentally questioning the film aid schemes around Europe. Having at its disposal a clear legitimization in the form of a cultural derogation enshrined in Article 87(3)(d) of the EC Treaty, the EU competition authority may well demonstrate that competition law is not blind to non-economic concerns and there are market failures or structural problems in sensitive sectors it has to address in a specific way.

Antitrust Rules versus Film Policy Considerations

In areas of competition law other than state aid control, cultural policy considerations figure less prominently. Nevertheless, there have been a few European cases illustrating both some difficulties in applying classic antitrust tools to the film sector and a tendency to treat cinema in a differentiated manner. They may be signs of a specific and inclusive approach towards cultural diversity imperatives within EU competition law.

---

16 So far, three block exemptions were granted, concerning state aid to small and medium-sized enterprises (SME), training aid and '*de minimis*' aid respectively. See 'Commission adopts group exemptions for State aid', Rapid press release IP/00/1415, 6 December 2000.

17 Council Regulation (EC) No 994/98 of 7 May 1998 on the application of Articles 92 and 93 of the Treaty establishing the European Community to certain categories of horizontal State Aid, [1998] OJ L142/1. For the moment, the EC can grant group exemptions for aids to small and medium-sized enterprises, research and development, environmental protection and employment and training.

18 In order to allow time for completion of the study and a subsequent possible revision of the criteria, the validity of the 2001 criteria was further extended until the moment when the potential new rules come into effect, or until 31 December 2009; see European Commission (2007), Communication concerning the prolongation of the application of the Cinema Communication, [2007] OJ C 134/5. The further steps by the Commission in that respect will thus depend on the results of the study commissioned.

Hence, although the market apparently cannot alone respond to the exigencies of cultural diversity, the negation of the free market by powerful operators, either through monopoly, oligopoly or through collusive behaviour, can have damaging repercussions for the quality and character of the range of cultural products on the market. Therefore, competition law, even though its primary objective is to keep markets open and not to defend cultural diversity *per se*, can nonetheless enhance diversity of supply. The antitrust control can ensure that media markets which are constantly evolving and access to which is often rendered difficult by substantial barriers of entry, are not closed off by excessive reinforcement of dominant positions leading to their abuses (sanctioned by Article 82 of the EC Treaty) or by anticompetitive collusions between market players (governed by Article 81 of the EC Treaty).

It has to be borne in mind, however, that from the consumer point of view, which involves not only the price but also the quality and the diversity of the offer, behaviour of media operators on the film market is to a large extent ambivalent. Thus, the assumption of a positive contribution of competition law to the success of European film policy remains elusive and one needs to analyze this contribution through an examination of specific European antitrust cases. This section is an attempt to demonstrate such an actual – and potential – contribution of antitrust policy to diversity in the European film sector.

The UIP Case: Inclusion or Rejection of Cultural Concerns?

An outstanding example of a case where the EC attempted to take account of film policy considerations in its competition decision making practice, (for some debatably and for many less than sufficiently), is the UIP exemption.

United International Pictures (UIP) is a joint venture created in 1981 by three of the main Hollywood film studios, Paramount Pictures Corporation, Universal Studios (forming part of MCA) and Metro Goldwyn Mayer, with the purpose to bring together their distribution activities. UIP was granted exclusive rights to the films of its parent companies in order to jointly distribute and licence them, thereby avoiding administrative duplication and considerably lowering costs.

When submitted to the EC for clearance under Article 81 of the EC Treaty, the agreement was considered to restrict competition. Indeed, the parent companies, which were previously competing with each other, would cease distributing films independently and would be able to coordinate their behaviour. As a joint distribution and licensing venture, UIP falls in the traditional category of joint sales organizations that are generally disfavoured by the EC since they are viewed as embodiments of 'classic horizontal cartels'.

An exemption was nevertheless granted under Article 81(3) of the EC Treaty.[19] The joint venture was considered as allowing for a more rational and efficient distribution in a market subject to considerable financial risks. However, the parties were forced to revise the notified agreements and to provide a number of positive undertakings to minimize the restrictive effects of the UIP.

---

19   *United International Pictures*, [1989] OJ L226/25.

From the cultural point of view, the UIP agreement seemed to affect the European film industry and the EC imposed conditions in the hope of countering that risk. The UIP promised to reinvest some of the profits it made from promoting European made films back into the EU industry.[20] Some commentators considered these conditions to be insufficiently connected to competition objectives (Waelbroeck 1998, 585). Others fiercely criticized and attacked the EC for its insensitivity to the needs of the European cinema sector, which would be heavily affected by the creation of the UIP distribution network.[21] The UIP exemption was renewed in 1999, by means of an administrative comfort letter (Rapid press release 14 September 1999). Again, the renewal was subject to enormous controversies (Agence Europe 1999). More resolutely this time, the critics argued that, despite the fact that the EC was to conduct an investigation of the agreement's impact on the film distribution market, it did not sufficiently analyze whether the advantages (including the cultural policy benefits) that motivated the initial exemption had materialized (Györy 2001). These voices demonstrated, without having recourse to emotional arguments amounting to cultural protectionism, that the perceived benefits had not been brought out in practice: neither the economic advantages for consumers nor an increase in European film production.

It would seem, indeed, that the UIP's 'cultural' undertakings had largely remained a dead letter but also that the renewed exemption in the new sound market conditions could have been damaging to the potential development of the EU cinema distribution market (FERA 1999; Györy 2001). The EC, however, did not see any particular impact of the UIP network on the market and could not find any proof of anticompetitive practices on the part of the UIP. It appears that the EC did not regard it necessary to examine the effect of 'cultural' undertakings given by UIP and instead focused, when requesting further modifications, on lessening the anticompetitive effects of the UIP agreement, on ensuring the highest possible autonomy of the parties to the agreement, and fair treatment of competitors (Toft 1999).

Once it was established by the EC that the agreement continued to yield competition benefits, the renewal did not come as a surprise. However, it came as a surprise in the film industry circles, more so as prior to its decision the EC had repeatedly stated that there would be little reason to allow UIP to continue benefiting from the exemption (*Variety* 1994; Chapman 1999). It was also claimed that the EC's final favourable verdict was, to some extent, due to political factors, the EC's change of heart being connected to the long story of trade tensions between EU and US over hormone treated beef and the EU banana regime. There were also suggestions that the positive decision had more to do with the brilliant performance of the UIP lawyers and weak or absent complainants (Chapman 1999).

---

20   Other undertakings referred to the support for the professional development of European filmmakers and film festivals, and the commitment to produce, finance, co-finance or acquire distribution rights to local films in the European Economic Area (EEA).

21   The criticisms were raised, among others, by Société de Auteurs, Réalisateurs et Producteurs – ARP, Eurocinéma and European Federation of Audiovisual Producers – FERA.

Notwithstanding these controversies, it seems that even if the EC decided to consider non-economic factors in its competition analysis of the UIP case, it appeared hardly imaginable for it to deny an exemption or its renewal solely on cultural grounds. Another theoretical option for the EC would be to interpret Article 81(3) of the EC Treaty in light of the cultural diversity objective (Article 151 of the EC Treaty), by a broad application of the consumer welfare concept. In fact, most recently there has been a certain shift in the EC approach towards a greater emphasis on consumer welfare. It seems however that the EC understanding of consumer welfare as including low prices, high quality products, a wide selection of goods and services, and innovation (European Commission, DG Competition Paper 2005) is rather narrow and would not entail cultural diversity concerns as such. Thus, it remains rather improbable that cultural diversity as an element of consumer welfare alone would be enough to justify or deny an exemption.

The EC is inevitably constrained by the language of Article 81 (3) of the EC Treaty and had to focus in this case on 'whether UIP has contributed to improving the production and distribution of films, while allowing users and consumers a fair share of the benefit' (Van Miert 1996).

Being so, it may seem that when considering the exemption renewal, the EC did not pay enough attention to evaluating the advantages, which the UIP exemption was supposed to produce. It may be true that the European film production sector had not benefited in a way expected from the UIP 'cultural' investment commitments. More importantly, however, the usually expected consumer benefits arising out of the agreement[22] were not borne out in practice (Györy 2001).

The controversy over the UIP exemption points more generally to the problem of effectiveness of the exemption decisions that incorporate cultural objectives. The UIP decision shows that on the one hand, the EC in its competition practice attempts to take into account the needs of the EU film industry (Van Miert 1996), and in doing so it is perfectly in line with its obligation set out in Article 151(4) of the EC Treaty and the positive film support policy. On the other hand, it also demonstrates the limits of competition law as a tool to purport cultural policy objectives. It appears extremely difficult to use competition policy to further the cultural aims of EU film policy. It might be reasonable and justified to require the parties of the agreement not to coordinate release dates, or to renounce block booking practices, yet asking them to invest in the European film industry might seem more questionable under competition law (FERA 1999). At the same time, however, the EC should be aware of the specificity of the sector and carefully check whether the consumer benefits expected to arise under competition law from a joint distribution network can be realized in the (different in many respects from other commodities) film distribution market.

The UIP decision is an example where, despite appearances to the contrary (the exemption and particularly its renewal being seen as having consolidated US dominance on the EU market), the cultural policy concerns did play a role in granting an exemption. Competition law, however, could not serve as an ultimate antidote for market failure in the cinema market and revealed its limits as an instrument of

---

22 These benefits are commonly perceived in terms of price, quality and offer.

active promotion for cultural diversity in the film sector. Thus, one would augur for the future – decentralized – competition scrutiny of the film distribution market around Europe, less 'cultural' (and not implemented) undertakings when considering potential exemptions, but instead a more profound evaluation of their potential effects on the structure of this market. This would provide a genuine response to the competitive advantages enjoyed by the US majors in EU film distribution and their constant tendency towards greater horizontal and vertical integration (London Economics and BIPE 1994). In all probability, opportunities to evaluate what needs to be done to enhance both competition in the supply of feature films and the access by European filmmakers to EU markets will not be lacking.

Towards a New Avenue: 'Output Deals'

The UIP theatrical exhibition case demonstrated, in the view of some, the EC's incapacity (or unwillingness even) to protect the EU film industry, and in the view of others its helplessness vis à vis the US hegemony in the European film market; and in the view of others still, this reflected an unjustified inclusion of cultural protectionism into the competition law methodology. The EC's 'victory' over the UIP pay-TV hegemony (Rapid press release 14 May 1997) did not change these divergent impressions. The UIP story marked, on the one hand, the confines of competition law as an instrument of cultural policy, and deficiencies in the EC competition analysis of the EU cinema distribution and exhibition market, on the other.

The recent EC *ex officio* investigation into the EU pay-TV markets and the supply of films to them by the US majors may indicate a new impetus for a more decisive, legitimate and potentially successful intervention in the film market by the EC as regards the – at least likely – anticompetitive behaviour by American film majors in the EU market, already reprimanded by the above mentioned UIP pay-TV dissolution.

In the new case, at stake are the so called 'output deals' between Hollywood studios and European pay-TV firms, involving the sale of television rights to recent films, which may be in breach of EU competition law. 'Output deals' is a jargon designation for agreements between big film production studios and the pay-TV operators for licensing of film rights, encompassing usually every title in a film distributors' catalogue for a specified number of years into the future.[23] Output deals are mostly the province of Hollywood majors because of the breadth and volume of their productions, and thus their commercial attractiveness for pay-TV operators (Marich 2004).

The EC's probe began after it had its attention drawn to the length of such contracts between European pay-TV companies and several Hollywood studios. Reportedly, it was prompted by a complaint from a French pay-TV operator TPS about alleged anticompetitive practices from its rival Canal Satellite (*Financial Times* 15 January 2003). An initial investigation into the matter was launched by the EC in 2001 and

---

23 Mostly five years in the EU context. A formula specifies minimum requirements for films to qualify and a license fee is calculated according to a foreseen method (see Marich 2004).

was followed by a second probe in 2002. As part of its inspection, the EC has raided a number of EU based pay-TV companies.

As reported repeatedly by the press (McLeod January 2004; Gonzales 2004), the EC was about to file its charges against the studios in the form of a formal statement of objections targeting the studios' anticompetitive practices to boost film profits by exploiting titles in foreign (that is, EU) television markets.

The EC's scrutiny centred on the so called 'most favoured nation' (MFN) clauses,[24] which are used by the studios to set the minimum prices for film contracts with European pay-TV operators. The clauses in question require pay-TV companies to extend the best price and terms for a set number of films for one Hollywood studio to all studios it has contracts with, giving them a sort of price protection in the EU pay-TV market. As a result of such clauses, any major studio benefits automatically from any more favourable commercial term granted by the pay-TV operator to another studio. The MFN clauses can also be applied to non-financial terms, such as definition of what films qualify to be included in film output deals, whereby pay-TV platforms would be obligated to purchase all qualifying films over the term of the contract (Marich 2004, 20).

The EU probe was supposed to cover all of the Hollywood major film suppliers because, given their bargaining power, they all negotiate MFN clauses for their benefit with the main European pay-TV operators. The European investigators believed that the 'cumulative effect' of the clauses might have entailed a horizontal effect keeping the prices of Hollywood films artificially convergent and higher than a free competition price, resulting in higher pay-TV subscription fees for customers in the EU. If a pay-TV platform increases prices for one film supplier, all pre-existing contracts with MFN clauses immediately soar to a higher level, thus creating a broad price upsurge (Marich 2004). In short, the MFN clauses may well be distorting competition in the EU market by eliminating competition between Hollywood studios and forcing European consumers to pay inflated prices.

Moreover and more importantly in terms of cultural diversity, it seems that such clauses may be further reducing competition by raising barriers to entry for other (mostly European) film producers, which is due to their combined effect on prices together with the volume of films to be purchased and the duration of the agreements. The pay-TV operators would be 'locked in' by the studios as they need the highly attractive film content (blockbusters) produced by them. The clauses would imply that operators have to buy not only at a higher prices but a bigger quantity of films and for a longer time, which definitely would affect their purchasing strategy. Thus, by means of the MFN clauses, the US majors could also prevent independent producers entering the European market for pay-TV, thereby violating EU competition rules.

Prior to the EC investigation, it was suggested that it would be the behaviour of EU pay-TV companies that would require more attention by the EU competition authority and the most significant legal issue within the EC's investigation framework would be the cumulative examination of series of vertical film licensing agreements concluded by single pay-TV operators (Sage 2003). This was deemed to be a natural

---

24   The MFN clauses are named after the status granted by the US Congress to trading partners.

consequence of a series of intensive investigations of premium contents' licensing, related at the EU level so far exclusively to sport rights (Rapid press release 24 July 2003; Herold 2003). Also the Hollywood studios would have wanted the EC to concentrate rather on the behaviour of pay-TV companies, arguing that MFN clauses are not illegal and can have equally adverse effects on their own position.[25]

This notwithstanding, the EC took a different stance and innovatively focused on the collusive behaviour of Hollywood studios acting as suppliers, both as far as pricing and the setting of contractual terms is concerned. The MFN issue, as a mechanism to elevate film prices in the pay-TV arena, was tackled from the viewpoint that EU pay-TV and consumers are injured (Marich 2004, 21). The EC definitely is aware that it must ensure proper functioning of competition between broadcasters and programmes' suppliers, which means tackling all restrictive behaviour, be it on the supply or demand side. Undoubtedly, the position of pay-TV broadcasters on the relevant markets has been taken into account in the EC's competition analysis. However, it would be inconceivable to use the pay-TV operators' position as a justification for anticompetitive practices by the studios. The dependence of studios on pay-TV providers is rather limited, as they rely on various sources of revenues, ranging from theatrical exploitation through DVD and videocassette income. Also, pay-TV broadcasters, even if reaching a considerable position in the markets, would remain localized operators, whereas major studios are unquestionably global players.

Hence, the EC's investigation addressing the horizontal collusion by the studios marks a first attempt by the European competition authority to challenge anticompetitive practices by Hollywood majors in the EU film distribution market. If the EC's allegations had been confirmed, the studios would have had to amend their contracts with pay-TV companies, easing pricing and other contractual terms of the deals and thus allowing other producers to enter the market more easily. Moreover, the studios could have faced fines and lawsuits by consumers.

For the time being, six out of eight major studios involved have avoided this risk. As reported recently, the EC closed its investigation in respect to the studios that decided to withdraw the MFN clauses in their contracts with pay-TV operators.[26] The majors have not admitted a violation of EU competition law, and did not agree with the EC's preliminary assessment, claiming that they are in fierce competition abroad which virtually rules out any collusion in pricing (Guider and Stern 2004). However, at an early stage of the investigation, one of them withdrew its clauses, indicating that it would not seek to implement such provisions in future agreements. Later on, five other studios also decided to waive the clauses in their existing agreements. Insofar as they do not deviate from this new behaviour, the EC declared that it would take no further action against them concerning this issue. The investigation remained open with regard to NBC Universal and Paramount that still held to the clauses in question, and which have been called to follow the other majors' decision (Rapid press release 26 October 2004; McLeod 26 October 2004). The case has not,

---

25   The studios claimed, for example, that the clauses prevented them from reselling a package of films for a lower price to another pay-TV platform.

26   On the problems with the EC statement of objections, see Dombey 2004.

however, been further pursued by the EC. The reasons for this have never been made public.

In any case, the 'output deals' case has become, at least to a certain extent, an exemplification of an active contribution of competition law to cultural diversity. By persuading the market players to renounce the MFN clauses, the EC ensures proper functioning of the EU film distribution market. In this way, the EC not only assists the pay-TV operators in the European market, but also lends a hand to the independent (including European) producers in accessing this market. The actual persuasive effect of the EC investigation in the practices of the majors definitely is to benefit of EU pay-TV providers by making it easier for them to agree to deals with a particular studio without having to offer the deal to other studios, but also to enable them to change their purchasing strategy into a more favourable one to third (mainly and most probably European, given the audience preference for local film content) producers. Thus, the actual (and potentially future in case it appears that MFN clauses are still used by some majors) EU action would not only help to liberalize the European market for pay-TV film rights but, more importantly, it can actively contribute to furthering cultural diversity in the EU film sector. It can reduce prices for consumers, but, more importantly from the cultural point of view, it can also guarantee them a more balanced and diverse range of films.

The Microsoft Case: Opening a Real Battle Over the Film Industry?

In the context of the future of the European audiovisual industries, a further significant sign of a more proactive approach of the EU competition authority could be found in the most prominent of recent EU antitrust cases resulting in the EC's ruling against the US software company Microsoft Corporation, widely reported by the press. Taking the cinema perspective, it is argued that the Microsoft decision has launched a battle over the future technical standards for online delivery of music, feature films and other forms of digital entertainment (Agence France Presse 2004).

The issues at stake are not negligible. An In-Stat study projects that 280 million consumers worldwide by 2008 will have equipment to produce their own media, such as films or music, and over 247 million will be connected to broadband connections, while among the companies most likely to benefit most is Microsoft, followed by Intel and Disney (Instat 2004). At the same time, it seems that Microsoft's strategy is to become an 'indispensable partner' to the content industry, including streaming audio and audiovisual, games and other new forms of content. Reportedly, Microsoft plans to use its Windows Media to dominate the film industry's distribution technology, from digital dailies to theatrical releases to digital cable and DVDs (*The Age* 2004). Microsoft's strategy is apparent both in the feature upgrades of its Windows Media and in the partnerships and projects it has announced since the technology was unveiled. Indeed, as openly admitted by the Microsoft management itself, it is working very closely with the film industry standard setting organizations, such as the Society of Motion Picture and Television Engineers (Sinnreich 2003).

Although, currently, competition for the technical standards of online content still exists, it is feared that, if unchecked, the US software giant could use its dominance in PC software to gain a stranglehold on the emerging online delivery field. As computer technology and home entertainment converge, it is thus essential to maintain competition in order to prevent Microsoft from 'locking in' its Windows Media Player (WMP), which is used for digital video and audio content delivery and proprietary format as the *de facto* standard (Lever 2004).[27]

This is one of the underlying reasons for the EC's ruling and one of the main conditions imposed therein, relating to WMP unbundling. In its decision, the EC has found that Microsoft violated EU competition rules by abusing its near monopoly (Article 82 of the EC Treaty) in the PC operating system (Rapid press release 24 March 2004). The nature of this abuse was established as twofold: according to the EC, Microsoft not only abused its market power by deliberately restricting interoperability between Windows PCs and non Microsoft work group servers, but also by tying its Windows Media Player (WMP), a product where it faced competition, with its ubiquitous Windows operating system. In response, the EC ordered Microsoft to offer a European version of its all conquering Windows operating system without its Media Player programme. Microsoft retained the right to offer a version of its Windows client PC operating system product with WMP. However, Microsoft must refrain from using any commercial, technological or contractual terms that would have the effect of rendering the unbundled version of Windows less attractive or functional. In particular, it must not give PC manufacturers a discount conditional on their buying Windows together with its media player.[28]

It is precisely this second finding of the EC, and the remedy imposed in its context, that might have a positive impact on the European – or more generally – non-US cinema market and, in particular, on the diversity of films to be offered, in the future, on the Internet (Herold 2004). Innovation in content delivery is unpredictable and the battlefield is still open. However, allowing the ongoing abuses to continue would act as a brake on the this innovative process and harm the competitive process and consumers, who might ultimately end up with less choice and facing higher prices. In the context of cinema, it might mean translating the hegemony of the US majors in the world theatrical distribution film market into domination (together with Microsoft) of the delivery of film content in cyberspace. Arguably, the Microsoft ruling might well have prevented or diminished the probability of such a scenario.

Concentration in the Media Sector and the European Film Market

As far as merger control is concerned, the contribution of EU action towards diversity in the film sector may be even less clear than in other competition law areas. No European merger has concerned the cinema sector as such, but feature

---

27   Ed Black, of the Computer and Communications Industry Association, was reported to claim that, by requiring Hollywood and other film industries, the music and game industries to use the Windows format and its WMP, Microsoft would be able to impose a sort of 'tax' on audiovisual (and audio) online content.

28   European Commission Decision of 24 May 2004 relating to a proceeding pursuant to Article 82 of the EC Treaty and Article 54 of the EEA Agreement against Microsoft Corporation (Case COMP/C-3/37.792 – Microsoft), [2007] OJ L 32/23.

films are often considered a form of premium content, control of which may create competition problems when considering approval of a given concentration. Needless to say, cultural considerations as such are never directly referred to in the merger decisions and these decisions are not intended to favour any particular type of content. The European merger control's sole objective is to ensure that no excessive concentrations are established which could be harmful to effective competition.[29] Yet, EU merger control, as it plays a role in enhancing media pluralism, may also have an impact on the diversity of the film sector, namely by preventing the creation of media monopolies, which would dominate certain dissemination channels of films, and, in cases where the merger is allowed, by imposing conditions on the restructuring of groups, facilitating thus a more favourable framework for content dissemination (CNC 2003).

In concreto, this positive role would consist, on the one hand, in ensuring access for all distributors to films as valuable content and, on the other, in guaranteeing access of all films, not only US productions, to the distribution infrastructure. The actual contribution of EU merger case practice to diversity in the film market is provided mainly by remedies imposed in mergers between multimedia companies that are active in downstream markets, mainly in various television markets, but also, and at least potentially, in online delivery markets. The consolidation of pay-TV platforms examined by the EC in some recent complex cases showed the paramount importance of EU merger control for both access to film rights and access of diverse film content to screens.

The *Vivendi/Canal+/Seagram* decision may serve as a good example of EU merger practice having a positive, even if indirect, impact on the diversity in the EU film sector by ensuring access to films.[30] The aim of the decision was, among others, to avoid one dominant operator eliminating competition by cumulating too much American content, or, in other words, rights to an excessive number of Hollywood films. The will to reduce anticompetitive effects of such a monopolization of rights was the underlying (usual in the merger investigation context) economic motivation for the EC to demand undertakings from the parties. At the same time, a reinforcement of a dominant position by one operator without such undertakings could have indirectly produced serious adverse effects on the European film industry residing in the danger of 'cultural' homogenization of the dominant player's offer. Therefore one can equally distinguish a value added effect of this decision on the supply side from the cultural point of view.

In casu, Seagram (which controlled Universal, hence one of the most important world film and music producers) notified a merger with Vivendi (a media and telecommunications company active in pay-TV with Canal+, mobile telephony with Cegetel, and multi access Internet portal with Vizzavi). As a result of the market investigation, the EC concluded that the concentration would create or strengthen the dominant position of Canal+ in the pay-TV markets of several European countries, as the newly integrated group could leverage its position from the film

---

29 In particular, by creating or reinforcing dominant positions, allowing the merged entities to act independently from their clients, competitors and suppliers.

30 *Vivendi/Canal+/Seagram*, [2000] OJ C311/3.

content rights. As regards these rights, Canal+, whose portfolio of 'output deals' was already considerable, would become more closely linked to Universal (itself linked with Paramount and MGM through UIP JV) and Fox (through BSkyB), so that any competing pay-TV operator would be deprived of access to the rights for a large percentage of US feature film output.

The merger between the parties was nonetheless rendered possible thanks to the conditions imposed. To meet the concern in the pay-TV market, the parties agreed to provide access to Universal's 'first window' films[31] on a non-discriminatory basis, to limit, for five years, up to 50 per cent of what Canal+ may receive, and to sever the links with Fox/BSkyB. These undertakings significantly reduced the capacity of Canal+ to influence other US film studios in their market behaviour and eliminated the serious doubts as to the reinforcement of a Canal+ dominant position after its integration with Universal.

The *Vivendi/Canal+/Seagram* case demonstrates that the EU merger control may play a role, even if less obvious than in other competition law areas, in enhancing cultural diversity in the film sector. By imposing strong behavioural remedies on the parties willing to merge, and nevertheless authorising the merger, the EC shows its favourable and dynamic approach towards integration strategies between EU and global media companies, while countering at the same time the risks of market foreclosure. By preventing concentration of too much US film content in the hands of a single dominant operator and ensuring access to valuable (so called premium) content, the EC contributes positively, although only indirectly, to diversity in the EU film market.

Another valuable contribution of the EU merger practice to diversity in the European cinema is to ensure access of all films, regardless of their origin, to distribution infrastructures. A good example where such a positive input can be recognized is provided by the EC decision in the *Newscorp/Telepiù* case,[32] in which the merged entity was obliged to grant third parties access to their satellite platforms under equitable, non discriminatory and cost oriented terms, such as to allow for intra platform competition. The obligation extended to the supply of technical services that are necessary and instrumental to offering pay-TV channels. Thus, the new media entity assumed an obligation of entering into simulcrypt agreements as soon as reasonably possible and in any event within nine months from the written request from an interested third party (Mendes Pereira 2003).[33]

These conditions ensured that access to different forms of content, including other films than those to which the rights were owned by the merged entity, to the new pay-TV platform would be facilitated. Hence, diversity in audiovisual content

---

31 Under 'first window', films are usually understood those showed on pay-TV shortly after cinema exhibition and video rental, that is, before they are widely available on free TV.

32 *Newscorp/Telepiù* [2004] OJ L110/73.

33 As an additional safeguard in respect of pricing, the parties were required to implement separate accounts for all the activities arising from the services related to the access to platform. Also, a clear separation between the parties' activities at wholesale and retail level in this respect was to be introduced.

available to the final consumers was, at least potentially, enhanced and potential access of EU films to distribution channels was rendered easier.

The contribution of EU merger control to cultural diversity in the cultural industries *sensu largo* may be, however, not always as evident as the above cases seem to demonstrate. A good example is provided by the *Sony/BMG* decision,[34] which can be seen as going against the cultural diversity objectives. It seems that the EC has not paid enough attention to the question of whether the concentration between Sony and BMG could have a negative impact on cultural diversity. As it has been argued, the EC should have assessed whether the possibly that the increased marketing power of the merged entities would have diminished the supply of recorded music from a variety of cultural origins in terms of competitive marketing investments. Furthermore, it appears that the EC should have evaluated the effect of collective market dominance resulting from a more concentrated oligopoly on cultural diversity (Germann 2006). By the judgment of 13 July 2006, the Court of First Instance (CFI)[35] annulled this decision on the grounds that the EC did not correctly assess the relevant facts and erred in law with respect to the question of a collective dominant position.[36] The Court did not raise the question of the impact of the merger on cultural diversity, and the Commission confirmed recently its approval of the joint venture (Rapid press release 3 October 2007). However, Impala (an independent music companies association) has announced that it would appeal against this decision, ask for damages and lodge a complaint with the European Ombudsman. What is more, Impala expects the Commission to review competition rules in cultural markets and issue new guidelines in 2008.[37] Thus, the saga is not over yet and the Commission may be forced in the future to explicitly take account of cultural diversity concerns in the music market in its practice.

This notwithstanding, some positive impact of European merger controls on diversity in the European film markets is difficult to deny. Furthermore, the general trends in the EC's merger control indicate that more recently it is more willing to accept big mergers in the media industry than before, as exemplified by the cases discussed above, and instead make extensive use of conditions and undertakings. Also, the EC tends to approve of the creation of *de facto* monopolies in some media markets (Ariño 2004). In this more general context, the subtle interplay of contradictory interests in the EU concentration control comes clearly to the fore: the EC is inclined to favour concentration of European media groupings in order to enable them to face US and Japanese competition, while ensuring respect for free competition and pluralism. On the one hand, the EC is aware that sizeable media corporations are essential with a view to accomplishing internal market objectives

---

34   19 July 2004, C(2004) 2815, Case No COMP/M.3333, *Sony/BMG*, [2005] OJ L62/30.

35   *Independent Music Publishers and Labels Association (Impala)* v. *Commission* (T-464/04) ECR [2006] II-2289.

36   The view of the CFI is likely to be upheld by the ECJ, see Opinion of Advocate General Kokott, *Bertelsmann AG and Sony Corporation of America* v. *Impala* (C-413/06P).

37   See http://www.impalasite.org/docum/04-press/Press%20Release%2013-12-07%20Background.htm.

and the strengthening of European competitiveness. On the other hand, these holdings should be deterred from taking advantage of their power to undermine competition, hinder the emergence or participation of newcomers and small companies, and damage social and cultural living conditions (Pauwels 1998). All that bearing in mind the specific and unbalanced situation in the EU film market. As for the film sector *sensu stricto*, the dilemmas may be rather disguised so far, and the choices not so pressing as in the broadcasting or press sectors, nevertheless the EU film industry interests will continue to come into play – and hopefully would be safeguarded in the future EU merger policy considerations.

Conclusions

The above outline of EU competition practice seems to indicate that the relationship between competition and film policy might be much more harmonious than the common opposition between culture and free market would suggest. It appears that competition law can accommodate to a certain degree cultural considerations and genuinely contribute to preserving, and promoting, cultural diversity in the film sector.

First of all, EU state aid law provides a compromise solution taking full account of cultural aspects of public film support policies while endeavouring to respect the fundamental competition imperatives of the internal market. The EC thus accepts a certain level of protection in cultural markets, and approves of national government measures to support the domestic audiovisual industry, provided they do not run contrary to the common market.

However, the role of competition law in enhancing cultural diversity does not and should not stop there. With respect to private economic behaviour, EU antitrust law gives the EC some leeway to take account of non economic concerns in its decisions. The EC has already previously acknowledged that 'competition law is not purely a matter of dissuasion or punishment ... [but] has an indispensable role to play in facilitating ... progress towards economic and social cohesion' (European Commission 1992, 47). At the same time, the EC recognizes the special nature of cultural goods, including film and television industries, which constitute important parts of the European cultural landscape. Consequently, it would seem that the EC is allowed, if not obliged, to take extra competition concerns, including cultural interests, into consideration when making competition law decisions, the more that the cross sectional clause of Article 151(4) of the EC Treaty compels the EU institutions to take cultural aspects into account in all their actions (Monti 2002). In fact, the EC Competition Directorate General has frequently stressed that cultural considerations have always been taken into account in applying Articles 81 and 82 of the EC Treaty (European Commission 1992, 97).

However, this approach may be constrained by the wording of Article 81(3) of the EC Treaty and the economic parameters of competition policy. The negative condition of Article 81(3) may be taken to mean that the EC cannot promote cultural diversity if that would lead to the eliminating of competition (Holmes 1998, 110). The EC itself recognized long ago the inherent boundaries of competition policy, admitting that 'all the participants in the process of cultural creation' are also economic actors competing with each other 'for audiences, advertisers and outlets' (European Commission 1992, 97). In the context of book agreements, it clearly stated that Articles 81 and 82 'were not designed to protect cultural objectives' and that in any case 'promotion of cultural objectives' cannot on its own constitute 'a basis for an individual exemption' (Bouterse 1994; Monti 2002). Thus, it may seem that, if an agreement cannot be exempted on cultural grounds alone under Article 81(3), mere cultural policy grounds could not justify denial of an exemption (so Holmes 1998, 114).

This is, among other reasons, why the EC's discretion with respect to cultural policy was limited in the UIP case re-investigation to take account 'of the main economic indicators underlying the previous decision and the extent to which UIP's conduct was in line with the undertakings given' (Van Miert 1996). The accuracy of the economic analysis carried out may be questioned, because of the specificity of the sector and its economic conditions, but the UIP's apparent failure to comply with the 'cultural' undertakings seems to indicate that the exemption decisions are not the right instrument to actively purport cultural policy objectives. Instead, the EC's input would be (and still can be) more valuable if it monitored more closely UIP's commercial behaviour in order to prevent it from concerting film releases or engaging in block booking practices. The EC's real responsibility may be to intervene more decisively in the film distribution market, taking account of its special (also cultural) characteristics and fully assessing the impact of the existing joint selling arrangements on its structure, which would ensure fairer access for all filmmakers to distribution chains.

The genuine contribution of competition law would thus reside not in using economic criteria to arbitrarily further cultural policy objectives, which can turn out to be, as the 'cultural' undertakings in the UIP case have shown, a risky and fruitless exercise, but rather concentrating on the core objectives in its antitrust analysis, although without ignoring cultural concerns. In fact, the non-economic interests are often, even if only implicitly, kept in the optic of the EC competition analysis. They could thus be more openly recognized by the EC as supplementary factors to be taken into account when granting/denying exemption. They cannot, however, prevail over competition factors or jeopardize the goals of undistorted competition and the internal market.

Yet, such a full opposition of cultural and market logic is, as the above survey demonstrates, very rarely the case. Not all competition interventions in the film market have to be controversial. The 'output deals' case (at least potentially) and indirectly also the Microsoft case are excellent examples where competition objectives go in line with the cultural interests of the European film industry and where reaction to anticompetitive practices in the EU media markets can perfectly serve the goal of promoting cultural diversity around Europe. What competition law could not achieve in the UIP case through an attempt to insert 'cultural' undertakings into the competition law practice, might well be better achieved by means of 'pure' competition analysis in the 'output deals' or Microsoft case. This is how the EC's action may ultimately have a positive impact on cultural diversity within the film sector: through the preservation of economic efficiency and preservation of an economic environment favourable to cultural creation.

As for the EU concentration control, it would seem that it also recognizes, at least to a certain extent, the cultural needs of the European film industry, as exemplified by the *Vivendi/Canal+/Seagram* and *Newscorp/Telepiù* cases. Using extensive undertakings in its merger scrutiny, the EC makes – even if only indirect – a contribution to cultural diversity of the range of audiovisual products and services in Europe, ensuring both access to premium films and access of all films to distribution channels. At the same time, the EC is perfectly aware of the fact that some concentration in the media sector can enhance the development of EU audiovisual industries, especially in view of their structural weaknesses. The EU merger control parameters seem to be apt to grasp the contradictory policy objectives in the film market, where a need for stronger European groupings meets the demand for keeping markets open.

In sum, it appears that EU competition law not only tolerates the specificity of the film sector by providing exceptions from the state aid regime but also can actively favour cultural diversity through its antitrust and merger instruments. After all, cultural products, film being an emblematic example, are designed to entertain, for which reason they are demanded and consumed. It might remain true that the (in)famous concept of the 'cultural exception', laying the basis for cinema policies around Europe, opposes the market logic and its forces; it does not mean, though, that cinema and competition policy objectives are contradictory and irreconcilable. For consumers (often culturally motivated) interest in a diverse range of cultural goods and services, films being the most popular and most influential among these, is nothing else than a central concern of competition law.

Hence, it seems that competition policy can contribute to the cultural aims of EU film policy, without confusing, though, their respective objectives (Van Miert 1996). Competition law, although tolerant of government intervention in the film sector and supportive of the development of the European film industry by private actors, cannot lose sight of its fundamental objectives, under which cultural diversity falls outside. Promoting cultural diversity *per se* may be an objective of the EU audiovisual policy but not one of EU competition policy, which cannot be treated as a tool for achieving cultural diversity and shows its inherent limits in action in favour of the European film industry. Cultural diversity in the film market cannot be attained solely through competition law instruments. The competition logic, residing in ensuring diversity of supply, does not respond automatically to the cultural goals of film policy. This is why intervention through audiovisual policy remains imperative in order to remedy market failure, by implementing support programmes and creating a favourable regulatory framework for European creativity.[38]

However, the EU lacks power in the field of media or cultural policy, which remain an area of national competence. Cultural policy is continuously considered

---

38 For example through the disputed instrument of quotas. The choice of the right instruments is of course subject to controversies, but falls outside the scope of this chapter.

an area of 'support, co-ordination and complementary action',[39] while audiovisual policy instruments remain based mostly on internal market and industrial policy provisions of the EC Treaty. This legal situation makes the contribution of competition law to cultural diversity at the EU level even more critical. Competition law is one of the most powerful EU legal instruments, where sweeping enforcement deeply impacts not only on the cinema market structure but also on the cultural policies designed across Europe. Indeed, the EC as the EU competition authority has been accused of taking far reaching decisions with profound constitutional implications and therefore interfering with national cultural policies (Schwarze 2002, 800). The actual and potential positive role of competition law in enhancing cultural diversity is far less widely realized. It is therefore all the more important that competition policy makers are made aware of their at least potential contribution to cultural diversity and legitimized in their efforts in that respect.

As this chapter has demonstrated, cultural concerns are not only present in the EU competition legal framework in the form of the cultural derogation of Article 87(3)(d) of the EC Treaty, but are also taken into consideration in the EC's antitrust and merger analysis. Their explicit recognition, without eroding the existing competition law constitution or altering its focus from the core values of market integration, consumer welfare and efficiency, would not do any harm to the EU competition doctrine, but may do some good to cultural diversity in the film market on our continent.

References

The Age (2004), 'Windows Could Lose Media Player in EU Tangle', 8 March 2004, www.theage.com.au.

Agence Europe (1999), 'European Directors Urge Prodi Commission to Review Approval of UIP Agreement', 17 September 1999.

Agence France Presse (2004), 'Microsoft Battle in Brussels is About Hollywood, Digital Entertainment', www.spacedaily.com,1 April 2004.

Ariño, M. (2004), 'Digital War and Peace: Regulation and Competition in European Digital Broadcasting', *European Public Law Journal* 10(1), 135–160.

Bouterse, R.B. (1994), 'Competition and Integration: What Goals Count? EEC Competition Law Goals of Industrial, Monetary and Cultural Policy' (PhD thesis), Florence: European University Institute.

Chapman, P. (1999), 'Van Miert Rewrites the Film Industry Script', *European Voice*, 23 September 1999.

CNC (Centre Nationale de la Cinématographie) (2003), *Rapport du groupe de travail sur le cinéma face au droit de la concurrence*, www.cnc.fr, 31 January 2003.

Dombey, D. (2004), 'Hollywood Scores Point in Brussels Dispute', *Financial Times*, www.news.ft.com, 9 May 2004.

Dony, M. (1996), 'Les aides à l'audiovisuel à la lumière du Traité de Maastricht', in

---

39   See new Article 2E introduced into the EC Treaty by the Treaty of Lisbon, see above, note 2.

Doutrelepont C. (ed.), *L'actualité du droit de l'audiovisuel européen*, Bruxelles: Bruylant.

European Commission (1992), XXIId Report on Competition Policy, COM(1993)162 final.

European Commission (2005), DG Competition Discussion Paper on the application of Article 82 of the Treaty to exclusionary abuses, December 2005.

FERA (1999), 'La FERA demande au Commissaire Van Miert de différer la décision de la Commission européenne dans l'affaire UIP en attendant la constitution de la nouvelle Commission présidée par Romano Prodi', 8 April 1999, www.fera-matin.org.

France (2002), 'La place de la culture dans le futur traité'contribution to the debate on the future of Europe', 17 December 2002, CONV 460/02, annex.

Germann, C. (2006), 'Towards a "Cultural Contract" Against Trade Related Cultural Discrimination' in J. Smiers and N. Obuljen, *UNESCO Convention of the Protection and Promotion of the Diversity of Cultural Expressions - Making it Work*, Zagreb: Culturelink.

Gonzales, P. (2004), 'Hollywood dans le collimateur', *Bloomberg*, 14 January 2004.

Guerrera F. and Burt T. (2003), 'Brussels Probes Hollywood TV Deals', *Financial Times*, 15 January 2003, available at www.ft.news.com.

Guider, E. and Stern, A. (2004), 'EC Drops Its Studio Probe', *Variety*, 26 October 2004.

Györy, M. (1996), 'La décision UIP: un defi juridique?' in Doutrelepont C. (ed.), *L'actualité du droit de l'audiovisuel européen*, Bruxelles: Bruylant.

Györy, M. (2001), 'Une derogation qui fait discuter', *Cinecittà Rivista*, no. 1, http://www.cinecitta.com/holding/rivista/rivista.asp.

Hancher, L., et al. (1999), *EC State Aids*, London: Sweet and Maxwell.

Herold, A. (2002), 'Rules Governing the Acquisition by Third Parties of Television Rights for Sporting Events under Eurovision in Breach of the European Competition Law', *International Journal of Communications Law and Policy*, issue 7, winter 2002–2003.

Herold, A. (2003), 'Future of Digital Cinema in Europe: Legal Challenge for the EU?', *Journal of Research into New Media Technologies* 9(4), 99–115.

Holmes, A. (1998), 'Culture and Competition: The Case of United International Pictures' (LLM thesis), Florence: European University Institute.

Klejver Aas, N. (2001), 'Challenges in European Cinema and Film Policy', European Audiovisual Observatory, www.obs.coe.int/online_publication/reports/aas.html.

La Tribune (2004), 'Le cinéma français défend son système d'aide a Bruxelles', 19 January 2004, available at www.latribune.fr.

Lever, R. (2004), 'Microsoft Battles Over Future Digital Hollywood', Technology Brief, 1 April 2004, http://www.gmax.co.za/feel/tech/2004/040401-MSbrussels.html.

London Economics and BIPE Conseil for Media Salles (1994), *White Book of the European Exhibition Industry*, vol. 2, chapter 3.3, www.medisalles.it.

Marich, R. (2004), *The EC versus the Hollywood Studios*, London: Informa Media Group.

McLeod, R. (14 January 2004), 'EU to Scupper "Cartel"-Like Studio Scam', 14

January 2004, *The Age*, www.theage.com.au.

McLeod, R. (26 October 2004), 'Paramount, NBC-Universal face EU probe on contracts', 26 October 2004, *Bloomberg*.

Mendes Pereira, M. (2003), 'Recent Consolidation in the European Pay-TV Sector', *Competition Policy Newsletter*, no. 2, 29–40.

Monti, G. (2002), 'Article 81 EC and Public Policy', CMLR 39(5), 1057–1099.

Pauwels, C. (1998), 'Integrating Economies, Integrating Policies. The Importance of Antitrust and Competition Policies within the Global Audiovisual Order', *Communications & Strategies*, 103–122.

Puttnam, D. (1997), *The Undeclared War: The Struggle for Control of the World's Film Industry*, London: HarperCollins.

Rapid Press Release (14 May 1997), IP/97/227, European Commission, negative clearance without publication, *UIP Pay Television+3*.

Rapid Press Release (14 September 1999), IP/99/681, European Commission, individual exemption without publication, *United International Pictures*.

Rapid Press Release (24 July 2003), IP/03/1105, Commission decision, *UEFA Champions League*.

Rapid Press Release (24 March 2004), IP/04/382, *Commission concludes on Microsoft investigation, imposes conduct remedies and a fine*.

Rapid Press Release (26 October 2004), IP/04/1314, *Commission closes investigation into contracts of six Hollywood studios with European pay-TVs*.

Rapid Press Release (3 October 2007), IP/07/143, *Mergers: Commission confirms approval of recorded music joint venture between Sony and Bertelsmann after re-assessment subsequent to Court decision*.

Sage, E.D. (2003), 'Series of Film-Licensing Agreements and the Application of Article 81', *ECLR* 9, 475–480.

Schaefer, K., Kreile, J. and Gerlach, S. (2002), 'Nationale Filmförderung: Einfluss und Grenzen des europäischen Rechts', *Zeitschrift für Urheber- und Medienrecht*, vol. 3, 182–194.

Schwarze, J. (2000), 'Medienfreiheit und Medienvielfalt im europäischen Gemeinschaftsrecht', *Zeitschrift für Urheber- und Medienrecht*, vol. 10, 779–800.

Scottsdale A. 'Disney, Microsoft and Intel Likely to Win as Entertainment Moves Online, Reports In-Stat/MDR', 31 March 2004, Business Wire, http://goliath.ecnext.com/coms2/gi_0199-186306/Disney-Microsoft-and-Intel-Likely.html.

Sinnreich, A. (2003), 'Microsoft Plays to Film Industry', 9 June 2003, www.wired.com.

Slot, P.J. (1994), 'State Aids in the Cultural Sector', in *Europäisches Wirtschaftsrecht nach Maastricht*, Bonn: Rheinische Friedrich-Wilhelms-Universitä.

Toft, T. (1999), 'Commission Renews Exemption of United International Pictures BV', *Competition Policy Newsletter*, no. 3, 26–28.

Van Miert, K. (1996), Answer to MEP's question by Anne Andre-Leonard, [1996] OJ C217/127.

Variety (1994), 'Euro Commissioner; R.I.P. UIP', 23 February 1994, www.variety.com.

Waelbroeck, M. (1998), in C.D. Ehlermann and L.L. Laudati, *European Competition*

Law Annual 1997: Objectives of Competition Policy, Oxford: Hart Publishing.

Zekaria S. (2004), 'EU in Talks Over Cinema Subsidies', 19 January 2004, available at http://www.theparliament.com/EN/News/200401/ed897ca5-67d2-4990-8439-7a9665823990.htm.

Chapter 3

The European Commission's State Aid Regime and Public Service Broadcasting

David Ward

The European Union's (EU) member states have a long tradition of allocating public subsidies to certain sections of the media industry to meet a number of public policy and strategic goals. These have historically covered a wide range of sectors, from support to the film industry, taxes or forms of licence fees to television and radio broadcasters, press subsidies and the development of network infrastructure, to mention just a few of the areas in the culture industry that receive some form of state support throughout the EU. Taken as a whole these subsidies represent significant levels of revenues and have generally supported a range of social, cultural or economic objectives and at times all three of these. It is perhaps surprising given the large amounts of public funding granted to the broadcasting industry, as the largest single recipient of public funding in the cultural sector, that it was not until the 1990s that the position of public funding of public service broadcasters became an increasingly contested issue at the EU level as the European Commission (EC) received a raft of complaints from commercial operators who claimed that the funding and range of activities undertaken by public service broadcasters was incompatible with the EC Treaty and the rules on competition in the common market.

This chapter investigates the approach of the EC to the questions posed by these complaints in respect of the balance between the right of member states to fund public service broadcasters, and the obligations placed on the EC as the guarantor of the EU Treaty and its rules on competition that, in this context, revolves around the key question of financial support and how this support is both established and employed by the public service broadcasters in an increasingly complex set of dynamics, with the growing amount of activities undertaken by these broadcasters. This development has been paralleled with the case law of the European Court of Justice (ECJ) and together the approaches require a number of procedural measures based on transparency and proportionality to be met by the member states. At the same time, the principle of subsidiarity has been respected by the EC and the member states retain a wide area of manoeuvre to establish the remits and activities of public service broadcasters, though this is likely to become far more complex in a world of multichannel television and the Internet.

It outlines key areas in the EC and ECJ's approach to public service broadcasters and concludes that it is unlikely that the current culture of complaint from commercial operators against the funding and activities of public service broadcasters will abate in the near future. Indeed we can expect the question of the Internet and public service broadcasters' move into new markets such as niche television channels, websites and associated markets to be crucial areas of disagreement in the absence of legal certainty. In this context, to date the EC has generally accepted distortions to the common market and respected the right of member states to define services of general economic interest, but the lack of a clear regulatory framework foreseeing the expansion of the range of services supplied by public service broadcasters, at the EU level, will continue to act as a source of contest between public and commercial operators as the debate about the funding and activities of public service broadcasters is played out on the EU stage.

General Principles of State Aid Policy

The EEC Treaty established the Community rules for the control of state aid in the EU based on the principle that funding allocated by the state to an entity which distorts or threatens to distort competition by conferring advantages on an undertaking is incompatible with the common market pursuant to Article 87(1). This is not to say that state aid is not permitted in the EU, but the basic rationale for a state aid regime at the EU level is the need to maintain a fair and level playing field for operators to ensure treatment favouring individual companies does not distort market conditions and normal market behaviour and erect entry barriers to companies in the common market. The provisions in the Treaty grant the EC wide ranging powers to investigate the allocation of state aid though the Treaty does not define state aid. This has been open to the EC and the ECJ to develop through case law together with other Community instruments which have gradually refined the concept and methodological framework for assessing cases involving public funding granted to undertakings.

Although the EC's role in this area is therefore to ensure that member states do not provide funding or other favourable conditions to individual companies and create unfair distortions to the internal market there is a degree of flexibility in the Treaty to ensure public funding of certain kinds of services that are defined by the member states is compatible with the EU Law. These include non-economic activities that receive state funding such as hospitals and the provision of social housing as well as some economic activities. In terms of economic activities an undertaking that carries out, what the EU terms, a service of general economic interest that is defined by a member state qualifies for compatible state aid as long as a number of criteria are met. The provisions for services of general economic interest in the EC Treaty allow exemptions from the ban on state aid pursuant to Article 87(1) EC Treaty. These areas are where: (1) the purpose of the aid fulfils clearly established objectives of common interest where trade is not affected that is contrary to the common interest; (2) state aid is used to correct market failure and enhance the competitiveness of the region; (3) in the promotion of social cohesion, development and cultural diversity. Although the EC Treaty, pursuant to Article 86(2) and Article 87(2) *et seq.*, as interpreted by the ECJ, allows certain derogations to competition rules the fact that an undertaking may be funded by state aid under certain conditions does not mean that the rules on competition set out in the Treaty are disregarded, hence:

Undertakings entrusted with the operation of services of general economic interest or having the character of a revenue producing monopoly shall be subject to the rules contained in this Treaty. In particular to the rules on competition, in so far as the applications of such rules do not obstruct the performance, in law or in fact, of the particular task assigned to them. The development of trade must not be affected to such an extent as would be contrary to the interests of the Community. (Article 86(2) of the EC Treaty)

There is therefore a balancing act between member states allocating state aid to sectors to achieve certain social, cultural and economic and non-economic objectives and the possibility of distortions to the internal market (Ward 2004). Whilst distortions to the internal market created by state aid are accepted as part of the need to supply state funding for services of general economic interest this funding should not allow undertakings that are recipients of public funding to disproportionately distort the internal market beyond what is necessary for the achievement of the objectives set out in public policy.

State Aid and Public Service Broadcasting

The background to the development of an EU dimension in the broadcasting sector is a case concluded by the ECJ in 1974 that set out a number of key interpretations for further activities of the EC in the field of television broadcasting. In *Sacchi*, the ECJ established two key principles in its approach to broadcasting in its interpretation of the EEC Treaty.[1] The complainant in the case against the Italian public service broadcaster, RAI, argued that the monopoly RAI enjoyed over advertising was in breach of the principle of the free movement of goods throughout the common market zone. The monopoly of advertising revenues, Sacchi argued, constituted an obstacle to the free flow of goods as it made it far more difficult to sell products from other member states in Italy, which contravened Article 3(a) of the EEC Treaty.[2]

The ECJ dismissed Sacchi's complaint that RAI's monopoly constituted a restriction on the movement of goods and services that was incompatible with the EEC Treaty. However, the case raised the question of whether television services came under the competition rules and the ECJ ruled that television broadcasting did come under the terms of the EEC Treaty, as broadcasters carried out activities of an economic nature (advertising in particular was stressed as important in this regard), and it reasoned that broadcasting was carried out for purposes of remuneration and therefore came under the competence of the EEC Treaty as a tradable service. The ruling is not without some nuance and the ECJ also recognized that as a service, broadcasting could not simply be understood as one which was established for the purposes of remuneration alone. The central function of broadcasting, as argued by the German government's submission to the Court, was the provision of a television service to carry out a social and democratic function. The ECJ concluded RAI's monopoly over broadcasting and advertising granted by the Italian state was lawful under Community law pursuant to Article 90(2) of the EEC Treaty (now Article

---

1   *Sacchi* (155/173) [1974] ECR 409–445, 30 April 1974.
2   *Ibid.*, 435–436.

86(2) EC). As a result the Court concluded certain derogations to the EEC Treaty were applicable on grounds that the nature of the institutions entrusted with the provision of a television service to promote general interests of a non-economic nature, such as news and educational programming, were important considerations in the democratic life of the citizens of the member states. The ECJ therefore acknowledged the legitimate monopoly status of broadcasters granted by the state in its decision on RAI and *ipso facto* the right of member states to establish measures in support of public service broadcasters. However, it also established that broadcasting came under the terms of the EEC Treaty and was a service carried out as an economic activity and this important dualism is a crucial foundation for further developments in EU media policy and its application to the area of state aid and public service broadcasting.

Given the framework established in the EEC Treaty for state aid measures and the decisions of the ECJ in *Sacchi*, together with the competence of the EC in this area, it is perhaps unsurprising that the funding of public service broadcasters became an ever greater issue at the EU level in the 1990s as competition in the sector between commercial and public service broadcasters increased. The television sector is a large recipient of public funding in the form of funding solutions for public service broadcasters that is largely unmatched in any other field in the culture industries. Licence fees, taxation revenues and ad hoc payments represent over €15 billion annually across the EU member states according to estimates (Association of Commercial Television 2004). Put in context, the total amount of state aid in 2004, excluding the aid granted to services of general economic interest for the 25 member states amounted to €61.5 billion, 59 per cent of which was allocated to manufacturing and 23 per cent to agriculture (EC 2006a).

Since the 1990s there have been numerous complaints submitted to the EC about the activities and funding of public service broadcasters across the EU member states and generally, these complaints fall into three categories:

- funding from public revenues in the form of licence fee and taxation revenues and ad hoc payments such as tax exemptions or capital investments;
- public service broadcasters developing new services on the Internet and niche channel/digital services;
- public service broadcasters exploiting public funding to distort the market for services either in cross subsidising commercial services, undercutting market prices or simply providing services that distort the market.

Public Service Broadcasting Cases in the 1990s: the Question of Public Funding

Based on the *Sacchi* decision, the public service broadcasters had enjoyed relative security until the 1990s. This changed with the submission of a number of complaints submitted to the EC claiming that state funding constituted state aid that was simply incompatible with the Treaty. Three of the cases were raised against France Télévisions,[3] RAI in Italy[4] and RTP in Portugal[5] and lodged by the commercial broadcasters who claimed that both the ad hoc payments received by these broadcasters (new aid) and the traditional funding these broadcasters received (existing aid) constituted state aid that was incompatible with the provisions of the Treaty.[6] The distinction between new and existing aid has important procedural consequences. When the EC concludes an undertaking that receives existing aid, which was established before the coming into force of the Treaty a cooperative procedure is followed and the EC will provide proposals to the member state in order to bring about the alignment of their framework to the provisions of the Treaty. If the member state agrees to undertake the recommendations it is legally bound to implement the measures and if it refuses then this can lead to a formal investigation. In sum the existing aid procedure aims to amend the system of funding under review for future compliance with the Treaty. In investigating new aid, however, if the EC concludes that the aid is incompatible with the Treaty because it is likely to distort competition and the aid is not justified under the provisions of the Treaty then it can either block the aid or if the aid has already been granted to an undertaking request that the aid is recovered. These cases should therefore be seen as having a dual nature, questioning the compatibility of, firstly, traditional funding and, secondly, ad hoc payments and measures.

The complaints against RAI, RTP and France Télévisions were technically nearly identical in that they were comprised of complaints against both ad hoc funding (new aid) and the funding of the public service broadcasters through more permanent measures such as licence fees and state grants (existing aid). The first case was against the Portuguese public service broadcaster RTP, submitted by the largest commercial broadcaster SIC. In 1993 the most popular French commercial broadcaster TF1 submitted a complaint concerning the methods used to finance the public service channels France 2 and France 3 and in 1996 Reti Televisive Italiane (Mediaset) also submitted a similar complaint about RAI, and this was further supported by another complaint submitted by Mediaset in 1998. It was not until a decade later that these cases were finally concluded in 2005 (existing aid) and

---

3   *Decision de la Commission relative aux aides d'Etat mises à exécution par la France en faveur de France 2 et de France 3*, C(2003) 4497 final.

4   *Commission Decision on Measures Implemented by Italy for RAI SpA* (2004/339/EC) OJ L85/1, 23 April 04.

5   *Commission Decision on State Aid Financing of Public Television in Portugal*, SG (96) D/9555, 1996.

6   *Commission Decision on State Aid Financing of Public Television in Portugal*, SG (96) D/9555, 1996; *Decision de la Commission relative aux aides d'Etat mises à exécution par la France en faveur de France 2 et de France 3*, COM(2003) 4497 final; *Commission Decision on State Aid Implemented by France for France 2 and 3* (2004/838/EC) [2004] OJ L361/21, 8 December 2004; *Commission Decision on Measures Implemented by Italy for RAI SpA* (2004/339/EC) [2004] OJ L85/1, 23 April 04; *RAI (annual fee)*, Object: State aid n. E 9/2005 (ex C 62/1999), COM(2005) 1164 final, Brussels, 20 April 2005; *France Télévisions (annual fee)*, Object: State aid E 10/2005 (ex C 60/1999), COM(2005)1166 final, Brussels, 20 April 2005.

2003 (new aid) and whilst they were being assessed a number of other cases were concluded in parallel.

The complainants in the three cases alleged firstly that the funding of the public service broadcasters represented illegal state aid and secondly that a whole range of anti-competitive measures related to the public funding or some form of advantage conferred on the public service broadcasters by the authorities of the member states, was against competition rules. SIC claimed these included tax exemptions, payment facilities, rescheduling of debt due by RTP to the Portuguese social security system, and non-recovery of fines owed by RTP to the Portuguese state. In France, the complaint against the two channels France 1 and France 2 and in the Italian case involving RAI similar allegations ranged from incompatible state aid derived from the licence fee to ad hoc measures including capital injections and grants. Amongst a range of anti-competitive behaviour SIC, TF1 and Mediaset argued, in the respective cases, that the aid enabled the public service broadcasters to outbid commercial operators for programme rights and undersell the commercial rates for advertising sales.

The EC concluded in all three cases that the funding received by the broadcasters was state aid and moved to an assessment as to whether it was compatible with the EC Treaty according to the principles laid out in cases dealt with in parallel as well as those set out in the Communication on public service broadcasting (EC 2001). These include:

1. There must be a clear definition of the service of general economic interest by the member state.
2. The public service activity must be entrusted by an act of state.
3. The public funding should be proportional and not exceed the net costs of the undertaking in carrying out its public service mandate.
4. There should be clear and separate accounts for undertakings that provide public service and commercial activities.

After an assessment of the funding and activities of the three broadcasters against the above criteria the public funding received by the public service broadcasters from the respective member states was understood to be compatible with the terms of the EC Treaty under Article 86(2). In a final conclusion to the RTP case, after a protracted investigation that included an annulment by the Court of First Instance (CFI)[7] of an initial ruling of the EC on procedural grounds after an appeal, the EC finally closed the case in 2006 confirming that the financial arrangements enjoyed by RTP were in fact in line with the state aid rules as was an agreement signed by the Portuguese authorities and RTP aimed at reducing the debt of RTP which was accumulated through 'constant under financing of RTP's public service tasks' (EC 2006b). The basis of such a decision was that both the funding of RTP was proportional to the net costs of providing a public service as defined by the Portuguese authorities and the

---

7   *Gestevisión Telecinco* v. *Commission* (T-95/96) [1998] ECR II-3407; *Financing of Public Television Channels: Failure to Initiate the Procedure Under Article 88 (2) Action for Annulment* (T-46/97) [2000] ECR II-02125.

reduction of the debt of RTP estimated to be approximately €1 billion did not exceed the debts that had accrued from carrying out of its public service tasks in previous years. This finally closed the second part of the case concerned with existing aid.[8]

Although concluding that the French and Italian broadcasters' receipt of state aid was compatible with Article 86(2) of the EC Treaty, the EC did have reservations about the regulatory frameworks which had been established by the French and Italian authorities that it suggested should be reviewed in order to ensure compliance to EU standards. These criticisms included the lack of guarantees against over-compensation, the absence of an explicit statement and any legal provisions establishing that commercial activities of France Télévisions and RAI should be undertaken according to market rates and standards (programme acquisitions and advertising rates).

In terms of the French and Italian cases the EC also assessed the ad hoc measures that were received by these broadcasters under new aid measures as in the RTP case. This component of the complaints was concluded in 2003 on very much the same grounds as the Portuguese case. After an assessment of the criteria of entrustment and clear obligations the net costs were measured against the ad hoc measures and permanent funding and no over-compensation was found in both cases. Furthermore, the complaint that these broadcasters had actively undercut pricing on the advertising market was not supported by the EC investigations and therefore the aid was cleared as compatible. The EC has therefore concluded the cases concerning the use of ad hoc measures against RAI and France Télévisions, and the Portuguese case was finally closed in 2006. It has also concluded that the existing aid (licence fees) granted to the respective public service broadcasters was acceptable, though with a caveat that the systems did not fully meet EC requirements in terms of a separation of commercial and public activities of public service broadcasters, transparency and guarantees against over-compensation.

The EC however, went a step further to also state that independent regulatory authorities should be established to monitor compliance with the above principles to guarantee that the activities of France Télévisions in the commercial market did not abuse public finance to distort the markets for advertising and programme sales and there was no over-compensation. The French authorities committed to implement such recommendations through revisions to their legal framework and a system of control of the French parliament over the allocation of the annual budget for the public channels. With this agreement reached the EC concluded that the system of

---

8   SIC challenged the EC decision in 1997 and took the case to the European Court of First Instance. SIC complained that the EC had not followed the correct procedure in evaluating whether RTP's funding was contrary to the EC Treaty rules on state aid and had therefore failed to move to the second stage of procedure. The second stage would have allowed all parties to submit observations in reference to the case, pursuant to Article 88(2) of the EC Treaty. On this issue the Court ruled that technically the original EC decision, which was favourable to RTP, should not have been granted at the first stage of the inquiry under Article 88(2) of the EC Treaty unless it was in no doubt as to the compatible nature of state aid granted to RTP. Appeals were also submitted to the CFI in the cases lodged by TF1 and Gestevisión Telecinco against France Télévisions and RTVE, in which the CFI concluded that the EC were also guilty of inaction.

funding was compatible with the EC Treaty under Article 86(2). In the Italian case, with the adoption of the highly controversial Gasparri law in 2004 the EC noted that the Italian authorities had introduced sufficient guarantees for the control of transparency and proportionality of state financing by the licence fee to meet EC criteria.

Public Service Broadcasters and New Media Services

A second batch of complaints was assessed by the EC in parallel to the funding cases above related to the expansion of new services provided by public service broadcasters. One of the most significant trends in the European communications landscape over the last 15 years has been the introduction of greater bandwidth for the delivery of audiovisual and ancillary services and the development of new services through mediums such as the Internet. Whether through the development of compression technology allowing greater use of spectrum and digitalization or the roll out of delivery technology with a greater capacity for storing and delivering content the developments are seen to fundamentally change the services that can be delivered by the broadcasting sector. Following a pattern of historical development, public service broadcasters have embraced both the world of niche channels and the Internet and in some cases such as the UK these broadcasters have become driving forces in the world of new media. In line with the general tendency for commercial broadcasters to attempt to stifle the expansion of public service broadcasters on a member state level and raising the stakes by appealing to EC instruments there has been a number of complaints about new services established by public service broadcasters from the private sector.

With the development of new services the EC dimension was triggered by two cases that challenged the right of public service broadcasters to supply niche services in the latter part of the 1990s, against the Federal Republic of Germany, ARD and ZDF, and against the BBC. The cases were raised by a consortium of private broadcasters Verband Privater Rundfunk und Telekommunikation e.V. (VPRT) against ARD and ZDF, and in the UK the satellite broadcaster BSkyB raised a complaint against the BBC. Both complainants alleged that the rules on state aid were infringed by the introduction of new thematic channels by public service broadcasters, on grounds of unfair competition against existing commercial channels. It has been further explored in decisions in 2003, with the EC concluding cases involving a proposal for a French international news channel and a specialized online educational service provided by the BBC as well as a range of new BBC digital niche channels, whose themes ranged from a children's channel to one aimed at the youth audience.

In the German case,[9] the commercial broadcasters argued two children's channels, Kinderkanal and Phoenix, established by ARD and ZDF represented unfair competition on grounds that they were granted privileged access to state aid as

---

9   *Commission Decision on State Aid Financing of Kinderkanal and Phoenix Specialist Channels* (NN 70/98) [1999] OJ 238, 21 August 1999.

well as preferential access to cable networks.[10] These arrangements, according to the complaint, went beyond the terms of the definition of the services of general economic interest criteria and gave the public service broadcasters an unfair competitive advantage over private channels that were already active in these markets.

The first part of the case was raised in regards to the financing arrangements of Kinderkanal and Phoenix that were both financed through licence fee revenues. The complainant argued that the advantageous conditions granted to the two channels went beyond the definition of a basic service in German law. The requirement of German law to provide a basic service, they argued, was to provide a universal service to the German public and although the licence fee received by the broadcasters for their generalist services was understood as compatible with the EC Treaty under Article 86(2) the principle underpinning the provisions of Article 86(2) could not be applied in the same terms to the specialist channels and they were therefore incompatible with the Treaty. As the specialist channels (by the very fact that they were aimed at niche audiences), did not cater for the whole population, this meant that the criteria of a basic service, as understood in German broadcasting law, could not be invoked, in order to reconcile the new services with a service of general economic interest in Community law. In attempting to distinguish between the generalist and specialist channels, the complainant argued that the justification for funding through state aid did not apply and thus could not be understood as coming under the derogations pursuant to Article 86(2) of the EC Treaty as was the case for the generalist channels.

The EC rejected the claims made by VPRT although it did conclude the funding of the channels constituted state aid. It judged the aid granted to the channels was compatible with the common market under Article 86(2) of the EC Treaty. The reason for this exemption to the competition rules of the Treaty was that the argument presented by VPRT was based on a distinction between delivery forms. This overlooked the service provided by the broadcasters, regardless of different delivery platforms and how these services were packaged. The EC did draw a distinction between services of general economic interest and the basic service classification, but stated, based on the Protocol annexed to the Amsterdam Treaty on public service broadcasting, it was outside the scope of the Community to define whether special interest channels formed part of the service of basic provision or not.

The EC therefore restricted itself to the question of whether or not the specialist channels could be understood as a service of general economic interest, regardless of the debate on whether or not the notion of basic services could be extended to thematic channels. Again drawing on the Amsterdam Treaty, the EC recognized it was the member states that retained the prerogative to define a service of general economic interest and the functions and obligations, which the particular service should pursue. The crucial point being that the undertakings must officially be

---

10 A further complaint was submitted against the commercial activities of ZDF concerning its investment, through a subsidiary, in a theme park. The EC rejected the complaint as it concluded ZDF had acted according to market rates and in a manner as that of a normal private investor would have in similar circumstances.

entrusted by the member state, with the provision of a specific service. The EC stated:

> The German authorities consider a channel for children, free of advertising and violence and with a high degree of information, and a channel, also free of advertising, providing background information on political and social issues and direct transmissions of political debates as 'services of general economic interest' and entrust such undertakings with the provision of these services.[11]

In strictly legal terms, the EC questioned whether the German definition of the public service remit encompassed specialist channels, but it noted that a public act by the state was sufficient in defining the nature of a public service. Due to the federal structure of German broadcasting law, the agreement by the Länder authorities to establish the channels had already recognized the extension of the public service broadcasters into new delivery forms, thereby legitimizing the enterprise in the EC's interpretation of Community law. The question of funding and proportionality was therefore the crucial issue that the EC presided on and whether or not the granting of state aid was proportional to the remit set out for the services. The Community dimension was therefore restricted to the question of the nature of state remuneration to the broadcasters for them to provide the new services.

As a consequence of the nature of the channels, that is, they would be free of advertising as established by the Länder authorities, the second part of this question was axiomatic. The very fact that the services were established free of advertising revenue meant that without a large subscription base it was highly unlikely that the channels would be provided by the commercial sector. The task of providing an advertising-free channel would therefore be precluded without some form of state aid. The subsequent question of proportionality therefore rested on the amount of state aid the broadcasters received in order to provide the new channels. In this context, the EC also judged in favour of the public service broadcasters, acknowledging that the funding set by the Kommission zur Ermittlung des Finanzbedarfes der Rundfunkanstalten and the method for evaluating the funding for the specialist channels conformed to the EC's criteria of proportionality.

The second aspect of the Kinderkanal/Phoenix case consisted of an assessment of the priority carriage granted to the two channels over the already congested cable networks. VPRT alleged the access to the networks constituted another form of state aid and excluded competitors from accessing the networks. The EC again rejected this argument as it ruled in the case of priority carriage of the channels the state neither conveyed financial advantage to the channels or preferential treatment, which was not also enjoyed by the other broadcasters carried over the cable network and therefore the applicability of state aid in this area was unsupported.

With these two conditions met, the EC ruled the exemption pursuant to Article 86(2) of the EC Treaty was relevant, even though the establishment of the two channels could distort competition in the market. In a clear statement of its acceptance of the services the EC suggested 'Article 90(2) (now Article 86(2) EC) accepts a certain

---

11 *Commission Decision on State Aid Financing of Kinderkanal and Phoenix Specialist Channels* (NN 70/98) [1999] OJ 238, at p. 11, 21 August 1999.

effect on competition and trade as a consequence of ensuring a public service remit to be provided'.[12] Therefore the state aid granted to the public broadcasters was deemed not only acceptable by the EC, but the EC's interpretation of the Treaty rules on state aid, unequivocally suggests distortions to the common market, because of activities which are seen to benefit the public interest, are acceptable.

BSkyB filed the second complaint against the 24-hour news channel established by the BBC in September 1998.[13] The case has obvious parallels with the Kinderkanal/Phoenix one, in that the complaint consisted of a challenge to the move of the BBC into specialized channels, which was already catered for by a commercial broadcaster. As in the German case, BSkyB alleged the funding of the BBC channel from state resources constituted state aid and therefore conferred a competitive advantage over the existing commercial news channels, particularly BSkyB's own news service, Sky News. Moreover, BSkyB claimed the funding of the news channel affected trade between member states, as it hindered the potential development of commercial news channels across the common market zone. The complainant also questioned whether specialized channels could be legitimately understood as part of the basic service of public service provision and therefore whether it qualified as a service of general economic interest, and as a consequence qualified for derogations to the competition rules. The central argument presented by BSkyB was that because the BBC was granted permission by the secretary of state to provide the channel as an ancillary service, as defined in the BBC's Royal Charter, it therefore could not be understood as part of the primary public service activities of the BBC. The complainant also pointed out an important part of the licence agreement was to provide a universal geographic service; something which BBC News 24 did not achieve for most of the UK, for the majority of its airing.

As in the Kinderkanal/Phoenix decision the EC agreed with the complainant that the provision of funding from the licence fee constituted state aid. The EC was, therefore, again called upon to decide whether the granting of state aid to the news channel was compatible with the services of general economic interest criteria. The EC again acknowledged that it was a member state prerogative to define the actual nature of these services, particularly in the broadcasting sector, pursuant to the Protocol on Public Service Broadcasting annexed to the Amsterdam Treaty. The Protocol states:

> The provisions of the Treaty establishing the European Community shall without prejudice to the competence of the member states to provide for the funding of public service broadcasting insofar as such funding is granted to broadcasting organizations for the fulfilment of the public service remit as conferred, defined and organized by each member state, and insofar as such funding does not affect trading conditions and competition in the Community to an extent which would be contrary to the common interest, while the realization of the remit of that public service shall be taken into account. (Treaty of Amsterdam 1997, 87)

---

12   *Ibid.*, at p. 17.

13   *Commission Decision on State Aid Financing of a 24 Hour News Channel out of the Licence Fee by the BBC*, SG (99) D/10201, 1999.

The EC dismissed the first two points on grounds that the question of whether an ancillary service could be understood as an integral part of the public service mission was a member state issue. The fact that the secretary of state had already granted the BBC permission to establish the channel, as part of its public service remit, was confirmation that the channel was part of the service, even if it was ancillary to the core services. The second point, on the universality of the service the EC also failed to support, and reasoned it was sufficient that BBC News 24 attempted to reach as many households as possible. The fact that it failed to reach the whole of the population due to technical constraints outside its control did not undermine the overall nature of the service provided by the BBC.

On the final issue of state aid and proportionality the EC ruled no extra revenues had been granted to the BBC for the news channel and its costs were proportional to the service that it provided. As the service was therefore defined by the secretary of state as part of the public service remit, the terms of the Amsterdam Treaty and the provision on services of general economic interest were therefore applicable. In conclusion, the EC ruled the introduction of BBC News 24 acted as a distortion to the market and may well have an impact on the development of the existing commercial news channels, but this was to be accepted as a necessary consequence of the provision of a service of general economic interest. In an explicit endorsement of this logic the EC reasoned:

> Even if the state financing of BBC News 24 would have led to more serious economic difficulties for its competitors, such effects could be accepted ... In order to allow a service of general economic interest to be delivered. Article 90(2) of the EC Treaty (now Art 86(2) EC) ... accepts a certain effect on competition and trade as a consequence of ensuring the provision of a public service remit.[14]

By rejecting all aspects of the complaint against the BBC, the EC acknowledged the significant role of the member states in defining the public service remit of broadcasters. As in the Kinderkanal/Phoenix case the EC supported the definition of public service established by the UK government and therefore the extension of its services into new areas of broadcasting.

Following on from the previous case the UK government sought approval for two new BBC services that the secretary of state had consented to as auxiliary services. The first of these was a batch of nine new digital thematic channels and the UK government notified the EC in 2001 that it had approved the channels (EC 2002). A further notification was submitted in 2003 together with a complaint about the BBC and its plan to establish the Digital Curriculum from Research Machines plc. (EC 2003). The BBC's Digital Curriculum consists of a group of interactive online educational services for students. It is funded by licence fee revenues that the BBC receives and provided free of charge to the end consumer and is one of the few cases that the EC has been called upon to assess concerning Internet services of public service broadcasters. A number of strict provisions were attached to the permission granted by the secretary of state for the service (a total of 18) in terms of distinctiveness from commercial services that existed on the market at the time

---

14   *Ibid.*, at p. 17.

(Department for Culture, Media and Sport 2003). The nine digital channels had similar thresholds of distinctiveness and innovation as a condition for clearance by the secretary of state.

Both of these cases satisfied the requirements set down in the Treaty and were cleared by the EC. Whilst both investigations followed similar lines as the previous BBC case, in both there was a departure. In the case of the new digital channels the EC ruled that the funding actually did not constitute state aid within the meaning of Article 87(1) as the funding from the existing licence fee was understood as compensation, but showing a degree of ambiguity, also stressed that even if the funding was state aid it would qualify under the exception granted by Article 86(2). Curiously this decision comes before the ECJ ruling in the Altmark case[15] (see below) and breaks with the approach in the previous cases. In the latter case of BBC Digital Curriculum the EC decided that although the service met all the requirements to qualify as compatible state aid it could not be understood as one of the traditional activities of the BBC as it represented an extension into a new market for the broadcaster as it represented a 'non television and radio' service. However, it also recognized that it was the right of the member states and a matter for national legislation to define which services could be defined in the public service mandate in line with previous decisions.

The most recent case of this kind to be concluded in 2005 concerned a request from the French authorities as to the compatibility of a joint venture between France Télévisions and TF1 to create an international satellite news channel that would be funded from public revenues.[16] The proposed channel would initially be funded entirely by a state grant lasting for a period of five years with the possibility of another period of renewal for a similar term. The plan envisaged a budget of €30 million for 2005 and rising to €70 million for the following years of the agreement based on inflation of goods and labour costs. It also envisaged the channel collecting advertising revenues to supplement state funding from 2008. A complaint was submitted to the EC that the proposed funding of the channel infringed competition rules and the funding represented a breach of the terms of the EC Treaty as it did not qualify for the derogations set out in Article 87(3) of the EC Treaty and could not be considered as a service of general economic interest within the terms of the Treaty as the channel was not intended for an audience in France. Further arguments were that the establishment of the channel by state aid would further consolidate the two operators' positions in the French television market, and as well as distorting the commercial market for television, there were no adequate provisions to ensure there would be no cross subsidies from France Télévisions.

A now familiar pattern to the EC investigations followed and in a first stage the EC concluded the measures were state aid. In a second stage it assessed whether the state aid was compatible with the EC Treaty. Concluding that the French authorities

---

15 Opinion of the Advocate General Delivered on 19 March 2002. *Altmark Trans GmbH and Regierungspräsidium Magdeburg* v. *Nahverkehrsgesellschaft Altmark GmbH* (C-280/00) [2003] ECR I-7747, 24 July 2003.

16 *Chaîne française d'information internationale. Aid d'Etat*, N 54/2005, COM(2005) 1479 final.

had provided adequate guarantees that there would be no over-compensation (the agreement stated that in such cases there would be reinvestment or either a reimbursement or a reduction of the annual state funding), as well as provisions to ensure that market prices would not be unfairly distorted, the funding of the channel was in compliance with Article 86(2) of the EC Treaty.

Compensation and State Aid

Whilst there has been a general tendency to understand public funding as state aid there are some ambiguities in the decision on the BBC digital channels demonstrating a level of uncertainty in areas of the EC's approach to new services that was also evident in the first conclusions in the RTP case before the annulment by the CFI. The ambiguity is part of a broader debate on the legal framework for the public funding of services of general economic interest and the question of whether revenues granted to an undertaking that carries out such a service is actually state aid or compensation. In the *Preussen Elektra* and *Ferring* cases,[17] the ECJ appeared to open up a sphere of respite for public service broadcasters. In *Ferring* the ECJ ruled that not all public funding or favourable conditions granted to an undertaking constituted state aid in the meaning of Article 87(1). The ECJ reasoned that there were cases where an undertaking receives some form of advantage for a service of general economic interest where the public funding or measures granted by the state in return for a specific public service to be fulfilled by an undertaking that was imposed by the state did not exceed the costs of that said obligation.

In order to be classified as state aid, Advocate General Tizzano stressed that some form of economic advantage needs to be granted to the recipient. In the absence of evidence that an economic advantage was granted to an undertaking the judgement concluded the advantages granted to the undertaking represented compensation rather than state aid. In such a situation the ECJ ruled the measures introduced by France that favoured Ferring did not actually constitute state aid but actually compensation. The ramifications of such an approach for the funding of public service broadcasters would be profound if they met the criteria set out in the case as based on a compensation approach the measures fall outside the scope of the state aid rules and there is no need to notify the EC of such measures.

In 2003, amidst some significant differences in the approaches of a number of Advocate Generals of the Court the ECJ decision in the *Altmark* case[18] developed the distinction between compensation and state aid attempting to partially clarify the concepts of compensation and state aid as well as establishing qualifying criteria for a compensation approach. The judgment emphasized, building on case law that:

> Where a state measure must be regarded as compensation for the services provided by the recipient undertakings in order to discharge public service obligations, so that those

---

17 *Preussen Elektra* (C-379/98) [2001] ECR I-2099, 13 March 2001; *Ferring* (C-53/00) [2001] ECR I-9067, 22 November 2001.

18 *Altmark Trans and Regierungspräsidium Magdeburg* (C-280/00) [2003] ECR I-7747, 24 July 2003.

undertakings do not enjoy a real financial advantage and the measure thus does not have the effect in putting them in a more favourable competitive position than the undertakings competing with them, such a measure is not caught by Article 92 (1) (now Article 87 (1)) of the Treaty). (paragraph 87)

However, in the *Altmark* case the ECJ also laid down four criteria for measures to qualify for a compensation approach rather than state aid. Where the four criteria are met the measures would qualify as compensation and where they were not established they would be understood as state aid. Such criteria would in effect make it extremely difficult to envisage the funding granted to institutions such as public service broadcasters being classified as compensation. These included:

- There must be entrustment of the obligation and it should be clearly defined
- The parameters on the basis of which the compensation is calculated must be established in advance in an objective and transparent manner
- The compensation cannot exceed what is necessary to cover all or part of the costs incurred in the discharge of public service obligations
- Where the undertaking is not chosen pursuant to a public procurement procedure which would allow for the selection of the tenderer capable of providing those services at the least cost to the Community, the level of compensation needed must be determined on the basis of an analysis of the costs which a typical well-run undertaking in the same market. (paragraphs 89–93)

Undoubtedly aware of the wider repercussions of the development of a compensation and state aid division, the Opinion of Advocate General Léger discussed two concepts for assessing state measures granted to undertakings on the basis of a 'net' and 'gross' approach distinguishing between the general provisions of the EC Treaty which are based on a concept of gross aid and the concept of aid that has developed in the area of public services where a net concept of aid has evolved. Stressing such a distinction would lead to grey areas and confusion throughout the member states as to the procedures laid down for state aid derogations in the EC Treaty Advocate General Léger suggested such a system was unsuitable as it was possible to foresee that some measures would fall into both categories of net and gross aid.

Following the *Altmark* decision all of the cases related to aspects of public service broadcasting have been assessed by the EC against the above four criteria and all have failed to meet the requirements to be classified as an undertaking that qualifies for compensation within the meaning handed down by the Court. In the French case the definition and establishment of the funding was assessed as inadequate and in the other cases assessed against the *Altmark* criteria the lack of an adequate procurement procedure to select the undertaking to provide the service of general economic interest led the EC to conclude that the manner in which public funding was granted to public service broadcasters failed to meet these requirements and therefore remained state aid in the terms of Article 86(2). The lack of fit with the accumulative requirements in *Altmark* seems to confirm that the funding of public service broadcasters will continue to be treated as state aid by the EC in the absence of any Court rulings that further define the framework for public funding in this field rather than be treated as compensation.

The Negative Decisions

Although all of the cases discussed above demonstrate that the EC have accepted the right of member states to support public service broadcasters by granting the broadcasters a range of state aid measures there have been two negative decisions concluded against TV2 in Denmark and NOS in the Netherlands.[19] Both cases concerned a combination of an assessment of the ad hoc and traditional funding enjoyed by these broadcasters and the compatibility of these measures with the EC Treaty and the key issue of proportionality. In both cases the measures were assessed as state aid and therefore qualified for a second stage of investigation under the three criteria for compatibility for state aid measures. However, whilst following a similar line of reasoning as in the previous cases the EC concluded that in both cases funding measures had been in excess of the net costs of the broadcasters in order for them to fulfil their public service obligations.

The case of TV2 in Denmark had further implications as in 2003, as part of a plan to privatize the broadcaster passed by the Danish Parliament, the company's status was changed and it became a private company with limited liability that was wholly owned by the state and the process of selling on the company was stalled whilst the investigation was in progress. The Danish authorities argued that the sums of money transferred to TV2 were necessary in order to build up the company's equity as well as to ensure the company's stability in a fluctuating advertising market. However, the EC ruled that this extra funding could have been used to cross-subsidize TV2's commercial activities, allowing it to undercut advertising rates and thereby distort the real market for advertising in the Danish television sector, and as a result TV2 was ordered to pay back a sum of €84.4 million representing over-compensation for the period 1995–2002.

In a further twist following the EC decision to instruct recovery of the over-compensation, the Danish authorities calculated that if TV2 was forced to repay the illegal state aid then the company would be forced into bankruptcy as the repayment exceeded TV2's equity. Three options to prevent bankruptcy were considered by the Danish authorities: to sell the company's assets, to sell the company to a private investor together with the debt and finally recapitalization. The first of these options was dismissed as the price received for the assets would not solve the problem of bankruptcy and the second option was seen to reduce the value of the company on the eventual sale of TV2 with the debt in place to the disadvantage of the state as the vendor. The Danish authorities opted for the third option of recapitalization that included a debt/equity exchange, capital injection from the state budget and the company agreeing loans with the commercial sector, arguing that this is how a

---

19 *Commission Decision on Measures Implemented by TV2/Denmark* (2005/217/EC) [2006] OJ L85/1, 23 March 2006; *Commission Decision on the Ad Hoc Financing of Dutch Public Service Broadcasters* (C2/2004) (ex NN 170/2003) COM(2006) 2084 final.

normal private investor would behave in a similar situation. As a result, it developed the scheme to recapitalize the company and in 2004 notified the EC of the plan (EC 2004). The EC cleared the scheme as compatible with the EC Treaty and notified the Danish authorities that it was compatible with Article 86(2) as the measures enabled TV2 to fulfil its public service mandate and were proportional to the costs of these obligations. In reality the recapitalization scheme wiped out the repayments due from TV2 for its over-compensation in previous years. The Courts will make the final decision on the case after a number of appeals for annulment were submitted in 2004 and 2005 against both of the EC decisions and in the meantime the sale of TV2 is cancelled pending the outcome of these cases.

The second negative decision represents one of the most complex cases involving public service broadcasters and state aid. The case had multiple aspects and complainants accused the Dutch public service broadcasters and the state owned advertising agency STER that sells advertising on behalf of the public service broadcasters, of a range of activities incompatible with the EC Treaty. This included receiving state funding from a number of sources that distorted competition in the advertising market and the market for the acquisition of rights to televise football. Furthermore, the complainants also argued that the state aid received by the public service broadcasters distorted inter community trade and a range of new services introduced by the public service broadcasters were outside of the public service mandate. A final aspect of the complaints was related to must carry obligations as well as uncompetitive measures related to copyright arrangements between the public service broadcasters and cable companies.[20]

Whilst central parts of the case were set aside by the EC for further examination of the use of existing aid measures in the funding of the public service broadcasting system in the Netherlands, the EC did investigate the use of ad hoc measures in the form of new aid granted to the public service broadcasters, which it argued had been introduced following the entry of the Netherlands into the European Community. In this respect, the main focus of the case was the compatibility and proportionality of a number of financial measures granted to the public service broadcasters. These ad hoc funding measures included: (1) Funds from the General Broadcasting Fund (GBF) that are allocated by the state and administered through the regulatory authority to cover fluctuation in prices and the possibility of under funding within a specific tax year due to depressed advertising prices or increased costs; (2) the Matching Funds that are allocated from the state budget to provide co-financing for the public service broadcasters in cases where the prices of programme rights increase; (3) the Co-production Fund that derives revenues from copyright payments of Belgium and German cable operators for distribution of the Dutch public service broadcasters' television channels and (4) the final ad hoc measure under investigation was a more general fund that could be withdrawn from the GBF and allocated to the NOS on an individual project basis, with the agreement of the secretary of state, to strengthen the Dutch audiovisual industry in areas as wide as encouraging quality programming

---

20 *Commission Decision on the Ad Hoc Financing of Dutch Public Service Broadcasters* (C2/2004) (ex NN 170/2003) COM(2006) 2084 final.

to investment in domestic programmes. Moreover, as in the case of the GBF the scheme also allowed NOS to offset fluctuations in prices.

The EC concluded that the measures constituted new aid and therefore should meet the principle of proportionality in a similar manner as in previous cases. In this respect, the EC concluded over-compensation had been paid to the NOS through the transfer of monies from the state budget that it calculated was not necessary for the NOS to fulfil its obligations as a service of general economic interest. The EC did not conclude that Dutch public service broadcasters could not retain reserve funds, indeed it recognized that the provisions in the Media Act of the Netherlands[21] specifically allowed for such a fund capped at ten per cent. However, the EC concluded that NOS had received over-compensation in the form of new aid of a total of €76.3 million for the period 1994–2005 that was incompatible with the common market and the Dutch authorities were requested to recover this sum from NOS.

The Danish and Dutch authorities have, as in all of the other cases discussed above, subsequently agreed to put in place a more adequate system of monitoring against any over-compensation whereby if over-compensation takes place the governments will be able to recover the excess revenues. In the NOS case the second part of the investigation concerned with existing aid remains ongoing, but given the ongoing reform of the Media Act of the Netherlands it is likely that a similar pattern of commitments to reform the regulatory framework will be required by the EC in its conclusions to the case and the regulatory system in the Netherlands will be tightened to ensure future compliance with the state aid regulations.

Conclusion

In the Communication on public service broadcasting 2001 the EC clearly recognized the right of member states to support public service broadcasters though with certain conditions (EC 2001). The central problem that continues to persist at the Community level is that the EC requires three qualifying criteria: a definition of activities, an official act entrusting the tasks to a specific body, and a system of proportionality and assessment to evaluate whether the activities of the broadcasters that receive state aid is consistent with the obligations imposed on them. It has accepted a general and wide definition of public service, acknowledging that public service broadcasters should maintain a mixed programme schedule as well as the compatibility of new niche services, as long as they are based on public service principles and on an official act of the relevant member state.

The EC's understanding of the Community dimension in these cases suggests it is mainly concerned with the question of the distribution and application of state aid granted to public service broadcasters and whether public funding is proportional to the services provided by the individual broadcaster and where they have extended their activities into commercial services there is a clear distinction between the public activities and the commercial arms, to ensure that the commercial services

---

21 AVT01/OW62028. 1. Media Act (Bulletin of Acts and Decrees of the Kingdom of the Netherlands (Staatsblad van het. Koninkrijk der Nederlanden) 1987, 249.

are carried out on grounds of fair competition. The EC has, also, however, required alignment of the regulatory frameworks in a number of member states in order for them to fully comply with the EC Treaty and Transparency Directive[22] and this is likely to be a growing trend. At the time of writing the Belgium authorities had been notified by the EC that its system of accountability and transparency was inadequate and was in need of reform to align it to the EC Treaty (EC 2006d) and in April 2007 the EC announced the closure of its formal investigation into the financing of the German public service broadcasters after the German authorities agreed to introduce amendments to align the legal and financial frameworks of these broadcasters to EC requirements (EC 2007). Whilst a number of decisions made by the EC have rejected the claims against public service broadcasters, a couple of cases have found the funding of public service broadcasters in Denmark and the Netherlands breached competition rules. The negative decisions suggest the EC remains firm in its implementing framework and the key areas of controversy continue to be questions of the proportionality of funding for public service broadcasters and the allocation of these funds and the move of public service broadcasters into new media services, the latter of which whilst not a problem in itself, may indicate the EC could raise, at some future point in time, the nature of some of these new services, in the absence of regulatory or policy intervention on the member state level.

In terms of new media and the expansion of public service broadcasters into new areas of delivery, the EC concept of manifest error will be a key tool for the future scope of public service broadcasting as these broadcasters continue to expand both their public service and commercial activities. Initial signals are evident in the EC's formal proceedings outline in the NOS case and in its TV2 decision with the EC concluding that some of the Internet services developed by NOS and TV2 should be considered commercial services. These services included games and chat rooms in the case of TV2 and SMS services supplied by NOS. The EC reasoned that these services were already supplied by commercial operators and the services offered by TV2 could not be distinguished from the pre-existing services offered by the market. Such reasoning is not without contradictions especially considering the fact that public service broadcasters have historically provided many services that have also been offered by commercial broadcasters and in previous decisions a broad understanding of the member states' interpretation of public service broadcasting has been accepted by the EC.

However, the crunch came when the EC stated that these services could not be understood as 'addressing the democratic, social and cultural needs of society' and as a result could not be defined as a service of general economic interest. The EC concluded that some of the Internet services provided by TV2 could be seen as part of the broad public service mandate of the broadcaster, but this was narrowly defined in the conclusions drawn by the EC and it did not include certain games and chat

---

22 *Commission Directive 2005/81/EC of 28 November 2005 Amending Directive 80/723/EEC on the Transparency of Financial Relations between Member States and Public Undertakings as well as on Financial Transparency with Certain Undertakings* [2005] OJ L312/47.

rooms in such a mandate. The fact that the Danish authorities also considered these activities outside of the scope of TV2's public service mandate certainly gave the EC assessment greater weight, but it does not detract from the potential importance of the distinction made between information society services and electronic services and television broadcasting for future cases. Together with the refusal of the EC to categorize the BBC Digital Curriculum as part of the BBC's 'public service broadcasting mission' (Depypere and Tigchelaar 2004) the EC have clearly continued to employ the concept of technological neutrality when assessing the cases of the public service broadcasters, but at the same time it has laid the foundations for the possibility of some restrictive measures placed on the state funding of certain types of activities of public service broadcasters through the concept of manifest error. It is not that the EC is suggesting that the public service broadcasters should not operate in all areas, but implicit in its apparent reasoning is that there are limits and areas where public funding should not be used to supply certain services. Where this is the case then the activities of the public service broadcasters should be undertaken by a commercial arm with clear and transparent separation between the commercial and public service activities. This could be a very difficult argument to sustain in certain area such as games with an educative function or chat rooms that provide advice to the public that clearly have public value, but the EC does not rule out such use of public funding, but it will increasingly look at the services to evaluate them against the definition of a service of general economic interest. It also raises the question of audience legitimacy and long-term funding strategies and the marriage between popular and high brow programming as public service broadcasters rely on popular mass programming and services to ensure mass audiences as a mark of their universalism.

The Internet services of the public service broadcasters and their move into new markets is likely to increase the conflict between the public sector and commercial operators. Indeed, we can also expect operators outside the television industry, such as newspaper providers and Internet news providers, to become involved, and who may well argue that public service broadcasters are distorting competition in markets such as local advertising. A second question may arise where the member states define a service as a service of general economic interest in law that the EC disagrees with, or has ruled in another member state is not a service of general economic interest. In such a scenario the protocol on public service broadcasting in the Amsterdam Treaty will then play a pivotal role as will the concept of manifest error. Both areas represent a potential collision course for the member states and the EC without adequate and clearly defined regulatory parameters.

There are pending cases against Belgium, Germany, Ireland and the Netherlands that are yet to be resolved by the EC as well as the appeals submitted to the Courts against some of the EC decisions with actors from both the public and commercial sectors appealing. The State Aid Action Plan also foresees in its roadmap a Communication on state aid to public service broadcasting in the near future. The conclusions to the outstanding cases and an assessment of public service broadcasting as part of the roadmap together with the conclusions to the legal challenges to the EC's decisions in the Court should provide greater legal certainty and clarity as to the framework that public service broadcasters and member states should comply with to ensure that public funding is compatible with the EC Treaty. However, until the question of new services is clarified by the authorities in the EU the uncertainty as to the range of services that member states may establish for public service broadcasters remain unclear. It should also be noted that member states are also taking a similar line in their reviews of the activities of public service broadcasters and although the EC has been criticized for applying a market failure approach to this important part of the television sector the member states are increasingly requiring justification for new services that are supported with public revenues in terms of novelty, originality and services that are clearly distinguished from those already available to consumers through the commercial sector.

At the present time, as long as the three criteria of proportionality, an official act of state and transparent accounting systems are maintained, the EC is likely to clear cases concerning public service broadcasters as compatible with the EC Treaty. However, there seems to be grey areas that persist. The ambiguity as to what constitutes a public service and therefore a service of general economic interest will continue to be a source of uncertainty as new services are developed in a dynamic industry and will require a legal framework that takes account of the growing range of public and commercial activities undertaken by public service broadcasters which could have crucial consequences for the communications industry.

References

Association of Commercial Television in Europe (2004), *Safeguarding the Future of the Audiovisual Market: A White Paper on the Financing and Regulation of Publicly Funded Broadcasters*, http://www.epceurope.org/presscentre/archive/safeguardingaudiovisual_market_300304.pdf, accessed 2 May 2006.

Department for Culture, Media and Sport (2003), *Tessa Jowell Gives Approval to BBC Digital Curriculum*. Press Release and Schedule of the Secretary of State of Conditions.

Depypere, S. et al. (2004), 'State Aid and Broadcasting: State of Play', *Competition Policy Newsletter* No. 1, Spring 2004, 71–73.

Depypere, S. and Tigchelaar, N. (2004), 'The Commission's State Aid Policy on Activities of Public Service Broadcasters in Neighbouring Markets', *Competition Policy Newsletter* No. 2, Summer 2004, 19–22.

European Commission (1998), *DGIV Discussion Paper on the Application of Articles 90, Paragraph 2, 92 and 93 of the EC Treaty in the Broadcasting Sector* (unpublished).

European Commission (2001), *Communication from the Commission on the Application of State Aid Rules to Public Service Broadcasting* [2001] OJ L320.

European Commission (2003), *State Aid N 37/2003 United Kingdom. BBC Digital Curriculum*. COM(2003) 3371 final, (N37/2003) OJ 271.

European Commission (2004), *State Aid No N 313/2004-Denmark, Recapitalisation of TV2/Danmark A/S*. COM(2004) 3632 final.

European Commission (2006a), *State Aid Scoreboard*, http://ec.europa.eu/comm/

competition/state_aid/scoreboard/, accessed 10 June 2006.

European Commission (2006b), *State Aid: Commission Endorses Financial Restructuring Plan for Portuguese Public Broadcaster RTP*. Press Release IP/06/932, 5 July 2006.

European Commission (2006c), *State Aid: Commission Orders Dutch Public Service Broadcaster NOS to Pay Back €76.3 Million Excess Ad Hoc Funding*. Press Release IP/06/822, 22 June 2006.

European Commission (2006d), *State Aid: Commission Requests Belgium to Clarify Financing of Public Broadcaster VRT*. Press Release IP/06/2006, 20 July 2006.

European Commission (2007), *State Aid: Commission Closes Investigation Regarding the Financing Regime for German Public Service Broadcasters*. Press Release IP/07/543, 24 April 2007.

European Court of Justice (2002), Opinion of the Advocate General Delivered 30 April 2002. *Ministre de l'économie, des finances et de l'industrie* v. *GEMO SA* (C-126/01) [2003] ECR 3454.

European Union. *Treaty of European Union*. http://europa.eu.int/eur-lex/lex/en/treaties/index.htm, accessed 30 July 2006.

Selmayr, M. and Kamann, H.G. (2004), 'Public Broadcasting and EC State Aid Law: No Carte Blanche after Altmark Trans', *Kommunikation & Recht*, 2/2004, 51–58.

Ward, D. (2004), *The European Union Democratic Deficit and the Public Sphere: An Evaluation of EU Media Policy*. Amsterdam: IOS Press.

Chapter 4

Media Pluralism and Enlargement: The Limits and Potential for Media Policy Change

Beata Klimkiewicz

Media pluralism is one of those normative concepts in European media policy that generates a broad respect for its undisputed value and importance for the democratic process as well as cultural identity formation at the European level. At the same time, the complexity of media pluralism leaves ample scope for interpretation and constitutes fertile ground for a variety of ways how the concept itself is being used in the formulation of policy objectives and rationales, as well as in policy implementation.

Undoubtedly, media freedom and pluralism have been perceived as basic conditions for successful transformation of media systems and consolidation of democracy in Central European (CE) countries during the European Union's (EU) eastward enlargement. A specific historical resonance of these issues in Central Europe can be best illustrated by the long experience of censorship, propaganda and state control over the media during the communist era. EU enlargement provided a framework of governance in which a process of democratic consolidation at the national level has simultaneously adjusted to supranational integration.

In the post-accession period, the issue of media pluralism still raises a question of different regional and national perspectives. The Final Report summarizing the debate of the Group on Media Pluralism at the Liverpool Audiovisual Conference devoted to revision of the Television without Frontiers Directive,[1] observed: 'New member states tended to have different notions of what pluralism means than the older members of the Union. There is a danger of applying double standards when dealing with media pluralism issues'. (Working Group 5 2005, 1)

The aim of this chapter is to examine how the concept of media pluralism has been used, operationalized and exposed during the accession process in European media policy. Three dimensions will be observed in this respect: vocabulary used – in particular standards promoted within a policy of conditionality, a way of reasoning and development of a monitoring process itself (especially the European

---

1   Directive 89/552/EEC on the coordination of certain provisions laid down by law, regulation or administrative action in Member States concerning the pursuit of television broadcasting activities [1989] OJ L298/23, as amended by Directive 97/36/EC [1997] L202/60.

Commission's (EC) Regular Reports). The inclusion of the post-enlargement period provides a possibility to analyze EU rule transfer and transposition of EU standards in CE institutional structures and political practices in the context of current policy change concerning media pluralism at the European level.

The chapter focuses on the fifth 2004 eastward enlargement and includes examples from the following CE countries: Czech Republic, Hungary, Poland, Slovakia, Slovenia. In addition to a conceptual dimension, these cases help us to understand media pluralism in a rapidly changing media environment affected by intense and rudimentary media reforms, many of which have caused unexpected problems. The chapter argues that problematization of media pluralism during the EU accession lacked distinct visibility and a clear message, thus resulting in the ambiguity of language and ambivalence of the policy-making process.[2] Paradoxically, the tension between different approaches to media pluralism and its role in consolidation of democracy has also stimulated a possibility of change in the post-accession period.

The Potential of Media Pluralism: A Problem of Conceptualization

Media relations and interdependencies with the political system and larger society define the way, and discourse through, which media pluralism is conceptualized and operationalized as a policy rationale. Its complexity manifests itself in a number of layers: a macro level of media systems (media ownership and service structures, entry costs and conditions), a meso level of media institutions (media performance, professional practices, user access and the way users interact with the content and services) and a micro level of media contents. Media pluralism is also being interpreted through conceptual dichotomies or alternatives such as external/ internal, proportional/open, organized/spontaneous, polarized/moderate, evaluative/ descriptive or reactive/interactive/proactive.

In the context of media policy, an operational definition of media pluralism has most notoriously developed around the axis of external/internal dimension. An instructive example would be the notion of media pluralism, which was elaborated by the Council of Europe and its advisory committees (later successively used and modified by other European institutions). The Council of Europe's Committee of experts on media concentration and pluralism (MM-CM) conceived pluralism as 'internal in nature, with a wide range of social, political and cultural values, opinions, information and interests finding expression within one media organization, or external in nature, through a number of such organizations, each expressing a particular point of view' (MM-CM 1994).

The frequently drawn distinction between *external* 'plurality of autonomous and independent media' and *internal* 'diversity of media contents available to the public', reveals a problematic relationship between the two dimensions. Namely, that research has not so far unanimously proved that a strong link between plurality of ownership and diversity of content is casual and direct. Although some researchers sustain

---

2   A close relationship between ambiguity of lannguage and ambivalence of political conduct was distinguished and conceptualized by Michael Oakeshott (1996).

that, extensive media concentration leads to the promotion of corporate values and political preferences of media owners and advertisers in media contents (Bagdikian 2000; FCC 2003), others convincingly argue that a direct link between media concentration and content diversity cannot be identified in quantitative terms (Ward 2006). Most commentators also agree that media pluralism is a multidimensional issue and should not be confined to mere plurality of ownership and diversity of content.

The traditional concept of media pluralism is being challenged by the reconfiguration of media systems and societal transformation resulting from the impact of digital revolution, convergence and multiplicity of media platforms and services. In this new and very dynamic context media pluralism presents a **Potential** the full usage of which depends on individual users, their ability to: critically read media content, distribute their own content and generate individual ways of interaction with the media services. The potential of media pluralism can be conceived through 'building blocks' and capacities which these components are able to mobilise in given circumstances. Thus it is to be thought of as a condition conducive to the balance between multiple centres of media control, compensation of multiple sources of information, competition between multiple viewpoints, socialization through multiple forms of media participation, recognition of multiple values and a choice between multiple forms of interaction (see Table 4.1).

Table 4.1 Potential of media pluralism: key components and capacities

Components	Capacities
Multiple centres if media control	Balance
	Shared Control
Multiple sources	Complementarity
	Compensation
Multiply viewpoints	Competition (discursive not instrumental)
Multiple access and participation	Socialisation
Multiple values	Recognition and representation
Multiple forms of interaction	Choice

The centres of media control vary in the extent to which they balance ownership control with a content producer's autonomy and journalistic independence, as well as with regulatory requirements. An increasing variety of services offered by media providers does not create a plural media environment, if limited by the exclusive use of proprietary solutions, lack of service interoperability and thus, if constraints are exercised both over users and content producers (Nissen 2006). Secondly, media pluralism may be used more effectively if source diversity meets the needs of users, and especially those who are compelled to compensate a disadvantage with respect to one source of information by exploiting their access to different sources. Thirdly, viewpoint diversity and competition between different opinions remains a principal rationale for media pluralism.

Fourthly, multiple forms of citizen access to the media define a process of socialization and models of social behaviour. In highly media-pervaded societies, the potential of media pluralism depends on a quality of socialization accompanied and strengthened by media literacy skills. Fifthly, media pluralism is often described through the capacity of recognition and representation of multiple, often conflicting values. Finally, the full exploitation of media pluralism depends on a choice between multiple forms of interaction with the media. The fact that citizens may increasingly control the way how and when they interact with media services stimulates diversity. Yet, an interactive future is certain to produce new types of monopoly (bottlenecks controlled by providers) and new forms of exclusion (a low level of media literacy) (Graham and Davies 1997; Freedman 2005).

Media pluralism comes into being through relations and context in which it is involved. In media policy, the relevance of the concept itself is marked by its potential. In other words, it is important, how the potential of media pluralism is seen to be activated and how connections between its 'building blocks' and capacities are to be stimulated in policy language, ways of reasoning and development of a policy process itself. Two readings of the term itself may be extracted from the current media policy debate: media pluralism is regarded in the broader social and political context – as a contribution to deliberative democracy or as a fundamental condition for a public sphere formation (Habermas 1995, 1996; McQuail 1992; Cavallin 2000). Such diversity being primarily about variety of viewpoints and attitudes of a political, cultural, ethical nature, serves as a founding rationale for defenders of public service broadcasting, and other structural measures promoting a more interventionist articulation of pluralism. Yet pluralism is also seen in economic, technocratic or professional terms – as increasing freedom of choice for the consumer, freedom of activities for industry, right to self-regulation and institutional autonomy; in other words, in opposition to interventionist public regulation.

The two perspectives also conceptualize media pluralism through different functional positioning of the media in a larger social system. In the first, inclusive, approach, the media are not seen as functionally differentiated from other spheres of social life (politics, culture, civil society), and thus they are expected to identify political and social problems and provide fertile ground for possible solutions. In this model, media pluralism is to be best structured at the level of a media system as a whole, through the existence of a range of media outlets reflecting diverse viewpoints or cultural representation rooted in different traditions of a society. Such a system characterized by a dominant presence of external pluralism will obviously be considered to have a high level of political and cultural parallelism (the extent to which a media system reflects the major political, cultural divisions in a society) (Hallin and Mancini 2004, 28).

The autonomous approach assumes that the media are in a process of becoming autonomous systems and networks due to functional differentiation, while this trend is driven mainly by economic and technological factors. Media pluralism could be best manifested through the dominance of internal pluralism – achieved within each individual media outlet. Such a model can be characterized by the growth of professional norms, self-regulation, low levels of political and cultural parallelism and universal provision reflecting the experience and perspective of the 'common' citizen (Hallin and Mancini 2004, 79). Inclusive and autonomous approaches to media pluralism conceptualization have evoked, to the certain extent, a main tension that has marked not only EU accession policy as regards freedom of expression and media pluralism, but more importantly, it has defined also current media pluralism policy debates.

Enlargement, Conditionality and Monitoring

In normative terms, media pluralism served both as a catalyst for the process of democratic consolidation in CEE and as a policy objective during the post-communist media reforms. Legacies of media censorship and tight media control during the communist era led to a broad political and public acceptance of deregulatory policies after 1989. There was widespread agreement that the best media policy is no policy and that the invisible hand of the market would be a perfect regulator and guarantee for media pluralism.

Although a membership in the Council of Europe and EU was an important point of reference for the changing media policy process in CEE, the pace of media system transformation took on an uneven speed. The pressure of time for the substantial reconstruction of media systems ended in some cases in rapid changes, some of which appeared to be superficial, while others irreversible and out of control. Some institutions were introduced too early (commercial broadcasters), while others were not given enough time for restructuring such as the state broadcasters' reform policies (Jakubowicz 2004). Certain policies proved to be premature when introduced (privatization of the print press), while others incomplete (especially new legal arrangements concerning the print press).

The prompt response of the Council of Europe (CofE) to democratization processes in CEE – Hungary became a member in 1990, Czech Republic and Slovakia in 1991, Poland 1991 – took the form against the internal redefinition of priorities in a media-related field. In this respect, CofE's objectives concerning media pluralism were historically linked to democratization of media systems in CEE. One of the fundamental incentives has been a positive action approach with regard to freedom of expression and the media as guaranteed by Article 10 European Convention of Human Rights (ECHR). The European Court of Human Rights has increasingly encouraged member states to ensure it is a citizen right to be fully and impartially informed, and to receive information from diverse and independent sources (Voorhoof 1998). Also an impressive volume of resolutions, recommendations and declarations adopted by the Parliamentary Assembly and the Committee of Ministers, many of which stressed the importance of the active implementation of Article 10 ECHR for the appropriate development of media pluralism, referred repeatedly to the situation in CEE.

The activities of the Committee of Experts on Media Concentration and Pluralism (MM-CM), established in 1991 to conduct an in-depth examination of media concentration, coincided with the drafting and adoption of new broadcasting laws in a number of CEE countries (Czech Republic 1991, Slovakia 1991, Poland 1992, Hungary 1996), aiming at the formation of a more diverse and plural media space. Media pluralism had been recognized as a central pillar of these regulations and many of these documents addressed the need to safeguard media diversity. For example, the Polish Broadcasting Act (1992) distinguishes 'an open and pluralistic nature of radio and television broadcasting' as one of the three main objectives to be ensured by the principal regulator – the National Broadcasting Council.[3] The Council of Europe's involvement in the protection of freedom and pluralism of the media provided an important normative basis for the EU to build on, not only when defining the EU's own membership conditions for new candidates, but also during the period of EU internal media pluralism policy debate (1992–1997), before the accession negotiations had begun.

The EU accession process entailed the adoption of EU rules and policies (the audiovisual acquis, competition and state aid policy) as well as incorporation of EU standards (formulated in the Copenhagen criteria (EC 1998) and Charter of Fundamental Rights of the European Union (European Parliament, Council and Commission 2007) into the level of domestic law, political institutions and practices. EU accession policy towards CEE has been generally described as a policy of conditionality, involving a bargaining strategy of reinforcement by reward, under which the EU provided external incentives for a target government to comply with its conditions (Schimmelfennig and Sedelmeier 2004, 662). The formulation by the European Council of the criteria for membership in Copenhagen in 1993 offered two normative dispositions in the context of media policy: political and economic. These were reinforced by the European Council in Madrid in 1995 by underscoring implementation and institutional function.

Since 1998, the EC has systematically assessed the fulfilment of the membership criteria through its principal monitoring instrument – annual Regular Reports. The structure of the Reports transcribed the Copenhagen criteria in order to indicate main achievements and problem areas in defined categories. For the fifth enlargement countries,[4] the EC issued Comprehensive Monitoring Reports in 2003, which abandoned the political component and focused solely on *acquis*. The chapter on Copenhagen political criteria was closed then, and the EC accepted the credibility of commitments made by the candidate countries in this area.

The issue of media pluralism was not recognized and distinguished as an independent category for evaluation, unlike freedom of expression, monitored under the section of 'Human Rights and Protection of Minorities' (political criteria). Apparently, the issue of media pluralism has been addressed in different sections of the reports and cut across both principal problem areas: the Copenhagen political criteria (with reference to freedom of expression) and *acquis* (culture and audiovisual policy).

---

3   Broadcasting Act adopted on 29 December 1992, *Official Gazette* No. 7, item 34, 1993, Article 6(1). See also Klimkiewicz 2005.

4   Previous enlargements included: 1973 (Denmark, Ireland and UK), 1981 (Greece), 1986 (Spain and Portugal) and 1995 (Austria, Finland and Sweden).

Monitoring Media Pluralism under the Political Criteria of the Copenhagen Document

The political Copenhagen criteria stipulated that a candidate country must have achieved 'stability of institutions guaranteeing democracy, the rule of law, human rights and respect for and protection of minorities.' As these criteria were not based on the *acquis* as such, the EC had to conduct its monitoring and assessment following a set of values and standards derived from non-EU documents, such as ECHR (Sasse 2004). These prerequisites perhaps help to explain why 'freedom of expression' was extracted from a wider and more complex body of communication rights (that also encompassed cultural, economic and social rights) and why media-related issues were operationalized within the category of civil and political rights only. Yet, the Regular Reports provided exceptionally large space for the description and interpretation of freedom of expression and, to a certain extent, illustrate the lack of well defined yardsticks in this field.

In general, the Reports covered a diverse patchwork of issues, demonstrating a lack of coherence between different elements of the empirical assessment. On the one hand, attention focused on fundamental matters for the protection of media freedom such as the high degree of government control over the public radio and television networks, criticized by the EC in the case of Slovakia (1998, 11). On the other hand, concerns were raised about the small number of radio stations in the case of Hungary (1998, 10) and the lack of stability in the television sector in the case of the Czech Republic (2002, 28–29). It is apparent, that some phenomena attracted significant attention in the case of particular countries (for example, the development of private media in Hungary), while in the case of other countries, they remained almost unnoticed (for example, the Czech Republic). Similarly, most of the reports in the case of Poland focused on libel laws offering politicians a higher level of protection than that afforded to the general public. At the same time, other problematic issues including political parallelism with respect to the composition of the regulatory authority and political influence on public service media remained overlooked. The issue of media pluralism emerges mainly from four problem areas that can be distinguished under the section of civil and political rights:

- demonopolization and robustness of media systems (a structural dimension);
- political influences on independence of regulatory authorities and public service media (this area is reflected also in the section on *acquis*);
- a crisis of the public service media;
- media coverage (mainly with reference to elections and political communication).

The Regular Reports gave an uneven prominence to structural diversity of media landscapes. The 1999 Composite Paper summarizing the achievements of all candidate countries, emphasized that 'most candidate countries have a robust and lively media' (1999, 15). Undoubtedly, the most detailed account of structural media developments can be found in the case of Hungary. It is interesting to note that the criteria evaluating the robustness of the Hungarian media system focused mainly on economic performance factors, such as a competitive pressure and competitiveness of the media market, broadcasting licence allocation to foreign consortia and the number of media outlets operating at different geographical levels of the media system.

The structural dimension of media pluralism was articulated much more modestly in the case of other countries. The 1998 Regular Report on Poland concluded that Poland continues to have 'a lively and active press' (1998, 12). In similar vein, the 2000 Report on Slovenia recorded, that 'the media is pluralist and represents a variety of opinions' (2000, 18). In general, the interpretation of the structural dimension gravitated towards economic and macro-level factors leaving out such important aspects as unresolved problems resulting from spontaneous media privatization, media ownership concentration (especially monopolies and duopolies of regional press markets) or unproportional asymmetry between the lack of domestic capital and dominance of foreign investment.

A problem of political influence on media regulatory bodies and public service media, which are supervised by these institutions, is well known from the substantial body of available research (Price 2002; Sükösd and Bajomi-Lázár 2003; Jakubowicz 2004; Petković 2004; Open Society Institute 2005). The EC's Regular Reports focused mainly on an assessment on the appointment procedures and composition of the media regulatory authorities. The crisis of the public service media, as recognized in these reports, has been naturally connected with this area of concern.

It should be recalled that after 1989 newly established public service media in Central Europe were regulated by new broadcasting acts, listing among the main duties of public service institutions an obligation to provide diverse programme content and plurality of information and opinion. Successful adoption of internal pluralism depended, however, on two normative prerequisites: one aimed at achieving a full independence both from the state and party politics; the second assuming a partial independence from market forces through the dual source of financing public service broadcasters (advertising as well as licence fees or some form of state support for the public mission parts of its service).

These aspirations met many practical difficulties, which were partially reflected in the Regular Reports. In sum, the Reports devoted most significant space to the crisis of the public service broadcasters in Hungary and the Czech Republic. The 2001 Report on Hungary described difficult financial conditions of the Hungarian public service broadcaster (MTV). In particular, the Report noticed that basic capital of the public television 'has been reduced to one tenth, outstanding public debts have doubled and numerous staff has been dismissed over the past two years in an attempt to render it more competitive' (2001, 20–21). These circumstances resulted not only in a significant drop in audience share (almost to 10 per cent), but also threatened public service remit requirements. Moreover, the abolition of television licence fees in 2002, by a legally questionable procedure (Open Society Institute 2005, 794), disclosed vulnerability of the public service broadcaster in its relation to ruling political parties. During the post-accession period, the situation has not significantly improved. Annual allocation of sources from the state budget determined by the political decision making process has rendered MTV's performance highly dependent on political choices. The September 2006 siege of MTV demonstrated that the public service broadcaster has been perceived, at least by some parts of the population, as a symbol of the ruling party's political power.

In the case of the Czech Republic, the 2001 Report summarized events that revolved around the staff strike in December 2000 and massive protests of the Czech public in January 2001. In December 2000, the Czech Council for Radio and Television Broadcasting dismissed the Director General of the Czech public broadcaster (ČT) and swiftly appointed a new candidate politically affiliated to the Civic Democratic Party (ODS). The employees responded to this situation by calling a strike and started to produce an alternative news service. The conflict itself was perceived by many citizens as a protest against political interference. Thus, it was not surprising, that on 3 January 2001, several thousand people gathered in Václav Square in Prague to demand the resignation of the newly nominated Director General and to express support for the journalists on strike. New legislation has since been adopted, enabling the election of the new Council for Radio and Television Broadcasting. As a result of these legal and institutional changes, the composition of the new Council reflected a relatively wide range of political organizations, civic associations, and also regional, social, cultural, religious and ethnic communities. The 2001 Report appreciated these changes and stressed that the spirit, in which they were made should be maintained (2001, 16). The 2002 Report reaffirmed the need to maintain the political independence of the Czech Council for Radio and Television Broadcasting (2002, 28–29).

The description of media coverage in the Regular Reports rested predominantly on data provided by other international institutions or NGOs. The 2000 Regular Report on Slovakia noted: 'monitoring of state-owned television has indicated that the opposition is not given sufficient and objective coverage' (2000, 19). Likewise, the 2002 Report on Hungary observed that 'during the election campaign, the presence of Government parties was more evident in public service media, while private media generally provided a more neutral coverage of events, as underlined by the OSCE' (2002, 29).

The picture of media pluralism in Central European countries emerging from the EC's Regular Reports under the section of political Copenhagen criteria (see Table 4.2), was painted rather cautiously. The Regular Reports avoided strong criticism in order to sustain progress along the envisaged 'road map' (Sasse 2005) and given the fact, that similar problems to those hindering media pluralism in Central European countries, remained unresolved in the older member states (for example, Italy). A milestone, by which candidate countries met political Copenhagen criteria (2003), stands symbolic rather than pragmatic in the area of freedom of expression and media pluralism. Many problematic issues indicated in the Reports (most notably political independence of regulatory authorities and public service media) have endured enlargement momentum and continued to define the reality of the media landscape in the post-accession period.

Table 4.2 Monitoring of political Copenhagen critieria: extracts from composite/strategy papers and country regular and comprehensive reports, 1998–2002

	1998	1999	2000	2001	2002
Strategy	*the independence of radio and television to be strengthened	*a robust and lively media, but fragile independence of radio and TV *media boards should represent a broad political spectrum	*no reference to media or freedom of expression	*the Copenhagen political criteria continue to be met by all negotiating candidate countries.	*all negotiating countries continue to meet the Copenhagen political criteria
Czech Republic	*freedom of expression was improved	*no reference to media or freedom of expression	*the Council for Television and Radio Broadcasting criticized for an ineffective action in addressing an ownership dispute	*the Council for TV and Radio Broadcasting replaced the Director of the public TV *the staff of the public TV on strike *new legislation adopted	*little progress in transparency and stability in the television sector *the Council for Radio and TV Broadcasting should maintain its political independence
Hungary	*competition between commercial TV channels *small number of private radio stations	*the board of trustees of public service TV formed solely by pro-Government members	*competitive market for news *in 1997 national television licenses granted to two Western private consortia	*80% of the print media and 70 % of radio and TV stations in private hands *financial situation in public service television is at risk *the supervision of the public service media not properly ensured	*equal political representation in the supervisory organs of public service media *election campaign coverage favours Government parties in public service media
Poland	*lively and active press *"slander and abuse" provisions in Penal Code do not cause problems	*"slander and abuse" provisions in Penal Code do not cause problems for journalists' rights	*concerns about the "slander and abuse" provisions of the Penal Code	*continued concerns about the use of the slander laws and stronger protection of politicians than the general public	*slander laws offer politicians a higher level of protection than to the general public
Slovakia	*the government exercised a high degree of control over the public radio and television	*changes in the composition of the boards controlling radio and television criticized as politically motivated	*the opposition is not given sufficient and objective coverage in the state-owned TV *the public service nature of state-owned media should be ensured and improved	*the freedom of expression enshrined in the Constitution of the Slovak Republic	*ineffective provisions of the Criminal Code concerning defamation of the State President, the Government and the Constitutional Court
Slovenia	*no reference to media or freedom of expression	*no reference to media or freedom of expression	*media is pluralist and represents a variety of opinions *support scheme for political pluralism in printed media	*freedom of expression enshrined in the Slovenian Constitution	*the Constitution guarantees *freedom of expression*

Media Pluralism as an 'Added Value'

It would be instructive in this context to see how EU accession and its monitoring exercise in particular, have pushed for a rethinking of EU's internal objectives and policies regarding media pluralism. During the 1990s media pluralism has been conceptualized by the EC almost exclusively through anti-concentration and media ownership policies (in fact, stimulating external pluralism). Overall, media pluralism was not seen as a value to be generated through EU media policy instruments, but rather as an 'added value' to be addressed by other European (Council of Europe) or national institutions.

In 1992, at the request of the European Parliament, the EC published a Green Paper: Pluralism and Media Concentration in the Internal Market to assess the need for Community action on the question of concentration in the media (television, radio and the press) (EC 1992). The unsuccessful results of the follow-up consultation process are well described in the field of media policy research (Doyle 2002; Ward 2004). Underscoring the difficulty in proposing any kind of rules harmonization between the EU member states on media pluralism, the EC has withdrawn from this policy area emphasizing the importance of added value of additional European actions (EC 2005a). For many members of the European Parliament supporting the regulatory change, media pluralism appeared to be 'without doubt the biggest failure of the EP' (Sarikakis 2004, 132). Even though the Parliament has renewed efforts to address this issue, the media pluralism regulatory initiative did not prove successful in the 1990s. The failure in this case stemmed not only from profound tensions between contradictory policy agendas of the involved parties, but also from conceptual ambiguity. In the regulatory debate the concepts of media pluralism and media ownership elided, although they are obviously not identical. Media pluralism served as a conceptual shell used most often in reference to anti-concentration measures and media ownership.

The drafting of the Charter of Fundamental Rights of the EU (2000) has provided an opportunity to revisit concerns for media pluralism in a new setting. Notwithstanding the Charter generally transcribes ECHR provisions, there was some room for redefinition. Hence, the second paragraph of Article 11 finally acquired the wording: 'The freedom and pluralism of the media shall be respected.' Unlike Article 10 ECHR, Article 11(2) refers explicitly to freedom and pluralism of the media, though the expression 'respected' has a much weaker weight than the term 'guaranteed', proposed in earlier drafts of the Charter (Westphal 2002, 486). The signing of the Charter in December 2000 has not significantly modified procedures of EU conditionality and monitoring exercises in the field of freedom of expression and media pluralism. The structure of Regular Reports generally followed previous templates and media pluralism has been further assessed indirectly under the category of freedom of expression.

More prominent orientation on media pluralism can be, however, found in the Reports prepared by the EU Network of Independent Experts on Fundamental Rights. The Network was set up upon a request by the European Parliament to monitor fundamental rights in the member states and its annual reports present, to a certain extent, continuation of the EU's Regular Reports. Some of these reports so far identified not only areas of concern (for example, the Gaspari Law in Italy, growing inter-media concentration in Portugal, insufficient impartiality and independence of the Polish regulatory agency – National Broadcasting Council, unequal obligations imposed on foreigners and Slovak citizens with regard to the Act of Periodic Press), but also positive aspects and good practices (Synthesis Report 2003; 2004; 2005). These include such practices as a requirement to offer a balance in programmes for all inhabitants without discrimination, which is imposed on broadcasters in the Czech Republic. Another example would be the control of media ownership consolidation in the UK, introduced in order to ensure a sufficient number of views in each market (Synthesis Report 2003).

The Reports also demonstrate clearer benchmarks in the area of media pluralism: the issue is monitored from a human rights perspective – as a right of each citizen to be fully and impartially informed from a diverse range of sources. The coverage of both old and new member states shows that, despite national specificities, many problem areas are similar and might require harmonized solutions, or at least a more formalized monitoring exercise at the European level.

The European Parliament's Resolution on the risks of violation, in the EU and especially in Italy, of freedom of expression and information (2004)[5] and the drafting of the Audiovisual Media Services Directive (AVMS) provided another opportunity for the redefinition of the EU's approach to media pluralism in the post-accession period. Some organizations claimed that the issue of media pluralism is back on the political agenda and requires not only national, but also a European response (Council of Europe 2002; 2004; Petković 2004; European Federation of Journalists 2006). 'The European response' to repeated claims of the European Parliament and interest groups, however, took on a slightly different direction. It certainly resulted from accommodation of heterogeneous interests, but more importantly following the logic of the 'autonomous approach', in which all policies affecting the media are to be tested against the economic performance and autonomy of the media industry (EC 2005d; DG Information Society and the Media 2006).

In a series of meetings with the publishing industry,[6] it became apparent that the industry representatives clearly aimed at preventing any new legislation at the European level to regulate media concentration and pluralism (European Publishers Council 2005), and demanded a recognition of a publisher's competitive position in a process of drafting policies aimed at other media market players (such as AVMS Directive) (European Publishers Forum 2005). The publishing industry also reminded the EC that there has not been and there should continue not to be any competence for the EU to intervene on matters of media pluralism other than its current rules on competition and merger regulation (ENPA 2005).

---

5   The Resolution was followed by the publication of the Final report of the study on the information of the citizen in the EU: obligations for the media and the Institutions concerning the citizen's right to be fully and objectively informed, prepared by the European Institute for the Media on behalf of the European Parliament, 31 August 2004.

6   These included: European Publishers' Forum 2005 (annual meeting), 6 December 2005, Brussels; Editors-in-Chief meeting with Information Society and the Media Commissioner Viviane Reding, Brussels, 23 September 2005 and the second meeting on 23 October 2006.

The EC's approach concerning competitiveness of the EU publishing sector plainly demonstrates that this is the key perspective that media policy is being 'filtered through.' The Staff Working Paper on Strengthening Competitiveness of the EU Publishing Sector recognizes that publishers have not yet been able to build the business models necessary to exploit online distribution and their online publications are frequently cross-subsidized by print revenues (EC 2005d). Thus, media policy should support sustainable competitiveness, bringing together the economic, environmental and social (high rates of employment) objectives of the EU, in order 'to enhance pluralism and culture at the European level' (EC 2005d, 30).

The audiovisual industry has raised equally strong arguments, emphasising that broadcasters do not strive for favourable treatment, but seek for equal regulatory mechanisms as other media businesses (ACT 2006). This framing of the policy debate puts media pluralism in a contradictory relation with global competitiveness of European media companies. On the one hand, European institutions (mainly the European Parliament and Council of Europe) have repeatedly highlighted the importance of media pluralism for the democratic nature of the European media landscape and expressed the need to formulate a common regulatory approach at the EU level. On the other hand, the European media industry has demanded regulatory solutions that would increase competitiveness of European media companies on a global scale.

Yet, the conflict between the inclusive and autonomous approaches to media pluralism has not only reactive, but also proactive potential in multi-level EU media policy-making processes. EC policy activities and discourses benefit from adding the 'value of media pluralism' to strengthen the EC's bargaining position vis-à-vis external actors (both industry representatives and various interest groups). A good example can be the addition of the 'value of media pluralism' to the project of the new AVMS Directive, promoted through the three major measures which contribute to media pluralism: an obligation for member states to guarantee the independence of national regulatory authorities, the right of broadcasters to receive 'short reporting' and promotion of European works and content from independent European producers (EC, DG Information Society and the Media 2005c).

On 16 January 2007 the EC published a staff working document Media Pluralism in the Member States of the European Union, indicating further steps in a policy process regarding this matter (EC 2007b). The document sustains a familiar argument against submitting a Community initiative on pluralism at present, but it emphasizes the necessity to closely monitor the situation. The monitoring process is to involve an independent study on media pluralism indicators and Communication from the Commission concerning these indicators. Thus, 'concrete' indicators of assessing media pluralism present a crucial methodological category used for developing a more sophisticated risk-based monitoring mechanism, including such areas as: (1) policies and legal instruments that support pluralism in MS; (2) the range of media available to citizens in different MS and (3) supply side indicators on the economics of the media (EC 2007b, 17–18).

The idea to monitor conditions of media pluralism in the EU member states integrates the EC decision making with the European Parliament's and Council of Europe's priorities concerning policy on media pluralism, at the same time, this integration is compensated by gains in autonomy vis-à-vis the media industry and interest groups. The monitoring is not likely to bring a significant qualitative change in current EU media policy-making, but will present a potential base (the EC may or may not use) for more substantial policy change depending on a critical mass of information needed for an initiation of new solutions.

Monitoring of the Audiovisual *Acquis*

The 1993 Copenhagen European Council indicated that the ability to take on the obligations of membership requires the adoption and implementation of the *acquis*. The European Council of Madrid highlighted the importance not only of incorporating the *acquis* into national legislation, but also of ensuring its effective application through appropriate administrative and judicial structures (EC 2000, 21). In the area of media policy, the conditionality implied a legislative alignment with the principal legal instrument – Directive 89/552/EEC, commonly referred as the Television without Frontiers Directive.[7] The Television without Frontiers Directive sought to create a European media space through the free movement of audiovisual services within the EU and the promotion of European and independently produced programmes. During the initial phase of the monitoring exercise, many Central European countries had been already involved in a process of the ratification of the Council of Europe's Convention on Transfrontier Television (ECTT) and in the ratification of its amending protocol. Although the Convention has covered similar areas as the Directive (removal of national barriers to cross-border broadcasting, promotion of European and independently produced programmes, minimum rules for the protection of minors, advertising, sponsorship, right to reply and human dignity), Karol Jakubowicz argues that the two legal instruments displayed differences in their fundamental philosophy:

> In one, emphasis was placed on the social, cultural and political function of broadcasting, while the other was geared more to the economic needs of the market, though some of those provisions also had clear cultural implications. (Jakubowicz 2006, 3)

As regards media pluralism, the Television without Frontiers Directive did not contain any provisions specifically aimed at safeguarding media pluralism, but some of its measures contributed indirectly to cultural diversity of media content. The ECTT included a specific provision on media pluralism (Article 10*bis*) stipulating that:

> The parties, in the spirit of co-operation and mutual assistance which underlines this Convention, shall endeavour to avoid that programme services transmitted or retransmitted by a broadcaster or any other legal or natural persons within their jurisdiction, within the meaning of Article 3, endanger media pluralism. (Council of Europe 1989)

---

7   Directive 89/552/EEC on the coordination of certain provisions laid down by law, regulation or administrative action in Member States concerning the pursuit of television broadcasting activities [1989] OJ L298/23, as amended by Directive 97/36/EC [1997] L202/60.

A very general formulation of the Article 10*bis* emphasized responsibility of the parties to take into consideration the importance of media pluralism, but did not impose any specific obligations on them (Council of Europe 1998). The EC deemed the ratification of ECTT by the candidate countries as one of the main benchmarks in their progress towards full transposition of the audiovisual *acquis*. Media pluralism was not distinguished as a specific area of concern during the monitoring exercise, but a short examination of overlapping issues seems instructive. The relevant problem areas exposed in the Regular Reports include:

- independence of regulatory authorities and some aspects of administrative capacity (for example, transparency concerning frequency allocation and distribution of support measures);
- ownership rules;
- promotion of European and independent works and proportionality of measures promoting works in national languages.

Until 1999, the reports described sectoral divisions of the *acquis* in a rather general setting. Since 2000, culture and audiovisual policy has been monitored systematically under Chapter 20. The Reports generally followed a route towards progress. A cumulative success has been described in a gradual manner; the efforts of each candidate country were evaluated through repeatedly used formulaic expressions: 'progress in the audiovisual sector is very limited', 'no significant progress', 'a moderate level of alignment with the acquis', 'a substantial degree of alignment with the acquis'.

The transposition of the Television without Frontiers Directive into national legislation stood at the centre of Chapter 20, including observance of subsequent amendments and legal procedures involving parliamentary discussions. In the case of some countries, a significant turning point has marked a new direction of the assessment. The 2002 Report on Slovakia concluded: 'Since the Opinion, Slovakia has made a considerable progress, and has reached, overall, an advanced level both in terms of legislative alignment and administrative capacity' (2002, 97). Likewise, the 2001 Report on Slovenia emphasized that substantial progress has been made on alignment with the audiovisual *acquis* and that the 2001 Mass Media Act brings Slovenian legislation into line with the Television without Frontiers Directive (2001, 71). The most problematic in this respect, appeared to be an alignment process in Poland. The 2003 Comprehensive Report warned that, 'unless rapid action is taken to catch up delays in amending the Broadcasting Act, there is a risk that Poland will not fulfil these requirements and not be able to implement the acquis by accession' (2003, 46).

The problems with the Polish legislative alignment stemmed from a disclosure of a corruption scandal, widely referred to as *Rywingate*, which ultimately resulted in the resignation of Leszek Miller's government in 2004. In 2002, the National Broadcasting Council (KRRiT) and Ministry of Culture in Poland proposed the Draft Amendment to the Broadcasting Law that was publicly promoted as a set of measures to protect media pluralism through constraints on cross-media concentration. An important objective of the Act was also the transposition of missing provisions of the audiovisual *acquis* in order to enable full alignment with the Television without Frontiers Directive. In 2002, one of the largest media companies in Poland, Agora, was approached by a film producer Lew Rywin representing a 'group in power' and was asked by him to pay a bribe in order to gain regulatory favours. The leading Polish daily and Agora flagship title *Gazeta Wyborcza* exposed the scandal. In consequence, the Sejm Investigation Committee disclosed several worrying irregularities concerning the legislative work on the Draft Amendment. These circumstances led to the withdrawal of the problematic document by the Sejm[8] and to serious delays in legislative transposition of the audiovisual *acquis*.

As late as in April 2004, another amendment (commonly referred to as the 'small' or 'European' amendment) to the 1992 Broadcasting Act was passed by the Sejm. The document itself did not contain anti-concentration provisions, nor did it address transparency of media ownership, but focused mainly on the implementation of the Television without Frontiers Directive requirements: European quotas (Article 15), definition of *European works* (Article 15b), advertising (Article 16a, b), sponsoring (Article 17), and protection of minors (Article 18). Article 35 of the amended Act also ensured that broadcasting licences may be granted to foreign persons or entities permanently resident in the EU.

All these circumstances have not been explained in the Regular Reports on Poland (in 2003 investigations were still pending), but the language of the assessment makes it clear that the EC was concerned about these issues. The 2003 Comprehensive Report on Poland suggested that 'Poland must pay attention to ensuring a stable, predictable, transparent and effective implementation of the broadcasting regulatory frameworks' (2003, 46). The corruption scandal showed the risks of political interference in the legislative process: it demonstrated how political and economic interests of the ruling elites, seeking support for their activities from media businesses, have distorted not only technical legislative procedures but the very texture of the law as well. *Rywingate* also demonstrated a fragile independence of the regulatory authority and once again proved that autonomy from politics and economics presents a necessary condition for maintaining media pluralism.

The Regular Reports devoted substantial space to regulatory authorities in the candidate countries, focusing mainly on their administrative effectiveness, competences, powers and composition. The 2000 Report on the Czech Republic noted that 'particular importance should be attached to the establishment and strong supervision of a transparent and predictable regulatory framework in this field' (2000, 79). In some cases regulatory bodies were praised for their effectiveness (1999 Poland) and independence (2000 Hungary), whereas in other cases, the EC suggested that strengthening in terms of staff and equipment (2000 Slovakia) or powers (2000 Slovenia) was needed. In the case of Hungary, the EC also underlined the need to increase transparency of activities affecting structural dimensions of media pluralism including frequency allocation and the distribution of the Broadcasting Fund (2002, 99).

The promotion of European and independent works, as well as proportionality of measures promoting programmes in national languages were specifically mentioned

---

8   The lower chamber of the Polish Parliament.

in the case of Poland (Regular Reports 1999; 2000; 2001; 2002; 2003), Hungary (1999) and Slovenia (2002). When introducing new broadcasting laws in the 1990s many Central European countries have acknowledged that a national presence in the audiovisual sphere (through original content produced in national languages) is crucial and should become a stable component of new regulatory designs. An obligation to adopt the audiovisual *acquis* added the European dimension to it, not by replacing the national production quota, but by completing it proportionally. For example, the Polish Broadcasting Act (1992), transposing the audiovisual *acquis* by the 2004 amendment, has stipulated that both private and public broadcasters are required to reserve at least 33 per cent of their quarterly transmission time (excluding news, advertising, teleshopping, sport events, teletext service, games) to programmes originally produced in the Polish language (Article 15.1) and more than 50 per cent of time to programmes produced by European producers (Article 15.3).

In general, the adoption of the European quota clause did not raise a contentious policy debate in Central European countries, as it has been the case in old member states (especially before the measure took its final shape and was inserted into the Television without Frontiers Directive). Available data from the post-accession period demonstrates that private broadcasters in Central European countries have devoted more or less a required portion of programming for European and independent production, while public service broadcasters have generally provided a higher proportion of these programmes (Open Society Institute 2005; EC 2006). A modest difference between the share of European and national productions also indicates that the European quota has, in fact, promoted national productions. Notwithstanding, the EC appreciated the application of Article 4 by new members from Central European countries as an encouraging success (a combined average transmission of European works in these countries amounted to 61.7 per cent during the first post-accession period (EC 2006, 5–6).

Media Diversity and Competitive Globalization

It would be useful in this context to follow post-accession developments in audiovisual policy and examine the EC's approach towards media pluralism. Some aspects of media diversity (especially cultural diversity of content) have been defined and used to protect a common European media space against US imports and to support dominant European media companies. In this logic of *competitive globalization* media diversity has been as important as it contributed to competitiveness of European ideas, cultures, languages and most crucially media and communication industries as a whole, on the global scene.

The concept of cultural diversity has served as an argument for state aid to the film and audiovisual industries as well as support for measures concerning European works and requirements for independent production during the drafting of the new AVMS Directive.[9] In its issue paper on cultural diversity, the EC called for the creation

---

9   National aid to the film and audiovisual industries is one of the chief means of ensuring cultural diversity, Council Resolution on National Aid to the Film and Audiovisual

Table 4.3   Monitoring of audiovisual (AV) acquis: extracts from composite/strategy papers and country regular and comprehensive reports, 1999–2003

	1999	2000	2001	2002	2003
strategy	*limited progress in the AV sector and few of the candidate countries have fully aligned to the TVWF Directive	*culture and audiovisual policy - a priority scheduled for the first half of 2001	*the need to set up or strengthen independent regulatory structures in audio-visual policy field	*no special reference to media and audio-visual policy	*The Czech Republic, Hungary and Poland must finalise alignment with the AV acquis; in the case of Poland particular efforts are still required
Czech Republic	*legislation is not compatible with the TVWF Directive	*some limited progress *the existing legislation is still not in line with TVWF Directive *particular importance should be attached to the strong supervision of a transparent and predictable regulatory framework in this field	*significant progress in terms of legislative alignment but no particular progress on administrative capacity	*a lack of transparency and stability in relation to ownership *some development of administrative capacity *supervision of a transparent regulatory framework needed *regulatory authority should ensure objective and effective application of broadcasting regulation	*The Czech Republic is meeting the majority of the requirements for membership in the area of the audio-visual policy *efforts should be focused on the establishment of a stable, transparent and effective regulatory framework.
Hungary	*Hungarian legislation is already to a large extent aligned with the acquis *Hungary must define the programming of European works	*limited progress in alignment with the Community acquis *The National Radio and Television Board is independent from the executive	*Hungary's legislation is still not fully aligned with the acquis	*new Media Law approved *the acquis largely transposed *the independence of the regulatory authority continues to be respected *transparency should be increased (frequency allocation and distribution of the Broadcasting Fund)	*Hungary is partially meeting the requirements for membership in the area of audio-visual policy *the remaining legislative amendment must be completed
Poland	*a moderate level of alignment with the acquis *administrative and implementation structures are in place	*Poland has made significant progress but further progress needed (e.g. promotion of European and independent works) *the issue of foreign investment remains an area for concern	*further legislative alignment in the field of AV policy required before accession regarding jurisdiction, promotion of independent and European works, capital liberalisation	*little progress with regard to audio-visual policy *administrative capacity judged satisfactorily	*Poland is partially meeting the requirements for membership *unless rapid action taken, there is a risk that Poland will not be able to implement the acquis by accession
Slovakia	*no significant progress made with respect to the adoption of the adiovisual acquis	*approval of the new Broadcasting Act *a substantial degree of alignment with the AV acquis, administrative capacity has to be noticeably strengthened	*the new Act on Broadcasting and Retransmission has brought Slovakia's legislation largely into line with the TVWF Directive	*Slovakia has made considerable progress, and has reached an advanced level both in terms of legislative alignment and administrative capacity	*Slovakia has met commitments and requirements arising from the accession negotiations on culture and AV policy and will be in a position to implement the acquis by accession.
Slovenia	*legislation is still not in line with the acquis *administrative structures have limited powers for effective monitoring	*limited progress in alignment *The Broadcasting Council has limited powers for effective monitoring	*The Mass Media Act (2001) brings Slovenia's legislation largely into line with the TVWF Directive	*Slovenia has made some progress regarding legislative alignment with the AV acquis *some further fine-tuning necessary, in particular regarding definition of European AV works	*Slovenia is essentially meeting the commitments arising from the accession negotiations on AV policy and is expected to be in a position to implement the acquis by accession.

of incentives increasing the distribution of European co-productions: 'Positive likely impacts in cultural terms might be a deeper understanding of Europe's cultural diversity and richness and a wider acceptance of the European integration process' (EC 2005b, 4). In this sense, the promotion of European works and co-productions has been increasingly interpreted as an essential contribution to the nurturing of cultural diversity both within and outside Europe and as a way of correcting current levels of media representations of cultures in a global scale.

The global perspective has strengthened the view on cultural diversity as a key value shared by all Europeans that needs to be constantly reaffirmed in subsequent media regulatory designs. In this process, cultural diversity is seen to reinforce a common European awareness and feeling of collective belonging, determining in consequence the progress of the Union. Thus, once highly contentious, the European quota issue has evolved in the alchemy of media policy-making and implementation into a widely accepted instrument. Some criticism on a rather soft formulation of Article 4 ('where practicable and by appropriate means'), as well as on implementation and monitoring functions, have not undermined a gradual consensus that these content rules provide a stable and flexible framework for the protection of cultural diversity (seen of course from the perspective of European culture). Herein, cultural diversity has conceptually functioned as a European cultural projection: it has been the conscious effort by media policy-makers and industry to place recognizable images and representations of European culture (through diverse cultural expression) in the global scene.

Yet, the widening of the new AVMS Directive's scope to non-linear audiovisual media services brings far less agreement, although it can be perfectly justified from the position of European *cultural competitiveness* in the global context. A potential of non-linear audiovisual services to replace linear services, upholds, in a view of the EC, regulatory commitment to the promotion and distribution of European works – and thus promotion of cultural diversity on non-linear services. In its amended proposal for a new AVMS Directive, the EC has proposed that on-demand media services promote production of and access to European works (EC 2007a, Article 3f). Incorporating some legislative suggestions of the European Parliament (European Parliament 2006), the proposal stipulates that 'such a promotion could relate, inter alia, to the financial contribution made by such services to the production and rights acquisition of European works or to the share and/or prominence of European works in the catalogue of programmes proposed by the service' (EC 2007a, Article 3f).

Taking into consideration the risk of avoiding these regulatory requirements by the establishment of media services outside the EU, the weight of cultural diversity promotion carries a more symbolic than pragmatic significance and might be, in future, related more closely to public media services rather than on-demand services generally.

Industries, 12 February 2001, [2001] OJ C73, p. 3. See also: European Commission (2005), Impact Assessment – Draft Audiovisual Media Services Directive, COM(2005) 646 final.

Conclusions

The different and in many respects conflicting characteristics of the media pluralism problematization have led to 'seesaw' efforts to introduce and abandon media pluralism regulatory measures at the European level. The problem however does not only seem to be rooted in a structural asymmetry of EU policies that have made pro-market deregulatory 'negative integration' far easier to achieve than market-correcting regulatory and 'positive integration' (Scharpf 1999). Both pro-market and market-correcting measures may be used for the same rationale as is the case of competitive globalization. Namely 'this objective' has guided the EC's policies on media pluralism/diversity (as it is encapsulated in media policy language) in both deregulatory (reluctance towards harmonizing 'media pluralism' anti-concentration measures) and market-correcting directions (protection of cultural diversity through European quota, European co-productions and production by independent producers).

The dividing line comes rather from two different ways of perceiving and conceptualizing media networks in a context of larger societies or political systems: one seeing the media as increasingly politically *autonomous* and differentiated system; playing a central role in a process of competitive globalization. The second perceiving the media as an *inclusive* part of a deliberative democratic system. This tension has defined, to a significant extent, the process of conditionality during the EU's fifth accession and especially the EC's monitoring exercise in the area of media policy. The possible effects carry naturally both negative and productive potential: on the one hand they set limits on policy solutions, bring the risk of destructive institutional competition and policy deadlock. On the other hand, they may generate an impetus for media policy change and a potential for reform that would not be possible in a unified structure.

During the accession and post-accession period two levels of conditional policy-making have emerged (formal and informal). The formal monitoring and enforcement of the Copenhagen political criteria lacked a strong foundation in EU law and well-defined indicators providing a firm base for assessment in the area of freedom of expression and media pluralism. Although the Charter of Fundamental Rights of the EU and a monitoring initiative of the EU Network of Independent Experts on Fundamental Rights offered a new dimension in this respect, the effective policy impact has remained weak. The monitoring and transposition of the audiovisual *acquis* proved more effective for the rule transfer process than was the case of the Copenhagen political criteria. This resulted not only from a greater clarity and formality of the rules, but also higher compliance.

Nevertheless, the scope of audiovisual policy as defined through the Television without Frontiers Directive and its revised version is significantly limited in the area of media pluralism. In fact, the formal policy concerning media pluralism has been seen as one of the biggest failures of EU institutions (both the EC and Parliament). Despite the need for harmonized European rules on media pluralism, the EU still lacks the formal powers (especially if member states' interests strongly diverge) and the institutional capacities necessary to enforce compliance with the rules and their transposition in the member states. The most important regulatory instrument continues to be competition law, which, while strong and intrusive, is limited in scope and is a poor substitute for other regulatory powers and capacities (Grande and Eberlein 2005). The Council of Europe's continuous efforts to repeatedly address the need for common standards on media pluralism have not so far brought a legally binding outcome.

Yet the tension between the inclusive and autonomous approaches provides an alternative route for harmonization, especially through defining the limits of both standards in a process of informal policy-making. The idea to regulate media pluralism at structural level (the prevention of concentration through anti-concentration rules, imposing diversity on media actors) is being replaced by soft and indirect regulatory levers, such as monitoring, transparency and the promotion of media literacy. Through information exchange and networking, both EU institutions and the Council of Europe, develop harmonized strategies focusing predominantly on information and competence. An individualized and interactive character of media use amplifies the possibility to better safeguard media pluralism through supporting citizens and interest groups with know-how to establish their media relations, to get their messages heard, cultural expressions aired and opinions addressed. The fact, that media pluralism is approached in different ways does not decrease its potential and the chance for vital policy-making. The important question is, however, whether policy bridges are built between divergent practices and rationales, and whether they, in consequence, activate media pluralism potential. This multi-rationality and multi-functionality of the media policy process itself creates a complicated, multi-layered setting that in certain circumstances brings a harmonized solution and strengthens European institutions.

References

ACT (2006), *ACT Conference <TV 2010: Digital&Beyond>*, http://www.acte.be/ usermodule/en/act.asp, accessed 3 October 2006.

Bagdikian, B. (2000), *The Media Monopoly*, 6th ed. Beacon Press.

Cavallin, J. (2000), 'Public Policy Uses of Diversity Measures' in J. van Cuilenburg and R. van der Wurff (eds), *Media and Open Societies: Cultural, Economic and Policy Foundations for Media Openness and Diversity in East and West*. Amsterdam: Het Spinhuis, 105–170.

Council of Europe (1989), *European Convention on Transfrontier Television*, text amended according to the provisions of the Protocol (ETS No. 171), which entered into force on 1 March 2002.

Council of Europe (1998), *The Revised European Convention on Transfrontier Television and its Explanatory Report* DH-MM (98) 8. Strasbourg: Directorate of Human Rights.

Council of Europe (2002), *Media Diversity in Europe*, Report prepared by the AP-MD, H/ APMD (2003)001.

Council of Europe (2004), *Transnational Media Concentrations in Europe*, Report prepared by the AP-MD, AP-MD (2004)7.

Department for Culture, Media and Sport (2005), *Liverpool Audiovisual Conference:*

Between Culture and Commerce, 20–22 September, http://www.culture.gov. uk/NR/rdonlyres/FFFED5B0-24DA-4166-895F-82FDB7936FDC/0/Conf_ Audiovisual.pdf, accessed 3 March 2006.

DG Information Society and the Media (2006), *Task Force for Co-ordination of Media Affairs*, http://europa.eu.int/information_society/media_taskforce/index_ en.htm, accessed 15 October 2006.

Doyle, G. (2002), *Media Ownership. The Economics and Politics of Convergence and Concentration in the UK and European Media.* London: Sage Publications.

ENPA (2005), *ENPA Response to the Commission Issues Paper on Media Pluralism – What Should Be the European Union's Role?*, http://ec.europa.eu/comm/ avpolicy/docs/reg/modernisation/issue_papers/contributions/ip6-enpa.pdf, accessed October 10, 2006.

European Commission (1992), *Pluralism and Media Concentration in the Internal Market: An Assessment of the Need for Community Action*, Commission Green Paper, COM(92) 480 final, Brussels, 23 December 1992.

European Commission (1998), *Reports on the Progress Towards Accession by each of the Candidate Countries*, Composite Paper.

European Commission (2000), *Enlargement Strategy Paper: Report on Progress Towards Accession by Each of the Candidate Countries,* http://ec.europa.eu/ enlargement/archives/pdf/key_documents/2000/strat_en.pdf, accessed 9 February 2007.

European Commission (2005a), *Issues Paper for the Liverpool Audiovisual Conference: Media Pluralism – What Should be the European Union's Role?* Brussels: DG Information Society and Media.

European Commission (2005b), *Issues Paper for the Liverpool Audiovisual Conference: Cultural Diversity and the Promotion of European and Independent Audiovisual Production.* Brussels: DG Information Society and Media.

European Commission, DG Information Society and the Media (2005c), *Why and How Europe Seeks Pluralism in Audiovisual Media*, http://europa.eu.int/ information_society/services/doc_temp/tvwf-sht5_en.pdf, accessed 5 February 2006.

European Commission (2005d), *Commission Staff Working Paper: Strengthening Competitiveness of the EU Publishing Sector, The Role of Media Policy*, SEC(2005) 1287, Brussels, 5 October 2005.

European Commission (2006), Communication from the Commission to the European Parliament, Council, the European Economic and Social Committee and the Committee of the Regions: *Seventh Communication on the Application of Articles 4 and 5 of Directive 89/552/EEC on 'Television without Frontiers', as amended by Directive 97/36/EC, for the period 2003–2004*, COM(2006) 495 final, Brussels, 14 August 2006.

European Commission (2007a), *Amended proposal for a Directive of the European Parliament and of the Council amending Council Directive 89/552/EEC on the coordination of certain provision laid down by law, regulation or administrative action in Member States concerning the pursuit of television broadcasting activities ('Audiovisual Media Services without Frontiers')*, COM(2007) 170 final, Brussels, 29 March 2007.

European Commission (2007b), Commission Staff Working Document: *Media Pluralism in the Member States of the European Union*, SEC (2007) 32, Brussels, 16 January 2007.

European Federation of Journalists (2006), *Media Power in Europe: The Big Picture of Ownership*, http://www.ifj.org/pdfs/EFJownership2005.pdf, accessed 10 October 2006.

European Parliament (2004), *Resolution on the risks of violation, in the EU and especially in Italy, of freedom of expression and information*, [2004] OJ C104 E, 30 April 2004.

European Parliament (2006) *Draft Report on the proposal for a directive of the European Parliament and the Council, amending Council Directive 89/552/EEC*, Committee on Culture and Education, 2005/0260 (COD), 1 August 2006.

European Parliament, Council and Commission (2007), *Charter of Fundamental Rights of the European Union*, OJ C303, pp. 1–16, 14 December 2007.

European Publishers Council (2005), *Memorandum on Pluralism and Media Concentration addressed to the Members of the European Parliament's Intergroup on the Press, Communication and Freedom*, http://www.epceurope.org/issues/ MemorandumPluralismMediaConcentration.shtml, accessed 20 October 2006.

European Publishers' Forum (2005), *21st Century Publishing in Europe 'Promoting Knowledge, Information and Diversity': Calls for Action*, Brussels, 6 December 2005, http://europa.eu.int/information_society/media_taskforce/doc/publishing/ calls_for_action.pdf, accessed 20 October 2006.

Federal Communication Commission (2003), *Report and Order and Notice of Proposed Rulemaking*, FCC 03-127, Federal Register.

Freedman, D. (2005), 'Promoting Diversity and Pluralism in Contemporary Communication Policies in United States and the United Kingdom', *International Journal of Media Management* 7:1–2, 16–23.

Graham, A. and Davies, G. (1997), *Broadcasting, Society and Policy in the Multimedia Age*. Luton: John Libbey.

Grande, E. and Eberlein, B. (2005), 'Beyond Delegation: Transnational Regulatory Regimes and the EU Regulatory State', *Journal of European Public Policy* 12:1, 89–112.

Habermas, J. (1995), *The Structural Transformation of the Public Sphere. An Inquiry into a Category of Bourgeois Society*. Cambridge, Mass: MIT Press.

Habermas, J. (1996), *Between Facts and Norms: Contributions to a Discursive Theory of Law and Democracy*. Cambridge, Mass: MIT Press.

Hallin, D.C. and Mancini, P. (2004), *Comparing Media Systems: Three Models of Media and Politics*. Cambridge: Cambridge University Press.

Jakubowicz, K. (2004), 'Ideas in Our Heads: Introduction of PSB as Part of Media System Change in Central and Eastern Europe', *European Journal of Communication* 19:1, 53–74.

Jakubowicz, K. (2006), *Revision of the European Convention on Transfrontier Television in the Context of International Media Policy Evolution*, paper presented during the meeting of Working Group 3 of COST Action A30, Budapest, 22–23

September 2006.

Klimkiewicz, B. (2005), 'Media Pluralism: European Regulatory Policies and the Case of Central Europe', *European University Institute Working Papers*, RSCAS, 19, 1–21.

McQuail, D. (1992), *Media Performance: Mass Communication and the Public Interest.* London: Sage Publications.

MM-CM, Council of Europe's Committee of Experts on Media Concentrations and Pluralism (1994), *The Activity Report of the Committee of Experts on Media Concentrations and Pluralism*, submitted to the 4th European Ministerial Conference on Mass Media Policy. Prague, 7–8 December 1994.

Nissen, C.S. (2006), *Public Service Media in the Information Society*, the Report prepared by the Group of Specialists on PSB in the Information Society (MC-S-PSB). Strasbourg: Media Division, Directorate General of Human Rights, Council of Europe, February 2006, Doc. No. H/Inf. (2006) 3.

Oakeshott, M. (1996), *The Politics of Faith and the Politics of Scepticism.* New Haven and London: Yale University Press.

Open Society Institute (2005), *Television Across Europe: Regulation, Policy and Independence.* Budapest: OSI/EU Monitoring and Advocacy Program.

Petković, B. (ed.) (2004), *Media Ownership and its Impact on Media Independence and Pluralism.* Ljubljana: Peace Institute.

Price, M.E. et al. (eds) (2002), *Media Reform: Democratizing the Media, Democratizing the State.* London: Routledge.

Sarikakis, K. (2004), *Powers in Media Policy: The Challenge of the European Parliament.* Oxford: Peter Lang.

Sasse, G. (2004), 'EU Conditionality and Minority Right: Translating the Copenhagen Criterion into Policy', *EUI Working Papers*, RSCAS No. 2005/16.

Scharpf, F. (1999), *Governing in Europe: Effective and Democratic?* Oxford: Oxford University Press.

Schimmelfennig, F. and Sedelmeier, U. (2004), 'Governance by Conditionality: EU Rule Transfer to the Candidate Countries of Central and Eastern Europe', *Journal of European Public Policy* 11:4, 661–669.

Sükösd, M. and Bajomi-Lázár, P. (eds) (2003), *Reinventing Media: Media Policy Reform in East-Central Europe.* Budapest: CEU Press.

Voorhoof, D. (1998), 'Guaranteeing the Freedom and Independence of the Media', *Media and Democracy.* Strasbourg: Council of Europe Publishing, pp. 35–57.

Ward, D. (2004), *The European Union Democratic Deficit and the Public Sphere: An Evaluation of EU Media Policy.* Amsterdam: IOS Press.

Ward, D. (2006), *Final Report on the Study Commissioned by the MC-S-MD 'The Assessment of Content Diversity in Newspapers and Television in the Context of Increasing Trends Towards Concentration of Media Markets'*, MC-S-MD (2006) 001, Strasbourg: Council of Europe.

Westphal, D. (2002), 'Media Pluralism and European Regulation', *European Business Law Review* 13:5, 459–487.

Working Group 5 (2005), *Final Report on Media Pluralism*, Audiovisual Conference 'Between Culture and Commerce', Liverpool, 22 September 2005.

Chapter 5

The Changing Totems of European Telecommunications Governance: Liberalization, Market Forces and the Importance of the EU Regulatory Package

Seamus Simpson

Since the late 1970s, the telecommunications sector in Europe has undergone nothing short of radical and wholesale transformation in terms of its technologies, goods, services and market types. Through a complex evolutionary process the long established twin 'totemic' characteristics of state ownership and public service around which the sector was built and functioned have been replaced by those of liberalization and efficient market functioning. The sector also underwent a process of internationalization in terms of the outlook and strategies of its key commercial protagonists in each of Europe's historically highly national-centric and foreclosed markets, as well as in the key area of the sector's governance. An outstanding feature in the ensuing political-economic milieu of change has been the emergence and growth of the European Union (EU) as a prominent policy actor in the telecommunications field.

Drawing on the core theme of this volume – the role of the EU in regulation and the public interest in the communications industries – this chapter explores and evaluates the increasingly prominent role which the EU has played in the telecommunications sector in Europe over approximately 25 years. Telecommunications provides a case of extensive and well-developed EU policy activities in communications – it is arguably the most 'EU-ized' of the culture industries examined in this volume. It asks and seeks to answers two questions.

First, why has the EU assumed such significance in telecommunications? In brief, the chapter argues that this can be explained by two core reasons which underpin a rich and complex picture of policy activity: the opportunities, on the one hand, and threats, on the other, perceived by EU member states from economic internationalization couched within the globalization policy discourse; and the active role played by the European Commission (EC) as the key EU level institutional actor in the telecommunications policy arena. Second, how has EU telecommunications policy evolved over the period in question? The chapter explains this evolution as a still ongoing process of shifting policy equilibria reached between national and EU levels in which a plethora of national and European level governmental and private actors have played roles in the precise nature of the equilibrium point reached at core policy junctures explored in the chapter.

In undertaking its exploration and analysis in this way, the chapter illustrates how the role of public actors and public interest issues altered in telecommunications. The nation state, the historic key custodian and functionary in telecommunications, gradually – though not without controversy – ceded direct control of the ownership of key parts of the sector which were in its hands to private interests and the market. It also transferred governance of an increasingly liberalized sector to independent regulatory authorities at the national level and, very importantly – through agreeing a legislative package to harmonize and liberalize telecommunications markets – to the EU level. This has been delivered through an important developing regulatory relationship between the national and the EU institutional contexts which is explored in the chapter. The inexorable process of liberalization through phased re-regulation inevitably impacted upon the definition and treatment of traditionally very strong public interest issues in telecommunications which have become shaped by and expressed through the discourse and practices of the market increasingly: public interest issues are now formulated and delivered in terms of consumer rights rather than the broader conceptualization of public service.

The chapter is structured as follows: the next section provides a very brief overview of the traditional structure of, and justification for, the telecommunications sector in Europe. The section following this explores the evolution of EU telecommunications policy from the early legislative activity of the 1980s through to the agreement of a comprehensive liberalization package by member states in the early 1990s which entered into force in 1998. The chapter's third section explores the important period of refinement of the 1998 regulatory framework which the EU and its member states undertook leading to agreement on what came to be known as the Electronic Communications Regulatory Framework (ECRF), agreed in 2002. The penultimate section of the chapter explores the current ongoing review of the EU telecommunications policy framework, which is likely to lead to the next stage of policy equilibrium, making in the process some tentative predictions about its likely shape and significance. Finally, the chapter offers some conclusions on the importance of the EU in shaping regulation and public interest issues in telecommunications.

Regulation and the Public Interest in European Telecommunications: The Traditional Position

Historically, telecommunications was a sector with which the EU had little or no engagement. This was due to the striking nation state–centricity and nationally inward-looking nature of the sector, ironic given the potential of communications technologies and services to allow the world to become a 'smaller place'. In fact, the internationality of the sector in organizational terms was inherently intergovernmental in the shape of a minimal series of interface technical and commercial agreements detailing arrangements for the carriage of international telecommunications traffic worked out and administered at the European level in the European Conference of

Postal, Telegraph and Telephone administrations (CEPT) and globally within the International Telecommunication Union (ITU).

Within what came eventually to comprise the EU's member states, the governance of telecommunications was the embodiment of the traditional corporate state (Cerny 1996). Here, telecommunications service provision was entirely absent of market forces, a government owned administration being responsible for telecoms and postal services (the Postal, Telephone and Telegraph Administration). The justification for this sectoral structure was a conjunction of utility economics and public service provision. In respect of the former, the telecommunications service market – consisting essentially of fixed line voice telephony – was deemed to be an uncontestable natural monopoly (Spence 1983) due in the main to the prohibitive market entry costs for investment in a telecommunications infrastructure. In respect of the latter, it was argued that universal access to a basic telecommunications service at a uniform price was effectively a social right for citizens to be pursued as a goal of public policy by the corporate state well accustomed to interventions of this kind in a number of Europe's industrial sectors, not least those of the utilities (energy and telecommunications, principally). Taken together, it was contended that the state owned and regulated natural monopoly Postal Telegraph and Telephone (PTT) administration would be able, through cross-subsidization achieved through tariff re-balancing, to undertake a program of network roll out which would ensure eventually that every citizen wishing it would be able to access affordable and reliable telecommunications services (Simpson and Wilkinson 2002).

This stable system went largely, though not completely, unchallenged across Europe for most of the twentieth century. However, as has been thoroughly documented elsewhere, development in telecommunications technologies, not least of which was the digitalization of communications, provided the potential for new market and service possibilities undermining and calling into question the status quo. In particular, innovations which allowed computer terminals to be attached and to communicate with each other in conjunction with human users across the telecommunications network created a series of new service possibilities yielding three kinds of pressure for change in the organization of telecommunication. First, economically, the market for these new Value Added Network Services (VANS) bore no relation to the natural monopoly traditional voice telephony services and were argued therefore to be inherently contestable. Second, commercially providing these services – essentially a combination of IT and telecommunications – proved highly attractive to a series of firms outside the telecommunications sector. On the demand side, they also proved equally attractive to telecommunications customers, not least powerful multinational companies keen to expand internationally and aware of assistive potential of telecommunications for conducting their business in the most profit maximizing manner, yet equally, frustrated by what they viewed as the nationally constrained, costly and technically myopic series of services then available from PTTs. Third, telecommunications provided an important opportunity for political interests keen to spread the values and practices of new economic liberalism to the global level. The essential message promulgated here was that traditional corporate state sectoral intervention should give way to independently regulated market forces wherever possible: telecommunications, it was argued, was an exemplar of a situation where radical change needed to be effected nationally and internationally in order to reap the potential benefits in terms of economic output and consumer welfare gains from technological developments in the sector.

As the 1980s dawned, these arguments gradually gained increasing weight across EU member states, a number of which began to alter radically the structure of their telecommunications sectors along broadly neo liberal lines. Foremost in the vanguard of change was the UK – the leading 'regulatory state' in Europe at the time (Bartle et al. 2002) – which, by 1982, had created and ordered competitively new markets in VANS and mobile telephony, introduced duopoly competition in fixed link telecommunications, privatized the majority of its PTT and, lastly, relinquished regulatory responsibility for an increasingly competitive and complex sector to an independent regulatory authority, the Office of Telecommunications (Hulsink 1999). Similar, though less radical moves also occurred in continental Europe, notably in Germany but also France (see Thatcher 1999; Dyson and Humphreys 1986). As a consequence, clear signs of change appeared in the totemic characteristics underpinning telecommunications altering significantly perspectives on regulation and public interest issues. Inevitably, the more competitive states' outlook on telecommunications became, the more important became the, at that stage, very poorly developed international market context of the sector. It is from this juncture and within this broad context that the influence of the EU began to emerge and develop at a fast pace within the European telecommunications sector.

Liberalization, Re-regulation and the Europeanization of Telecommunications

The twin structural elements of technological opportunity and neo liberal economic globalization which were utilized by 'reformist' governments in Europe to alter the nature of telecommunications provision and regulation laid the ground for the EU to consider the sector as one within which it could, indeed should, develop policy responsibility. This process, begun in the early 1980s proceeded steadily through to a first 'equilibrium' point in EU telecommunications policy around the turn of the decade (see below). As in most policy areas of the EU, the role of European level institutional actors – in this case the EC – proved crucial (see Schneider et al. 1994). Noted for being an organization constantly alive to the possibility of expanding its competence and authority (see Cram 1994), the EC quickly developed into a skilful political actor in telecommunications (see Sandholtz 1993, 1998) in the process cementing the development of telecommunications policy authority to a significant and what has turned out to be irreversible extent. Here, the EC utilized its coercive powers, on the one hand, specifically enshrined in, and cleverly interpreted from, the Treaties establishing the EU (Humphreys and Simpson 2005). On the other, and for the most part, the EC actively pursued securing a consensus on the creation of EU telecommunication policy competences through what Thatcher (2001) has perceived as partnership building. In this respect, the development of EU telecommunications policy was far from merely a story of the EU and the EC specifically driving policy forward with only limited regard for member states' preferences. In fact, the character of policy in telecommunications at EU level at any one time has tended to reflect the thinking of most member states – or certainly the most influential and powerful of them – on how telecommunications should be ordered.

Early telecommunications policy activity of the EU provides evidence of the EC setting out its case for reform of the sector to incorporate the EU institutional context. Here, one the one hand, the economic threats from what were at the time the EU's two main industrial competitors – the USA and Japan – were used to urge member states to consider pooling resources of some kind at the EU level (EC 1984). On the other hand, the EC extolled the economic benefits to be derived from the creation of a Single European Market in telecommunications, part of a much wider policy initiative pursued in the latter half of the 1980s (EC 1985). The theme of an EU-wide market in telecommunications services was at the centre of the 1987 EU Green Paper which provided the first comprehensive indication of the EU's intent to develop a detailed legislative policy package of a liberalizing kind for telecommunications. Here, the EC declared its intention to propose legislation to create full EU-wide competition in telecommunications terminal equipment, on the one hand, and VANS on the other (EC 1987). The Green Paper also gave a strong indication of the liberal regulatory approach to the sector that would be pursued by the EU. For example, the paper argued that in markets subject to competition in the EU it was no longer tenable for the PTT administration (or the most recent incarnation thereof) to be both regulator and commercial player in the market in question. Indicative of the careful path which the EC knew it had to tread, the paper nonetheless made reference to maintaining certain of the well established elements of the telecommunications sector to which certain member states – notably those of the EU's southern states – were proving reluctant to countenance changing. Here, first, the EC affirmed member states' right to maintain voice telephonic markets as state-owned monopolies and, second, noted the continued importance of the public interest dimension of telecommunications pursued through universal service provision (EC 1987).

The EC indicated the seriousness of its liberalising intent soon afterwards through the publication of two directives whose purpose was to liberalize telecommunications terminal equipment and VANS respectively. The aftermath was a short but intense period of negotiation that eventually resulted in the first equilibrium point in the dynamic history of EU telecommunications policy. Very much aware that there were essentially two camps among EU member states on telecommunications policy liberalization – reformers and traditionalists – the EC took the seemingly rather bold decision to pass both directives directly into EU law, thereby bypassing the Council of Ministers and European Parliament. This it justified by citing Article 86 (then Article 90) of the Treaty of Rome, which it claimed required it to take direct remedial action in any instances where it found distortions of competition as a result of the granting by states of an exclusive dominant position to public undertakings in particular markets. Those of telecommunications terminal equipment and VANS were of this kind, the EC argued.

The EC's action precipitated two legal challenges in the European Court of Justice around each proposed directive from states opposed to both the substance of the directives and the manner in which the EC proposed to enact them. However, there were at the same time powerful EU member states, not least among which Germany and the UK, which supported the Directives' content, though being opposed to the EC's methods. It was also the case that as the 1980s ended, countries such as France began to become more attuned to the view that commercial opportunities from liberalising the newer parts of the telecommunications sector might outweigh the threats from so doing. Aware in classic neo-mercantilistic fashion of its leading position at the time in VANS delivered through the ambitious state funded Teletel programme, France was keen to capture any opportunities which might be gained from exporting its technologies and services internationally. The EU could even act as something of a tool for justifying liberalization to particularly resistant domestic interests (Thatcher 2002b).

As a consequence, a situation which had initially all the hallmarks of controversy and stalemate proved ripe for compromise, something which the EC took pains to secure by 1990. The 'settlement package' involved the passage of the two directives, the one on services[1] having been modified to allow member states to impose certain public service obligations on private telecommunications operators leasing lines on the public network (Woolcock et al. 1991). The second element was the passage of a framework Directive on Open Network Provision in telecommunications[2] which concerned creating harmonized conditions to allow free competition to be practised across telecommunications networks. The 'ONP compromise' as it came to be known provided an important balance between the liberalizing power of Article 86 of the Directive (the legal challenges to which were rejected by the European Court of Justice) and the harmonizing tenor of the ONP framework Directive. The latter would prove in the next phase of EU telecommunications policy an important focal point for reaching the next equilibrium point in the move towards further liberalization of telecommunications across the EU since it was able to facilitate competition promoting and public interest defending measures simultaneously (Humphreys and Simpson 2005).

The next significant period of development of EU telecommunications policy involved a much less controversial series of negotiations between member states in which the EC continued to be the key EU-level institutional actor. In 1992, it undertook the Telecommunications Services Review, which involved in part the canvassing of opinion from interested parties from the public and private sectors across Europe on how, if at all, telecommunications policy should be developed. In this way, the EC applied its by now well-established tactic of aiming to push the agenda of liberalization forward, yet at the same time proceeding as consensually as possible. The Review resulted in the presentation to EU member states of four possible options, which ranged from the least radical of stalling the liberalization process through to the liberalization of all voice telephonic communications services across the EU. The extent to which the liberalization 'bandwagon' was gaining speed across the EU was clear in the 1993 agreement by member states to proceed with the most radical proposal – itself favoured by the EC – to be achieved by 1998 by the

---

1   Directive on Competition in the Markets for Telecommunications Services, [1990] OJ L192/10, 90/388/EEC, 24 July 1990.

2   Directive on the Establishment of the Internal Market for Telecommunications Services Through the Implementation of ONP, OJ L192/1 (90/387/EEC), 24 July 1990.

majority of EU member states (European Council of Ministers 1993). This was soon followed by a further agreement – stimulated by the conclusions of an analysis of Europe's position in the emerging so called Information Society by the Bangemann Group (EC 1994) – to liberalize all telecommunications infrastructures across the EU by 1998, in complement to the earlier voice telephonic services liberalization agreement (European Council of Ministers 1994).

Nonetheless, despite the period lacking the intensity leading up to the previous stage of equilibrium in the development of EU telecommunications policy, there were a number of issues which required resolution before agreement could be reached on this quantum leap forward on liberalization and, thereafter, the necessary legislation be put in place to realize the 1998 liberalization deadline. Most significantly, several EU member states with less well-developed infrastructures were able to negotiate derogations to allow them until 2000 (in the case of Luxembourg) and 2003 (in the cases of Greece, Ireland, Portugal and Spain) to open their voice telephonic markets and telecommunications infrastructures to full competition. Others, notably France and fellow southern states, were able to ensure that the package of legislative measures enacted up to the 1998 deadline in order to lay out the basic parameters of the liberalized telecommunications market also contained measures to protect the provision of public interest in telecommunications through universal service provision.[3] It has also been argued by Thatcher (2001) that the EC took care to ensure that liberalizing legislation necessary to create the potential for competition in so-called alternative infrastructures – satellite, cable and mobile – kept pace with the domestic reform agendas of member states in these areas.

Overall, that EU telecommunications policy developed to such a significant extent to reach this second equilibrium point is indicative of nothing short of an attitudinal transformation among member states regarding the place of telecommunications in the global economy and the opportunities to be derived as a consequence. Even those with arguably least to gain from exposing their domestic markets to liberalization became convinced enough of the likely practical benefits of liberalization in terms of lower prices and better quality services for consumers to agree to the wholesale changes. The transformation was at times skilfully exploited by the increasingly sure footed EC. For example, it became involved in a negotiation to secure liberalization of alternative infrastructures in France and Germany two years ahead of schedule in return for regulatory approval of a proposed telecommunications services international joint venture between their increasingly commercially oriented former incumbents France Telecom and Deutsche Telekom (Bartle 2001). Nevertheless, it also became clear at the time that though a considerable transference of legislative sovereignty in telecommunications was occurring to the European level in the

---

3   Directive on Interconnection in Telecommunications with Regard to Ensuring Universal Service and Interoperablility through Application of Open Network Provision, 97/33/EC, [1997] OJ L199/32, 26 July 1997; Directive on the Application of Open Network Provision to Voice Telephony and on Universal Service for Telecommunications in a Competitive Environment (replacing European Parliament and Council Directive [1995] 95/62/EC), 98/10/EC [1998] OJ L101/41, 1 April 1998.

service of European wide competition, day-to-day responsibility for the regulation of telecommunications would be very much the remit of the national level thereby effectively remaining overwhelmingly under its control.

Refinement of EU Telecommunications Policy: The Creation of the Electronic Communications Regulatory Framework

Agreement on the 1998 regulatory framework for telecommunications meant that within the space of a decade a battery of legislation of both a competition creating (liberalizing) and harmonizing kind had been created at the EU level, over which the latter held shared responsibility with member states for implementing. Across the EU, a remarkable transition from the traditional telecommunications regime based on state owned natural monopoly to one of across the board neo liberal market competition had occurred. Here national governments relinquished their role as corporate states in telecommunications, replacing it instead with regulatory state (Seidman and Gilmour 1986) governance in which the key decisions about the functioning of the telecommunications sector were taken by a new series of publicly funded though operationally independent National Regulatory Authorities (NRAs) (see Thatcher 2002a, 2002b). At the EU level too, there is strong evidence in telecommunications policy of efforts to create a European regulatory state (Majone 1994, 1996, 1997) in which the EC working alongside regulatory committees composed of national representatives often from the NRA made technical decisions on the possible regulatory evolution of the sector on an EU wide basis. Outstanding here in the 1998 Framework was the ONP Committee.

Nonetheless, the second key stage of EU telecommunications policy equilibrium that the 1998 Framework represented was only in effect the point at which the fundamental *basic structure* of the European regulatory state in telecommunications was mapped out. Setting out the parameters of such a system was one thing; ensuring its effective implementation was another. So rather like the previous phases of EU telecommunications policy highlighted in the chapter thus far, the EC almost immediately set about examining how the framework might more effectively embed a comprehensive efficiently functioning liberalized market system. The by now well-utilized tool of a comprehensive sectoral review and consultation (EC 1999) in anticipation of further policy actions marked the commencement of the next developmental phase in EU telecommunications policy launched in 1999. The review itself undertook three main lines of enquiry: the functional efficacy or otherwise of the 1998 Framework; the possibility of making existing regulation in key parts of the telecommunications sector less burdensome and complex in response to evidence of the emergence of a competitive market; and the possibility of creating some kind of convergent regulatory framework for all communications networks and services. The latter issue stemmed from yet another policy review on the matter undertaken by the EC in 1997 (EC 1997) which proved highly controversial (see Levy 1997, 1999). In brief, member states decided that it would not be possible to create a convergent regulatory framework for all communications infrastructures and services since the latter would have to cover the highly sensitive area of broadcasting which it soon emerged member states were unwilling to treat as part of any convergent framework, let alone an EU-level one (see Simpson 2000). However, it was considered appropriate to develop a convergent regulatory framework where possible to cover all communications *infrastructures* including those of broadcasting and the Internet. The outcome of the 1999 Communications Review was largely a re-statement of this position and was much more interesting in terms of decisions taken regarding the first two of its core lines of enquiry.

The first main proposal to emerge from the Review was to create radical rationalization in what was perceived to be an over-elaborate regulatory framework for telecommunications. The new system – the Electronic Communications Regulatory Framework (ECRF) – would see a reduction in the number of directives making up the previous system from twenty to six in the process reducing the workloads of NRAs and making the system simpler and more cost effective to comply with for telecommunications companies operating in the Single Market. As the name suggests, the ECRF was convergent in scope, covering broadcast and Internet infrastructures alongside those of telecommunications. It was to consist of two measures of a liberalizing purpose – a general competition directive (EC 2002) and a regulation passed with some urgency in 2000 which mandated member states to take action to ensure unbundling of the local loop,[4] or last mile, of the telecommunications network in their jurisdictions, seen at the time to be a major impediment to the growth of competition. It would also be made up of five harmonizing directives dealing respectively with general framework issues,[5] data protection and privacy,[6] universal service,[7] authorization[8] and access and interconnection.[9]

Whilst the above rationalization element of the ECRF and its implied refinement of the recently established European regulatory state in telecommunications proved relatively uncontroversial, the movement towards the next equilibrium point in the history of EU telecommunications policy also involved significant disagreements requiring typical European compromises. A key indicator of the efficacy of the market liberalization project in telecommunications would be the extent to, and the

---

4   Regulation No. 2887/2000 of the European Parliament and of the Council of 18 December 2000 on Unbundled Access to the Local Loop, [2000] OJ L336/4–8.

5   European Parliament and Council Directive on a Common Regulatory Framework for Electronic Communications Networks and Services (Framework Directive), 4 February 2002, PE-CONS 3672/01.

6   European Parliament and Council Directive on the Processing of Personal Data and the Protection of Privacy in the Electronic Communication Sector (Directive on Privacy and Electronic Communications), 31 July 2002, OJ L201/31–57.

7   European Parliament and Council Directive on Universal Service and User's rights relating to Electronic Communication Networks and Services (Universal Services Directive), 4 February 2002, PE-CONS 3673/01.

8   European Parliament and Council Directive on the Authorization of Electronic Communications Networks and Services (Authorization Directive), 24 April 2002, OJ L108/21–32.

9   European Parliament and Council on Access to and Interconnection of, Electronic Communications Networks and Associated Facilities (Access Directive), 24 April 2002, OJ L108/7–20.

speed at, which *ex ante* sector specific regulation for designated markets within the telecommunications sector could be removed allowing them merely to be governed by general EU competition law, one of the areas in which the EU, and the EC in particular, has developed most authority.

The debate centred specifically on the designated threshold figure for determining the existence of Significant Market Power (SMP), thus calling forth *ex ante* regulatory measures. In the 1998 regulatory framework, any operator holding a 25 per cent or greater share of a particular market was subject to specific regulatory measures requiring it to offer interconnection arrangements to its network to competitors according to a cost-based formula. In the negotiations, the EC proposed the quite radical step of raising this threshold SMP figure to 50 per cent – operators with a market share below this would be free to negotiate arrangements for the provision of interconnection to their competitors privately. This would have reduced the regulatory burden on itself and NRAs and could also be seen politically as a measure which affirmed the efficacy of an albeit relatively new competitive market environment in telecommunications. The implication here was that market forces were strong enough to counteract anti competitive tendencies even in situations where one player held as much as 40 per cent of a particular market.

For a number of member states – not least the telecommunications neo liberal forerunner, the UK – this proved to be a leap of faith too far. Unsurprisingly, new entrant companies were also concerned that the potential looseness of the regulatory framework regarding SMP would deprive them of the protection necessary to ensure that they held on to their current position in key markets, let alone to develop it further. In the end, a compromise solution was reached: the SMP threshold proposed by the EC was raised to 50 per cent. However, alongside this the EU issued a detailed list of criteria, other than market share, to be used in an assessment of whether market dominance existed in any particular case, taking into account key issues voiced in the debate such as collective and leveraged dominance (Humphreys and Simpson 2008).

The negotiations on the ECRF also illustrated, once more, the extent to which the EC had become a key politico-institutional player in the regulation of the European telecommunications sector. As part of its proposals for the ECRF, the EC argued that it should be given a right of veto over certain decisions made by NRAs. Specifically, it argued that it should be granted the authority to prevent member states from making additions to the list of markets which the latter would draw up as being subject to sector specific ex-ante regulation. The EC also proposed that it should have the right to examine and if necessary veto NRA decisions on the withdrawal of *ex ante* regulation from any telecommunications market, necessitating either an amendment or complete withdrawal of the initial decision. Backed by the support of both established and newer telecommunications operators, the EC secured the significant increase in its power to obtain a veto right in respect of the decisions on whether operators held SMP and the classification of new telecommunications markets as needing sector – specific *ex ante* regulation. The EC was not able, however, to secure its desired veto over regulatory remedies proposed by NRAs in any particular instance, an issue which merely was placed on the EC's policy 'backburner' as a result rather than being dropped (Humphreys and Simpson 2008) (see below).

Another important issue requiring a compromise solution concerned the EC's role in EU-level regulatory committees for telecommunications. This matter gives a strong flavour of how far EU telecommunications policy had developed since its inception in the mid 1980s: the parameters of the European regulatory state having been established in the domain the detailed mechanics of the functioning regulatory state at the national and EU levels needed to be secured and augmented as necessary. In this regard, the 1999 Communications Review contained a proposal from the EC to create a High Level Communications Group (HLCG) under its auspices made up of the EU NRAs. This was interpreted by member states as an attempt by the EC to manoeuvre itself into a position something akin to a European telecommunications regulator (Michalis 2004), something which had been vaunted in the past but strongly resisted by both governmental (see Bartle 2001) and commercial interests in telecommunications at the national level. The compromise position eventually reached saw the establishment of the European Regulators Group (ERG) which had a similar composition to the proposed HLCG but with much less power being transferred to the EU level, the EC securing for itself the chair of the Group for which it also provided administrative support. Nonetheless, this role was enough to give the EC a better developed opportunity to monitor, and even possibly steer, the unfolding of the single European Market in telecommunications than was at its disposal before the initiative.

The extent of the development of EU telecommunications policy can be appreciated through a brief consideration of the kinds of activities which are required to take place at the EU level to ensure the smooth functioning and continued development of the single EU-wide market. It is important to note that whilst the EU has assumed considerable authority in the telecommunications sphere, it has by no means displaced the national level, which still maintains the lion's share of responsibility for the day to day functioning of markets. This dispersal of responsibility across the EU policy landscape in a qualitatively different fashion than in the past has created a pan European network of governance which has been associated with the growth of the regulatory state (Majone 2000). Within this network, which is essentially two-level – that is, EU and national – in nature, a broad series of quasi state actors tend to predominate. Crucial among these are the EC and NRAs, which take part in various technocratically organized committees and working groups at the EU level (Humphreys and Simpson 2008). The gravitation towards agreement on the ECRF both cemented and developed further this arrangement. As a consequence, there was a growth in EU-level regulatory committee governance in telecommunications: a Communications Committee, a Radio Spectrum Committee, a Radio Spectrum Advisory Group and an advisory working party to deal with data protection issues were created (Humphreys and Simpson 2005). The EC formed a task force of members from its Information Society and Media and Competition Directorates General to deal with pressing issues such as SMP and market definition, illustrating again its influence in orchestrating the mechanics of competition in the new liberalizing market scenario.

The more elaborate the regime of competition became in EU telecommunications policy the greater was the requirement for regulation to ensure that competition was nurtured and maintained. This has placed a highly significant regulatory onus on the new quasi state functionaries of telecommunications governance in the EU. Whilst the era of the corporate state in telecommunications has well and truly disappeared, intervention in the market has arguably increased, the desire of the EC and others to remove *ex ante* regulation notwithstanding. Here, for example, the EC has since before the agreement of the 1998 Framework conducted market reviews of the state of competition across the EU. It has also issued numerous proceedings against member states for non-compliance with EU legislation of various kinds from transposition to implementation. In general, the regulatory workload of the network of EU and national level regulatory players – from the drafting, transposition, implementation, monitoring and review of an increasingly complex system – is substantial. Telecommunications provides one of the most mature examples of the consequences of choosing to replace the domestically focused corporate state with a European oriented regulatory version.

Moving Towards the Next Policy Equilibrium in EU Telecommunications: The 2006 Communications Review

The agreement on, and operationalization of, the ECRF from 2002 onwards has not marked the end of the evolution of the EU telecommunications to a 'steady state' equilibrium. In fact, one of the paradoxes of early 21st century neo liberalism is the need for close management and ongoing refinement of the market mechanism (for the core of this idea see Vogel 1996). The result at this point appears far from the light touch or 'nightwatchman' (Gill and Law 1988) role for the public sector envisioned by advocates of a neo liberal governance order, albeit that the state is now clearly at one remove from the 'mechanics' of the telecommunications sector. For EU telecommunication policy this has been manifest in the 2006 review of the ECRF, which at the time of writing is still ongoing.

Many of the recognized characteristics of the politics of EU telecommunications are evident in its current phase, which is likely to lead to the EU and its member states gravitating towards another equilibrium policy position in telecommunications which further cements the regulatory state in the sector at national and European levels, though any new framework is unlikely to be in place before 2009. The review was launched by a consultation period based on discussion documents produced by the EC that drew in part on the findings of a number of consultancy studies of the telecommunications sector which it commissioned. In its proposals, there is yet more evidence of the EC wishing to consolidate further its position of influence in EU telecommunications, something that is likely to cause resolution through the kind of policy compromises which have characterized EU telecommunications policy since the late 1980s.

In its pre-consultation recommendations, the EC focused on four key areas, three of which relate specifically to ongoing refinement of the Single Market in telecommunications, the fourth introducing proposals for the creation of a competitive environment for spectrum management, an important consequence of the development of digitalization and the growth of mobile communications. The former three issues relate to: first, further reduction in the level of *ex ante* regulation applying to the telecommunications sector through its removal in six of the 18 markets defined by the EC (EC 2003a); second, making the market review procedure faster and less burdensome; and, third, measures to ensure that regulatory remedies for problems identified in the markets of telecommunications are consistent and applied in the same manner across EU member states (EC 2006).

Regarding the streamlining of market reviews, the EC noted the widespread view among NRAs that the undertaking of market analyses and notifications of regulatory action – classic burdens of the regulatory state in action – were proving onerous to the point of being counterproductive. As a consequence, the EC proposed the introduction of a simplified procedure for those telecommunications markets which were previously found to operate subject to a satisfactory level of competition and for those notifications, such as proposed remedies, which were only of a minor nature (EC 2006). The EC also proposed a rationalization and clarification of market review procedures. It noted how under the current ECRF these are spread between the Framework Directive and the 2003 EC Recommendation on markets and put forward the consolidation of arrangements into a single legislative instrument in the form of a Regulation.

Though not specifically mentioned by the EC, the use of a Regulation would negate the need for transposition of the measure into national law, once passed it being directly applicable to member states. The EC argued here that the Regulation 'could set a precise and legally binding timetable, using defined triggers, for initiating and for completing future market analyses and for the imposition or removal of remedies' (EC 2006, 16). The EC noted a current inefficiency in the system where NRAs have in certain instances split notification between the three key issues of market definition, SMP analysis and proposed remedies causing delays in the system. The Regulation would bind legally NRAs to undertake all three as part of a single process. The EC was critical of a lack of response from NRAs to the former's veto decisions on market reviews granted to the EC as a result of the ECRF negotiations (see above). It proposed that the Regulation should tighten up the requirements on NRAs to do this by mandating legally a response within a specified period of time. All of this does not suggest that the work of NRAs will be any less pressurized and would seem to point to a strengthening of the EU's regulatory grip (through the proposed Regulation) on the evolution of competition in the telecommunications market at the national level.

The most likely controversial area of the current communications review concerns the EC's proposal to extend its right of veto, itself secured controversially, as laid out in Article 7 of the 2002 Framework Directive. Commenting upon the functioning of the ECRF to date the EC noted, referring to one of the key elements of the Article 7 procedure that 'consistency has been improved in the way that markets are defined and SMP is assessed, but only to a lesser extent in relation to the choice of appropriate remedies' (EC 2006, 18) noting cases of inadequate and ineffective remedial action having been taken by certain NRAs. It also noted specifically that there were cases of different remedies having been applied to similar problems in different member states and also cases of differential implementation nationally of the same remedies.

As a consequence, the EC put forward the rather bold proposal that its right of veto be extended to remedies. Sensitive to the potentially controversial nature of this proposal and previous baulking by member states at the idea of transferring too much power into the EC's regulatory hands, it aimed to allay any such fears in this instance by arguing that it 'would not have the power to replace an NRA remedy by one of its own but would indicate the problems with the remedy proposed by the NRA in its justification for the veto decision' (EC, 2006, 18). By implication, the NRA would have to then produce a remedy to the EC's satisfaction, arguably increasing the regulatory burden it faces even further and emphasizing the growing regulatory power of the EC. The extent to which this proposal will be viewed, on the one hand as a sensible piece of pragmatism, or on the other, as a move to create the EC as a European telecommunications regulator 'by the back door' may determine whether or not the proposal is accepted in its current form, rejected out of hand or, perhaps most likely given past precedent, modified into a suitable compromise.

The EC also moved to close what it perceived to be the growing practice across the EU of using the legal system, through appeals against NRA decisions, to delay the operationalization of remedial action to rid abuses of competition in the single telecommunications market. Specifically, it proposed the amendment of Article 4 of the Framework Directive so that national courts could only suspend NRA decisions in the face of appeal where there was demonstrable 'irreparable harm to the appellant' (EC 2006, 19) as well as an EU wide procedure to monitor the incidence of suspensions. The EC's proposals also made reference to two other key areas where it noted inconsistency of approaches across EU member states. First, regarding what should have been in theory a light touch system of general authorizations to provide a service (as opposed to the more onerous system of licences which pre-dated it) it was apparent that 'most often individual rights of use are required at national level for using scarce resources' (EC 2006, 19) which tended to differ across member states. As a result, the EC proposed to introduce three measures at EU level: first, a system for determining that services had a pan-European scope in order to apply; second, a commonly defined system of authorization and selection; third, a series of commonly applied conditions for rights to use scarce communications resources. Decisions relating to these matters would be taken at EU committee level, an increasingly important aspect of telecommunications policy-making. The EC also addressed what it perceived as a problem of inconsistent use of Article 5 of the 2002 Access Directive which permits NRAs to take action against companies without SMP to improve access, interconnection and end-to-end connectivity. The proposed solution would involve devolving more power to the EU level in that NRAs would be required to submit their intentions in this regard to the EC which, using the aforementioned regulatory committee decision procedure, would adjudicate on the proposal.

Finally, the 'totemic' change in European telecommunications which witnessed the replacement of state ownership and public service provision with liberalization delivered through market regulation over almost 25 years has significantly altered the position of the telecommunications user. The emergence and development of the neo liberal project in telecommunications inevitably resulted in a focus on users as customers as opposed to citizens to an unprecedented degree though it must also be stated that universal service was ensconced as a key element of the 1998 Regulatory Framework and has remained so ever since. Through the original ONP Framework Directive, those member states of the EU, notably France, with very strong traditions of *service public* in telecommunications which they wished to see maintained and protected, were able to upload their preferences here to ensure that a harmonized system of universal service was established legally at EU level. The current review of telecommunications gives an indication of the state of the EC's thinking on universal service and its place within the maturing European regulatory state in telecommunications.

In 2005 the EU undertook a review of universal service involving a consultation exercise whose results suggested that member states did not wish to alter radically in the short to medium term the current stipulations for universal service. As a consequence, current EC proposals for developing universal service are modest in nature. In response to the emergence of Voice over Internet Protocol (VoIP) services, the EC's wish is to separate universal service obligations placed on infrastructure providers, on the one hand and service providers, on the other, the assumption being that the growth of VoIP will greatly increase user choice of voice service providers. The extent to which the market will provide the staples of universal service in the future is also clear from the proposal to remove the provision of directory enquiry services from the universal service package and leave its provision instead to the market (EC 2006). The EC's approach to universal service in the near and longer term future is underpinned by the rather optimistic view that where necessary the system 'could be adjusted to anticipate changes in markets and technologies ... [to] allow for regulatory obligations to be reduced once the market is shown to be meeting users' needs' (EC 2006, 34).

Conclusion

Telecommunications is arguably the most 'EU-ized' of the culture industries examined in this volume. As shown in the chapter, this has evolved as a complex process involving key institutional and private actors at the national and European level for the best part of a quarter of a century. Underpinning the development of EU telecommunications policy has been the replacement of the traditional core 'totemic' values of state ownership and public interest provision by the new practices of economic liberalization and market regulation and their associated values. As noted in the chapter, the internationalization of the governance of the sector to the EU level which has accompanied this fundamental change has proceeded as a steady movement along the scale of liberalization, reached through the attainment of a series of compromise temporary policy equilibrium points. It is important to point out that, though it has proceeded apace, the maturation of a liberalized telecommunications market through a comprehensive regulatory framework has not yet been completed fully. In fact, the chapter has shown that the creation of the regulatory state in telecommunications (replacing the historic corporate state) was only the beginning

– the evolving experiment of the regulatory state in action in telecommunications is still unfolding as illustrated by current ongoing negotiations among EU member states and the EC to modify further the ECRF.

How significant, then, has the EU been in this increasingly important part of the information and communications domain? There is little doubt that a re-ordered governance of the sector along the lines of the neo liberal model in Europe's political territories would have occurred without the existence of the EU: the powerful opportunities as well as threats associated with economic globalization (see Weiss 1998, 2003), would have ensured this. However, the EU has provided a vital means for its member states negotiating the complexities of globalization (see Wallace 2000), in this case the internationalization of the telecommunications sector. It has allowed them to upload their policy preferences at key junctures – and has provided a relatively familiar and secure environment within which to mark out and refine a single telecommunications market space in Europe, something recognized more widely as a classic set of policy responses to globalization (see Borzel 2002). The EU has been used to play an important role in synchronizing the liberalization of telecommunications to the different speeds of reform found across the EU. As in all situations of EU-ization, compromise outcomes have characterized the various equilibrium points reached in the development of EU telecommunications policy and it would also be realistic to assert that the point of policy lock-in in telecommunications for member states has been reached some time ago, probably by 1994, with agreements by then made to liberalize comprehensively all telecommunications infrastructures and services.

However, the development of EU telecommunications policy has not been driven completely by the intergovernmental exchanges and compromises of the EU's member countries. Any decision to use the EU institutional context to the extent exhibited by member states in telecommunications bears a 'cost' in terms of partially ceding governance authority. This has been most clearly illustrated by the prominent role played in an administrative and political capacity by the EC which has developed into one of the most skilful political actors on the European telecommunications policy landscape. It is also evident in the growth of a clutch of regulatory committees at EU level to deal with the many complex matters that arise from the decision to create competition across Europe in a former utility sector. The resulting pattern is a complex regulatory web (Radaelli 2004) of transnational network (Eberlein and Grande 2005) governance in which a plethora of public and private actors play a part in the evolution of the sector. Here NRAs working domestically and at the EU level interact with the EC as the core regulatory relationship in the sector. This has required the creation of an accommodative relationship between regulatory peers from different markets with different degrees of maturity as well as with the EC with its specifically European overview agenda. The robustness and continual development of telecommunications policy is testament to the realization by member states of the importance of the EU context as well as the various roles – policy entrepreneur, facilitator, monitor and administrator – astutely played by EU institutional actors – most significantly the EC – across its history. These key binding elements are likely to remain undiminished for the foreseeable future.

References

Bartle, I. (2001), 'Is the European Union an "agenda setter's paradise"? The Case of a Possible European Regulatory Authority for Telecommunications', *Current Politics and Economics of Europe* 10(4), 439–459.

Bartle, I. et al. (2002), *The Regulatory State: Britain and Germany Compared*. London: Anglo-German Foundation for Industrial Society.

Börzel, T.A. (2002), 'Pace-setting, Foot-dragging, and Fence-sitting: Member State Responses to Europeanization', *Journal of Common Market Studies* 40(2), 193–214.

Cerny, P. (1996), 'Globalization and Other Stories: The Search for a New Paradigm for International Relations', *International Journal*, LI, 617–637.

Cram, L. (1994), 'The European Commission as a Multi-Organisation: Social Policy and IT Policy in the EU', *Journal of European Public Policy*, 1(2), 195–217.

Dyson, K. and Humphreys P. (eds) (1986), *The Politics of the Communications Revolution in Western Europe*. London: Frank Cass.

Eberlein, B. and Grande, E. (2005), 'Beyond Delegation: Transnational Regulatory Regimes and the EU Regulatory State', *Journal of European Public Policy* 12(1), February 2005, 89–112.

European Commission (1984), 'Communication From the Commission to the Council on Telecommunications: Progress Report on the Thinking and Work Done in the Field and Initial Proposals for an Action Programme' (Communication), COM(84)277, 18 May 1984.

European Commission (1985), 'Work Programme for Creating a Common Information Market. Communication from the Commission to the Council'. (Communication) COM(85) 658 final, 29 November 1985.

European Commission (1987), 'Communication from the Commission - Green Paper on the Development of the Common Market for Telecommunications Services and Equipment Summary Report' (Communication), COM(87)290, 30 June 1987.

European Commission (1994), *Europe and the Global Information Society; Recommendations to the EC* (The 'Bangemann Report'). Brussels: European Commission.

European Commission (1997), *Green Paper on the Convergence of the Telecommunications, Media and Information Technology Sectors, and the Implications for Regulation. Towards an Information Society Approach*, COM(97)623, Brussels, 3 December 1997.

European Commission (1999), *Towards a New Framework for Electronic Communications Infrastructure and Associated Services. The 1999 Communications Review*, COM(1999) 539, Brussels.

European Commission (2002), *Commission Guidelines on Market Analysis and the Assessment of Significant Market Power under the Community Regulatory Framework for Electronic Communications Networks and Services*, OJ C165, Luxembourg, 11 July 2002, pp. 6–31.

European Commission (2003a), *Commission Recommendation of 11 February 2003 on relevant product and service markets within the electronic communications*

sector susceptible to ex ante regulation in accordance with Directive 2002/21/
EC of the European Parliament and of the Council on a common regulatory
framework for electronic communication networks and services, OJ L114, 8 May
2003, pp. 45–49.

European Commission (2003b), *Commission Recommendation of 23 July 2003 on
notifications, time limits and consultations provided for in Article 7 of Directive
2002/21/EC of the European Parliament and of the Council on a common
regulatory framework for electronic communications networks and services*, OJ
L190, 30 July 2003, pp. 13–18.

European Commission (2006), *Communication from the Commission to the Council,
the European Parliament, the European Economic and Social Committee and
the Committee of the Regions on the Review of the EU Regulatory Framework
for Electronic Communications Networks and Services – Proposed Changes*,
COM(2006) 334 final, Brussels.

European Council of Ministers (1993), Resolution on the Review of the Situation
in the Telecommunications Sector and the Need for Further Development in that
Market, 93/C213/01, 6 August 1993.

European Council of Ministers (1994), Resolution on the Principles and Timetable
for the Liberalisation of Telecommunications Infrastructures', OJ C379, 31
December 1994.

Gill, S. and Law, D. (1988) *The Global Political Economy: Perspectives, Problems
and Policies*. New York and London: Harvester-Wheatsheaf.

Hall, P.A. and Soskice, D. (eds) (2001), *Varieties of Capitalism: the Institutional
Foundations of Comparative Advantage*. Oxford: Oxford University Press.

Héritier, A. (1999) *Policy-Making and Diversity in Europe: Escape from Deadlock*.
Cambridge: Cambridge University Press.

Hulsink, W. (1999), *Privatization and Liberalization in European Telecommunications:
Comparing Britain, the Netherlands and France*. London and New York:
Routledge.

Humphreys, P. and Simpson, S. (2008), 'Globalization, the "Competition" State and
the Rise of the "Regulatory" State in European Telecommunications', *Journal of
Common Market Studies* 45(3), September (forthcoming).

Humphreys, P. and Simpson, S. (2005), *Globalisation, Convergence and European
Telecommunications Regulation*. Cheltenham, UK and Brookfield, USA: Edward
Elgar.

Humphreys, P. and Simpson, S. (1996), 'European Telecommunications and
Globalization', in P. Gummett (ed.), *Globalization and Public Policy*. Cheltenham,
UK and Brookfield, USA: Edward Elgar, pp. 105–124.

Kohler-Koch, B. (1999), 'The Evolution and Transformation of European
Governance', in B. Kohler-Koch and R. Eising (eds), *The Transformation of
Governance in the European Union*. London: Routledge, pp. 14–35.

Levy, D. (1997), 'Regulating Digital Broadcasting in Europe: The Limits to Policy
Convergence', *West European Politics* 20(4), 24–42.

Levy, D. (1999), *Europe's Digital Revolution: Broadcasting Regulation, the EU and
the Nation State*. London and New York: Routledge.

Majone, G. (1994), 'The Rise of the Regulatory State in Europe', *West European*

Politics 17(3), 77–101.

Majone, G. (1996), *Regulating Europe*. London and New York: Routledge.

Majone, G. (1997), 'From the Positive to the Regulatory State: Causes and Consequences of Changes in the Mode of Governance', *Journal of Public Policy* 17(2), 139–167.

Majone, G. (2000), 'The Credibility Crisis of the Community Regulation', *Journal of Common Market Studies* 38(2), 272–302.

Michalis, M. (2004), 'Institutional Arrangements of Regional Regulatory Regimes: Telecommunications Regulation in Europe and Limits to Policy Convergence', in E. Bohlin, S.L. Levin, N. Sung and C.-H. Yoon (eds), *Global Economy and Digital Society*. Amsterdam: Elsevier, pp. 285–300.

Mueller, M. (2004), 'Convergence: A Reality Check', in D. Luff and D. Geradin (eds), *The WTO and Global Convergence in Telecommunications and Audiovisual Services*. Cambridge: Cambridge University Press, pp. 311–322.

Radaelli, C. (2004), 'The Puzzle of Regulatory Competition', *Journal of Public Policy* 24(1), 1–23.

Sandholtz, W. (1993), 'Institutions and Collective Action. The New Telecommunications in Western Europe', *World Politics* 45(2), 242–270.

Sandholtz, W. (1998), 'The Emergence of a Supranational Telecommunications Regime', in W. Sandholtz and A. Stone Sweet (eds), *European Integration and Supranational Governance*. Oxford: Oxford University Press, pp. 134–163.

Schmidt, V.A. (2002), *The Futures of European Capitalism*, Oxford: Oxford University Press.

Schneider, V. et al. (1994), 'Corporate Actor Networks in European Policy-Making: Harmonizing Telecommunications Policy', *Journal of Common Market Studies* 32(4), 473–498.

Seidman, H. and Gilmour, R. (1986), *Politics, Position and Power. From the Positive to the Regulatory State*. Oxford: Oxford University Press.

Simpson, S. (2000), 'Intra-institutional Rivalry and Policy Entrepreneurship in the European Union: the Politics of Information and Communications Technology Convergence', *New Media and Society* 2(4), 445–466.

Simpson, S. and Wilkinson, R. (2002), 'Regulatory Change and Telecommunications Governance: A Neo-Gramscian Analysis'. *Convergence* 8(2), Summer, 30–51.

Spence, M. (1983) 'Contestable Markets and the Theory of Industry Structure: a Review Article', *Journal of Economic Literature* 2(2), September, 981–990.

Thatcher, M. (1999), *The Politics of Telecommunications: National Institutions, Convergence and Change* Oxford: Oxford University Press.

Thatcher, M. (2001), 'The Commission and National Governments as Partners: EC Regulatory Expansion in Telecommunications 1979–2000', *Journal of European Public Policy* 8(4), 558–584.

Thatcher, M. (ed.) (2002a), 'Analysing Regulatory Reform in Europe', a special issue of the *Journal of European Public Policy* 9(6).

Thatcher, M. (2002b), 'Regulation after Delegation: Independent Regulatory Agencies in Europe', *Journal of European Public Policy* 9(6), 954–72.

Vogel, S. (1996), *Freer Markets, More Rules: Regulatory Reform in Advanced*

Industrial Countries. Ithaca and London: Cornell University Press.

Wallace, Helen (2000), 'Europeanization and Globalization: Complementary or Contradictory Trends?', *New Political Economy* 5(3), 369–82.

Weiss, L. (ed.) (1998), *States in the Global Economy: Bringing Domestic Institutions Back In*. Cambridge: Cambridge University Press.

Weiss, L. (2003), *The Myth of the Powerless State: Governing the Economy in a Global Era*. Cambridge: Cambridge University Press.

Woolcock, S., Hodges, M. and Schreiber, K. (1992), *Britain, Germany and 1992: The Limits of Deregulation*. London: Royal Institute of International Affairs.

Chapter 6

Back to the Future: New Media, Same Principles? Convergence Regulation Re-visited

Monica Ariño and Carles Llorens[1*]

Convergence has been a buzzword that has been used widely over the last 20 years. It denotes a process in which two forces or things 'blend or come together at a point'.[2] In the communications sector, the term embraces many ideas and concepts but is generally used to describe the phenomenon, whereby the technological and market boundaries between previously distinct sectors, and by extension services and platforms used to deliver them, blur. Initially, convergence was presented as a motion towards a single universal network with converged services (Baldwin et al. 1996) and also as the meeting point between telecommunications and audiovisual through the information technology sector (Burgelmann 1995, 54; Bennet and Adamson 1995, 5). In 1997, the European Commission (EC) defined convergence as the ability of different network platforms to carry essentially similar kinds of services, or the coming together of consumer devices such as the telephone, television and personal computer (EC 1997). Today, these early definitions appear simplistic and even naïve, since convergence has proved to be a richer and certainly more complex phenomenon. In fact, as Wirth (2006, 445) and Wallis (1998) have pointed out, a major challenge when studying the phenomenon of media convergence is the multiplicity of concepts, from technological convergence, to companies and markets convergence, the convergence of services, platforms and devices, as well as policy and regulatory convergence.

Since the mid 1990s there has been an enormous range of literature and policy documents produced on the phenomenon of 'communications convergence' and its global economic impact. Many have seen convergence, or the broader concept of the 'Information Society', as the 'third industrial revolution', on account of the anticipated social, economic and political impact (see the Bangemann Report, EC 1994). Expectations were high. Amongst the various visions, the most ambitious portrayed the idea that *all* content and services would be distributed over *all* networks

---

1   * Monica Ariño is an international policy advisor for Ofcom. Any views expressed in this chapter are those of the author and are neither endorsed nor do they reflect Ofcom's policy position on any of the issues dealt with in the text. Carles Llorens is senior lecturer at Universitat Autònoma de Barcelona.
2   Webster's New World Dictionary.

and accessible through *all* platforms and devices with the full range of functions. It was proclaimed that 'distinctions between broadcasting and information services will become irrelevant'.[3] The different industries would come together as one and there would be 'no differences between broadcasting and telecommunications' (KPMG 1996, 8).

Although inspiring, forecasts surrounding convergence did not materialize in practice, and, when they did, they took much longer and often a different form than the one predicted. Convergence remained something 'high in concept but low in content' (OECD 1992, 13–14). Following a frantic merger period in the late 1990s, the enthusiasm subsided. The general economic downturn and, more importantly, the collapse of many 'dotcom' companies at the turn of the century, coupled with the financial troubles faced by telecom operators after the 3G auctions, were partly responsible. Crucially, many underestimated, or possibly misunderstood, consumers' perceptions of convergence and the central role that the *user* – and not the device – was meant to play in the new environment. For the most part, and for most of the time, people continued to use their fixed or mobile phone to communicate privately, the computer to browse the Internet, to work and to carry out commercial transactions, and the television for entertainment, and they received these services from distinct sector providers.

This is now rapidly changing. Today, voice, data and video services are delivered through a multitude of networks (fixed, wireless and IP-based), they are integrated and often offered in bundles, while receiving devices are multifunctional and increasingly portable. In the UK, 40 per cent of households take two or more communications services from one provider while converged platform services like VoIP and IPTV are rapidly taking off (Ofcom 2007). The digitalization and seamless integration of data, networks and services has brought together sectors and players that were inherently different and have traditionally been isolated from one another. In 2006 and 2007 we have witnessed how services providers such as BT, SKY, Vodafone, Virgin, Channel 4, and the BBC in the UK and Telefónica and Sogecable in Spain have moved into each other's territory, and are starting to deliver competing services. For their part, consumers are no longer prisoner of a particular network or platform to access video content or to communicate with one another, at home or on the move. They have access to telephony and messaging services, Internet access and email, radio and television broadcasts or streamed audiovisual content, time shifted or on demand, and they can increasingly alter that content, share it and even contribute their own. Community video portals such as You Tube and Dailymotion, social networking sites like MySpace and Facebook, and content sharing sites such as Flickr mushroomed in 2006, bringing in a whole new perspective of the potential of convergence. It is now commonplace to refer to the 'communications sector', which is widely understood to encompass not just fixed and wireless telecommunications and broadcasting, but also publishing, computing, gaming and the creative industries more widely. As high-speed broadband penetration grows, fibre networks are rolled out, and spectrum is freed up for new and varied uses, it is likely that the seamless

---

3   See the Declaration of the Union of Industrial and Employers Confederation of Europe (UNICE) at the 1995 G7 meeting in Brussels (Cited by Harcourt 2005, 77).

integration and combination of services and platforms will continue to increase. The long predicted and much discussed convergence is finally coming of age.

The economic, societal, organizational and institutional implications of these developments are without precedent in the communications industry. The impact of convergence goes beyond quality of service improvements, increased competition, innovation, choice and freedom for consumers, at better prices, or the advantage of portability and ubiquity of communications services. Convergence is altering the very foundations of information and communications exchanges, and thereby fundamentally affects societal structures. While the 'information and communications revolution' is a global phenomenon, its paths and outcomes are extraordinarily diverse, often determined by regional, national and local singularities. The challenges for regulators and policy-makers are paramount, not least because at times they might find it difficult, or even impossible, to keep up with the pace of technological evolution and fast changing markets.

In this context, this chapter will review European regulatory models and principles upon which initial responses to the challenges posed by convergence were constructed. It will assess their continued validity against the backdrop of new and somewhat unexpected developments (for example the avalanche of user-generated content), and will look in particular at the regulatory challenges posed by the increasing growth of content provision over Internet networks. We will argue that the centrality of the Internet and IP delivered content services calls for a fundamental re-assessment of regulatory structures and instruments to deliver consumer protection and other public interest goals. The traditionally distinct telecommunications and broadcasting regulatory paradigms confronted one another in this space, and so are sector specific regulators. Both will need to adapt if they are to encourage the development of this sector to its full potential.

The first part of this chapter provides an overview of the initial visions of convergence and the 'great expectations' surrounding it, as well as the 'hard times' that followed. We then look at Europe's regulatory response to such changes and challenges, as initially outlined in the Green Paper on Convergence in 1997, through the development of a minimal, technologically neutral and horizontal framework, for electronic communications and services. In the second part, we re-assess these regulatory approaches against the backdrop of new technological developments and the enhanced centrality of citizens both as consumers as well as providers of content. In particular, we question the principles that underlie the new Audiovisual Media Services (AVMS) Directive.[4]

We conclude with some general remarks about the different roles for regulators and industry in the new environment. We argue that, despite claims of regulatory withdrawal, regulators have rather invited new parties into regulatory dialogue, in a new form of 'collaborative regulation' where the role of regulators and regulation remains central, albeit of a fundamentally different nature.

---

4   Directive 2007/65/EC of the European Parliament and of the Council, OJ L332/27 of 18 December 2007.

Great Expectations

In the mid 1990s the terms 'digitalization' and 'technological convergence' were widely used to describe what were perceived to be huge shifts in the communications sector as technological developments blurred the boundaries between different sectors. The question was not whether the media and telecommunications sectors would change dramatically, but rather when and at what pace. As with any other technological change, there were opportunities, but also new risks to companies, arising from industrial uncertainty.

At that time, individual players faced different questions and challenges. While the big telecom operators were trying to decide which would be the best network for the future: cable, fixed, or mobile, the IT industry pondered about which terminal (the TV set, the PC, the set top box, the mobile handset, or a new yet to be invented, device) would be the best suited to become the home digital hub. In the meantime, the software industry was busy working on applications that would be best positioned to dominate the future. Content providers remained relatively quiet, watching this space with the reassurance that, after all, content was king and they would be the ones providing it. As uncertainty spread, some firms opted for developing new capacities internally. Yet a great majority chose to establish a strategy that allowed them to share risks and opportunities through alliances, mergers and acquisitions. Behind the merger and alliances frenzy in the 1990s, there was a feeling that companies needed to be present everywhere, while avoiding the distress of a lone failure (Tremblay 1995).

Telecommunications liberalization had brought competition in network provision, particularly as cable developed its own network across Europe. New entrants were benefiting from regulated access to existing networks or new infrastructures such as LMDS or mobile. Handset and terminal developers regularly upgraded their systems, with increasing emphasis on set top boxes and video consoles. Broadcasting, on its side, had been subject to a process of liberalization since the late 1980s, and the multiplication of players in the market placed increasing pressure on the sector, particularly in regards to advertising revenues and content rights, which often ended up in the hands of financially strong pay-TV operators.

All of the players appeared to believe that successful business models were heavily dependent upon access to content in any form: television programmes, videogames or other applications in order to foster subscriptions as well as sales of electronic equipment (Dang-Nguyen and Le Traon 1995). As a result of this perception, and because of their financial strength, some telecom operators decided to lead new digital pay-TV platforms and acquire content, whereas media companies were more prone to alliances and joint ventures in order to achieve a quick and easy rise in distribution capacity. The most powerful satellite players such as Canal+ and Sky integrated vertically.

In a convergent environment the incumbent European telecommunications companies needed to find new revenue streams, both to counter the effects of market liberalization and to avoid remaining mere carriers of others' content. If networks were doomed to become a commodity, the possibility to offer attractive and exclusive content became key to attract subscribers and increase network traffic.

Cable not really being option at the time,[5] they found the digital satellite pay-TV market as a good convergent – and yet safe – investment opportunity. They also had the technological and operational expertise to deal with a large customer base. Thus, the Spanish telecommunications operator Telefónica was behind the digital pay-TV operator Vía Digital, which launched in 1997; similarly, France Télécom supported the launch of TPS in 1996 while Telecom Italia was the main shareholder of Stream, launched in 1996. To ensure the viability of these new platforms, telecommunications operators needed to ensure exclusivity over content rights or to create new content production firms.[6] Sky and the French group Canal+ were major exceptions in this telecommunications-led convergence. They remained the primary operators in the French and British markets, but had a markedly different convergence strategy, based on vertical integration models, set top boxes with proprietary software and exclusive content (in particular premium movies and sports).

Internet players were at the heart of the convergence hype. The acquisition of Time Warner by AOL for $183 billion was at the time the largest acquisition ever seen, and a classic example of the 'multimedia convergence' phenomenon.[7] The idea was to combine AOL's multi-platform capacity with Time Warner's library of content, merging both companies' subscription base. The Internet allowed for a more direct relationship with clients and targeted advertising, delivering on a promise of profits from electronic commerce. Through the development and promotion of multimedia and interactive services, telecommunications operators saw an opportunity to increase network traffic, while for the computer industry it was an invitation to extend their hardware and software business. For media companies, the development of new interactive and multimedia services facilitated synergies and re-usability of existing content as a new revenue stream.

However, reality proved less rosy. As the next section illustrates, most of these attempts met with little success, if not complete failure, and the various marriages between inherently different operators collapsed, at best, as an amicable departure.

---

5   The decision in the review of the Competition Directive to divide the fixed telephone business from the provision of cable TV resulted in a loss of interest by telecommunications operators, which looked for alternative competition through new technologies as ADSL. See EC Directive 1999/64/EC of 23 June 1999 amending Directive 90/388/EEC in order to ensure that telecommunications networks and cable TV networks owned by a single operator are separate legal entities, OJ L175, 10 July 1999, pp. 39–42.

6   This is the case in the Spanish market with the Telefónica's acquisition of one of the main Spanish free to air (FTA) television channels, Antena 3 in 1997. It was the first time that one telecommunications operator bought a big FTA channel and assumed its management. Later on this strategy was completed with the acquisition of Endemol in 2001 and the creation of a specific firm called 'Telefónica de Contenidos' as a content subsidiary in 2004.

7   By the time it was cleared, however, the deal had been eclipsed by Vodafone's acquisition of Mannesmann, which broke the record.

Hard Times

After fewer than ten years of revenue losses, the entire European digital pay-TV sector collapsed or merged. A fundamental restructuring in the Spanish and Italian markets saw the merger of the two satellite TV operators, into a single platform in 2002 and 2003 respectively, with France following in August 2006 with the merger between TPS and CanalSat. Consolidation also took place in the cable market with, for example, the long anticipated merger between NTL and Telewest in the UK in March 2006. Many telecommunications firms decided to sell or to maintain a purely financial presence in media markets, without fully engaging in media activities, focusing instead on the development of their broadband and mobile strategies and trying to reduce their high levels of debt. In Europe, several incumbent operators such as KPN, France Telecom and Deutsche Telekom adopted strategies aimed at selling non-strategic assets, cutting down investment and expenditure in order to re-finance their debt. The 2002 net incomes meant that many of these companies balance sheets were still in the red: Deutsche Telekom (€–3.8 billion), Telefónica (€–5.5 billion), KPN (€–9.6 billion) and TeliaSonera (€–23.6 billion) (Pouillot 2003, 180).

The reasons leading to the failure of the first convergence wave were multifaceted. Contrary to most market predictions, business integration was not an automatic guarantee of success. Initial market convergence trends focused on bringing together services and platforms, with perhaps an underlying assumption that consumers would follow, and that network capacity would easily support the various applications. The general economic slowdown, the astronomical prices paid for exclusive content, the slow roll out of digital cable and unenthusiastic consumer take up partly explains the failure of some digital pay-TV ventures. The lack of a return path in satellite delivery meant that the television remained a limited device for interactive applications or Internet surfing. Furthermore, the difficulties in bringing together what had traditionally been very different corporate cultures and regulatory regimes seemed to have been underestimated, the failed AOL/Time Warner merger being a case in point. Although broadcasters might be experts in commissioning and sometimes creating content, they are less experienced in dealing with customers and providing personalized services, while the business model for telecommunications remained largely dependent on corporate markets and was less appropriate for the marketing of entertainment to a highly residential market. In this light, combining or integrating the different skills, know-how, customer relations and sector specific experiences was never going to be an easy task. After the Internet bubble bust in 2001, each sector's expansion was more focused on their core business, with telecommunications operators concentrating on mobile phone growth and broadband deployment through ADSL, and television operators developing digital transition strategies.

The overenthusiasm that surrounded the earlier phases of convergence is surprising when one considers that, in the past, all major technological developments were gradual. Scholars of economic history and technology development have analyzed how all technical revolutions (whether steam or the railways, electricity or steel) have gone through similar cycles until they eventually come of age (Perez

2002; Fidler 1997). And yet initial disappointment did not kill off convergence but simply slowed it down.

The New Convergence wave

Today, convergence is generally understood to be the possibility to access a mutltitude of services through one network or device, or similar services through different networks or devices, is fundamentally changing the competition paradigm. More and more services are delivered in combination as multiplay (and often bundled) offers. Imcumbents such as Telefónica and BT are now well established in the television market through IPTV services such as 'Imagenio' or 'BT vision', mobile operators are developing television services, and broadcasters are increasingly present in the Internet and mobile spaces. The development of high-speed broadband and next generation networks, the introduction of disruptive services such as VoIP, together with greater recognition of consumers and changing social attitudes, are all contributing to such rapid change. A wide range of players, including fixed network, cable TV, traditional broadcasters, pay-TV operators and mobile operators have started (or are preparing) to offer a combination of voice, data and television content over fixed or mobile networks. Sometimes services are provided over a single network (fully converged offer), or making use of another operator's infrastructure. At the other extreme, single services can be put together in a combined offer at the point of sale (normally with joint billing). In all of these cases, consumers purchase a distinct offer (bundled or not) of services that used to be provided to them separately.

Consumers are at the centre of change, and driving it and to a large extent it is the social engagement with new technologies that has promoted further innovation in content delivery. An example is the so-called Web 2.0 phenomenon, which can be described as a second generation of Internet based services that emphasize online collaboration and sharing among users based on the network effects created by an 'architecture of participation'. This concept has already played an important role in Internet success stories such as Flickr, eBay, Skype and AdSense, the successful advertising scheme of Google, and is fundamentally altering the audiovisual online space, to a point where traditional distinctions between pushed, pulled, professional and editorialized content are all blurring. With a few exceptions, such as Sky or the BBC, innovation has not come from traditional broadcasters but rather from the mobile, Internet, computing, telecommunications and entertainment industries. Operators such as Apple, Google, Sony, MySpace and Joost dominate the new audiovisual space. This is putting pressure on the traditionally cosy broadcasting industry, and particularly on public service broadcasters, which are suffering from a steady decrease in advertising-generated revenues and are finding it difficult to respond to new modes of content production and distribution, with the risk that they will be sidelined.Convergence might have taken longer than expected, and it may still travel in yet unexpected directions, but it is certainly a one-way trip, even if characterized by more fragmentary and evolutionary developments. The associated development of triple and quadplay offers is bringing about not only innovation, greater choice and better prices, but also greater (at times inevitable) complexity for consumers, who need to navigate their way around increasing amounts of information about different services, price offers, technologies and devices. It is also making the general competition and regulatory assessments more complex, highlighting deficiencies in current methodologies and challenging traditional approaches to regulation in this sector.

The Regulatory Response: The Quest for a New Model

Historically, governments have tightly regulated the telecommunications and broadcasting sectors. In most cases these industries were also nationally owned and managed. Such structures were justified in the case of telecommunications on account of the desire to achieve universal service goals, and in broadcasting to fulfil a public service remit aimed at protecting moral values, cultural traditions and pluralism. In contrast, the IT sector was relatively unregulated, although it was still subject to government intervention through competition and industrial policy. Traditionally, the communications infrastructure was regulated on the assumption that it would be used to provide specific services. In other words, the focus of regulation was the *service* element (for instance telephony) and the underlying infrastructure was regulated according to the characteristics of the service and related public policy objectives (for instance, universal service obligations), on the assumption that the network and the service were intertwined.

Digitalization broke down the distinction between networks and services, bringing together previously separate sectors. As telecommunications, broadcasting and information technology began to converge, the continued separation of the legal regimes for each sector seemed no longer viable. The existence of separate regulatory structures for increasingly similar services created the risk of overlap and conflict between regulatory regimes, and the possibility of incomplete legal coverage. Regulatory uncertainty, divergence and fragmentation were seen as potential obstacles for future market and technological developments (Holznagel 1999).

In Europe, the EC took the lead of a much-needed process of regulatory reform with the publication of the Green Paper on Convergence (EC 1997). This represented the first serious attempt to tackle the regulation of convergence. The challenge was to devise a new regime that would encourage, rather than forestall, the convergence process and the consumer and citizens' benefits associated with the so-called 'information society'. The options were: (1) to retain a separate vertical approach for the regulation of each sector; (2) to develop a new horizontal approach just for new services and (3) to create a new technologically neutral model comprising both traditional and new services, based on a reconsideration of fundamental principles and inspired by methods of competitive regulation. In other words, this was a policy response based on the idea that if technologies converge, regulation should also converge.

The third alternative was the preferred option, but also the most ambitious and it hinted at the creation of a single European regulatory authority. It was taken forward and opened the path towards subsequent proposals, in particular the 1999

Communications Review (EC 1999), and culminated in the regulatory package for electronic communications and services adopted in 2002. A key policy proposal that inspired the reform involved replacing sector specific regulation with general competition law, as competition became more effective, even if it was intended that regulation of general interest objectives should remain in place. The Communications Review was adopted at the peak of the drive towards convergence and signalled the obsolescence of technologically determined norms, thus making a strong case for the introduction of the principle of *technological neutrality* in regulation. Another fundamental principle was the separation of content and infrastructure for regulatory purposes. Other principles that inspired the communications reform included harmonization, while reflecting the differences in markets and national conditions, and greater cooperation between national regulatory authorities. The idea of a Euro regulator was abandoned.

In July 2003 a new Regulatory Framework for Electronic Communications and Services (the Framework) came into force in the member states, with one liberalization directive and five harmonization directives: the Framework Directive, the Access Directive, the Authorisation Directive, the Universal Service Directive and the Data Protection Directive. In addition, the EC issued a Decision on Radio Spectrum, a Recommendation on Relevant Markets and Market Assessment Guidelines.[8] It aimed to introduce as much flexibility as possible, for example by substituting licensing requirements for a general authorization regime and the commitment to periodic review. Crucially, the Framework Directive stresses that regulation should be the minimum possible, and should only be imposed if there is no effective competition (or if it is unlikely in the near future), if competition law remedies prove insufficient and/or when market forces do not satisfy the public interest. The Framework covers the electronic communications networks, including broadcasting networks, and associated services, but it does not include content or information society services, which are regulated by the Television without Frontiers Directive[9] and the E-Commerce Directive[10] respectively. The Framework is under review at the time of writing and the new Audiovisual Media Services Directive has just been adopted. Both have prompted the re-opening of a debate about the appropriate regulatory model for convergence.

Central to the new model established by the regulatory framework, is the principle of *technological neutrality* (regulation should neither impose nor discriminate in favour of the use of a particular type of technology) and, linked to this, a *horizontal approach* to regulation. This means that the same regulatory principles should be applied to all transmission infrastructures, irrespective of the services carried over

---

8   All texts are available at http://europa.eu.int/information_society/policy/ecomm/todays_framework/overview/index_en.htm.

9   Council Directive 89/552/EEC of 3 October 1989 on the co-ordination of certain provisions laid down by Law, Regulation or Administrative Action in Member States concerning the pursuit of television broadcasting activities (Television without Frontiers Directive) [1989] OJ L 298/23, as amended by Directive 97/36, [1997] OJ L 202/60.

10   Directive 2000/31/EC of the European Parliament and of the Council of 8 June 2000 on certain legal aspects of information society services, in particular electronic commerce, in the Internal Market (E-Commerce Directive) [2000] OJ L 178/16.

them. Regulation is thus structured along activity lines as opposed to the existing vertical framework structured around industries. What is important for the purposes of intervention is the service *regardless* of how it is delivered to the customer. This notion of regulating in a completely technology neutral fashion is attractive. If one service is substitutable for another, then it should be subject to roughly the same regulatory constraints, irrespective of the technologies used to deliver it, thereby promoting inter-platform competition. Yet, as we will argue later, the principle of technological neutrality, if broadly interpreted, might clash with other regulatory principles or with the formulation of certain national policies linked to content, with audiovisual policy clearly among these.

The second pillar of the convergence model created by the regulatory framework is the principle of *separation between the regulation of infrastructure and content*. This is partly the logical outcome of the current distribution of competences between the EU and its member states in the area of culture. Even if certain issues regulated by the Framework are intertwined with content-related public policy objectives at national level, the EU has limited competences in the area of content.

This is easier said than done as the content/network distinction underlying the directives is not straightforward; rather, there is a gradation from one end of the chain to the other (Larouche 2001). Content production and rights acquisition clearly belong to the content realm, whilst transmission for the purposes of delivery to consumers does not. However, there are various phases between both extremes in which the substance is unclear, such as the packaging of channels and the provision and distribution of technical services. Links between infrastructure and content are particularly prominent in the areas of must carry and associated facilities such as conditional access, electronic programme guides or application programme interfaces. Similarly, the concept of 'universal service' in broadcasting goes beyond mere geographical coverage, to encompass notions of quality and diversity of genres.

These issues are left to the member states for detailed implementation in accordance with the principle of subsidiarity. However, the primacy of Community law as well as the EC's powers in the monitoring of implementation and compliance with market freedoms could lead to conflicts in the interpretation of principles and the assessment of the 'proportionality' of national measures. It could be argued that despite attempting to strictly separate infrastructure and content, the principle of technological neutrality has deprived member states of their legitimate competence over the latter. At times, the fulfilment of public policy goals in the area of content might be unavoidably linked with the development of a particular delivery network or platform (on account, for example, of universal availability). Thus, the national championing of digital terrestrial platforms or the unconcealed European preference for the DVB-H standard for mobile TV (EC 2007), while inconsistent with the principle of technological neutrality, have been justified on public interest grounds. This possibility is recognized in the Framework Directive, which envisages that, in allocating spectrum frequencies, member states can legitimately consider criteria other than efficiency. Recital 19 lists a series of considerations that can be taken into account, such as 'the democratic, social, linguistic and cultural interests'. It should be noted, however, that regulation for social objectives would still need to be proportionate and balanced against efficiency considerations. In other words, the Commission and the member states must demonstrate that there is no other more efficient means available to achieve a particular objective, which effectively limits their hands in policy-making terms. As a result, despite the stated recognition that public interest considerations as regards the latter remain solely in the hands of the national authorities, the EC plays a significant role in 'specifying and at times re-conceptualising the alternatives among which member states will ultimately choose' (Smyrl 1998, 96), even in cases where the subsidiarity principle applies.

Four years into the implementation of the Framework, and unsurprisingly, the horizontal separation between infrastructure and content has resulted in administrative complications. There has not been sufficient rationalization of national broadcasting regulations (in some member states broadcasting regulation has been extended), with the result that there are overlapping regulatory regimes or additional content regulatory burdens on service providers (including on operators which merely re-transmit content already authorized). Most prominently, distribution issues (such as coverage obligations, platform presence, management of advertising gaps, must carry rules, channel selection or access to associated facilities) that are neither pure content nor pure transmission issues, are often regulated by more than one framework. This is becoming more evident with the emergence of new broadcasting technologies and platforms such as IPTV or mobile TV, which at times are regulated by a different authority. Indeed, if this separation is excessively rigid, for example in the case of the audiovisual broadband services market, the regulatory outcome is likely to be suboptimal. Cooperation and coordination amongst telecommunications, broadcasting and competition authorities becomes a necessity to avoid implementation inconsistencies. From this perspective, the existence of 'converged' regulators might be an advantage as it facilitates greater coherency between regimes.

The regulatory framework for electronic communications networks and services can be seen as an innovative and, in some respects revolutionary, response to the challenges raised by communications convergence. It was specifically designed to take account of convergence, in that it dealt with markets and services independent of the underlying technologies. Crucially, it was based on the premise (and the promise) of a progressive removal of regulation, which would be withdrawn when competition became effective. In that respect, the 2003 Regulatory Framework represented a fundamental paradigm change in the regulation of telecommunications, and it proved successful.

The recognition of the different policy concerns relating to content in the regulatory framework signalled a continuation of a distinctive regime for broadcasting. Issues relating to the licensing of broadcasting services, media pluralism or the definition of the public service remit remained separate, and exclusively in the hands of the member states, with minimum European harmonization of content standards in the areas of advertising, protection of minors and human dignity through the Television without Frontiers Directive. Thus, the European regulatory response to convergence was conceived as primarily economic in nature, with a strong focus on issues of competition and access at the infrastructure layer, while social regulation in the area of broadcasting remained relatively unaffected.

The development of high-speed broadband and next generation networks, and the increased availability of audiovisual content through networks and platforms, which have little in common with traditional broadcasting, is bound to break such a carefully designed balance. The question remains, is a change of paradigm equally necessary – or even feasible – for content? Are the principles upon which regulatory convergence was initially designed applicable in this area? Is the new Audiovisual Media Services Directive the appropriate response to the challenges posed by multi-platform distribution of content in a global manner? These questions are addressed in the remainder of this chapter.

The Impact of Convergence on Content Regulation ... or Vice Versa?

The delivery of audiovisual content today presents itself at the heart of the convergence process, and by extension at the heart of regulatory debates around convergence. Content regulation is perceived as the last bastion of regulatory reforms initiated with the 1997 Convergence Green Paper. Regulators and policy-makers, both at the European and at national level, are under pressure to design a regulatory framework that will encourage, rather than forestall, the development of audiovisual services that are seen as a key driver of competition and innovation in this sector. With this objective in mind, the EC initiated a reform of the Television without Frontiers Directive, aimed at modernizing the traditional rules that apply to television broadcasting, in particular advertising rules, as well as to address the challenges posed by new video content delivery. The intention was to provide the basic framework for the regulation of new audiovisual services in a converged and technologically neutral manner.

In 2005, the EC put forward proposals for a new Audiovisual Media Services (AVMS) Directive.[11] It was felt that, just as with networks, there was a need for a more consistent and horizontal approach to deal with the challenges created by digitalization and convergence in the area of content. In addition, the EC argued in favour of the creation of a 'level playing field' between traditional broadcasters and providers of video-on-demand services, so far categorized as 'information society services' under the E-commerce Directive, and therefore excluded from the application of minimum content rules. As with any other internal market initiative, the primary objective of the EC was the removal of cross border barriers to trade in the European audiovisual content sphere. After two years of intense negotiations the Directive was finally formally adopted on 18 December 2007.[12]

---

11   See Proposal for a Directive of the European Parliament and of the Council amending Council Directive 89/552/EEC on the coordination of certain provisions laid down by law, regulation or administrative action in Member States concerning the pursuit of television broadcasting activities, COM(2005) 0646 final.

12   Directive 2007/65/EC of the European Parliament and of the Council of 11 December 2007 amending Council Directive 89/552/EEC on the coordination of certain provisions laid down by law, regulation or administrative action in Member States concerning the pursuit of television broadcasting activities, OJ L332/27 of 18 December 2007.

The European Commission proposed to extend the scope of the Directive to cover 'audiovisual media services', originally defined as any service providing moving images with or without sound, in order to inform, entertain or educate the general public by electronic communications networks (Article 1a of the draft EC proposal). This was a very wide definition, which could potentially have resulted in the extension of regulation far beyond traditional television broadcasting to a wide array of other content services including video blogs, or websites hosting or sharing user generated content, mobile multimedia applications, and even online games or gambling websites. After discussions in both the Council and the Parliament, the scope of the Directive was narrowed down to so called 'television like' services. In other words, regulation has only been extended to cover services that are essentially similar in form and content to television broadcasting, but delivered on demand, and in respect of which users might expect some kind of regulatory protection. The Directive has the aspiration of being technologically neutral, and would therefore cover any such services, irrespective of the technology used to deliver them, or the platform through which they are accessed.

As a recognition that users exercise greater choice and control over on-demand offers, the Directive distinguishes between linear and non-linear services, and applies different regulatory requirements: linear services are defined as analogous to television broadcasting, with scheduled content pushed by the broadcaster to the viewer, while non-linear services are delivered 'on demand' at the time chosen by the viewer. Linear services are subject to a higher tier of regulatory controls, similar to the ones currently applied to television broadcasting, albeit with some modest liberalization of advertising restrictions, insertion rules and product placement, while on-demand services are subject to lower levels of regulation, primarily designed to provide protection for minors and against incitement to hatred, promote European works and meet qualitative content requirements in terms of advertising, sponsorship and product placement (for example, general prohibition of tobacco advertising and restrictions on advertising of alcohol to minors).

There are a few considerations to make at this stage. First, the fact that regulatory requirements significantly differ depending on the nature of the service casts doubts about the real meaning of a 'level playing field' between broadcasting and video-on-demand services trumpeted by the EC. Similarly, it is difficult to see where, if any, are the additional internal market benefits from the application of the country of origin principle to non-linear services, since member states have retained their current competence to derogate from that principle on the same public interest grounds that exist under the E-Commerce Directive. In other words, the minimum harmonization of content standards for non-linear services has not been accompanied by additional protections for providers under the country of origin principle, and member states will continue to be able to block services from providers lawfully established in other member states. Thus, the Directive's internal market rationale that is the basic premise for EU intervention in this sector seems to have been fundamentally undermined.

The Directive puts a strong emphasis on self and co-regulation as effective means for implementation of the non-linear tier. Indeed, in the new media environment where technology and markets change rapidly and where viewers are taking greater responsibility for their media consumption, self- and co-regulation schemes can prove to be a better and more flexible means of delivering a high level of consumer protection. Debates in the Council and in the Parliament also highlighted the importance of media literacy, understood as the skills, knowledge and understanding that enable people to use media effectively, as a necessary condition for the success of self- and co-regulatory initiatives.

It is beyond the scope of this chapter to provide a detailed account of the various issues raised by the new AVMS Directive, and there are other chapters in this book entirely devoted to specific questions such as jurisdiction, European quotas or protection of minors. Therefore, we would limit ourselves to raise a few points of particular relevance in considering the role of content regulation in the context of an overall regulatory model for convergence.

Traditionally, the case for regulating television broadcasting to a much stricter and higher standard than other media such as the printed press or other forms of artistic expression rested principally on two grounds. Firstly, there was a technological rationale: the spectrum needed for terrestrial distribution was both a public resource and a scarce commodity, and this justified public intervention designed to achieve an efficient distribution of frequencies. In addition, in order to avoid signal interference and chaos it was deemed necessary to put in place some regulation or organization of the airwaves. Secondly, there was a public interest rationale linked to the immediacy and pervasiveness of the audiovisual medium (Feintuck 1999; Tambini et al. 2001). Television was regarded as a powerful medium with a privileged position in terms of access to mass audiences, and with a recognized capacity to influence the public debate and thereby directly affect political and democratic processes (Barendt 1995). It can also cause direct harm to individuals (and particularly minors) through, for instance, unfair representation of views, depictions of extreme violent or sexual material and intrusion of privacy.

Whether these arguments can (or should) be transposed to the new convergent media environment remains an open and highly controversial question (Ariño 2007). The AVMS Directive starts from the premise that, as television moves to other platforms, television regulation should follow. Though appealing as an argument, the reality is much more complex. First, television is not simply moving to other platforms, it is also *changing* along the way, and converging with other media. The question is, therefore, whether regulatory approaches designed for the traditional television environment are appropriate or should take priority over other regulatory approaches that might be better designed to address the challenges posed by new convergent technologies.

Many of the new convergent services are characterized by entirely new models of content production and distribution, and increasingly the focus is on the creative role of the user or private individual in generating, editing and sharing with others their own original content. As we move forward, and as broadband technology developments allow for greater bandwidth, the amount of video content and the degree of integration, sophistication and consumer empowerment of television and other audiovisual services will only increase.

As digitalization removes capacity constraints, the pervasiveness, impact and influence of the television medium becomes the prevalent regulatory rationale.

However, the critical – and yet unanswered – question is whether new audiovisual media services, particularly those delivered over the Internet, can be considered 'mass media' from the point of view of their impact and influence in society. A comparison with the press helps to illustrate this point. The original justification for the lack of regulation of the press had to do with the idea that a relatively large number of independent publications co-existed and covered a broad range of political and ideological views and that entry and competition was possible. It was argued that as newspapers were commercially competitive, other voices and other interests could counter biases. The task of governments in the print media was therefore limited to allowing the free expression of opposing views, rather than providing a single platform that would convey a national consensus. In contrast, there were only a limited number of television stations, and it was physically impossible to transmit more than one message on the same broadcast frequency without interference. Another reason for this differential (and deferential) treatment of the press related precisely to the immediacy and pervasiveness of the audiovisual medium. While printed content is actively sought by readers who are aware that newspapers carry politically relevant and biased information, television is readily available at the switch of a button.

It can be argued that, except for a minimum set of audiovisual services which are identical to television broadcasting but delivered using IP technology, most of the materials currently available on Internet platforms, despite the potentially global audience and despite the fact that they may integrate some 'moving images' or video, are actually consumed and perceived very differently by users, in a way which reminds us more of the press than the television medium. This consideration, at a minimum, challenges the assumption that new Internet services need to be subject to the highly strict regulatory controls traditionally imposed on television broadcasts. It rather makes the case for a re-consideration of the need to regulate broadcasting, beyond some enduring objectives such as the protection of minors or qualitative advertising controls.

An important challenge in this context has been the championing of the principle of technological neutrality (similar services should be regulated in a similar manner, regardless of the technology that is used to deliver them – cable, satellite, terrestrial networks or IP networks) to mean 'platform neutrality', in an attempt to address the future impracticality of technology based platform distinctions. This suggests that a television channel should be regulated in a similar manner regardless of whether it is delivered over a cable network, or through the Internet. The aim is to deliver a level playing field between incumbents and innovators, and to reduce the opportunities for regulatory arbitrage. Yet, if strictly applied to the content world, the concept of platform neutrality implies that the same piece of content or service should be regulated in a similar manner, regardless of the platform or device through which it is consumed or the conditions under which consumption takes place.

This idea, although attractive in theory, does not sit well with the basic principle that content rules need to be applied *in context*, and that the level of protection (and by extension regulation) that might be required critically depends on the conditions of access and use of the content service. Already today, the same single piece of content is subject to a wide range of different regulatory controls depending on whether it is broadcast on a free to air or pay-TV, delivered as video on demand, sold at a DVD store or shown in a cinema. Accordingly, restrictions (including advertising restrictions) that are suitable on free to air television broadcasting platforms might not be appropriate for on-demand platforms (online, mobile, and so on) where the consumer experience is inherently different. This highlights the need to reconcile the principle of technological or platform neutral regulation with the principle of regulation 'in context', and might require a certain degree of discretion for the regulator. More generally, the principle of technological neutrality should not be regarded as an absolute, but rather act as a guiding principle, since there are still differences in technologies that need to be recognized by regulators (for example, specific multiplex licensing and the use of specific spectrum).

When considering the extension of regulation to additional forms of media, it should not be forgotten that any intervention in this sector constitutes a restriction of the fundamental right to freedom of expression under Article 10 of the European Convention of Human Rights, and should therefore be carried out with extreme care and sound reasoning, always subject to proportionality constraints. It should also be noted that all audiovisual services are still subject to general copyright, criminal and privacy laws, and that there are ways of delivering specific protection to particularly vulnerable groups such as minors, which might constitute a more proportionate, and at times more effective means of protection.

In this respect, the recognition of the advantages of self- and co-regulatory schemes to deal with the challenges that convergence creates for content regulation is critical. The case for the introduction of self- and co-regulatory practices rests principally on considerations of expertise and efficiency. It is assumed that self- and co-regulation result in greater promptness and flexibility in responding to changing markets, and for that reason they are particularly well suited to deal with new media. Furthermore, the involvement of those most affected by the measures (in this case industry and consumers) is seen to ensure not only wider ownership of the policies, but also greater compliance. Major drawbacks are the lack of democratic legitimacy and external accountability, as well as potential risks of abuse of self-regulatory powers in order to restrict competition.

Though still nascent in most member states, with possibly the exception of Germany and the UK, governments and regulators around Europe are increasingly awakening to the idea that, in the area of on-demand content and new media, there is a need for a stronger emphasis on the responsibility of both content providers and recipients of services through the development of codes of conduct and self-protection systems such as filtering, labelling, ratings and access controls. The EC has also been very active in recent years in encouraging the development of self- and co-regulatory schemes, particularly in regards services on the Internet and mobile phones. In this context, the fact that the AVMS Directive encourages implementation through co-regulation should be welcomed, because it gives a political signal as to the importance of such mechanisms.

Getting the future of content regulation right is critical. At stake is the successful development of a truly convergent environment. If inappropriately designed, content regulation risks hindering the pace of convergence, without delivering on promises of consumer protection. Seen in this light, the question is not what convergence will do to content regulation, but, rather, what would an ill-conceived content regulatory framework do to convergence.

Conclusion

Convergence is no longer restricted to the realm of the public imagination or as a mantra of political discourses. After a small period of ostracism following the 'dotcom' bubble burst in 2001, the digital environment and the idea of convergence is now resurfacing strongly and becoming an everyday reality. As this chapter has illustrated, the reality of convergence has proved richer and certainly more complex than envisaged in the early 1990s. Today, consumers are faced with a myriad of options in networks, services and products and benefit from competition, choice and better prices. The societal implications are significant. There is no doubt that changes in communications structures induced by digitalization are without precedent and go beyond a mere quality improvement in the picture or sound resolution, altering the basic characteristics of communication, entertainment and information exchanges and even questioning their very foundations.

The dynamics of convergence are complex and the pattern of the convergence evolution (rather than revolution) remains uncertain. Convergence is taking place at different geographic levels and at different speeds across countries, sectors and services, and it remains a multi-purpose, multi-functional and multi-dimensional concept that encompasses continuous, processes of change, innovation and disruption. Regulators and policy-makers are faced with the challenge of designing a flexible regulatory framework that allows the different industry players, as well as users, to exploit the benefits that convergence brings, while ensuring consumer protection and a necessary degree of regulatory certainty.

After more than a decade of regulatory discussions around convergence, policy-makers and regulators still face significant uncertainties, both as regards its outcomes, as well as the speed at which convergence is occurring. We are still far from a coherent and consistent 'convergence regime', and this is particularly noticeable in the area of content. Institutionally, there seem to be important benefits in having a converged regulator to manage developments, but the experience has been so far limited, and open questions remain as to its form, structure and competences.

The media and communications industries remain inherently 'cyclical', and regularly undergo phases and processes of profound change, affecting technologies used to make and distribute content and services, business models, audience behaviour and regulatory responses. In such context, regulators are under pressure to keep the pace with developments, promoting innovation and competition, while ensuring that the race is fair and that consumers benefit from it. This requires a combination of a clear understanding of, and commitment to, first principles, with what should be prompt and flexible interventions. Importantly, regulating for convergence should not mean the replacement of a rigid vertical structure with a rigid horizontal framework. Principles of horizontality and technological neutrality should not encourage regulators to ignore the differences between networks and platforms, particularly in relation to their social impact.

We have argued that, the convergence model, as initially conceived, was one fundamentally based on the premise that regulation and regulators needed to withdraw, except for minimum intervention in cases of dominance or market failure (Clements 1998, 202). Public interest regulation to ensure universal provision of services or to achieve public interest goals in broadcasting would remain relatively untouched, subject to a careful balance between economic and social goals. Thus, in the early phases of convergence, infrastructure and content regulation continued in a separate though harmonious co-existence (Blackman 1998).

As convergence reaches maturity, and as new increasingly integrated services emerge, this model is called into question. While network access regulation under a modernized regulatory framework will continue to ensure competition and innovation at the infrastructure level, traditional broadcasting regulation is perceived not only as inappropriate, but also as potentially ineffective in delivering public service goals at the content level, in particular as content delivery over the Internet increases. The AVMS Directive will not, in and of itself, provide the appropriate counter balance that convergence requires, and it will remain insufficient to address the challenges that regulators face in the new environment.

It is therefore unsurprising that, in this context, self- and co-regulation have become central in contributing to the maintenance of a necessary degree of consumer protection in those areas where it is perceived that competition alone is insufficient (classically, the protection of minors). Self- and co-regulation are increasingly promoted as a preferred complement to network regulation, particularly as regards new and emerging services. Regulators and policy-makers are starting to realize that they need to engage with both industry and consumers not only to understand the changes in markets and social behaviour brought about by convergence, but also to respond to them in the most appropriate and effective manner.

In this context, the claim of regulatory withdrawal could be seen less as a retreat by the regulator to let markets and competition do the job, and rather, as an invitation to other parties into regulatory dialogue. In this game, the regulator is no longer setting out the rules, monitoring market behaviour and intervening as and when necessary, but also taking a more active role in orchestrating industry self-regulation and consumer engagement. Although some might claim that this type of 'multi-party' regulation constitutes a desperate attempt by regulators to continue to influence markets – and keep their jobs, beyond what is desirable and even legitimate, it can be argued that it represents a new mode of regulatory governance, which is inevitable and might indeed prove superior in a context of rapid market developments. Critically, this partnership could be seen as the only way to address the intrinsically global nature of Internet services. Convergence regulation seen in this light can no longer be described simply as 'minimum' regulation, but rather as 'collaborative' regulation where intervention and the role of the regulator is fundamentally different in nature.

This puts pressure on the need for greater transparency, representation and accountability in regulatory activity. The lack of transparency and democratic input would otherwise undermine the legitimacy of this new regulatory technique, and risks resulting in regulatory capture. There are new challenges around enforcement and greater reliance on stakeholder forces should not lead the state to abdicate its ultimate responsibility over the functioning of the system. Finally, this also highlights the vital importance of focusing on the consumer and ensuring that they understand and actively participate in this new environment.

References

Ariño, M. (2007), 'Content Regulation and New Media: A Case Study of Online Video Portals', *Communications & Strategies* 66, 115–135.

Baldwin, T. et al. (1996), *Convergence. Integrating Media, Information and Communication*. London: Sage.

Barendt, E. (1995), *Broadcasting Law. A Comparative Study* Oxford: Clarendon Press.

Bennet, P. and Adamson, M. (1995), *Convergence in Europe: The New Information Infrastructure*. London: Financial Times Management Reports.

Blackman, C.R. (1998), 'Convergence between Telecommunications and Other Media. How Should Regulation Adapt?', *Telecommunications Policy* 22(3), 163–170.

Burgelman, J.-C. (1995), 'Convergence and Réseaux transeuropéens: quelques problèmes politiques', in Noirhomme-Fraiture, M. and Goffinet, L. (eds) (1995), *Multimédia. Actes de la journée d'information sur le multimédia*. Namur: Presses Universitaires de Namur.

Clements, B. (1998), 'The Impact of Convergence on Regulatory Policy in Europe', *Telecommunications Policy* 22(3), 197–205.

Dang-Nguyen, G. and Le Traon, J. (1995), 'L'analyse de l'offre multimédia: un premier examen des stratégies d'alliances entre acteurs', *Communications et Strategies* 19, 203–226.

European Commission (1994), 'Europe and the Global Information Society: Recommendations to the European Council' (The Bangemann Report). Brussels, European Commission.

European Commission (1997), 'Green Paper on the Convergence of the Telecommunications, Media and Information Technology Sectors, and the Implications for Regulation. Towards an Information Society Approach', COM(97) 623, Brussels, 3 December 1997.

European Commission (1999), Communication to the European Parliament, the Council, the Economic and Social Committee and the Committee of the Regions, The Convergence of the Telecommunications, Media and Information Technology Sectors, and the Implications for Regulation. Results of the Public Consultation on the Green Paper [COM (97)623], COM(1999) 108 final.

European Commission (2007), European Commission: Communication to the European Parliament, the Council, the Economic and Social Committee and the Committee of the Regions on 'Strengthening the Internal Market for Mobile TV', COM(2007) 409 final.

Feintuck, M. (1999), *Media Regulation, Public Interest and the Law.* Edinburgh: University Press.

Fidler, R. (1997), *Mediamorphosis. Understanding New Media*. Thousand Oaks:

Pine Forge Press.

Harcourt, A. (2005), *The European Union and the Regulation of Media Markets.* Manchester: Manchester University Press.

Holznagel, B. (1999), 'New Challenges: Convergence of the Markets, Divergence of the Laws. Questions regarding the future communications regulation', *International Journal of Communications Law and Policy* 2 (IJCP Web-Doc 5-2-1999).

Larouche, P. (2001), *Communications, Convergence and Public Service Broadcasting*, Paper presented at the Workshop on PSB and European Law, EUI, Florence.

Noirhomme-Fraiture, M. and Goffinet, L. (eds). (1995), *Multimédia. Actes de la journée d'information sur le multimédia.* Namur: Presses Universitaires de Namur.

OECD (1992), *Telecommunications and Broadcasting: Convergence or Collision?* Paris: OECD.

Ofcom (2007), *The Communications Market Report.* London: Ofcom.

Perez, C. (2002), *Technological Revolutions and Financial Capitals: The Dynamics of Bubbles and Golden Ages.* Cheltenham, Edward Elgar.

Picard, R. (ed.) (1998), *Evolving Media Markets: Effects of Economic and Policy Changes.* Turku: The Economic Research Foundation for Mass Communication and Turku School of Economics and Business Administration.

Pouillot, D. (2003), 'Telecom Services and Operators in 2002: Slowdown in Growth and Structural Changes'. *Communications & Strategies* 51, 173–181.

Smyrl, M.E. (1998), 'When (and How) Do the Commission's Preferences Matter?', *Journal of Common Market Studies,* 36(1), 79–99.

Tambini, D. et al. (2001) *Communications Revolution and Reform.* London: IPPR.

Tremblay, G. (1995), 'Los medicos audiovisuales en un entorono de turbulencias. Una reorganización necessaria', *Boletin de las Fundación* 172, 7–9, Madrid.

Wallis, R. (1998), 'Unbundling the Bouncy Road towards Convergence: Myths, Rhetoric and Technological Determinism', in Picard, R (ed.) (1998), *Evolving Media Markets: Effects of Economic and Policy Changes.* Turku: The Economic Research Foundation for Mass Communication and Turku School of Economics and Business Administration.

Wirth, M.O. (2006). 'Issues in Media Convergence', in Albarran, A. et al. (eds) (2006), *Handbook of Media Management and Economics.* New Jersey: Lawrence Erlbaum Associates, 445–462.

Chapter 7

Jurisdiction in the Television without Frontiers Directive

Lorna Woods

One of the main aims of the European Community has been the creation of the European single market. In seeking to introduce a 'one-stop shop' for regulation, the Television without Frontiers Directive[1] reflected this market concern. The provisions allocating jurisdiction between the national authorities have proved contentious, a difficulty that has become more evident as technological developments such as satellite television facilitated the evasion (whether deliberately or accidentally) of national television regulatory systems (Woods and Scholes 1997). This issue raised questions about the balance of power between the member states and the European Union (EU), as well as tensions between different policies within the EU at these different levels. Further developments in technology, and the realisation of convergence of technology and services, raise further difficulties regarding the notion of jurisdiction (Harrison and Woods 2000). This time, however, the question was less 'who should regulate' but rather, 'who (or what) should be regulated.'

This chapter looks at these two issues but considers the issue of the subject matter of regulation first, that is the question of whether the Television without Frontiers Directive (or the Audiovisual Media Services Directive (AVMS Directive) when it is implemented) applies, before going on to consider the scope of that provision. In doing so, this chapter identifies the difficulties with the operation of the Television without Frontiers Directive in a changing broadcasting environment, its interrelationship with other directives, particularly the e-Commerce Directive,[2] and, finally, identifying the extent to which the proposed amendments to the Television without Frontiers Directive via the AVMS Directive are likely to provide satisfactory solutions to these problems. In assessing the satisfactory nature or otherwise of the clause, this chapter particularly bears in mind those who might be expected to benefit from a regulatory regime, that is, the viewers.

---

1   Directive 2007/65/EC of the European Parliament and of the Council of 11 December 2007 amending Council Directive 89/552/EEC on the coordination of certain provisions laid down by law, regulation or administrative action in member states concerning the pursuit of television broadcasting activities, OJ L332/27 of 18 December 2007.

2   Directive of the European Parliament and of the Council (EC) 2000/31 of 8 June 2000 on certain legal aspects of information society services, in particular electronic commerce, in the Internal Market [2000] OJ L178/1.

So what is Television Anyway?

It seems that the question of what television and broadcasting are was considered self-evident when the original Television without Frontiers Directive was enacted. The original Green Paper (EC 1984) certainly did not feel the need to address the scope of broadcasting as a service directly. Problems were perceived to relate to the different national regimes and the development of cross-border broadcasting, rather than the nature of the service itself. Thus Article 1(a) defined 'television broadcasting' as:

> the initial transmission by wire or over the air, including that by satellite, in unencoded or encoded form, of television programmes intended for reception by the public. It includes the communication of programmes between undertakings with a view to their being relayed to the public. It does not include communication services providing items of information or other messages on individual demand such as telecopying, electronic data banks and other similar services.

The nature of 'programmes' was presumably at that stage assumed to be obvious, although as the first revision process in 1997 illustrates, with several different definitions being put forward for the term, none of which were ultimately accepted, industry practice at least was challenging accepted understandings of broadcasting.

The increasing commercialization of the sector, itself encouraged by the impact of EC law and the four freedoms, particularly the free movement of services, also contributed to this trend as the commercial sector sought to maximize profits and minimize regulatory constraints. These developments seem to have been reinforced by the introduction of digital technology and the consequent convergence of the communications sector. The changes in hardware, services and market structure undermined traditional legal distinctions between broadcasting and one to one information services. Whilst the boundaries of broadcasting had initially been non-contentious, technological changes made the scope of the Television without Frontiers Directive less clear.

The difficulties in this area were becoming apparent even by the time of the review of the Television without Frontiers Directive in 1997,[3] which introduced the definition of the term 'broadcaster' to supplement the definition of 'broadcasting' in the attempt to clarify the scope of the Television without Frontiers Directive. The definition, that '"broadcaster" means the natural or legal person who has editorial responsibility for the composition of schedules of television programmes within the meaning of (a) and who transmits them or has them transmitted by third parties', is

---

3   Council Directive (EC)97/36 of 30 June 1997 amending Directive 89/552/EEC on the coordination of certain provisions laid down by law, regulation or administrative action in member states concerning the pursuit of television broadcasting activities [1997] OJ L202/30. See EC (1995), pp. 25–26, where the Commission expressed caution about over-regulating new services. The EP ultimately concurred with this view, although the Barzanti Report expressed some reservations in this regard: see Doc A4-0018/95 p 34 and 47. Contrast the views in the Committee of Ministers of the Council of Europe: Explanatory Memorandum as amended by the provisions of the Protocol amending the CTT, para. 45.

dependent on the notion of editorial responsibility. That concept operates, or seeks to operate, so as to determine the boundary between content and transmission, that is responsibility for complying with content regulation lies with those who make decisions about content. This issue becomes increasingly significant with the introduction of new transmission networks, such as web-TV. We will see the same idea within the determination of geographical jurisdiction. Here, the use of the term leaves open the question of what sorts of content-based services fall within the terms of the Television without Frontiers Directive.

Despite the original proposal that the Television without Frontiers Directive should include radio, it always had focused on just television, or audiovisual services, other services falling outside its scope. If we look at the definition of broadcasting, it takes what might be termed a hybrid approach. It identifies both the services that fall within the definition (essentially point to multi-point programmes) and gives examples of those that do not (one-to-one data services). The second part of the definition thus operates to limit the scope of the first part. Problematically, this second limiting class of service is not exclusively defined; Article 1(a) gives examples rather than an exhaustive list leaving open the suggestion that other services would likewise fall outside the scope of television broadcasting and thereby introducing an element of uncertainty. Nonetheless it is possible to suggest that in this second limiting element we see the key criterion; individual choice, or rather choice limited to opting out, rather than as tailoring to individual demand.[4]

The reverse side of this picture can be seen in the e-Commerce Directive. Information Society Services are defined generally as 'any service normally provided for remuneration, at a distance, by electronic means and at the individual request of a recipient of services.' The Transparency Directive[5] additionally has an 'indicative list' of services not included within information society services, which includes broadcasting (whether television, radio or teletext). Although it has not been entirely clear whether all content-based communication services are comprised in the two types of service (broadcasting and information society service), the two identified categories seem to be mutually exclusive, the boundary line drawn by the concept of individual demand. The distinction is sometimes referred to as the distinction between push services and pull services. This concept also suggests that the content is personalized, as well as the timing. Given the freedom to choose viewing time, this constitutes an opposing notion to the 'simultaneous reception' required by television broadcasting (including pay-TV).

Despite the fact that the boundary between the two types of service seems clear, in practice it was problematic, as illustrated by the *Mediakabel* decision by the European Court of Justice (ECJ).[6] The argument turned on the technical nature of the

---

4   There are other elements making up the definition: the notion of programme, the requirements of transmission and the issue of reception by the public.

5   Directive of the European Parliament and of the Council (EC)98/34 of 22 June 1998 laying down a procedure for the provision of information in the field of technical standards and regulations, [1998] OJ L204/37.

6   *Mediakabel BV* v. *Commissariaat voor de Media* (c-89/04) [2005] ECR I-nyr, judgment 2 June 2005.

service, which involved two separate signals, that of the encrypted film and that of the decryption code necessary to view the film. Whilst the former might fall within the definition of television broadcasting, as the film could in principle be watched by more than one viewer, the payment and encryption system was individualized. Was this, therefore, an information society service? The ECJ concluded that it was not. Although the first two elements of the definition of an information society service (provision at a distance and transmitted by electronic equipment) were satisfied, the service was not provided 'at the individual request of a recipient of services.' The ECJ pointed out that the list of films available is at the choice of the service provider, and the selection is offered to all subscribers on the same terms and at times determined by the service provider. On this basis, the ECJ concluded that the service was not 'commanded individually by an isolated recipient who has free choice of programmes in an interactive setting'.[7] Article 1(a) Television without Frontiers Directive, requires reception by 'an indeterminate number of potential television viewers, to whom the same images are transmitted simultaneously',[8] a requirement satisfied in this case. Thus:

> a pay-per-view television service, even one which is accessible to a limited number of subscribers, but which comprises only programmes selected by the broadcaster and is broadcast at times set by the broadcaster, cannot be regarded as being provided on individual demand.

What is problematic about this argument is that the regulatory protection offered to viewers might vary depending on such technical matters, when in terms of the viewers' perception there is no difference in the service offered. As the referring court raised in its questions to the ECJ, in determining the boundary between different types of service, should priority be given to the standpoint of the subscriber or to that of the service provider? Perhaps surprisingly from the fact the service provider was unsuccessful in its arguments, the ECJ held that the standpoint of the service provider should be prioritized. Such an approach is particularly worrying from the perspective of viewers, as they may well assume that television-like services are regulated in the same way as television.

The Convergence Review had suggested a horizontal approach to regulation, so that all communication networks were subject to a common set of regulatory principles irrespective of the content they carried (Communications Package, now under review).[9] The same logic could be applied to content services, and certainly the question arises about the boundary of broadcasting and the justification for a

7   *Ibid.*

8   *Ibid.*

9   Green Paper (communication) on the Convergence of the Telecommunications Media and the information Technology Sectors and the Implications for Regulation COM(97) 623, December 1997. The package from 2002 (EC 2002a, 2002b, 2002c, 2002d, 2002e) is under review, as can be seen in the Commission Communication Report on the Outcome of the Review of the EU regulatory framework for electronic communications networks and services in accordance with Directive 2002/21/EC and Summary of the 2007 Reform Proposals, COM(07) 696 final, 13 November 2007. A website provides information on the

distinctive sector specific regulation. Under the current regime, audiovisual content in the same format as that broadcast but supplied by non-traditional means, such as the downloading of television programmes, podcasts and the delivery of news bulletins to mobile phones, even when supplied by the same companies, would fall outside the scope of the Television without Frontiers Directive. As suggested above, this might be confusing for a viewer. The EC had other concerns, not based on viewer protection but rather concern for industry players and the desire for a level playing field (EC 2005b). Against this background, we come to the second review of the Directive and the proposed transformation of that Directive into the AVMS Directive (EC 2005b and 2007a). The question is, to what extent have the institutions succeeded in balancing the different interests at play in this field and, importantly, have the viewer's interests been overlooked or minimised in the interests of industry participants and the i2010 agenda?

The AVMS Directive deals with both the country of origin principle and the issue of the scope of broadcasting. The scope of the Television without Frontiers Directive has consequently been broadened, though not necessarily to a constant depth. In some respects the proposal for an AVMS Directive was surprising. First, rather than submit to a deregulatory argument based on a horizontal approach to content regulation, it accepted, to some degree, the argument that like services should be treated alike, but used that argument to extend the scope of regulation to some non-broadcasting services.[10] Secondly, it re-opened the debate about the country of origin principle, which the EC had defended as central to the internal market, and in particular raised the question of abuse of Community law.

The AVMS Directive requires the extension of a basic tier of regulation to all audiovisual media services. A second tier of regulation remains, based on a simplified version of existing rules in Television without Frontiers Directive, which applies to television broadcasting. There are thus two categories of service within the AVMS Directive: linear (traditional broadcasting) and non-linear (on-demand), which are services which would otherwise fall outside the Television without Frontiers Directive and, probably, within the e-Commerce regime, which has lower levels of obligation (though more flexibility for member states to take action in the public interest). Whilst the legislative process has worried over drafting issues, it seems that at a general level the expanded scope of the Directive and the boundary between linear and non-linear services is accepted. We need nonetheless to consider the extent the AVMS Directive:

---

progress of the review: http://ec.europa.eu/information_society/policy/ecomm/tomorrow/roadmap/index_en.htm#communication1.

10 The European Parliament had tried to extend the Television without Frontiers Directive to on-demand services at the time of the 1997 review when it proposed, unsuccessfully, the insertion of a definition of television programme as 'a moving or non-moving sequence of images which may or may not be accompanied by sound', (See Keller 1997).

1. successfully identifies the outer boundary of Audiovisual Media Services (AVMS);
2. clearly delineates the inner boundary between linear and non-linear services; and
3. clarifies the relationship between AVMS Directive and the e-Commerce Directive regime.

It has been argued that, as regards point 1, the definition of AVMS is not clear, leading to uncertainty in the application of the new regime (Ofcom 2006) (presumably affecting both industry and viewer) and that, regarding point 3, there is potential overlap between the AVMS Directive and e-Commerce regimes (Castendyk and Bottcher 2006). As the distinction between linear and non-linear is essentially that between push services and pull services, the problems in determining the old boundary for regulation under the Television without Frontiers Directive have just been relocated to within the AVMS Directive (Castendyk and Bottcher 2006; Lutz 2006), focusing this time on the boundary between the first and second tier of regulation. The viewer, it would seem, might still not be aware of the different regimes in issue affecting similar types of content.

The institutions seem to have been well aware of the difficulties in defining the scope of AVMS. In this, we see an example of the familiar problem of reducing a concept to words, and words which must be appropriate across all official languages. The EC in a 'non-paper', after commenting that the central definition, on which all others in the AVMS Directive were built, was that of AVMS, identified six elements in the definition (EC 2006b). These six elements cumulatively ensure that, according to the EC, the audiovisual regulatory system is kept within proper bounds. AVMS in the new directive are defined as:

> a service as defined by Articles 49 and 50 of the Treaty which is under the editorial responsibility of a media service provider and the principal purpose of which is the provision of programmes in order to inform, entertain or educate the general public by electronic communication networks within the meaning of Article 2(a) of Directive 2002/21/EC of the European Parliament and of the Council. Such an audiovisual media service is either television broadcasts as defined in point e) of this Article or an on-demand audiovisual media service as defined in point (g) of this Article.

This definition, which is supported by a number of recitals, has a number of elements, all of which must be satisfied to constitute an AVMS (Recital 25 AVMS Directive) and is also dependent on the definition of 'programme', inserted during the drafting process as Article 1(b), and of 'media service provider' (MSP) (Article 1(d) AVMS Directive), the amended proposal accepting the European Parliament's suggested changes. The final version of the definition of AVMS clarifies that there are only two possible service types within its ambit: television/linear services; or on-demand/non-linear services. This version of the definition avoids the difficulties caused by the inclusion in earlier drafts (EC 2007b) of a third type of service, 'commercial communication', seemingly existing as a separate category of service.

The reference to 'services as defined by the Treaty' is intended to ensure that non-economic activities are kept out of the regulatory regime (see also Recital 15

AVMS Directive). Whilst the intention is laudable, it should be noted that the ECJ has typically taken a very wide view of when the freedom of provide services has been engaged,[11] so it is far from clear how much protection this element of the definition will give.[12] The intention to distinguish between economic activities and non-economic activities was also seen in the definition of 'editorial responsibility' in the March working paper version of the amended proposal (EC 2007b), which referred to content being assembled 'in a professional capacity'. Whilst this requirement would exclude those who provided content as part of a hobby (typical user generated content), 'professional' could be interpreted as 'in the course of business' and not necessarily linked to a media business. This element has been removed from the definition of editorial responsibility. The change is an improvement, as the requirement for 'professional capacity' was not only unclear but seemed inappropriate in this particular definition. The definition of editorial responsibility is more about control of decision-making.

The EC also suggested that the definition excluded those services where the audiovisual element is ancillary, such as gambling websites and search engines.[13] Many of the examples in the recitals are qualified by wording such as 'provided that their main purpose is not that of distributing audiovisual content' and 'as long as the principal purpose of the audiovisual media service is not reached', which suggest that a service which falls within one of these categories can still be an AVMS if that is its main function. It remains possible, moreover, to think of cases in which the ancillary or otherwise nature of a service may be less clear, such as someone trying to sell their own songs (as a professional even if unprofitable activity) via, for example, MySpace and including a video. Although the revisions to the draft introduced a specific exclusion of 'content generated by private users for the purposes of sharing and exchange within communities of interest' (Recital 16 AVMS Directive) as a result of some concerns expressed, *inter alia*, by the UK government, the boundary of this term is fluid.

The original EC proposal required the 'delivery of moving images with or without sound.' The current version of the definition refers to programmes, an element retained from the original Television without Frontiers Directive, though expanded. As noted, 'programme' is now defined, though as we shall see, it is not entirely unproblematic. The current text specifies in Article1b AVMS Directive that a programme is:

---

11 *Deliège* v. *Ligue Francophone de Judo et Disciplines Associées ASBL, Ligue Belge de Judo ASBL and others* (C-51/96 and C-191/97) [2000] ECR I-2549; *Françoise de Coster* v. *Collège des Bourgmestres et Echevins de Watermael-Boitsfort* (C-17/00) [2001] ECR I-9445

12 In the *Hieronymi Report*, EP Doc A6-0399/2006, the European Parliament proposed that Recital 13 be clarified to specify 'the economic element must be significant to justify the application of the Directive. Economic activities are normally provided for remuneration, intended for a certain period and characterised by a certain continuity; the assessment of the economic element is subject to the criteria and rules of the country of origin.'

13 Recital 18 AVMS Directive gives a non-exhaustive list of examples.

a set of moving images with or without sound constituting an individual item within a schedule or a catalogue established by a media service provider and whose form and content is comparable to the form and content of television broadcasting.

The reference to moving images excludes radio and newspapers, a point which is reinforced in the recitals (Recital 21 AVMS Directive). During the legislative process this recital was changed. In the March 2007 working paper version, Recital 16 as it was then also excluded 'stand-alone text-based services'. The meaning of 'stand alone' is open to interpretation: are we concerned with the content of the service or the way it is delivered? Teletext could fall either side of the line but, seeing as teletext fell within the scope of television broadcasting within the existing regime, it would appear to remain within the scope of the AVMS Directive.

Whether the definition operates to exclude private pop videos as not forming part of a catalogue of content remains unclear. For example, whilst we might say that a catalogue is a listing, does it matter whose listing it is, or for what purpose it was made? Further, must the catalogue entries comprise only audiovisual works? The scope of the term 'catalogue', which is also found in the definition of an 'on-demand service' (Article 1g AVMS Directive) and 'editorial responsibility' (Article 1c AVMS Directive), will be essential to determining the boundary of audiovisual media services.

One of the principal questions has been to determine what constitutes a television-like service: the basis of the definition of 'programme' is that the broadcast content is comparable to television broadcasting. It seems that what is key here is impact;[14] that what the AVMS Directive seeks to regulate is the mass media (again raising questions why certain mass media are excluded). Recital 16 AVMS Directive suggests that there is a two-fold element to identifying the mass media: those services which are both intended (presumably by the provider of the service) to be viewed by a large number and are so viewed.[15] The mass media aspect is reinforced by the requirement that the service be available to the general public, a requirement that would exclude private emails, or internal correspondence even of media companies themselves (Recital 18 AVMS Directive). This aspect is reinforced by the fact that according to the definition in Article 1a AVMS Directive, an audiovisual media service can only be provided 'under the editorial responsibility' of an MSP.

MSP then constitutes an element of audiovisual media service and raises the question of whether there is content that is excluded from the scope of the Directive because it has not been provided by a MSP. MSP is defined as 'the natural or legal person who has editorial responsibility for the choice of the audiovisual content of the audiovisual media service and determines the manner in which it is organised'

---

14   This approach seems to have been popular in the German literature: see Lutz (1996, 143) citing Gounalakis, G., 'Regulierung von Presse, Rundfunk und elektronischen Diensten in der zukünftigen Medienordnung' [2003] ZUM 180, pp 183, 186 and Blaue, A., 'Meinungsrelevanz und Mediennutzung – Su Konvergenz und Regulierung elektronisher Medien' [2005] ZUM 30, p. 34.

15   Interestingly, Recital 16 also suggests that such services 'have a clear impact' on viewers. It is to be hoped that this is a statement of the perceived impact of mass media services rather than as a requirement to have one, as this seems difficult to prove.

(Article 1d AVMS Directive). This is not particularly helpful, as potentially anyone providing content falls within it. The terms 'choice' and 'organised' could cover a number of levels of decision making within the media sector, (see also van den Bos 2006 on the difficulty of what is meant by organisational control) and it is not tied in to the provision of content to the public (whether as a linear or non-linear service) (Gibbons 2005). Contrast Gibbons's suggestion, which limits the scope of content providers to those who provide relevant content which 'is organised for the purpose of being accessed by the public'. Whilst this author is not sure that the phrase 'by the public' would not apply to fully on-demand services, this definition identifies the link between provider and viewer, which is where we might assume that regulation should most appropriately bite.

There are further drafting problems, which derive from the circularity of the definitions. To define programmes we need to understand broadcast services, and also MSP, but these terms depend on the meaning of programmes. Whilst to a certain extent definitions tend to be closed circuits, this is an extreme example. Furthermore, in including the requirement that programmes essentially are content that is television-like, an element of subjectivity is also introduced. In many cases, the matter may not be contentious, but the outer edges of the Directive will be where the difficulties will always lie. In this context, the recitals, an aid to teleological interpretation, are weak. They give examples of the sort of thing that will be a programme,[16] but assume that these types of programming (such as children's programmes) are themselves clear. Once again we are abandoned where the difficulties start and despite the Council's point that the definition of programme must be flexible,[17] we are left with the choice of a list based in television's past or a definition that is so 'dynamic' (Recital 17 AVMS Directive) it has little to grasp hold of.

Editorial responsibility is another term that occurs repeatedly. It is also one of the factors identified in the EC's list of six cumulative elements (EC 2006b). It is arguable that the reference here to editorial responsibility is unnecessary, given the definition of MSP, which is also based on editorial responsibility. Nonetheless, editorial responsibility suggests some intention to provide content that will be watched and this aspect is reflected in the requirement in the definition of audiovisual media service that the material be designed to 'inform, entertain and educate' and thus excludes, for example, traffic webcam footage (EC 2006b). Such an approach raises questions of what happens when that footage (or part of it) is turned into a fly on the wall so-called documentary, as increasingly seems to be the case these days. This example illustrates the point that the Directive's definitions are not based on the inherent nature or type of content, but are more connected with the way content, which fulfils certain physical criteria (i.e. being audiovisual), is disseminated. Pure

---

16   This list seems to originate from the Council: see Council of the European Union, Proposal for a Directive of the European Parliament and of the Council amending Council Directive 89/552/EEC on the coordination of certain provisions laid down by law, regulation or administrative Action in Member States concerning the pursuit of television activities (Television without Frontiers – General Approach', Note from the Presidency to the Council, 7 November 2006, Doc 14616/06, annex p. 3).

17   *Ibid.*

transmission, nonetheless, remains outside the Directive, as are services such as video stores and DVD rentals (EC 2006b), even those which have only an Internet presence.

We noted earlier the role of 'editorial responsibility' in identifying the boundary between content and transmission, and now, in the new definition, in identifying mass media content from other forms of audiovisual content. Despite its significance, the term has been problematic. Prior to the current revision process, the question had been raised as to whether the term identified the place in the distribution chain of content most appropriate/effective for regulatory purposes (Gibbons 2005). Of course, this to a certain extent depends on how we view 'editorial responsibility' and a number of possible interpretations could be put forward. In particular, the distinction between editorial responsibility on the level of the making of an individual programme; editorial responsibility in terms of the scheduling of programmes; responsibility in terms of the branding of a channel; and even the choice of the channels to make available (Harrison and Woods 1999). Whilst in a traditional environment all these activities might be carried out by the same legal entity, privatization, digitization and convergence have challenged that assumption.

The AVMS Directive recognizes the significance of the term:[18] following the European Parliament's first reading (European Parliament 2006) of the proposal (EC 2005), that institution's suggested definition of 'editorial responsibility' was accepted. This has been rephrased in the final version of the Directive as Article 1(c), together with Recital 23. Article 1(c) AVMS Directive seeks to clarify the point in the distribution chain at which the regulatory obligation will take effect, that is:

> the exercise of effective control both over the selection of the programmes and over their organisation either in a chronological schedule, in the case of television broadcasts, or in a catalogue, in the case of on-demand audiovisual media services.

Whilst this excludes both the making of individual programmes and also very general policy choices, it still seems to leave the possibility that a company responsible for a bouquet of channels and the company creating a channel could both be responsible for specific content. This double possibility existed also in Recital 17 of the March 2007 working version of the draft (EC 2007b). Indeed, Recital 17 in that version specified that editorial responsibility 'may apply to an individual content or a collection of contents.' Whilst this may be considered unproblematic in the context of what is regulated, if the same terms are used to determine geographical jurisdiction, conflicts, as to which regulatory has the responsibility to regulate, could arise.

The second main issue about scope relates to the internal boundary between linear and non-linear services. The AVMS Directive equates linear services to television broadcasting, which is a phrase used throughout the current version of Television without Frontiers Directive. Indeed, the AVMS Directive barely used the term 'linear' in its operative parts, referring instead to the old terminology of the Television without Frontiers Directive. Presumably, this is to avoid excessive

---

18   The Presidency note also suggested an amendment to the recitals clarifying the meaning of editorial responsibility, Doc 14616/06, Annex p. 2.

changes throughout the text of the Directive. Initially, the EC proposed that a linear service be defined as a service, 'where a media service provider decides upon the moment in time when a specific programme is transmitted and establishes the programme schedule', by contrast to the situation where a viewer chooses the time from a range of content made available by the service provider. The issue of timing which the ECJ identified in *Mediakabel* are thus reflected here.

There were concerns that the EC's proposal was not particularly clear (Castendyk and Bottcher 2006) and the amended proposal specifies that a linear service is one provided 'for the simultaneous viewing of programmes on the basis of a programme schedule' (Article 1e AVMS Directive). A non-linear service (or 'on-demand audiovisual media service'), by contrast, is one 'for the viewing of programmes at the moment chosen by the user and at his/her individual request on the basis of a catalogue of programmes selected by the media service provider' (Article 1g AVMS Directive). Technologies such as personal video recorders as well as services that allow for the personalization of schedules, pose difficult questions here. It is possible to pick further holes in this drafting, suggesting that the boundary between the two categories remains unclear. The definition of non-linear comprises three elements (timing, user request and catalogue). Is it possible for some but not all elements to be satisfied and if so, how will the service be regulated, especially given that only the two types of service identified are possible within the framework provided by AVMS Directive? As we have noted earlier, much will depend on the notion ascribed to 'catalogue', which will, presumably, be consistent in its usage in the AVMS Directive. Whilst this might raise some problems for the industry, the lack of clarity for viewers as to their level of protection in regard to different services is particularly problematic, as the point about the two types of service is that they are both by definition television-like. Further, it is possible, if not likely, that the same content could be delivered under both regimes.

The final problem concerning the scope of the AVMS Directive principally affects the industry and member states' regulators, as it concerns the extent to which non-linear service providers subject to the base level of regulation in the AVMS Directive could be caught by national rules aimed at protecting public interests not identified in Article 3b and 3h, but allowable under the e-Commerce Directive. In response to concerns expressed about this possibility, the redrafting of the proposal seeks to clarify the relationship between the two provisions. As Recital 2 to the original proposal noted, the derogation provisions of the e-Commerce Directive may contribute to different standards across the EU and consequently to barriers to trade. The implication from the recitals is that the AVMS Directive should be regarded as *lex specialis* in relation to non-linear audiovisual media services, providing for a higher degree of coordination of national laws than existed in relation to other information society services. This implication is given expression by Article 3(8), which deals with attempts to circumvent higher national standards (discussed below) specifies that in the event of a conflict between the AVMS and e-Commerce directives, the provisions of the AVMS Directive are to prevail. Further, Recital 35 now specifies that, with regard to on-demand audiovisual media services, 'restrictions on their free provision should only be possible in accordance with conditions and procedures replicating those already established by Articles 3(4), (5) and (6) of Directive

2000/31/EC'. Whilst this is not as clear as the earlier drafts (see Recital 24, EC 2007b), the implication is that the procedures in the AVMS Directive should replace the possible measures which could have previously been taken under either Article 3(4) and/or Article 12(3) of the e-Commerce Directive, at least so far as matters covered by Article 3b and 3h are concerned.

Jurisdiction: Which Member State Should Regulate?

The jurisdiction clause in its original version of the Television without Frontiers Directive was problematic. Essentially, it stated that jurisdiction fell to the responsibility of the member state that has jurisdiction, which is not helpful in the case of a dispute as to how one determines jurisdiction in the first place. That there were different possible interpretations of this point[19] became clear as a number of cases came before the ECJ. The dispute centred on whether the issue of jurisdiction was concerned with formal criteria of establishment or took into account where the transmission was intended to be received. This issue has significance for the effectiveness of a regulatory regime, if we assume that one of the functions of such a regime is to protect viewers in the light of the culture of the member state of citizens' residence. Disconnecting the regulatory regime from content seen in an area disconnects the viewer from the regime to which they are habituated.

The EC's view was unambiguous. In its first Report on the Application of Directive 89/552/EEC, it stated that the member state in which the broadcasting body was established would have jurisdiction 'irrespective of the destination of the broadcast' (EC 1996, Explanatory Memorandum, para. 101). This was not so clear to the member states. The UK government took the view that Article 2 should be interpreted in line with the Council of Europe Convention on Transfrontier Television, the terms of which broadly paralleled those of the Television without Frontiers Directive. On this basis, the UK suggested that jurisdiction had more to do with which member state had responsibility for the radio frequency used for the transmission as well as the country of destination.[20]

The EC brought an enforcement action against the UK.[21] There, the ECJ took an approach that favoured the formalistic model of country of origin, which looked to the member state in which the broadcaster was established, rather than the model based on control of the airwaves or country of destination model. In some sense recognizing the 'special' nature of broadcasting, the ECJ adapted the 'standard' test for establishment found in the *Factortame* case[22] by introducing an element

---

19 *Commission* v. *UK* (C-222/94) [1996] ECR I-4025, para. 46. The Advocate-General in his opinion in this case gives a thorough review of the possible interpretations of the jurisdiction clause.

20 *Ibid.*

21 *Ibid.*

22 *Factortame and Others* (C-221/89) [1991] ECR I-3905. The test is usually expressed as 'the actual pursuit of an economic activity through a fixed establishment in another Member State for an indefinite period' (para. 20). Interestingly, Wattel suggested, albeit in 1995, that a company that had no economic substance in the host member state and was a 'brass plate at

of editorial control. Thus, establishment arises for the purposes of the Television without Frontiers Directive in 'the place in which a broadcaster has the centre of its activities, in particular the place where decisions concerning programme policy are taken and the programmes to be broadcast are finally put together'.[23] The use of this test only becomes relevant if there is more than one possible location within the EU for the broadcaster and establishment remains irrelevant. In this we see the focus of regulation on the broadcaster rather than the broadcast itself, which has potential adverse consequences for the viewer in the state of reception. This approach was maintained, with the exception of the *De Agostini* case,[24] in subsequent cases which came before the ECJ and was applied in cases of double control, such as *VT4*[25] and *Denuit*.[26]

VT4 raised another issue, which periodically resurfaces in discussion on the regulation of television within Europe: that of the so-called abuse or circumvention of Community law. Essentially, abuse is perceived to occur when someone takes advantage of free movement rights to circumvent the national regulatory regime of the member state that contains the target market (audience). This concern had arisen in earlier broadcasting cases decided under the freedom to provide services. In its early jurisprudence in *van Binsbergen*,[27] the ECJ had accepted that Union law should not be used to avoid national regulation, but the scope of this principle was somewhat contentious as it undercuts the right of free movement and is therefore antithetical to the internal market ideal.

The ECJ addressed the matter in a number of broadcasting cases under Article 49 EC Treaty, notably *Veronica*[28] and *TV10*.[29] The ECJ's approach to the scope of the principle has not been consistent. In some cases it focused on the intent of the broadcaster rather than on the effect of the broadcaster's actions, and in other cases limited the doctrine's scope by reference to the interests which the member states

---

the front of some lawyer's office' should not be treated as satisfying the *Factortame* test, and its formal seat should be ignored in favour of economic reality, that is, the company would then not have exercised its right of free movement: Wattel (1995), pp. 1265–1267. Whether this is arguable post-*Centros* (*Centros Ltd* v. *Erhvervs-og Selskabsstyrelsen* (C-212/97) [1999] ECR I-1459) is debatable: see further below.

23 *Commission* v. *UK* (C-222/94) [1996] ECR I-4025.

24 *Joined Cases C-34-36/95 Konsumerntombudsmannen* v. *De Agostini (Svenska) Forlag AB and Konsumentombudsmannen* v. *TV-shop i Sverige AB* (C-34-36/95) [1997] ECR I-3843.

25 *VT4* v. *Vlaamse Gemeenschap* (C-56/96) [1997] ECR I-3143.

26 *Criminal Proceedings against Paul Denuit* (C-14/96) [1997] ECR I-2785.

27 *Van Binsbergen* v. *Bestuur van de Bedrijfsvereniging voor de Metaalnijverheid* (C-33/74) [1974] ECR 1299, para. 13: '... a member state cannot be denied the right to take measures to prevent the exercise, by a person providing services whose activity is entirely or principally directed towards its territory, of the freedom guaranteed by Article [49] for the purpose of avoiding the professional rules of conduct which would be applicable to him if he were established within that state ...'.

28 *Vereniging Veronica Omroep Organisatie* v. *Commisariaat voor de Media* (C-148/91) [1993] ECR I-487.

29 *TV10 SA* v. *Commissariaat voor de Media* (C-23/93) [1994] ECR I-4795.

sought to protect. In all cases, however, the ECJ has taken a narrower approach than in *van Binsbergen* (Woods and Scholes 1997, 57). The national regulator in *VT4*, another broadcasting case, put forward two arguments: that to rely on the freedoms, the service must be provided in the host state; and that, following *TV10*, where an operator directed all its output at another member state, it should be considered to be established there. The ECJ rejected both these arguments, but in terms that did not discuss the scope of the anti-avoidance doctrine, but rather focussed on the rights of the individual.[30] Some have seen this as implicitly overruling the anti-avoidance doctrine (Jones 1999/00), though this is open to debate. It could also be that member states still have the possibility to take action in the case of abuse, but the meaning of abuse was itself uncertain. In any event, the member states' freedom of action in this regard has been constrained.

One of the central revisions to the Television without Frontiers Directive in 1997 was the changes introduced to the jurisdiction clause. Relying heavily on the jurisprudence of the ECJ, it details various factual situations and the impact these differences might have on the determination of jurisdiction. The provisions in the revised Directive are more sophisticated than their predecessor and much clearer about the connecting factors to establish jurisdiction. The AVMS Directive is modelled closely on this provision, the changes firstly reflecting the extension to AVMS; and secondly, concerning satellite frequencies.

As already noted, of central importance to the determination of jurisdiction is the issue of editorial control, reflecting the approach taken by the ECJ in *Commission v. UK*. Thus Article 2(2) identifies jurisdiction as being where the broadcaster (or, under AVMS Directive, the MSP) has both head office and makes editorial decisions. Where these two factors do not occur in the same place, then other factors are taken into account, such as location of the workforce. The formal criterion of establishment, which focuses on the broadcaster, and the question of editorial control, which takes into account the content broadcast, seem thus to be equally weighted. Although some effort has gone in to taking account of the realities of the audiovisual industry in the EU, the final fall-back position in the jurisdiction clause at Article 2(5) AVMS Directive is the use of the *Factortame* test for establishment, re-emphasizing the formal model for country of origin, which permits the disassociation of a service's regulatory regime from the cultural expectations of viewers, as the underlying model for the Directive. That the primary concern of the Directive is the needs of industry is re-emphasized by the recitals.[31] The only reference to the viewer in this context is in Recital 9 AVMS Directive, which expresses viewers' needs as being met by having the right 'to choose from a wide variety of European programmes', an assumption which reflects the approach taken by the ECJ to consumer protection. There the view is that consumers are best served by choice, without consideration of whether the consumer is placed to make an informed choice, or has a meaningful choice. This does not protect those most in need of protection and a similar point can be made here (Harrison and Woods 2007).

---

30 *Commission* v. *UK* (C-222/94) [1996] ECR I-4025.

31 Recitals 27 and 28 AVMS Directive. Recital 29 AVMS Directive is particularly abstract in its language to the point where this author is not sure what it means.

We have already seen, in relation to the definition of audiovisual services, that a central question is the level at which editorial policies might be expected to be taken. Similar issues arise in relation to jurisdiction. If we look back at the ECJ's views then it seems that either programme-based decisions or more general policy level decisions could constitute 'editorial decisions.'[32] As noted above, different levels of decision making take place at different levels of corporate structure, which may in these days of multinational corporations, take place in different countries. The determination of what an editorial decision is may have significance for the question of which member state has jurisdiction over a given operator. We now have the additional question of whether editorial decision has the same meaning for Article 2 as it does in determining the meaning of audiovisual media service. Whilst common sense suggests that it does, it should be noted that the most recent round of amendments tie the definition of editorial responsibility in to the definitions sections alone.

Concerns have always existed about the possible misuse of the country of origin principle, as expressed in the jurisdiction clause. The AVMS Directive introduces provisions which allow member states to counter 'abuse or fraudulent conduct', subject to compliance with certain procedural requirements (EC 2005) though the wording of these provisions has changed during the drafting process. There are thus two exceptions to the principle of freedom of retransmission in Article 2a: the derogation provisions triggered by manifest, serious and grave infringements of the negative content rules provisions (Article 22(1) or (2), Article 3b);[33] and the anti-avoidance rules now proposed in Article 3(2) *et seq.* which relate to the higher standards which member states under Article 3(1) may impose on those established within their respective jurisdictions.

The proposal has been controversial and there have been a number of changes to the drafting through the legislative process. Significantly, the EC's original proposal did not define what was meant by 'abuse or fraudulent conduct', specifying that the requirement to act is to be proven on a case-by-case basis. Whilst the AVMS Directive no longer refers to 'abuse or fraudulent conduct', the recitals suggest, however, that the provision was intended to codify the ECJ's jurisprudence in this regard (Recital 32 AVMS Directive). We have seen that the jurisprudence was far from clear (Harrison and Woods 2007). In particular, the level of intent on the part of the person seeking to abuse Community law to justify member states' action was uncertain from the case law, as was the scope of the public policy objectives which might justify a member state seeking to take action against such a person.

The European Parliament's amendments sought to clarify that a member state may take action to protect only certain interests: 'public policy, including the protection of minors or public security or public health or the protection of cultural

---

32   Whether there is any significance in the difference in terminology between Articles 2(3)(a) and (b) AVMS Directive on the one hand and Article 2(3)(c) AVMS Directive on the other is also not clear.

33   There is also a special emergency procedure available in relation to non-linear services: Article 2a(4) AVMS Directive. As noted, for non-linear services this replaces the possibilities for Member States' actions in the e-Commerce Directive.

diversity' (EC 2007b, Article 3(2)(b)). The AVMS Directive as adopted refers once again only to 'rules of general public interest' (Article 3(2)(a) AVMS Directive). If we accept that *VT4* repudiates the anti-avoidance doctrine, this is wider scope for member states than under the EU Treaty. Alternatively, we can say *VT4* says nothing about the existence or scope anti avoidance doctrine, and discuss where the other cases lead us. In so far as the AVMS Directive deals with the grounds on which member states may take action, it follows of the line taken by the more limiting case, *Veronica*.

As regards the intent of the broadcaster, the original proposal for the AVMS Directive referred only to some of the ECJ's case law: *van Binsbergen*, *TV10* and *Centros* (a company law case), suggesting that the EC was taking a partial view of the ECJ's jurisprudence. These cases are now no longer referred to in the recitals. Instead, the test of when a member state may take action has been clarified and tightened up. The procedure involves two stages. The first permits a member state to request the member state with jurisdiction to take action against a broadcaster, and arises when a broadcaster[34] is acting in an abusive or fraudulent manner. The determination of this point, in the first instance, lies in the power of the member state, though presumably always subject to Community law (whatever that, in this context, might require). The second stage allows the recipient member state itself to take action. Here the test has changed during the legislative process. At one point, the wording suggested that a member state would be able to rely on this provision if avoidance were the sole motivation for the broadcaster's location in that state (EC 2007b). Under this version, when a broadcaster established itself elsewhere partly to avoid recipient state rules, Article 3(3) would not have applied. In the final version, however,. a member state may take action where the service provider 'has established itself in the member state having jurisdiction in order to avoid the stricter rules …' (Article 3(3)(b) AVMS Directive). The use of the word 'solely', which was inserted at the request of the European Parliament, and which took no account of the relative weighting of other reasons has been removed. This seems closer to the existing case law. Even in *TV10*, the ECJ's formulation was that the company must have been established 'in order to' enable it to avoid the relevant mandatory rules in the receiving member state. Although this formulation suggests that motive must be established *ab initio*, it does not require that avoidance be the sole motive.

In any event, the issue of proof in this regard will always be difficult. It seems that the burden of proof will fall on the member state seeking to rely on the provisions. Proving intent is difficult, although Recital 33 AVMS Directive lists some examples of factors member states could take into account: the origin of the television advertising and/or subscription revenues; the main language of the service; or the existence of programmes or commercial communications targeted specifically at the general public in the member state. Assumptions about where broadcasters might 'normally' be established given the language spoken or the nationality of the employees comes

---

34   There was ugly drafting in this document in the March 2007 version (EC 2007b) to the effect that whilst Article 3(2)(c) refers to 'broadcaster', Article 3(3) then refers to audiovisual media services provider. Whilst as a matter of law this probably worked, the reference to 'audiovisual media services provider' has been replaced by the word 'broadcaster'.

close to nationality discrimination, however, and, following *VT4*, the mere fact that a broadcaster is established in one member state and directs its transmissions at another does not take the broadcaster outside Community law.

Conclusions

As the history of the Television without Frontiers Directive shows, regulation of the media has always been contentious, and the now not-so-new media have proved to be no exception. Member states and the different institutions have had different views on the appropriate balance to be drawn, based on many considerations – the market, the need to protect culture and even other societal values. Whilst the main compromise to extend the scope of the Directive may have been reached, questions still remain about the detail. The boundaries of the Directive remain unclear, partly due to the changing nature of the audiovisual sector. The terminology in the Directive, however, compounds the difficulty as it is subjective and circular and, in seeking to be technology neutral and produces definitions which are capable of meaning anything. One might criticize drafting which repeatedly relies on the same terms, so that the definitions provisions, rather than nesting neatly inside one another like Russian dolls, more resembles an abstract watercolour on which water has been spilt. With goodwill, many of the difficulties might resolve themselves; the alternative is, as Ofcom has suggested, that there are too many gaps for the national regulators to fill in, resulting in uncertainty and inequality.

In discussions about the detail, a point of principle may be lost. As Commissioner Redding argued in relation to the extension of the Directive to non-linear services, it is hard to justify different regulatory regimes for similar content. Yet, with the introduction of a two-tier system, different regulatory regimes remain. Whilst the definitional difficulties may create uncertainty for the industry, many of whom can afford to pay for legal advice, the viewer is not so fortunate. It seems likely that many will judge the media companies providing non-linear services to be playing by the same rules as their linear counterparts. The *Mediakabel* case, and the arguments about the boundary between NVOD and VOD there, is a particularly telling example of the problems in this area. Such an approach is hardly taking much account of viewer protection, particularly in respect of vulnerable viewers who are not necessarily media literate.

Questions of viewer protection also arise in relation to a discussion of the jurisdiction clause, which famously allows the dislocation of content from the regulatory culture of the viewer. The prioritizing within the EU of trade concerns over non-trade values is well known. With regard to the amendments to the jurisdiction clause, a narrow formulation (though not the narrowest formulation in all cases) has been proposed to all the exceptions. This is not surprising. What is surprising is the re-introduction of the anti-avoidance doctrine at all, a re-weighting, however slight, in the balance between national control and free movement. What seems likely is that any such exception will be for exceptional use only and should not trouble industry too much. The change may therefore be significant in principle, but in practice the protection it would grant to viewers applies only in extreme circumstances and is therefore of only limited value.

References

Castendyk, O. and Bottcher, K. (2006), 'The Commission's Proposal for a New Directive on Audiovisual Content – A Feasible Solution', *Ent. L. Rev* 17(6), 174–180.

Council of the European Union (2006), Proposal for a Directive of the European Parliament and of the Council amending Council Directive 89/552/EEC on the coordination of certain provisions laid down by law, regulation or administrative Action in Member States concerning the pursuit of television activities (Television without Frontiers – General Approach, Note from the Presidency to the Council, 7 November 2006, Doc 14616/06.

European Commission (1984), Green Paper on Television without Frontiers COM(84) 300, Brussels, 14 June 1984.

European Commission (1995), Report on the Application of Directive 89/552/EEC and a Proposal for a European Parliament and Council Directive amending Council Directive 89/552/EEC COM(95) 86 final, Brussels, 31 May 1995.

European Commission (1996), Amended proposal for a directive amending Council Directive 89/552/EEC on the coordination of certain provisions laid down by law, regulation or administrative action in Member States concerning the pursuit of television broadcasting activities COM (96) 200 final, Brussels, 7 May 1996.

European Commission (2002a), Directive of the European Parliament and of the Council (EC) 2002/21 of 7 March 2002 on a common regulatory framework for electronic communications networks and services [2002] OJ L108/33.

European Commission (2002b), Directive of the European Parliament and of the Council (EC) 2002/19 of 7 March 2002 on access and interconnection [2002] OJ L108/7.

European Commission (2002c), Directive of the European Parliament and of the Council (EC) 2002/20 of 7 March 2002 on the authorisation of electronic communications networks and services [2002] OJ L108/21.

European Commission (2002d), Directive of the European Parliament and of the Council (EC) 2002/22 of 7 March 2002 on universal service and users' rights relating to electronic communications networks and services [2002] OJ L108/51.

European Commission (2002e), Directive of the European Parliament and of the Council (EC) 2002/58 of 12 July 2002 on data protection and privacy [2002] OJ L108/37.

European Commission (2005a), *Commission Proposal for a Directive amending Directive 89/552/EEC, COM(2005)646 final*, 2005/0260 (COD), SEC (2005).

European Commission (2005b), Proposal for a Directive of the European parliament and of the Council amending Council Directive 89/552/EEC on the coordination of certain provisions laid down by law, regulation or administrative action in Member States concerning the pursuit of television broadcasting activities COM

(2005) 646 final, Brussels, 13 December 2005.

European Commission (2006a), *Communication on the Review of the EU Regulatory Framework for electronic communications networks and services*, Communication from the Commission to the Council, the European Parliament, the European Economic and Social Committee and the Committee of the Regions COM(2006) 334 final, Brussels, 29 June 2006.

European Commission (2006b), *Definition in the proposal for an Audiovisual Media Services Directive*, non-paper, February 2006, available on http://europa.eu.int/comm/avpolicy/regul//regul_en.htm#4.

European Commission (2006c), *Definitions in the proposal for an Audiovisual Media Services Directive*, non-paper.

European Commission (2007a), Amended Proposal for a Directive of the European parliament and of the Council amending Council Directive 89/552/EEC on the coordination of certain provisions laid down by law, regulation or administrative action in Member States concerning the pursuit of television broadcasting activities COM (2007) 170 final, Brussels, 29 March 2007.

European Commission (2007b), *Non-binding Working Doc rev.* 2, March 2007.

European Parliament (2006), Hieronymi Report, EP Doc A6-0399/2006.

Gibbons, T. (2005), Gibbons, T. (2005), 'Jurisdiction Over (Television) Broadcasters: Criteria for Defining "Broadcaster" and "Content Service Provider"', in H. Rossnagel (ed.), *Die Zukunft der Fernsehrichtlinie/The Future of the 'Television without Frontiers' Directive* (Schriftenreihe des Instituts für Europäisches Medienrecht (EMR), Saarbrücken, Band 29), Baden-Baden: Nomos Verlagsgesellschaft.

Harrison, J., and Woods, L. (2000), 'Broadcasting Regulation in the Internal Market: An Analysis of EU Audiovisual Policy', in T. Lees et al. (eds) *Is Regulation Still and Option in a Digital Universe.* Luton: University of Luton Press.

Harrison J., and Woods, L. (2007), 'Introduction' in *EC Broadcasting Law and Policy.* Cambridge: Cambridge University Press.

Jones, C.A. (1999/00), 'Television without Frontiers', *Yearbook of European Law* 19, 299–345.

Keller, P. (1997/8), 'The New Television without Frontiers Directive', *Yearbook of Media and Entertainment Law* 3, 177–195.

Lutz, H. (2006), 'the Distinction between Linear and Non-linear services in the New Proposal for an Audiovisual Media Directive', C.T.L.R 12(5) 141–144.

Ofcom (2006), 'Assessing Indirect Impacts of the EC Proposals for Video Regulation', Commissioned report by RAND: Marsden, C., Cave, M., et al., available at http://www.ofcom.org.uk/research/tv/reports/videoregulation.

van den Bos, J.W. (2006), 'No Frontiers: The New EU proposal on Audiovisual Media Services', 17(4) *Ent. L Rev.* 109–113.

Wattel, P.J. (1995), 'Note on Case C-23/93 *TV10 SA* v. *Commissariaat voor de Media*: Circumvention of National Law; Abuse of Community Law?', *Common Market Law Review* 32, 1257–1270.

Woods, L., and Scholes, J. (1997), 'Broadcasting: The Creation of a European Culture or the Limits of the Internal Market?' *Yearbook of European Law*, 17 47–82.

Chapter 8

Content Ratings Harmonization and the Protection of Minors in the European Information Society

Oliver Carsten Füg

While minors have always sought exposure to media deemed to be unsuitable for children by adults, a number of developments in the media industries has both facilitated and encouraged shifts in media usage that affect minors' behaviour. The pathways in which this influence plays out ultimately depends on individual circumstances and therefore do not allow for schematic predictions based on the type of content, the age of the viewer or any combination of the two. Still it is maintained here that developments in the structural features of the media landscape have increased both usage opportunities and risk potential for minors. The salient factors in this respect are the changing strategies of content development as well as developments in content production and content access technologies. As content consumption opportunities have multiplied and increased in quality minors have emerged as one of the most financially viable target groups (Strasburger and Wilson 2002) as media products have become increasingly differentiated. In the print media, specialist journals now cater to a wide range of minors' interests, including comics, lifestyle, music, sports or games magazines. Other examples of such content differentiation include the production of new children's programmes and the growth of special interest channels targeted at young audiences. The latter strategy is complemented by differentiation efforts in the games industry, one of the largest and most lucrative markets for audiovisual content.

It is also in the games industry that the question of how media content shapes minors' behaviour has become most relevant. Based on advances in microchip design and computing power, ever more sophisticated means of virtual representation have become possible, lending a degree of realism that has far outstripped the pixelated worlds of early computer games. In addition to creating parallel worlds for minors to explore, computer based production technologies also enable the editing of real world materials in ways that may yield unrealistic, yet strongly suggestive depictions capable of exerting a relatively stronger influence on the impressionable minds of the young than on those of seasoned media users. Combined with an ever earlier exposure to such content, a frame of reference emerges in which the distinction between the 'real' and the 'virtual' is less succinct, thus contributing to an impoverished understanding of the real world and its effects, which may amplify the consequences of undesirable conduct such as aggressive behaviour (Villani 2001).

However, the ability to discriminate between the two realms and accurately grasp the meaning and implications of on-screen representations becomes crucially important where representations can endanger the health and safety of those imitating them in 'real life'. Negative effects may be stronger still when minors participate in the enactment of violence through computer or video games. Where game consoles further include Internet capabilities, they allow for the embedding of simulated in-game reality into the virtual reality of cyberspace.

This points more generally to changes in the content that access technologies make available to minors: whereas children in many families did not have access to their own television set two decades ago, today general media usage and thus exposure to audiovisual content is far higher. Minors are often at the vanguard of employing new media technologies, their playfulness and curiosity making them more open to new forms of media usage than the average consumer. At the same time, their inherent tendency towards experimentation leads them to explore new, unanticipated ways of using media technologies. With the advent of mobile phones capable of receiving both multimedia messages and television broadcasts, handheld gaming devices with similar reception capacities, and the emerging uptake of computer and Internet usage among primary schoolchildren, the media environment for children has been considerably enlarged beyond television.

The risk profile of children's media consumption is therefore continually evolving, mediated by cognitive precepts and socially conditioned taste as well as by the platform through which the content reaches the child (Eveland 2003). The same audiovisual work may be delivered through a handheld device or shown on the screen of a movie theatre, yet the ability to elicit intense reactions among members of the audience by virtue of the overpowering effect of the visual dimension alone is more pronounced in the latter case. On the other hand, devices that are subject to a child's own control without the moderating role of an adult or the limiting selection of a pre-scheduled programme may more readily be employed for exploratory media behaviour that can confront children with unforeseen and potentially unpleasant or shocking content.

Taken together, the media environment surrounding minors has gained significantly in complexity with the emergence of new media outlets, changes in production technology and diversification of access technologies. The financial attractiveness of youth audiences to producers of audiovisual content and commercial derivatives, content packagers and distributors, and the advertising industry adds an additional layer of potential risk comprising threats such as abusive marketing techniques and violations of privacy rights. The new media landscape of the information society places every conceivable type of content only one click away – including the new dangers associated with it.

Both at the national and European levels, policy makers are faced with the challenge of devising solutions that allow minors to benefit from participation in the information society while being adequately protected against information that threatens their development. Given the variety and mutability of possible threats, it is little wonder that a wide variety of institutions are now attempting to address different aspects of the threat scenario. At the European Commission (EC) alone, protecting minors in the information society spans the services of the Directorates

General for the Information Society, Health and Consumer Protection, Education and Culture, and the Internal Market who deal with issues as diverse as media and information literacy, media violence, advertising and child obesity, commercial communications, data protection, and so on. The tools employed to cope with these issues are equally diverse, ranging from legislative and regulatory measures designed to impose obligations on service providers to 'soft' measures such as reliance on industry self-regulation and a variety of pragmatic efforts to strengthen technological solutions. While the policy mix employed by different member states to meet their obligations under European Union (EU) law regarding the protection of minors from potentially harmful content varies across jurisdictions, the commitment to this objective has remained strong throughout the development of European audiovisual and information society policies and is articulated as such by its member states in the wider context of the Council of Europe.[1]

Against this background, the following analysis traces the concern for the protection of minors in European audiovisual and information society policy and explicates how this has developed in terms of regulatory emphasis and the range of supporting mechanisms promoted to develop a safe media environment for minors. Distinguishing three broad stages of policy development, it focuses on the role that content classification and notably the idea of a unified regulatory approach across different delivery platforms has played as a mechanism at the European level. A first section briefly establishes the background to Community level regulation with the advent of the Television without Frontiers Directive[2] and its approach to the protection of minors. In a second step, the conceptual development spurred in reaction to the rise of the Internet and its distinct threats to minors is mapped and the concomitant widening of the policy toolkit at European level explored, highlighting the establishment of an overarching approach to the protection of minors parallel to continued sectoral developments in the broadcasting field and the emergence of new initiatives with regard to the Internet. Considering the further development and consolidation of this policy framework, and the amendments proposed in the context of the Television without Frontiers Directive's expansion to cover audiovisual media services, which constitute the main features of the third period of European policy development moves the debate into contemporary terrain. A final section concludes by re-examining the regulatory tools available with a view to assessing the future feasibility of a unified pan European content classification system.

---

1   Most recently with the adoption of Recommendation Rec(2006)12 of the Committee of Ministers to Member States on empowering children in the new information and communications environment on 27 September 2006.

2   Directive 89/552/EEC on the coordination of certain provisions laid down by law, regulation or administrative action in Member States concerning the pursuit of television broadcasting activities [1989] OJ L 298/23, as amended by Directive 2007/65/EC [2007] OJ L332/27.

Period 1: The Television Age

The first discussions of how to incorporate the regard for an audiovisual environment responsive to the special needs and requirements of minors into a European regulatory framework arose with the deregulation of national television broadcasting systems and the introduction of commercial television broadcasting services across member states in the late 1980s. Following a failed attempt at establishing a European television programme, Community broadcasting policy embraced a regulatory approach envisaging a single market for television broadcasts. As national broadcasting laws had evolved historically without regard to the object of an overarching European broadcasting market, the provisions of national regulations, and especially those pursuing public interest objectives, were seen to be so divergent as to possibly impede the emergence of a pan European market. In order to facilitate the provision of broadcasting services in a trans-border context, the Council adopted the Television without Frontiers Directive for the coordination of national broadcasting laws in a number of areas. The protection of minors became part of this regulatory effort both as an area of coordination in its own right and as part of the provisions relating to television advertising. Under the first of these two regulatory strands the Directive addressed the core concern of safeguarding minors against exposure to unsuitable material, whereas the second interjected a prohibition against the exploitation of minors' credulity in the context of commercial communications.

The mechanism to achieve a safe viewing environment for children and youth comprised a complete ban on programmes perceived to seriously impair the physical, mental or moral development of minors, notably pornography and gratuitous violence, and a conditional ban on those likely to impair their development, unless exposure of minors to such programming could generally be prevented by virtue of scheduling or the use of technical means. The rules for television advertising addressing minors mirrored the thrust of the rules for programme content in requiring that such advertising in general did not cause any moral or physical detriment to minors, and specifically prohibited advertising of alcoholic drinks to minors and advertising depicting minors consuming such beverages.

Compliance with these rules was to be ensured in line with the country of origin principle, according to which each member state would have to enforce the rules laid down by the Directive vis à vis broadcasters operating within their jurisdiction, even where these did not target domestic audiences. The special importance afforded to the well being of minors was highlighted by providing for the only exception from this principle. A receiving state could thus suspend retransmission of broadcasts from another member state where these broadcasts manifestly, seriously and gravely infringed the provisions on the protection of minors concerning programming content. By allowing for this exception, member states were ultimately empowered to bring their own understanding of what constituted content likely to impair the development of minors to bear on broadcasts originating outside their jurisdiction.

Rating and labelling of television content for the protection of minors was to occur exclusively on the basis of national assessment schemes embedded in their respective cultural backgrounds. Although legislative attention in this sense did not rest on embedding particular technical measures for the protection of minors in Community legislation, the provisions concerning precautionary mechanisms for ensuring suitability of content for underage audiences demonstrated that one possible starting point for a shared regulatory technique could be the notion of temporality and its implied link to social expectations about the proper time for televising potentially harmful content. While the implementation of such a watershed would differ according to socio-cultural circumstances, the category as such proved to be immediately recognizable to policy makers and capable of implementation.

Period 2: Labelling Internet Content

During the early to mid 1990s, Community policy, following the move towards liberalization in the regulation of telecommunications, laid the foundations for the concept of a European information society. Parallel to the convergence of delivery platforms facilitated by digitalization, the Community at this time witnessed the emergence of a range of new services delivered over these converged networks, including near video on demand, pay per view and digital television in the field of broadcasting, and the delivery of various types of content over the Internet.

In October 1996, the EC issued two policy documents intended to address the challenges that these new services were seen to pose to public interest objectives, and notably the protection of minors. A Green Paper on the Protection of Minors and Human Dignity in Audiovisual and Information Society Services (EC 1996a) was drawn up to generate a discussion of the guiding principles for the proper regulatory approach to sustaining these values in the medium to long term, whilst a Communication on Illegal and Harmful Content on the Internet (EC 1996b) embedded this discussion in the context of a more short term–oriented, action-focused approach to a wider range of Internet related issues. The specific problems concerning the protection of minors raised at this point related to abusive marketing and violent and pornographic content – concerns that had already been aired in the discussions preceding the adoption of the Television without Frontiers Directive, but which were now presenting themselves anew in a potentially less controllable environment.

The Green Paper defined the challenges associated with these new services as deriving primarily from their special propagation and diffusion characteristics. While the content transmitted could remain the same as in traditional broadcasting, the technological capacity to transform recipients into retransmitters posed severe challenges to centralistic regulatory solutions that had been developed with the traditional point to multipoint transmission model in mind. In response to these challenges, the EC proposed a wide range of possible measures, including self-regulatory arrangements alongside educational efforts and the development of parental control systems (EC 1996a, 1).

The Communication, on the other hand, was based on the key conceptual distinction between illegal and harmful content. The meaning of this distinction becomes clear when placing it in the context of the topics addressed by the Green Paper: the concept of harmful content was tied to the protection of minors, whereas illegal content per definition was considered a threat to human dignity. By this non self evident definition of the two key categories for content classification, the EC implied that rating systems designed for the protection of minors would cover all of the content considered to be harmful, whereas outside that remit only illegal or harmless content was to be found.

Rating mechanisms were discussed both in the overarching Green Paper and in the Internet-specific discussion of the Communication, albeit each of these documents placed different emphases on their utility as a tool for dealing with problematic content. The Communication portrayed rating mechanisms as a supplementary tool to be used in addition to labelling based software to restrict access to content deemed inappropriate by a parent or legal guardian. Particular reference was here being made to the Platform for Internet Content Selection (PICS) initiative launched by the W3 consortium in May 1996 and its use of 'value neutral labelling' which due to the wide extent of industry support enjoyed by it and the self reported immunity to manipulation was seen to proffer an especially promising means of addressing the challenge of harmful Internet content.[3] While the Green Paper agreed to the potential offered by PICS to assist parents in making informed content choices on behalf of their children, it recognized at the same time the possibility of developing common standards for rating systems as a way of reinforcing the protection of minors. As part of the effort to define the future regulatory strategy to accommodate the emergence of new services, the EC raised a number of questions that it regarded as crucial in this regard to be addressed in the subsequent consultation. Among these was the question of whether a future approach to parental control devices was to be based on legislation or self regulation, and which role there was for the Community in this regard, as well as the question under what circumstances parental control should be automatically integrated into a service, and whether or not this should be compulsory.

In conclusion, the Communication adopted a heavily self-regulatory approach focused on industry led cooperation in conjunction with supporting technical measures, in which the development of rating mechanisms was recognized only as part of a purely technical adjustment strategy to deliver localized content evaluation. The emphasis here was on end user responsibility, and this extended to the protection of minors as well. The Green Paper presented a more balanced approach to the question of how to balance regulatory and user centred technology solutions to protect minors, although this might arguably have been a simple reflection of the fact that the remit assigned to the paper, and notably its long-term orientation, facilitated a more balanced approach. In as far as the Communication was meant to define short-term priorities of European public policy towards the evolving information society, it signalled a turn towards self-regulation as the predominant regulatory mode.

As the debate on the Green Paper continued, the EC negotiated, under the impression of an increased uptake of satellite broadcasting technology, an amendment of the Television without Frontiers Directive, which brought the issue of technological solutions for the protection of minors back into the remit of regulatory policy. During the discussions preceding the adoption of an amending Directive on 30 June 1997, both the European Parliament and Council thus focused on the possibility of linking a systematic classification of content to a parental control mechanism inspired by the proposed introduction of the V -Chip in the United States, a technology pioneered by

---

3   For a specification of the PICS system, see Miller et al. (1996).

the Canadian legislature to facilitate filtering of violent television content.[4] This chip was regarded by Parliamentarians as a useful device to counter what was perceived to be an increase in the amount and intensity of violent television programming, and by that token enforce the Directive's prohibition against violent television content likely to seriously impair the development of minors as well as to help parents in making prudent viewing choices for their children. As the Council and Parliament could not reach an agreement on the compulsory usage of this or any other particular parental control technology, the Directive instead entrusted the EC with carrying out of a study on possible technical devices to be fitted on new television sets to enhance parental viewing control. Additionally, the investigation was to consider the appropriateness of setting up rating systems and promoting educational and awareness measures to bolster a safe media environment for minors. This compromise solution was accompanied by an extension of advertising related safeguards and efforts to further clarify the distinction between different levels of threat posed by certain content for the well being of minors.

The Directive responded to the advent of teleshopping by replicating the protective standards applicable to television advertising and adding the requirement that minors must not be exhorted to purchase or rent goods or services by teleshopping offers. On the issue of programmes that were likely to have negative consequences for the moral, physical or mental development of minors, and therefore could either be banned completely from screening or made subject to a requirement of suitable technical precautions, the Directive clarified that neither one measure depended on prior control of programming for its effectiveness. It further added to them a third provision demanding the identification of un-encoded broadcasts containing potentially harmful material by way of an acoustic warning or through a visual symbol. Given the state of the European broadcasting landscape at the time of the revision, this requirement applied to the vast majority of television channels. It made it clear that the popular watershed technique that had been adopted in several member states in response to the requirements of the original Television without Frontiers Directive was no longer sufficient to protect minors where the broadcast signal was not encrypted. Simultaneously, the new provision served to illustrate what type of technical measure might be sufficient to adequately prevent harmful audiovisual material from being accessed by minors, thereby illustrating one intersection of legal and technological form that could be amalgamated into a regulatory provision.

Although the compromise thus reached was met with criticism by a number of broadcasters that felt that the provision was unable to accommodate the specific character of their activities,[5] the Directive was generally well received. With the addition of the new provision the Community legislature demonstrated how a higher degree of technical specification for the mechanisms to protect minors from unsuitable audiovisual content could be achieved in regulatory terms, without excessively constraining broadcasters' freedom of expression. With regard to the role of European policy in securing the protection of minors the field of emerging new services, the follow up communication on the Green Paper concluded that emphasis

---

4   For an overview of the evolution of the V -chip in the US, see Kamarck (1996).
5   For an example of such criticism, see the statement by Stock (1997).

was to be placed on ensuring coherence between national self-regulatory schemes and encouraging cooperation at the European level. To this end a recommendation covering both audiovisual and information society services without regard to the medium of transmission was proposed, suggesting:

- the development of a specific methodology to deal with issues of protecting minors and human dignity;
- the adoption of a set of common guidelines for the implementation of national self-regulation schemes; and
- the enactment of initiatives to promote access to new services and the production of quality content for minors, to fight illegal content and to develop new means of parental control.

Already at this point, the questions posed by the Green Paper regarding possible approaches to the normative embedding of parental control devices, the EU's role in determining the shape of parental control regimes and the compulsory integration of parental control features into specific services had been abandoned in favour of a clear emphasis on national industry-led, self-regulatory schemes as the solution to the question of how to best construct a viable scheme for the protection of minors. Indeed, the EC's summary of the responses received did not make any explicit reference to the original questions raised and left the issue of additional binding legislative initiatives untouched. Instead, the Recommendation was to act as a complement to existing Community legislation and provide a structuring, but not obliging measure for new online services. It suggested that new activities across both industries were to be built around the principle of voluntary action on behalf of service providers to further the application of protective technology solutions, with member states adopting a facilitating role in this respect that might have an encouraging effect on the uptake of new technologies for the protection of minors. After the recent completion of the Television without Frontiers review, television broadcasters were unlikely to incur additional obligations unless technological developments promised to improve their competitive standing or national governments provided significant incentive measures for doing so.

Online services, on the other hand, were to find their frame of reference in self-regulatory efforts by service operators themselves who would make technology choices as these were deemed appropriate to their business activities. With regard to the nature of the self-regulatory schemes to be instituted, the Recommendation pointed towards the adoption of codes of conduct to address the protection of minors and human dignity. Specifically for the protection of minors, the guidelines envisaged the working together of four distinct measures complemented by a wider effort to heighten awareness and media literacy among young users. In addition to general information being provided to adult users about the content or services and the setting up of complaints handling procedures in the form of hotlines, the guidelines suggested, where possible, a range of technical means to alter the presentation of legal, but potentially harmful content and the enhancement of opportunities for parental control. Echoing the results of the review, these featured the use of visual or sound signals to highlight problematic content, plus the introduction of warning pages, descriptive labelling and/or classification of content as well as age verification systems. For the purpose of strengthening parental control of content accessible to minors, filtering devices either activated by parents themselves or implemented by operators at a higher level of the content supply chain were recommended in line with the earlier Communication on Harmful and Legal Content on the Internet (EC 1996b).

Whereas the draft Recommendation discussed a larger menu of technological means, it did not reflect further on the regulatory options available. Its main emphasis lay on the general facilitation of further development in this area by enabling exchange between stakeholders within the structural parameters of a shared framework. Enabling the interaction between different sides of the market could be interpreted as crucial in a period when online services were not yet a mass phenomenon, but service provision was in need of a framework capable of promoting trust in the online environment, especially with regard to the protection of minors. Given a relative lack of experience in regulating the Internet in member state jurisdictions, a preponderance of self-regulatory models in those countries where frameworks had been established and the striking down of the Communications Decency Act in the United States earlier that year,[6] a solution on which subsequent bottom-up harmonization could build constituted a response adequate to the young age of the medium and open to future elaboration, while receptive to national sensitivities. Thus strengthening the effectiveness of national self-regulatory regimes through the introduction of common standards promised both immediate benefits in the short term and kept alive the prospect of future Community regulatory involvement in this field.

In 1997 the EC published the Green Paper on the Convergence of the Telecommunications, Media and Information Technology Sectors, and the Implications for Regulation (EC 1997c). Drawing on the wide range of activities carried out by the EC services during the preceding 18 months, the Green Paper cut across these specific discussions by establishing a distinction between content and infrastructure as the organizing framework for regulatory activity. Arguing that the technologically conditioned character of service delivery might call for a re-evaluation of the manner in which existing normative rules for the realization of these objectives should be applied, the Green Paper made it clear that an unaltered extension of the old broadcasting rules to new services was unlikely. Indeed, appropriate sensitivity to differences between services was seen to constitute a major precondition of ensuring adequate protection of minors in the new audiovisual environment. Pervasiveness of service delivery was here invoked as a possible starting point for moderating the level of intensity of regulatory obligations: to the extent that end users themselves were able to exercise individual control of the services delivered, lighter touch regulation might be sufficient for the fulfilment of public interest objectives. By proposing a regulatory mix for Internet services characterized by self-regulatory practices in conjunction with technological means of aiding parents in assuming greater responsibility in controlling viewing behaviour, the EC sought to strike a balance between conceding the continued relevance of public interest objectives, and the prospective unfolding of the nascent online economy.

---

6   Communications Decency Act, enacted by the US Congress on February 1, 1996, Title V, USC, Section 501.

Based on the EC's proposal, the Council of Ministers on 24 September 1998 adopted a Recommendation on the development of the competitiveness of the European audiovisual and information services industry by promoting national frameworks aimed at achieving a comparable and effective level of protection of minors and human dignity. The Recommendation, while incorporating a substantial amount of the arguments put forward by the EC, departed from its line of reasoning in a number of ways. This became most clearly apparent when the Council redefined the protection of minors as a problem of single market integration, basing the Recommendation on the EU Treaty's provision on industrial policy. Consequently, the justification for the proposed coordination of national self-regulatory schemes was derived explicitly from the anticipated positive effect on the competitiveness of the European audiovisual and information services industries, in addition to the increased leverage this would give the Community internationally by allowing it to promote a unified set of European values in the international arena. In terms of the underlying regulatory philosophy, the Council replaced the EC's central contention that harmful and illegal content necessitated categorically different regulatory approaches by softening it to allow for such differentiation without prescribing it.

Where the results of the consultation had identified a consensus concerning the need to address the ethical aspects of a shared approach towards the regulation of new services, the Recommendation conceptualized the challenges to be dealt with as impediments to the development of online services and uptake of new technologies. In terms of regulatory approach, it upheld, however, the path outlined by the EC consisting of supplementary Community action to coordinate national measures designed to address these problems. Concern for technical measures that might be employed to prevent exposure of minors to unsuitable audiovisual content had been relegated to the status of ancillary considerations in the sense that the Community would consider supporting the development of innovative solutions under one of its funding streams, but the choice of technology would remain decentralized, preferably to the end user, but certainly to the member state level.

The following year signalled the maturation of the Community's policy towards the protection of minors in the new online environment. Early that year, Council and Parliament adopted a decision for the Safer Internet Action Plan (SIAP), a multi-annual financing instrument designated to address the problems of harmful and illegal Internet content under three main action lines dedicated to the creation of a safer Internet environment, the development of filtering and rating systems and the promotion of awareness building measures. At the level of technological support mechanisms, the Decision continued previous Community policy initiatives, stressing the advantages of enabling protective technologies such as PICS and software and rating systems for the control of children's media use.

March 1999 saw the publication of the results of the study on rating and filtering technologies mandated by Article 22b of the Television without Frontiers Directive following the inter-institutional compromise over the obligatory use of V chip technology. The study underlined the importance of digital technology to the development of future-proof filtering mechanisms for the protection of minors. In the face of disintegrating viewing patterns and heightened saturation of minors' media environments with new technical devices, the study suggested the need for increasing coherence among platform specific rating systems to ensure that young people were granted an even level of protection. While a harmonization of content ratings was ruled out due to differing cultural sensitivities, the report suggested a possible alternative in the development of a set of common content descriptors that could be applied in line with national preferences. These findings were endorsed by the EC who identified cooperation with the Digital Video Broadcasting Group (DVB) as a means of assessing the technical and commercial viability of the proposed solutions for the enhancement of parental and guardian control over the content accessible to minors. Simultaneously, the EC announced its intention to further promote work on the development of descriptive rating systems among relevant stakeholders, and discuss the contribution of media literacy and awareness initiatives in this context.

Before Parliament could express its support for this line of action, the EC presented a Communication on the guiding principles for future Community policy in the audiovisual field (EC 2003c). The Communication defined the remit of European audiovisual policy as encompassing the services communicating audiovisual content to the public with the potential to affect general interest concerns attached to the societal function of the media. Regulatory intervention was to be based on market failure in attaining public interest objectives, 'except in certain cases ... where market forces are not adapted to the achievement of such objectives', including the protection of minors. In this field, the diffusion of new technologies, for example, hard disk recording, threatened to undermine the effectiveness of established regulatory practices such as the watershed, with the ubiquity of content available through the Internet putting further strain on regulation. Initiatives to enhance and promote responsibility among all stakeholders were seen as central to meeting this challenge, in addition to technological measures like filtering and blocking technologies and greater transparency in rating practice. Notwithstanding their perceived importance, no attempt was made to link these measures to binding regulatory obligations. Instead, the Communication stressed the flexibility of self-regulatory schemes as an appropriate remedy for volatile market developments, not without underlining the need to embed such self-regulatory activity within a wider overall legal framework.

As an endpoint to a series of evolutionary responses to the changing nature of audiovisual markets, the Communication marked the first comprehensive statement of the principles and considerations guiding European audiovisual policy, notably in its regulatory aspects. With the completed review of the Television without Frontiers Directive, the Recommendation on the Protection of Minors and Human Dignity and the SIAP Decision,[7] the Community had created a range of policy tools that provided different regulatory approaches for dealing with different types of content associated

---

7   Council Recommendation of 24 September 1998 on the development of the competitiveness of the European audiovisual and information services industry by promoting national frameworks aimed at achieving a comparable and effective level of protection of minors and human dignity, OJ L 270, 7 October 1998, p. 48; Decision No. 276/1999/EC of the European Parliament and of the Council of 25 January 1999 adopting a multiannual Community action plan on promoting safer use of the Internet by combating illegal and harmful content on global networks, OJ L 33, 6 February 1999, p. 1.

with the old and new media as well as a range of overarching considerations that ensured a certain consistency between Community actions. Having conducted an internal review and consulted widely on various aspects of Community audiovisual policy, the presentation of a number of sector-specific policy principles heralded a period in which the primary emphasis would be one of studying the implementation of these new initiatives and preparing the second review of the Television without Frontiers Directive scheduled for December 2002. The protection of minors constituted one of the core principles of the emerging Community policy mix, with all three instruments addressing the topic in considerable detail. Despite this central role, the associated regulatory burdens increased only modestly during this period with the addition of requirements for the unencrypted broadcasting of potentially harmful content, while the Internet remained largely unregulated, with Community action focusing exclusively on the promotion and coordination of national self-regulatory solutions. On both platforms content providers were encouraged to consider the adoption of guidance technologies that could proffer additional protection by enabling parental viewing choice, but on neither one was there an evident willingness to couple technological tools with legal form. The SIAP with its various action lines provided a starting point for the development of new tools, but did not offer any strategy for the effective entrenchment of new technologies. Therefore even where shared standards for the classification and/or labelling of audiovisual content were to emerge as a result of Community funded actions, the incentive for their actual usage would have to evolve along other lines. In this sense, the period represented a strong belief in the appropriateness of self-regulation as a way of fostering new solutions attuned to the changing nature of the audiovisual sector.

Period 3: Adapting to New Services

The third and final period in the development of the Community's audiovisual policy following the establishment of the general principles revolved primarily around the second review of the Television without Frontiers Directive and the assessment of the policy framework developed thus far more generally. The impetus for the second review had originally been created with the adoption of the 1997 Directive, which required the EC to produce a report on the effectiveness of the quota for European works to be completed no later than five years after the entering into force of the amending act. That report was also to take into account the first evaluation of the Recommendation on the Protection of Minors. When the evaluation finally was published in February 2001, the European media landscape had undergone significant change, with strong increases in Internet penetration in several jurisdictions and the concomitant proliferation of new services such as chat room and instant messaging functionalities. Under the impression of these changes, Commissioner Reding spurred the debate on possible future regulatory options by suggesting as possible alternatives a drastic remodelling, a more cautious fine tuning and the drafting of a work programme to draft a proposal at a later date, while maintaining the realization of a number of public interest objectives, including the protection of minors, as 'the primary purpose of regulation in the audiovisual sector' (Reding 2002, 3). A substantial delay of the report on the functioning of the quota regime led to the postponing of the drafting exercise and the adoption of a set of Council conclusions in December 2002 which stressed the need for extensive preparation of prospective changes to the Directive and announced the Council's 'intention to take stock regularly of the progress of [the associated] discussions'.[8]

The end of 2002 also marked the expiry of the Safer Internet Action Plan. Following an intermediate evaluation in 2001, the EC submitted a proposal for its extension until the end of 2004, arguing that more time was needed to generate results, enhance networking and address new emerging technologies. The proposal extending the Action Plan was accepted by a joint decision of the Council and Parliament in June 2003 that explicitly recognized the need to address harmful content in the development of industry self-regulation and content monitoring schemes, seeking to expand upon the notion of safer Internet use more generally with the aim of strengthening the protection of minors. With the decision came a decisive shift in funding prioritization towards awareness raising activities that resulted in nearly half the projects supported during the 2003/2004 period being awareness measures, with a comparable number of hotline projects gaining support, while development of labelling and rating mechanisms were represented by one project each. The creation and implementation of rating systems responsive to both national differences and the challenge of convergence was seen to be a task to be accomplished through the networking of the parties concerned rather than through EC action.

At the same time the discussion over adequate protective mechanisms was reignited by the fourth implementation report on the Television without Frontiers Directive, which set out a work programme for the future review process. This included a consultation exercise organized around six thematic papers, one of which addressed the protection of minors in conjunction with the protection of public order and the right of reply. Taking account of the findings of the first round of consultation, the EC issued in December 2003 a Communication on the future of European regulatory audiovisual policy, in which it laid out the priorities for imminent policy reform (EC 2003c). Reviewing the Directive's provisions on the protection of minors, the Communication concluded that these had proved their appropriateness in terms of precision and proportionality. Countering concerns over the effectiveness of enforcement, the EC announced a proposal for the updating of the Recommendation on the Protection of Minors that was to take account of co- and self-regulation as possible flanking measures especially in the online environment. Evaluations of the Recommendation had established that the labelling obligation of the 1997 Directive had been transposed in all jurisdictions, with half of the member states considering it necessary to enact supplementary measures to effectively protect children from undesirable content, and some suggested necessary improvements of the mechanism's operational design and implementation.

In this regard, the use of filtering devices for digitally encoded television broadcasts to bar access to unsuitable content met with scepticism regarding effectiveness and

---

8   Council Conclusions of 19 December 2002 on the Television without Frontiers Directive, OJ C 13, 18 January 2003, para. 7.

public awareness. A lack of involvement of the DVB group that had earlier been identified as one of the key partners in promoting the development of this technology further slowed uptake. Without a common legislative framework, Internet content regulation remained fragmented among jurisdictions not only in terms of 'how' but also with regard to the 'if' of specific regulation. Almost all member states did choose, however, to supplement their considerations of different legal options with the setting up of a national reporting hotline for illegal content. While self-labelling of Internet content had made little progress since the introduction of the PICS standard, earlier that year the Interactive Software Federation of Europe had launched the Pan European Game Information System (PEGI), which combined graphic descriptors of content types and age categories.[9] With only a minority of member states having enacted specific legislation on the issue, PEGI presented an exemplar of an industry led, pan European effort for content labelling and rating that, in conjunction with the concerns expressed by a number of member states over the incoherence of existing rating systems, refocused attention on the possibility embraced by the Parental Control study to devise shared descriptive standards applicable throughout member states in the national evaluation of content.

The successful establishment of PEGI coincided with the findings of an EC study that had compared rating practices between European countries in a cross-platform perspective, arriving at the conclusion that neither industry nor consumers were exerting pressure to achieve homogeneity in age rating or a unified labelling approach. In light of these developments, the EC maintained in the conclusion of its second evaluation report the option of bottom up harmonization of rating systems through the collaboration between national self- and co-regulatory bodies as a possible approach to a horizontal pan European content labelling mechanism. This idea was soon thereafter taken up in the 2004 proposal for a new Recommendation to complement the 1998 Recommendation on the Protection of Minors, which called upon industry to explore the definition of a common set of content descriptors allowing viewers to independently assess content and to strengthen cooperation between self and co-regulatory bodies as a means of promoting safe access for minors to audiovisual and information services. This emphasis on an industry led approach to the promotion of common filtering and labelling standards also shaped the 2005 revised version of the Internet Action Plan, which in adjusting the action line previously devoted to the development of filtering and rating systems shifted its emphasis to familiarizing users with existing solutions and increase the uptake of labelling practices on the supply side of the market rather than to promote development of additional technical solutions.

The EC proposal for an amending Directive presented in December 2005 took as its basic premise the undiminished importance of protecting minors in the face of technological developments, defining it as one of the constitutive elements of the basic regulatory tier to be applied to television broadcasts and new audiovisual media services alike. This approach was subsequently supported by the Council as

---

9   Spanning a total of seven content and six age descriptors, the system allowed for an unprecedented richness in the description and classification of video gaming content for different age groups through the combination of up to six icons with an overall age label reflecting the intensity of gaming content in both the offline and online gaming environments.

well as by Parliament, who both reaffirmed the core elements of the EC's draft in this area, namely to institute protective requirements against modes of delivery for audiovisual media services that are prone to impair the development of minors and to extend the content restrictions applicable to television advertising to audiovisual advertising communications, for example, prohibitions against targeted marketing of alcoholic beverages to minors and against marketing that appeals to the credulity of minors, exploits their trust in or their ability to persuade others, or depicts them in dangerous situations. The Parliament furthermore suggested extending the Directive's protective remit by prohibiting all audiovisual content likely to seriously impair the development of minors.

As regards the specificity of regulatory requirements, the amendments proposed by Parliament were simultaneously both more comprehensive and demanding than those of the other institutions. Neither the EC nor the Council included specific demands concerning technological aspects in their positions, signalling that the implementing choices should be left to the market. In the Council, protecting minors and consumers more generally appeared as a rather uncontroversial topic and as such was not included among the priority issues to be addressed by the review process.[10] The Parliamentarians' proposal on the other hand focused explicitly on the possible linkages between general legal requirements for the protection of vulnerable viewing groups and the possibility of employing technological means available for their implementation. References both to the use of filtering and labelling were incorporated with due regard to their respective functions and context specific application, yet without favouring a particular standard or product such as the PICS labelling system that had previously figured prominently in European policy debates.

At the overarching level, member states were called upon, in conjunction with the EC, to promote a Community wide labelling, assessment and filtering system for the protection of minors. The encouragement of market players to contribute toward the development of such a unified solution was placed in the context of member states' obligation to prevent distribution of audiovisual media services in a manner likely to harm minors. Specifically, providers of audiovisual media services were to offer appropriate filtering technology for harmful content and make users aware of its availability. On the other hand, audiovisual service providers, regulatory bodies and other stakeholders were to contribute to an assessment of the legal and technical feasibility of a cross platform content labelling system. These proposals were coupled with content specific measures such as the introduction of legal sanctions against child pornography and an appeal to service providers to run information campaigns for the prevention of violence against women and minors. Finally, in the context of audiovisual commercial communications, Parliament's efforts went beyond clarifying and broadening the normative basis of Community regulation to incorporate specifications with regard to the separation of commercial and editorial content. The proposed actions in this regard included both the regulation of sound

---

10   The four priority areas for inter-institutional deliberation set out by the Council in a background note for a meeting of the Education, Youth and Culture Council were the scope of the Directive, establishment of jurisdiction, product placement and quantitative advertising rules; cf. Background note of 9 November 2006.

levels between audiovisual commercial communications and programming content, and the mandated demarcation of editorial content and particular types of commercial communications by either acoustic, optical or spatial means.

With regard to implementing the provisions designed to ensure the protection of minors, Parliament highlighted the need to guarantee effective enforcement capacities on behalf of national regulatory authorities. Moreover, it supported the Council's emphasis on self-regulation as an additional means of implementing the obligations for audiovisual media service providers alongside the co-regulatory measures proposed by the EC. This combination was reaffirmed by the EC in its consolidated legislative draft, which did not accommodate, however, any of the technological demands made by Parliament, including only a brief mention of labelling among the Directive's recitals.[11] This position remained largely unchanged with the adoption of the final version of the AVMS Directive, whose only substantive change in this respect consisted in the additon of filtering sstems to the list of means mentioned in the Recitals for the protection of the physical, mental and moral development of minors and human dignity.[12]

Conclusion

Ten years after the idea of a common classification mechanism made its debut in Community policy, what are the prospects for its realization? The preceding analysis of the range of instruments developed to protect minors from unsuitable content has identified a considerable increase in the number of tools designed to ensure the safe use of minors of audiovisual content. This expansion of the regulatory toolkit has followed the steady evolution of new services that have been integrated into the Internal Market economy. Following the growth in the diffusion of the Internet during the mid to late 1990s, more recent developments have included the advent of mobile television services and a variety of on demand delivery solutions. The increase in the amount of content available and the detachment of delivery from particular devices and geo-spatial situations of consumption have on the one hand challenged traditional regulatory logic and at the same time increased the need for guidance and information on behalf of viewers. Under these circumstances, the protection of minors from unsuitable content has developed into a far more complex endeavour spanning multiple regulatory venues, with a varying number of content originators and varying technical means of intervention and control that legislators can dispose of.

With the effective regulatory framework for traditional television broadcasting having come under pressure as a result of the increase in the number of broadcast operators, the adoption of a command and control–like style of regulation towards new service delivery platforms did not present itself as a viable strategy for the attainment of regulatory objectives, including the protection of minors, given that especially the Internet produced a structure of interaction between content originator

---

11   Recital 34 of the Draft Audiovisual Media Services Directive (consolidated text) of 8 March 2007, http://ec.europa.eu/comm/avpolicy/docs/reg/modernisation/proposal_2005/avmsd_cons_amend_0307_en.pdf.

12 Recital 45 of the Audiovisual Media Services Directive.

and recipient that did not conform to the one-way mode of communication embodied by television broadcasting. Responses at the European level were therefore centred on the encouragement of self-regulation by industry actors in conjunction with the enforcement of national rules as these applied to the Internet, and the prospective opportunity for a harmonization of approaches from below. While this meant a dissociation of regulatory approaches to information society services, including Internet communications, and television broadcasting services, a shared underlying commonality in the recognition as services in the sense of the EU Treaty remained.

At the same time there was an attempt to strengthen the possible role of technology in promoting the attainment of regulatory objectives under both strands, without jeopardizing responsiveness to national cultural sensitivities. The suggestions for the adoption of labelling and/or filtering mechanisms originated in this context, and were later supplemented by discussions of technological access control opportunities in the form of electronic programme guides and application programming interfaces. The adoption of the Safer Internet Action Plan provided a support framework within which possible answers to these challenges could be developed, and the creation of a solution potentially applicable at a pan European level could be pursued. The PICS standard that the EC had emphasized as the possible foundation for a comprehensive labelling effort to protect minors from unsuitable audiovisual content online failed to attract the necessary support of Internet content providers who were slow to engage in a process of self-labelling.[13] The incentive problems connected to self-regulatory approaches to the protection of minors were explicitly recognized by the Council and Parliament when adopting the 2006 Recommendation on the Protection of Minors and Human Dignity and on the Right of Reply, which both institutions preface by emphasizing that self-regulation 'is not sufficient to protect minors from ... harmful content'.[14]

While the history of content labelling so far has thus been one of incentives for content producers, of regulatory competition between jurisdictions and differing national cultural sensitivities, it might legitimately be maintained that the demand side of the market still stands to potentially reap substantive benefits from a harmonized labelling approach. The introduction of (ambient) user information and classification systems presents one possible way of addressing an increasingly complex range of content offerings available for individual consumption, and the possibility of instituting a uniform approach across platforms promises to establish an ordering structure that is easily recognizable while acting as a counterweight to the proliferation of content across a diversity of usage contexts. What then are the prospects of such a solution being developed and implemented?

European policy discourse has consistently emphasized respect for the principles of subsidiarity and cultural specificity as an incontestable feature of any policy effort in this field, as expressed by the prohibition against the adoption of harmonizing

---

13   The standard never attracted a critical mass of participants despite the flexibility it allowed with regard to content description and the definition of rating preferences on behalf of end-users. Schindler (2000) estimated that only 2 percent of web content had been labelled. Today the standard is considered outdated for technological reasons (non-compliance with XML-standard, lack of explicit trust structure, and so on), Kato et al. (2004).

14   Recommendation 2006/952/EC of 20 December 2006, Recital 12, OJ C 310, p. 73.

legal acts contained in Article 151 of the EU Treaty. While the wording of the current Directive as well as that of the future constitutional Treaty[15] both imply that there is no direct competence for the Community to enact harmonizing measures from the perspective of cultural policy, an alternative possible regulatory strategy might seek to subsume content classification under the remit of the existing Directive, arguing that common standards were needed to realize the Internal Market.

The European Parliament, in its legal resolution on the proposed Audiovisual Media Services Directive, suggested the introduction of a clause that, if adopted, were to ensure that an assessment of the feasibility of a common approach in technical and legal terms were to be carried out. The rejection of this clause by the EC does not of itself prejudice the possibility of such a study being carried out, or indeed a particular answer to the question concerning the scheme's feasibility. Indeed, the feasibility of such a scheme, in both its legal and technical dimension, was already at the heart of the conclusions of the Article 22b study implemented after the last revision of the Directive. As the PEGI scheme illustrates, a coherent system at the pan European level does not constitute an insurmountable obstacle in technical terms where there is an impetus for concerted action among relevant stakeholders. The scheduled completion of the switch over to digital broadcasting in member states by 2012 will further improve chances for the adoption of an effective harmonized content labelling system by offering a uniform transmission standard on which to build.

As far as legal feasibility is concerned, the current regulatory framework for television broadcasting is characterized by a relatively low level of integration between technical specifications and legal requirements. The protective measures ordered to avoid exposure of minors to harmful content are defined in categorical rather than in typical terms and leave transposing member states a substantial amount of discretion in determining whether to require the implementation of a particular approach or leave broadcast operators to choose from among the options identified by the Directive. Especially where broadcasts are being offered in encoded format, operators are unlikely to offer additional content labelling for protective purposes if this is perceived as a burden that neither heightens safety levels nor provides exploitable value for consumers, since encoding itself qualifies as a technical measure in the meaning of Article 22(1). To the extent that national labelling systems for television broadcasting are exclusively protective in orientation, this is likely to reinforce reluctance on behalf of broadcasters. Yet even broadcasters transmitting their programmes in un-encoded format can eschew visual labelling by employing acoustic warnings to indicate harmful content instead. From the diversity of national approaches to transposing and enforcing this provision, it is apparent that the current legal framework provides little foothold for a distinctively European approach to identifying harmful broadcasting content.

Further narrowing the provisions to prescribe a specific pan European system of content classification are likely be met with severe reservations regarding the proportionality of such legislative change. For such change to be justifiable under European law, a case would have to be made for the Directive's minimum harmonization

---

15   Article III-280 of the Treaty establishing a Constitution for Europe, OJ C310, 16 December 2004.

approach to be raised to this level by arguing that this would be in the interest of the establishment of the Internal Market for television broadcasting services. Given the current status of broadcasting markets in the EU, this argument might prove difficult to bear out empirically. Even where sufficient empirical evidence could be presented for free to air broadcasting markets, this would not necessarily lend justification to abolishing the differentiated treatment given to encoded and non-encoded broadcasts by the Television without Frontiers Directive. At the same time, national jurisdictions would continue to have the option of deviating from such a European standard by imposing stricter national regulations given the character of the harmonization measure at issue. As the process leading to the recent adoption of the Audiovisual Media Services Directive[16] demonstrates, there is little appetite among Member States to support a regulatory model that imposes stricter rules by way of legislation, be it by extending in full the existing content standards from linear to non-linear services, or by linking the protection against unsuitable methods of distribution for non-linear services under Article 3h of the Directive to the adoption of a labelling system.

Absent such justification for introducing more restrictive legislative requirements, member states remain free to pursue a common approach to content classification on a voluntary basis. However, the window of opportunity for such a horizontal approach seems to be closing as an increasing number of jurisdictions move towards unifying existing content labelling and rating mechanisms within a horizontal framework at the domestic level. In addition to the Netherlands, the United Kingdom has recently signalled that the national communications regulatory authority Ofcom will be venturing to design a cross-platform system for content labelling (Mulholland 2007). These developments mirror the conclusions of the 2003 study conducted on behalf of the EC that the standard frame of reference for users of audiovisual content remains national, and that a unification of approaches is therefore likely to yield the greatest benefit to consumers at this level. While bottom-up harmonization, the model explicitly embraced by the Recommendation for the Protection of Minors and Human Dignity, thus remains a possible way in which to achieve a system covering all European jurisdictions, such coordination becomes progressively more difficult as individual member states introduce new content labelling approaches themselves, thereby impairing the feasibility of both a unified system for all content types and of media specific approaches at the European level. Since the wider implications of changes in media content delivery and transformation in usage patterns attributed to the proliferation of non linear services are only beginning to emerge, adopting a harmonized model at this point might prematurely exclude other options before allowing sufficient opportunity to establish their relative merit.

Ultimately, the character of labelling itself may be subject to change with future approaches relying less on actual evaluation of content, and more on accurate descriptions of content based on a multiplicity of content descriptors as the idea of a semantic web for content classification materializes. While this would not do away

---

16   Cf. Directive 2007/65/EC of the European Parliament and of the Council of 11 December 2007 amending Council Directive 89/552/EEC on the coordination of certain provisions laid down by law, regulation or administrative action in Member States concerning the pursuit of television broadcasting activities , OJ L 332, 18 December 2007, p. 27.

with the necessity of procedures designed to rate content, it might herald the end of a conceptual approach to content labelling and rating that posits protection as the sole or main function of content classification. From a regulatory perspective, the best possible answer under these circumstances might well be for European and national legislatures to signal a firm commitment to enforcing adequate levels of protection of minors in a changing media landscape and promote the uptake of new labelling initiatives by content providers.

References

BDRC (2001), *Intermediate Evaluation of the Safer Internet Action Plan.* Brussels: BDRC.

Buckingham, D. (2000), *After the Death of Childhood.* Cambridge and Malden, MA: Polity.

Bushman, B.J. and Cantor, J.R. (2003), 'Media Ratings for Violence and Sex: Implications for Policymakers and Parents', *American Psychologist* 58, 130–141.

Cantor, J. (1998), 'Ratings for Program Content: The Role of Research Findings', *Annals of the American Academy of Political and Social Science* 557: 54–69.

European Commission (1996a), Green Paper on the Protection of Minors and Human Dignity in Audiovisual and Information Services, COM(96) 483 final, 16 October 1996.

European Commission (1996b), *Illegal and Harmful Content on the Internet. Communication from the Commission to the Council, the European Parliament, the Economic and Social Committee and the Committee of the Regions*, COM(96) 487 final, 16 October 1996.

European Commission (1997a), *Communication from the Commission of 18 November 1997 on the follow-up to the Green Paper on the protection of minors and human dignity in audiovisual and information services, together with a proposal for a Council Recommendation concerning the protection of minors and human dignity in audiovisual and information services*, COM(97) 570 final, 18 November 1997.

European Commission (1997b), *Action Plan on Promoting Safe Use of the Internet. Communication from the Commission to the Council, the European Parliament, the Economic and Social Committee and the Committee of the Regions. Proposal for a Council Decision adopting a Multiannual Community Action Plan on promoting safe use of the Internet*, COM(97) 582 final, 26 November 1997.

European Commission (1997c), *Green Paper on the Convergence of the Telecommunications, Media and Information Technology Sectors, and the Implications for Regulation Towards an Information Society Approach*, COM(97) 623, 3 December 1997.

European Commission (1999a), *Communication from the Commission to the Council, the European Parliament and the Economic and Social Committee: Study on Parental Control of Television Broadcasting*, COM(99) 371 final, 19 July 1999.

European Commission (1999b), *Communication from the Commission to the*

Council, the European Parliament, the Economic and Social Committee and the Committee of the Regions: Principles and guidelines for the Community's audiovisual policy in the digital age*, COM(99) 657 final, 14 December 1999.

European Commission (2001), *Evaluation report from the Commission to the Council and the European Parliament of 27 February 2001 on the application of Council Recommendation of 24 September 1998 concerning the protection of minors and human dignity*, COM(2001) 106 final, 27 February 2001.

European Commission (2002), *Fourth report from the Commission to the Council, the European Parliament, the European Economic and Social Committee and the Committee of the Regions on the application of Directive 89/552/EEC 'Television without Frontiers'*, COM(2002) 778 final, 6 January 2003.

European Commission (2003a), *Communication from the Commission concerning the evaluation of the Multiannual Community Action Plan on promoting safer use of the Internet and new online technologies by combating illegal and harmful content primarily in the area of the protection of children and minors*, COM(2003) 653 final, 3 November 2003.

European Commission (2003b), *Second evaluation report from the Commission to the Council and the European Parliament of 12 December 2003 on the application of Commission Recommendation of 24 September 1998 concerning the protection of minors and human dignity*, COM(2003) 776 final, 12 December 2003.

European Commission (2003c), *Communication from the Commission of 15 December 2003 on the future of European regulatory audiovisual policy*, COM(2003) 784 final, 15 December 2003.

European Commission (2004), *Proposal for a Recommendation of the European Parliament and of the Council of 30 April 2004 on the protection of minors and human dignity and the right of reply in relation to the competitiveness of the European audiovisual and information services industry*, COM(2004) 341 final, 30 April 2004.

European Commission (2006a), *Communication on the implementation of the Multiannual Community Programme on promoting safer use of the Internet and new online technologies (Safer Internet Plus)*, COM(2006) 661 final, 6 November 2006

European Commission (2006b), *Communication on the final evaluation of the implementation of the Multiannual Community action plan on promoting safer use of the Internet by combating illegal and harmful content on global networks*, COM(2006) 663 final, 6 November 2006.

Eveland, W.P. (2003), 'A "Mix of Attributes" Approach to the Study of Media Effects and New Communication Technologies', *Journal of Communication* 53(3), 395–410.

Funk, J.B. et al. (1999), 'Rating Electronic Games', *Youth and Society* 30(3), 283–312.

Kamarck, M.J. (1996), 'Television with Directions: The Implications Of V-Chip Technology', *Business of Film* October 1996, available from http://www.rmslaw.com/articles/art42.htm [retrieved 15 February 2007].

Kato, F. et al. (2004), *Content Labeling for Mobile Internet*, paper presented at the WWW2004 Workshop on Content Labeling – Technical and Socio-Cultural Challenges and Solutions, 18 May 2004, Sheraton Hotel, New York, available from   http://web.sfc.keio.ac.jp/~kaz/www2004/papers/fk.pdf   [retrieved   15

February 2007].

Miller, J. et al. (1996), *Rating Services and Rating Systems (and their Machine Readable Descriptions) Version 1.1*, W3C Recommendation 31 October 1996, REC-PICS-services-961031, available from http://www.w3.org/TR/REC-PICS-services [retrieved 11 February 2007].

Mulholland, H. (2007), 'Brown unveils classification system for new media', *Guardian Unlimited*, 7 March 2007, available from http://politics.guardian.co.uk/media/story/0,,2028490,00.html [retrieved 9 March 2007].

Olsberg SPI and KEA European Affairs (2003), *Empirical Study on the Practice of the Rating of Films Distributed in Cinemas Television DVD and Videocassettes in the EU and EEA Member States*. London: Olsberg SPI.

Ramsay, G. (2003), *The Watershed: Providing a Safe Viewing Zone*. London: Broadcasting Standards Commission.

Reding, V. (2002), *The Review of the Television without Frontiers Directive*, speech at the European Voice Conference on 'Television Without Frontiers', Brussels, SPEECH/02/120, 21 March 2002.

Resnick, P., and Miller, J. (1996), 'PICS: Internet Access Controls Without Censorship', *Communications of the ACM* 39(10), 87–93.

Scheuer, A. (2006), 'Jugendschutz im Fernsehen in Europa', *tv diskurs* 10(2), 4–7.

Schindler, F. (2000), Rating und Filtering. Zukunftstechnologien im Jugendschutz?!?', tv diskurs 11/2000, 56–61.

Stock, R. (1997), 'Don't rock the boat – A pan-European view of "Television without Frontiers"', *Commercial Communications Newsletter 6*, March 1997, available from http://ec.europa.eu/internal_market/comcom/newsletter/edition06/page20_en.htm [retrieved 11 February 2007].

Strasburger, V.C. and Wilson, B.J. (2002), *Children, Adolescents, and the Media*. Thousand Oaks, CA: Sage.

Valkenburg, P.M. (2004), *Children's Responses to the Screen*. Mahwah, NJ and London: Lawrence Erlbaum Associates.

Van Evra, J. (2004), *Television and Child Development*. Mahwah, N.J. and London: Lawrence Erlbaum Associates.

Van Rompaey, et al. (2002), Children's Influence on Internet Access at Home: Adoption and Use in the Family Context, *Information, Communication & Society* 5(2), 189–206.

Villani, S. (2001), 'Impact of Media on Children and Adolescents: A 10-Year Review of the Research', *Journal of the American Academy of Child & Adolescent Psychiatry* 40(4), 392–401.

Walsh, D. and Gentile, D. (2001), 'A Validity Test of Movie, Television, and Video-Game Ratings', *Pediatrics* 107(6), 1302–1308.

Chapter 9

The Quota Quandary:
An Assessment of Articles 4–6 of the
Television without Frontiers Directive

Tarlach McGonagle[1]

Under Articles 4–5 of the Television without Frontiers Directive,[2] television broadcasters in Europe are subject to a quota system for European, and independent European, works. The system is based on a rather convoluted definition of European works set out in Article 6 of the Television without Frontiers Directive. Controversy and contention have tended to characterize debates about this quota system – even prior to the adoption of the original Directive. It is therefore quite remarkable that Articles 4 and 5 have managed to weather the sustained criticism levelled at them over the years to remain essentially unchanged in the Audiovisual Media Services Directive (AVMS).[3]

This chapter will begin by situating Articles 4–6 in the general context of the Television without Frontiers Directive and explaining how the objective of promoting European works took hold during the drafting process of the original Directive. It will then trace the development of Articles 4–6 through the amendment of the Directive in 1997 up to the current proposals for the renaming and revamping of the Directive as the AVMS Directive. It will also examine the precise content and scope of the Articles before assessing their application by European Union (EU) member states and, ultimately, their actual impact on the European audiovisual industry.

1   The author would like to thank Rosanne van der Waal, Information Specialist at the Institute for Information Law (IViR), University of Amsterdam, for her very helpful assistance in locating various documents consulted during the preparation of this contribution. This text was completed in April 2007; the author is grateful for the editorial flexibility which allowed him to update and adjust references to provisions in the Audiovisual Media Services Directive after its adoption on 11 December 2007.
2   Council Directive 89/552/EEC on the coordination of certain provisions laid down by law, regulation or administrative action in member states concerning the pursuit of television broadcasting activities, OJ L332/27 of 18 December 2007 (as amended by Directive 2007/65/EC of the European Parliament and of the Council of 11 December 2007).
3   Directive 2007/65/EC of the European Parliament and of the Council of 11 December 2007 (amending Council Directive 89/552/EEC on the coordination of certain provisions laid down by law, regulation or administrative action in member states concerning the pursuit of television broadcasting activities, OJ L332/27 of 18 December 2007).

The Television without Frontiers Directive

The Television without Frontiers Directive is the EU's flagship regulatory text governing television broadcasting. The Court of Justice of the European Communities (ECJ) has repeatedly held that the pursuit of broadcasting activities constitutes a service within the meaning of the Treaty establishing the European Community.[4] The Television without Frontiers Directive re-affirms this approach (Recitals 6–8), while also seeking to distinguish broadcasting from other services on the basis of its additional social and cultural dimensions.[5] In keeping with Article 49 of the EC Treaty,[6] it seeks to remove obstacles to the free movement of television broadcasting services between member states, with a view to furthering the objectives of the establishment of 'an even closer union among the peoples of Europe' and the consolidation of the Internal Market. It considers that the abolition of restrictions on the freedom to provide broadcasting services within the Community must be accompanied by 'coordination of the applicable [national] laws'. The extent of the envisaged coordination is that required 'to achieve the essential harmonization necessary and sufficient to ensure the free movement of television broadcasts in the Community'. As such, the Directive purports to ensure only minimum harmonization in its coordinated fields: it fixes the basic requirements at Community level and allows member states the discretion to decide whether television broadcasters under their jurisdiction should be required 'to comply with more detailed or stricter rules in the areas covered by this Directive'. The fields coordinated by the Directive are: access to events of major importance for society (Article 3a); promotion of distribution and production of [European] television programmes (Chapter III); television advertising, sponsorship and teleshopping (Chapter IV); protection of minors and public order (Chapter V) and right of reply (Chapter VI).

The legal framework put in place by the Directive has as its fulcrum a principle which is often referred to as the 'country of origin'/transmitting state principle. It entails two crucial and related regulatory consequences:

- Each Member State shall ensure that all television broadcasts transmitted by broadcasters under its jurisdiction comply with the rules of the system of law applicable to broadcasts intended for the public in that Member State.
- Member States shall ensure freedom of reception and shall not restrict retransmissions on their territory of television broadcasts from other Member States for reasons which fall within the fields coordinated by this Directive (Articles 2.1 and 2a).

---

4   See *inter alia Sacchi* (155/73) [1974] ECR 409; *Procureur du Roi* v. *Marc J.V.C. Debauve and others* (52/79) [1980] ECR 833; *Bond van Adverteerders and Others* v. *The Netherlands* (352/85) [1988] ECR 2085.

5   Recital 3 of Directive 89/552/EEC, for instance, contains a reference to the public interest role to be discharged by television broadcasting services (this would, presumably, embrace cultural objectives), whereas Recital 4 of Directive 97/36/EC adverts to the cultural and sociological impact of audiovisual programmes.

6   Article 49 (ex Article 59) prohibits restrictions on freedom to provide services 'in respect of nationals of Member States who are established in a State of the Community other than that of the person for whom the services are intended'.

Thus, as long as a broadcast complies with the rules existing in the member state exercising jurisdiction over the broadcaster (the originating/transmitting state or 'country of origin'), its reception may not be restricted in another member state for reasons which fall within the Directive's coordinated fields. This approach necessarily requires that member states mutually recognize each other's relevant national rules (see McGonagle and Van Loon 2002).

Articles 4 and 5 of the Television without Frontiers Directive

As already mentioned, Articles 4 and 5 of the Television without Frontiers Directive establish a quota system for European, independent European and new, independent European works. The key parts of the articles read as follows:

> Member States shall ensure where practicable and by appropriate means, that broadcasters reserve for European works, within the meaning of Article 6, a majority proportion of their transmission time, excluding the time appointed to news, sports events, games, advertising, teletext services and teleshopping. This proportion, having regard to the broadcaster's informational, educational, cultural and entertainment responsibilities to its viewing public, should be achieved progressively, on the basis of suitable criteria. (Article 4)

> Member States shall ensure, where practicable and by appropriate means, that broadcasters reserve at least 10% of their transmission time, excluding the time appointed to news, sports events, games, advertising, teletext services and teleshopping, or alternately, at the discretion of the Member State, at least 10% of their programming budget, for European works created by producers who are independent of broadcasters. This proportion, having regard to broadcasters' informational, educational, cultural and entertainment responsibilities to its viewing public, should be achieved progressively, on the basis of suitable criteria; it must be achieved by earmarking an adequate proportion for recent works, that is to say works transmitted within five years of their production. (Article 5)

Articles 4 and 5 are governed by the definition of European works, which is provided in a detailed and relatively complex manner in Article 6. The definition essentially means works originating in one of the member states, though this has proved more complex than the drafters of the Directive foresaw. For instance, one of the criteria employed in Article 6 is the place of establishment of producers, a criterion that has proved somewhat vexed when applied to broadcasters (McGonagle and Van Loon 2002). Divergent or conflicting assertions of jurisdictional control by different national authorities over the same broadcaster (or producer) can be difficult to resolve and lead to protracted proceedings, like in the *RTL 4 & 5* case.[7] The

---

7   *RTL* v. *Commissariaat voor de Media*, Judgment of 6 August 2003, Case No. 200203476/1 (Dutch Council of State). In that case, the Dutch *Raad van State* (Council of State), while accepting (in principle) the claim of the Dutch *Commissariaat voor de Media* (Media Authority) that the stations RTL 4 and 5 ought to be under its jurisdiction, nevertheless ruled that the stations should remain under Luxembourg's jurisdiction in order to avoid a scenario of double supervision that would be counter to the objectives, system and spirit of the case and a summary of the judgment (see Steenbruggen 2003).

definitional waters are further muddied by recurrent reliance on vague phrases (for example, 'mainly made'/'made mainly', 'preponderant' [contribution]) and notions which do not lend themselves easily to practical application (for example, residence, establishment, actual control).

Under Article 6, works can be understood as 'European' if they satisfy certain criteria. The most clear-cut category is works originating from EU member states. Works originating from European states which are not members of the EU but are party to the Council of Europe's Convention on Transfrontier Television (ECTT) can also be considered 'European works', provided that works originating from member states are not subject to discriminatory measures in the countries concerned (paragraph 1). Works have to be 'mainly made with authors and workers residing in one or more of' those states. One of the following three conditions must also be complied with: (1) the works 'are made by one or more producers established in one or more of those States'; (2) 'production of the works is supervised and actually controlled by one or more producers established in one or more of those States', or (3) 'the contribution of co-producers of those States to the total co-production costs is preponderant and the co-production is not controlled by one or more producers established outside those States' (paragraph 2).

Works originating in other European countries can also be considered 'European works', again subject to the proviso that works originating from EU member states are not discriminated against in the countries concerned. Additionally, they have to be 'made exclusively or in co-production with producers established in one or more Member States by producers established in one or more European third countries with which the Community has concluded agreements relating to the audiovisual sector, if those works are mainly made with authors and workers residing in one or more European States' (paragraph 3). Finally, works can also be designated as 'European' in two other ways. First, when they are produced in the framework of bilateral co-production treaties between member states and other countries, as long as 'the Community co-producers supply a majority share of the total cost of the production and that the production is not controlled by one or more producers established outside the territory of the Member States' (paragraph 4). Second, when works do not fulfil the foregoing criteria, but are 'made mainly with authors and workers residing in one or more Member States', they 'shall be considered to be European works to an extent corresponding to the proportion of the contribution of Community co-producers to the total production costs' (paragraph 5).

Before proceeding to analyze the content and scope of Articles 4–6, it is useful to consider how they emerged and were developed during the various stages in the evolution of the Directive. It has been noted, perspicaciously, that the EU is 'grammatically singular' but 'institutionally plural' (Collins 1993, 371) and this observation is certainly borne out in the drafting of the Television without Frontiers Directive. Institutional perspectives and priorities differed, often sharply, as did those of the member states. The tale of the drafting process – complete with ample references to the various inter-institutional turf wars and horse trading between member states – has already been recounted many times (Dupagne 1992; Krebber 2002).

A further key feature of EC policy development around the quotas is that the strategy for strengthening and generally promoting the European audiovisual industry comprises two main prongs in terms of increasing the capacity for content production: the European content and independent European production requirements enshrined in Articles 4 and 5, and structured subsidization of European audiovisual works, as exemplified by the Media Programmes.[8] The Media Programme has been termed the 'positive' counterpart of the 'negative' quota rules of the Directive' (De Witte 1995, 107) and their *de facto* complementarity has been underscored by a noticeable political tendency to present the continuation and strengthening of the Media Programme as a means of compensating for the perceived weakness of the obligations contained in Articles 4 and 5. While the importance of the Media Programmes for the European audiovisual sector is obvious, it has not been free of criticism, *inter alia*, because of the budgetary strictures within which it perennially has to operate (Holmes 2004, 197–198).

Drafting History of the Television without Frontiers Directive

The initial impulse for the development of EC policy in audiovisual matters was provided by the European Parliament's so-called Hahn Report of 1982 (European Parliament 1982a),[9] which was primarily concerned with the establishment of a European television programme, either as 'an independent European radio and television broadcasting company', or as 'a joint European channel which would be transmitted by the existing companies in the member states via the fifth channel of their satellites, using the same picture but in the respective national language' (European Parliament 1982a, 10). In short, the Hahn Report perceived information and the mass media as being vitally instrumental for the realization of the twin projects of forging a European identity and facilitating European unification. The idea that the EC should give its backing to, and become involved in, plans by national television companies and the European Broadcasting Union (EBU) to establish a European television channel, was subsequently taken up in a Parliamentary Resolution sponsored by Hahn and others (European Parliament 1982b). Significantly, the Resolution also called on the EC to draft a report which would contain, in particular, information on the legal foundations for EU activities in this field within the terms of the EEC Treaty as well as the feasibility of establishing a pan European television channel.

It was at this moment that the development of EC policy in the audiovisual field really began to gather momentum. The EC presented an interim report in May 1983 (EC 1983), followed by a behemoth Green Paper in 1984 in parallel to the Hahn Report initiative (EC 1984). Whereas the EC's Interim Report dealt primarily with

---

8   MEDIA Programmes to date are as follows: MEDIA I (1991–1995); MEDIA II (1996–2000) (with focuses on development and distribution and on training); MEDIA Plus (2001–2005) (which prioritized development, distribution and promotion), and MEDIA 2007.

9   The European Parliament had made other – fleeting – forays into relevant issues prior to the adoption of the Hahn Report, but they were of little significance in terms of the subsequent development of European audiovisual policy (Goldberg et al. 1998, 42 *et seq*).

the scope for creating a European television channel, the Green Paper examined 'the question of how the common market for the national television channel could be established' (EC 1984, 1). A cursory enumeration of the main structural components of the Green Paper serves to illustrate its scope: Introduction/The brief for the Community; Technical aspects; Cultural and social aspects; Economic aspects; Legal aspects; Freedom to provide services; Harmonization of legislation. For all of its capaciousness, however, the Green Paper did not examine the question of the promotion of European works. Part Six of the Green Paper, entitled 'Harmonization of legislation' focused on three main areas: (1) Rules on advertising (2) Public order and safety, protection of personal rights[10] and (3) Copyright.

Two Parliamentary reports drafted in response to the EC's Green Paper, the Hahn Report (No. 2) (European Parliament 1985a) and the De Vries Report (European Parliament 1985b), both advocated, in a *general* way, measures for the promotion of the European audiovisual industry. On the back of these reports, two corresponding resolutions were adopted by the European Parliament (European Parliament 1985c, 1985d). Significantly, the texts of the resolutions, as adopted, differed from the draft motions included in the reports in that they called for the introduction of *specific* prescriptions for European content. The Hahn Resolution (No. 2) called on the EC to set out in its Proposal for a Directive:

> Measures to secure and promote the production of television programmes in the Community, encourage the emergence of Community programme makers independent of the broadcasting organizations and thereby provide a creative and cultural stimulus in Europe, more specifically by laying down that a large percentage – at least 50 per cent – of televised films should be Community-produced, reserving a specific percentage of programme-related expenditure each year for co-productions by programme-makers from at least two Member States. (European Parliament 1985c)

In the Resolution on the economic aspects of the common market for broadcasting in the European Community, the most relevant provision read:

> 12. Considers it necessary, in order to promote the European broadcasting industry and safeguard the European cultural area, to stipulate that at least 50 % of programmes should be indigenous European productions. Only the establishment of a Europe-wide internal market will enable the broadcasting industry to compete with international producers.

The EC's Proposal for a Directive in 1986 (EC 1986) did not simply track the recommendations of the two European Parliament Resolutions; while it did include specific prescriptions for European content, it opted to calibrate them differently. According to Article 2 of the Proposal, television broadcasters would have been obliged to reserve 30 per cent of their 'programming time not consisting of news, sporting events and game shows, advertising or teletext services' for the transmission of Community works. Furthermore, of that 30 per cent, 'in the case of initial transmissions at least one third shall be reserved for first broadcasts in the

---

10   This section comprised an introduction and the sub-issues, protection of minors and right of reply.

Community'. It was envisaged that the prescribed percentage would have to 'be progressively increased' to reach at least 60 per cent after the expiry of three years after the deadline for the transposition of the Directive into national law. Under Article 3 of the Proposal, broadcasters would have had to reserve at least 5 per cent of their programming budget for Community works created by independent producers, with that percentage rising progressively to at least 10 per cent after the expiry of three years after the transposition deadline.

The European Parliament's Committee on Legal Affairs and Citizens' Rights gave its response to the EC's Proposal for a Directive in the so called Barzanti Report (European Parliament 1987). It proposed that the EC's stipulation of 'at least 30%' of broadcasters' programming time be amended to read 'an adequate proportion' (Amendment No. 22), which it quantified as 'at least 60% of the programming time of each broadcaster', to be achieved 'gradually through appropriate criteria and timetables after the expiry of three years' from the transposition deadline (Amendment No. 23).[11] As regards the notion of independent producer embedded in Article 3 of the EC's Proposal, the Report underscored that what was meant was independence from 'television companies' (Amendment No. 26). The Report also stated that the target of reserving 10 per cent of the programming budget for independently produced European works 'should be achieved by allocating adequate time to recent works, i.e. works produced within a reasonable period (five years at most) before their transmission' (Amendment No. 27).

This approach only became palatable to the French by virtue of a concatenation of appeasement measures and diplomatic endeavours. The most important of these were the establishment of the EUREKA funding programme for the European audiovisual sector; the alteration of 'adequate' proportion to 'majority proportion' and the political negotiation of the non-roll-back (*'non recul'*) clause (Dupagne 1992, 111 *et seq.*; Humphreys 1996, 281; Krebber 2002, 150). The non-roll-back clause was later incorporated into the final text of Directive 89/552/EEC as its Article 4(2) and it can be considered a reflection of economic realities, that is to say, difficulties experienced by certain broadcasters, more pronouncedly in some countries than in others.

Constraints of space do not allow for all of the proposed approaches or, more concretely, proposed provisions or specific formulations mentioned, to be itemized and analyzed here. Nevertheless, it is worth dwelling on a number of general reflections prompted by the conceptual and textual twists and turns of the drafting process detailed above.

The development of EC policy in audiovisual matters generally, and the negotiation and drafting of the Television without Frontiers Directive, in particular, have been described as struggles between different, or rather, opposing, philosophies of broadcasting. Interventionist (*dirigiste*) and liberal perspectives clashed repeatedly, and often acrimoniously, during the deliberative process. Moreover, there has

---

11   It then added: 'However, a proportion equal to at least 30% of the programming time of each broadcaster shall also be considered adequate in the case of television programmes distributed on a subscription basis and programmes on specific and specialized subjects whose nature and variety justify such a proportion'.

always been an inherent tension in the conceptual hybridity of the Television without Frontiers Directive. Finally, the discernible shift in EU audiovisual policy from promoting an ideal of 'cultural unity' to prioritizing the value of 'cultural diversity' has also shaped the ideological and regulatory context in which Articles 4–6 operate (Collins 1994, generally).

Amendment of Directive 89/552/EEC

As with the previous section, this account of the process leading to the adoption of Directive 97/36/EC is selective as it aims merely to identify some of the main substantive ideas discussed in the context of the proposed amendment of Directive 89/552/EEC. Fuller accounts of the legal considerations and political dynamics at play in the process are available elsewhere (Krebber 2002, 149–156; Machet 1999, 35, 37–38; Dolmans 1995). This section will therefore concentrate on a selection of the proposals contained in the EC's 1995 Proposal to amend the Directive 89/552/EEC (EC 1995) to the extent that they illustrate or otherwise relate to the strengths and shortcomings of Articles 4–6 and their implementation.

In its 1995 Proposal to amend the Directive 89/552/EEC, the EC suggested a number of modifications to Articles 4–6. Those proposals were based on the approach taken by the EC in its first report on the monitoring of Articles 4 and 5 (see further, below) as well as consultations arising out of its 1994 Green Paper (EC 1994):

Article 4

1. Member States shall, by appropriate means, ensure that broadcasters reserve for European works, within the meaning of Article 6, a majority proportion of their transmission time, excluding the time appointed to news, sports events, games, advertising, teletext and teleshopping services.
2. In the case of channels which devote at least 80% of their transmission time, excluding the time appointed to advertising and teleshopping, to cinematographic works, drama, documentaries or animation, Member States shall allow television broadcasting organizations to choose between complying with the first paragraph or allocating 25% of their programming budget to European works within the meaning of Article 6. For the purposes of this Directive, 'programming budget' means the accounting cost of acquiring, commissioning, producing and co-producing all those programmes broadcast by the channel in question in any given year.
3. The proportions referred to in paragraphs 1 and 2 shall be attained progressively, in stages, no later than three years after the date of the first broadcast by the channel in question.
4. Channels broadcasting entirely in a language other than those of the Member States are not covered by the provisions of this Article or those of Article 5.

The main proposals made in respect of Article 4 may therefore be summarized as follows:

- retention of basic broadcasting obligations for general-interest channels
- deletion of the phrase, 'where applicable'
- extension of range of programme services considered as excluded transmission time (by mentioning 'teletext and teleshopping services')
- deletion of provision allowing for deference to the broadcaster's various generic responsibilities
- deletion of reference to the 'absolute minimum' clause in Article 4(2)
- introduction of prescriptions (majority of transmission time or 25 per cent of programming budget) for certain (themed) channels
- replacement of references to 'television programmes' with 'channels'
- definition of programming budget
- gradual introduction of obligations for new broadcasters over a three-year period
- non-applicability of Articles 4 and 5 to channels broadcasting entirely in a language other than those of the member states.

This package of measures, if adopted, would have brought welcome clarity to key terms used in Article 4, as well as their conceptual underpinnings. As such, the proposed measures would have greatly facilitated the entire monitoring process – both in terms of member states' reports and the EC's evaluation of the same (see further, *infra*). The proposed modifications would also have considerably reduced the discretion enjoyed by member states when determining the applicability of their Article 4 obligations to particular broadcasters (by removing the phrase 'where applicable' and the reference to the regard to be shown to the generic responsibilities of broadcasters to their viewers). One outcome of these proposed modifications would undoubtedly have been a tightening up of some aspects Article 4 and a concomitant whittling down of member states' discretion to move about within their obligations. On the other hand, another probable outcome of the EC's proposals would have been the safeguarding and enhancement of the flexibility offered by Article 4 in other important respects, for example, deletion of the 'absolute minimum' clause; gradual introduction of obligations for new broadcasters over a three-year period from their launch, and the possibility for special interest channels to choose between a transmission time requirement and an investment requirement (EC 1995, 35–36). The prospect of such outcomes was enough to re-ignite the interventionist-liberal debates which had inflamed, and even jeopardized, the drafting of the original Directive. The main institutional players and the more vocal member states regrouped largely along the same proverbial battle-lines as on the previous occasion.

Ultimately, only the exclusion of 'teletext and teleshopping services' from the calculation of relevant transmission time was incorporated into the minimally revised Article 4. The proposed non-applicability of channels broadcasting entirely in non-EU languages was reworded and repositioned in Recital 29 of Directive 97/36/EC, which reads as follows:

Whereas channels broadcasting entirely in a language other than those of the Member States should not be covered by the provisions of Articles 4 and 5; whereas, nevertheless, where such a language or languages represent a substantial part but not all of the channel's transmission time, the provisions of Articles 4 and 5 should not apply to that part of transmission time.

The EC's most controversial proposal relating to Article 4 was not actually set out in its proposed rewording of that Article; instead, it was put forward as Recital 17 to the proposed amending Directive. It read:

Whereas, if Article 4 of Directive 89/552/EEC, as amended by this Directive, is effectively implemented over a ten-year period, it should be possible, given the impact of the financial instruments available to the Community and the Member States, to achieve the objective of strengthening the European programme industry.

This is a bold statement which attests to a sense of confidence in the inherent strength and competitiveness of the European programme industry that is rarely articulated in official texts emanating from any EU institution, especially in such a forthright manner and in a context likely to give rise to very far-reaching consequences. In effect, the proposal would have limited the application of the revised Article 4 to ten years – the decisive period which the 1994 Green Paper had predicted would (to put it somewhat colloquially) 'make or break' the European programme industry on world markets. As such, it vested enormous faith in (1) the economic viability of the European audiovisual sector, and (2) the potential impact of financial measures for sustaining and stimulating the industry. The proposed Recital is clearly couched in economic terms and concepts, thereby further undermining the assumption that Article 4 is premised on economic *and* cultural rationales. Moreover, this reading also suggests that the underlying economic objectives of Article 4 hold the logic of the Internal Market to be less relevant than the overriding concern of ensuring the competitiveness of the European audiovisual industry at the international level.

Turning, then, to Article 5, under the EC's proposals, it would have been amended to read:

- Member States shall ensure, by appropriate means, that broadcasters reserve at least 10% of their transmission time, excluding the time appointed to news, sports events, games, advertising, teleshopping and teletext services, or alternately, at the discretion of the Member States, at least 10% of their programming budget, for European works created by producers who are independent of broadcasters.
- This proportion must be achieved by earmarking at least 50% for recent works, that is to say works transmitted within five years of their production.

In keeping with the proposals made in respect of Article 4, the flexibility afforded member states under Article 5 would also have been diminished by the removal of the qualifier, 'where practicable'. Likewise, a reference to 'teleshopping and teletext services' was also proposed. The most far-reaching change proposed, however, was that 50 per cent of the proportion of independent European works would also have to be 'recent works'. This proposal was prompted by the widely-held view (confirmed by the EC's monitoring exercise) that the 'adequate proportion' of 10 per cent of a broadcaster's transmission time or programming budget was less onerous than the obligations set out in Article 4 and that broadcasters generally had little difficulty in meeting it. Indeed, the lack of precision offered by 'mushy' or 'marshmallow' terms, such as 'adequate', 'reasonable' or 'substantial' amounts of programming has led to their general usefulness for regulatory and monitoring purposes to be called into question (Geller 1990, 306). The proposed ratcheting up of the minimum requirement for recent independent European works to at least half of the 10 per cent of a broadcaster's transmission time or programming budget can be explained by the desire to support and stimulate the production and distribution of such works in a meaningful way.

It is conspicuous that the sunset clause introduced in the proposed Recital 17 would apply only to Article 4 and not to Article 5. The discrepancy was deliberate: the EC described the value of Article 5 as 'ultimately structural' and referred to representations from audiovisual professionals, for whom it serves as a safeguard for 'pluralism in a world of media mergers' (EC 1995, 36). Relatedly, unlike under the proposed amendment of Article 4, the obligation would have been immediately binding on newly-established broadcasters. Thus, arguments for pluralism were invoked to explain why neither the sunset clause nor the provision for gradual introduction over three years for new broadcasters would only have applied to Article 5. The EC's substantive proposals concerning Article 6 were ultimately incorporated into the text of that Article as paragraphs 3 and 4.

As intimated at the beginning of this section, the inter-institutional process leading to the adoption of Directive 97/36/EC was carried along by political currents and counter currents involving not only the institutions themselves, but also member states and various stakeholders.

The Audiovisual Media Services Directive

One of the most important novel features to be introduced into the AVMS Directive is the distinction between linear and non-linear audiovisual media services, described in the Directive as 'television broadcasting' and 'on-demand audiovisual media service[s]', respectively. The former are defined as services 'provided by a media service provider for simultaneous viewing of programmes on the basis of a programme schedule' (Article 1(e)). In other words, these are so called 'push' technologies (because content is 'pushed' to viewers), such as traditional television broadcasting or other forms of scheduled broadcasting via the Internet or mobile phones. Non-linear audiovisual services, on the other hand, are defined as services 'provided by a media service provider for the viewing of programmes at the moment chosen by the user and at his individual request on the basis of a catalogue of programmes selected by the media service provider' (Article 1(g)). These are also known as 'pull' technologies (because viewers 'pull' content from networks) or on-demand services. The AVMS Directive will introduce a form of tiered regulation, with different tiers of obligations and responsibilities applying to media service providers, depending on whether they provide linear or non-linear audiovisual media services. A basic, minimum level of content regulation will apply to non-linear audiovisual media services, whereas additional regulation will apply to linear audiovisual media services. The distinction between the two is likely to be of capital importance in respect of the future realization of the objective of promoting the distribution and production of European audiovisual content.

Under the AVMS Directive, the definition of 'European works' in Article 6 of the Television without Frontiers Directive is repositioned in Article 1, alongside other definitions that are of importance to the Directive. The order in which the various elements of the definition are listed is altered somewhat, but its substance remains the same: only Article 6(5)[12] falls by the wayside and no new elements are introduced. The AVMS Directive also leaves Articles 4–5 virtually untouched. However, it does envisage that the goal of promoting European works would also be pursued in respect of non-linear audiovisual media services as well. In general terms, Recital 48 of the AVMS Directive reads:

> On-demand audiovisual media services have the potential to partially replace television broadcasting. Accordingly, they should, where practicable, promote the production and distribution of European works and thus contribute actively to the promotion of cultural diversity. Such support for European works might, for example, take the form of financial contributions by such services to the production of and acquisition of rights in European works, a minimum share of European works in video-on-demand catalogues, or the attractive presentation of European works in electronic programme guides. It is important to regularly re-examine the application of the provisions relating to the promotion of European works by audiovisual media services. Within the framework of the reports set out under this Directive, Member States should also take into account notably the financial contribution by such services to the production and rights acquisition of European works, the share of European works in the catalogue of audiovisual media services and in the actual consumption of European works offered by such services.

More substantively, Article 3i reads:

1. Member States shall ensure that on-demand audiovisual media services provided by media service providers under their jurisdiction promote, where practicable and by appropriate means, the production of and access to European works. Such promotion could relate, *inter alia*, to the financial contribution made by such services to the production and rights acquisition of European works or to the share and/or prominence of European works in the catalogue of programmes offered by the on-demand audiovisual media service.
2. Member States shall report to the Commission no later than 19 December 2011 and every four years thereafter on the implementation of paragraph 1.
3. The Commission shall, on the basis of the information provided by Member States and of an independent study, report to the European Parliament and the Council on the application of paragraph 1, taking into account the market and technological developments and the objective of cultural diversity.

---

12 Article 6(5) reads: 'Works which are not European works within the meaning of paragraphs 1 and 4, but made mainly with authors and workers residing in one or more Member States, shall be considered to be European works to an extent corresponding to the proportion of the contribution of Community co-producers to the total production costs'.

This new Article prompts a few remarks. First, the manner in which paragraph 1 extends the requirement to promote European works to on demand services is far-reaching, even if: (1) the provision is promotional and non-prescriptive, and (2) flexibility is offered by the formulae 'where practicable and by appropriate means'. Second, paragraph 2 creates new reporting obligations for member states concerning the promotion, by on-demand services provided by media service providers, of the production of and access to European works. These reporting obligations are additional to those already established pursuant to Articles 4 and 5, Television without Frontiers Directive. Third, paragraph 3 envisages a double-barrelled evaluation exercise on the part of the EC. The express linking of the EC's reporting task to the objective of cultural diversity is useful insofar as it provides conceptual grounding for the exercise. The explicit references to the need to factor in considerations of market and technological developments follow through on Recital 48's emphasis on the need for regular re-examination of 'the application of the provisions relating to the promotion of European works by audiovisual media services'.

Critique of Articles 4–6 of the Television without Frontiers Directive

Nature of Obligations

Around the time of the initial adoption of the Television without Frontiers Directive, a certain amount of confusion arose concerning the precise nature of Article 4. For example, it was contended in some quarters that Article 4 did not entail a legal obligation, but a political commitment. This contention was largely based on press reports of comments by Martin Bangemann, then EC Vice President with responsibility for Internal Market and Industrial Affairs (Lupinacci 1991, 116; Wallace and Goldberg 1989a, 721). The press also made reference to statements in the Council minutes pertaining to the adoption of the Directive. The comments and statements were elevated – at least implicitly – to the status of having interpretive relevance for the Directive. However, it is erroneous to confer such an elevated interpretive status on remarks that were extraneous to the text of the Directive. It has been noted by several authoritative commentators that the conferral of heightened interpretive status on the aforementioned comments was 'legally untenable' (Wallace and Goldberg 1989b, 192). Pursuant to Article 189 of the EC Treaty, directives are binding in their entirety – the only discretion available to member states concerns the choice of means employed to achieve the desired goal; that discretion does not extend to the result to be achieved.

The readiness with which some contemporary academic literature embraced the interpretive power of statements devoid of legal force served to exacerbate confusion about the precise nature of Article 4. Subsequent academic literature did not, by and large, make this mistake (Machet 1999, 41; De Witte 1995; but c.f. Krebber 2002, 150), not least because an opportunity quickly presented itself for the EC to set the record straight. In response to a written Parliamentary question, Bangemann clarified that the text of the Television without Frontiers Directive:

is, in its entirety, legally binding on the Member States. The latter's fulfilment of their obligations will consequently be monitored by the Commission; such monitoring can in principle always result in an action being brought before the Court of Justice.

As far as Articles 4 and 5 are concerned, however, the wording adopted, which is the result of a difficult compromise and departs from the Commission's initial proposal and Parliament's wishes, allows Member States a great deal of discretion in choosing the means of attaining the desired result ('by appropriate means'); furthermore, and above all, it introduces an element of flexibility ('where practicable'), indicating that the attainment of the objectives can be overridden by technical constraints or economic imperatives.

While the flexibility incorporated into the provisions renders assessment more difficult, it in no way detracts from the legal nature of what amounts to an obligation to behave in a certain manner. Admittedly, however, it is difficult to imagine specific cases of application of those Articles that could be the subject of a clear ruling by the Court of Justice. [...][13]

Bangemann's statement makes candid reference to the 'difficult compromise' brokered in order to secure the necessary agreement for Articles 4 and 5 to be adopted in their current form. As mentioned earlier, the difficulties in question stemmed from diametrically opposed positions on the inclusion of the provisions as a matter of principle, never mind their scope. As a country with a typically interventionist approach to broadcasting, France, for instance, insisted on the inclusion of the provisions and lobbied strongly for high prescriptions of European audiovisual content. Other member states, such as Germany and the United Kingdom, which espoused more liberal philosophies as regards broadcasting, opposed the provisions and favoured limiting their scope. It was against this background of heated contention that Bangemann's comments sought to assuage the fears of liberals and of economically disadvantaged member states that failure to comply with the obligations set out in Articles 4 and 5 could lead to legal proceedings.

Bangemann's statement also adverts to the flexibility offered to member states by the formulae, 'by appropriate means' and 'where practicable'. Bangemann neglected to mention that the wording of Article 4 confers additional flexibility on member states by providing for the progressive attainment of the core obligations 'on the basis of suitable criteria' and 'having regard to the informational, educational, cultural and entertainment responsibilities' of a broadcaster to its viewing public (Holmes 2004, 195). It has been argued that such flexibility or looseness ultimately serves to undermine the effectiveness of Article 4 (Holmes 2004). When the cumulative effect of each of the clauses offering measures of flexibility to member states is considered, it is difficult to refute such a conclusion.

For member states wishing to evade their obligations under Article 4, the vagueness of these phrases provides convenient smoke screens. The requirement of 'progressive achievement' should not be regarded as problematic *per se*: it denotes an obligation that is weighted more heavily towards conduct/performance than result (see also Machet 1999, 62). Nevertheless, the requirement here would be bolstered

---

13   Answer given by Mr Bangemann on behalf of the Commission (4 January 1990) to Written Question No 758/89 by Mr Kenneth Collins (S) to the Commission of the European Communities (23 November 1989) (90/C97/39), OJ C97/22 of 17 April 1990.

if appropriate indicators were to be devised in order to measure progress towards the 'majority proportion' target. The Weber Report for the European Parliament has called for 'the discretion which the member states are permitted in applying Article 4 to at least be compensated for by the communication of public, precise and transparent indicators' (European Parliament 2005, paragraph 7). In this respect, it could be instructive to consider analogously the increased reliance on indicators and various benchmarks to monitor governmental performance as regards the progressive implementation of economic, social and cultural rights.[14]

Extent of Coverage

It has not always been patently clear what the full extent of Article 4 and 5 obligations actually is. The qualification 'where practicable and by appropriate means', and the reference to the broadcaster's 'informational, educational, cultural and entertainment responsibilities to its viewing public', both of which are included in Articles 4 and 5, are relevant here. They would appear to suggest a certain amount of flexibility concerning the extent to which broadcasting initiatives would be bound by relevant obligations. The point is of practical importance as the obligations in question inevitably entail financial consequences.

While the text of Articles 4 and 5 offer little guidance for the resolution of abstract questions about the extent of their coverage, it is possible to identify a number of cases to which the two Articles do not apply. For instance, Article 9, Television without Frontiers Directive stipulates that Articles 4 and 5 'shall not apply to television broadcasts that are intended for local audiences and do not form part of a national network'. According to the EC's Suggested Guidelines for the monitoring of the implementation of Articles 4 and 5, 'local' should be interpreted restrictively and be taken to mean 'sub-regional' (EC 1999). Thus, to the extent that the target audience of a minority television broadcaster (for example) is locally constituted, Articles 4 and 5 would not apply. Furthermore, Recital (29) of Directive 97/36/EC makes the case for the non-applicability of Articles 4 and 5 to channels broadcasting entirely in a language other than those of the member states (See also EC 1999, 2).

Conversely, it is also clear from the ECJ's judgment in the *Mediakabel* case[15] that Articles 4 and 5 *do* apply to near video-on-demand services. The crucial reasoning is provided in the following excerpt from the Court's judgment:

> 51. That provision [Article 4(1) of Directive 89/552] sets a quota for European works in the transmission time of the television broadcaster in question but cannot be intended to require television viewers to actually watch those works. Although it is undeniable that the provider of a service such as that at issue in the main proceedings does not determine the works which are actually chosen and watched by the subscribers, the fact remains that that provider, like any operator broadcasting television programmes intended for

---

14 This approach involves measuring the willingness of a government to implement human rights against its capacity to do so; the dissociation of a lack of moral or political commitment from financial or technical incapacity reveals any real progress or regression. See further Eide (2001).

15 *Mediakabel BV* v. *Commissariaat voor de Media* (C-89/04) [2005] ECR I-4891.

reception by the public, chooses the works which he broadcasts. The films which are in a list that that provider offers to the subscribers to the service all give rise to the broadcast of signals, transmitted in identical conditions to the subscribers, who have the choice to unencode or not the images thus transmitted. The provider therefore knows his overall transmission time, and can thus comply with the obligation imposed on him to reserve for European works ... a majority proportion of [his] transmission time.

Conceptual Integration and Friction

Articles 4 and 5 have been roundly criticized by many commentators for being little more than EU cultural protectionism unconvincingly dressed up as promoting creativity and cultural diversity (Harrison and Woods 2001; Katsirea 2003). In reality, they pursue dual economic and cultural objectives, but that conceptual integration has led to considerable friction. Nevertheless, it must be said that Articles 4 and 5 constitute particularly blunt instruments as regards their purported cultural objectives, for a number of reasons. First, they lack any qualitative criteria. They would appear to be predicated on a deterministic view of the media as considerations of impact or audience reception analysis are conspicuous by their absence. As Monroe Price has argued, it is important to resist assertions that media effects are straightforwardly hypodermic and to challenge the 'simple equivalence of viewing and impact' (Price 1995, 77). Being purely quantitative in character, Articles 4 and 5 are only useful for raw and unrefined economic analysis. They cannot be evaluated in qualitative cultural terms.

Article 4(3) provides for biannual reporting by member states on the implementation of Articles 4 and 5 within their jurisdictions. The data provided in the context of that reporting process is primarily statistical. The collected data is processed and synthesized by the EC in biannual Communications on the overall application of Articles 4 and 5 in member states. In the EC's most recent Communications, the general conclusions have been positive: in its Fifth Communication, it noted the 'generally satisfactory application' of Articles 4 and 5 (EC 2002, 41); in its Sixth Communication, it concluded that the objectives of Articles 4 and 5 'have been achieved' over the reference period and compared with the previous reference period (EC 2004, 11), and in its Seventh and latest Communication, the conclusion was that the objectives of Articles 4 and 5 'have been comfortably met over the current reference period (2003–2004), as in previous reporting periods, both at European level and at level of member states, including the ten member states which joined the EU in 2004' (EC 2006, 9). Relevant sections of the EC's periodic reports on the general application of the Television without Frontiers Directive tend to merely summarize the most recent communications on the application of Articles 4 and 5.

These general conclusions and the more detailed statistical data on which they are based are not accompanied by any content-oriented analysis. As such, they tell us nothing about the extent to which such generally positive trends regarding the transmission by broadcasters of European, independent European, and recently produced independent European works are effective in their stated objective of stimulating cultural creativity. It cannot be assumed – one way or another – that such generally positive trends in any sense reflect the fortunes or failings of broadcasters in their transmission of cultural programming. Any evaluation of the latter type would necessarily require elaborate methodology which would disaggregate data in a way that would meaningfully identify and zone in on specific aspects of programming (for example, language, content, format, and so on). Such a re-aligned approach would also help to translate into practice one of the statements contained in Recital 31 to Directive 97/36/EC, *viz.* that 'with a view to promoting the production of European works, it is essential that the Community, taking into account the audiovisual capacity of each member state and the need to protect lesser used languages of the European Union, should promote independent producers'.

Second, Articles 4 and 5 lack any stipulations about time-scheduling and they lack any requirement to reinvest percentages of *profits* in new, independent European production. Such shortcomings increase the likelihood of mere *pro forma* compliance with Articles 4 and 5 by cost-conscious broadcasters who might prefer to meet their obligations by transmitting cheap, low-quality programming during off-peak hours. Such practices manifestly do disservice to relevant cultural objectives and are clearly in breach of the spirit of Articles 4 and 5, even if they would not, technically speaking, contravene the letter of the same articles. Again, the monitoring exercise lacks the methodological sophistication to be able to ascertain whether there is a tendency to rely on so-called 'quota quickies' (that is, programmes produced quickly and cheaply without much (if any) regard for their content and broadcast merely to fulfil quota obligations).

Legal Bases for Cultural Objectives

The European content requirement has been described as a '*corpus alienum*' in the Internal Market logic with which the Television without Frontiers Directive is infused (De Witte 1995, 106). One reason for this is that at the time of the adoption of the Television without Frontiers Directive, there was no specific basis in EU Treaty law for the EC to take action in the cultural field (Craufurd Smith 2004a, esp. 19–20; De Witte 1995, 117–119). Consequently, the legality of the Directive was deemed contestable, at least to the extent that it, or more specifically, its Article 4, could be considered 'an instrument of cultural policy' (De Witte 1995, 117). However, in relevant EC circles, there was a clear resolve not to allow the EC's lack of competence to implement a cultural policy to become an insurmountable impediment to its engagement with cultural issues. The strategy used to legitimize such engagement was to seize upon economic aspects of the so-called European culture industry (Collins 1994, 90). This strategy is exemplified by the Television without Frontiers Directive, insofar as the Directive 'provides a striking instance of an ostensibly economic Community policy having a major impact on culture' (Collins 1994, 91).

With the amendment of the EC Treaty by the Treaty on European Union in 1992, a new Article 128 (dealing with culture) was inserted into the former (Treaty on European Union 1992, Article G, para. 37). Article 128(4) read: 'The Community shall take cultural aspects into account in its action under other provisions of this Treaty' and thereby provided a legal basis for factoring cultural considerations into the decision-making processes governing a broad range of Community actions. The

Treaty of Amsterdam (1997) resulted in the following words being appended to Article 128(4): 'in particular in order to respect and to promote the diversity of its cultures'. It also led to the renumbering of Article 128 in its entirety as Article 151.

To conclude, Article 151 (ex-Article 128) of the EC Treaty establishing the European Community has become one of the most important legal bases for the protection of cultural heritage and diversity within the EU. Article 151(1) states: 'The Community shall contribute to the flowering of the cultures of the member states, while respecting their national and regional diversity and at the same time bringing the common cultural heritage to the fore'.

Article 22 of the Charter of Fundamental Rights of the European Union is entitled 'Cultural, religious and linguistic diversity'; it reads: 'The Union shall respect cultural, religious and linguistic diversity'. It is based on Article 6, TEU, and Article 151(1) and (4) of the EC Treaty.[16] Although the explicit reference to cultural diversity is welcome, it is hard to refute the suggestion that its importance is more symbolic than real. Pending the outcome of the stalled European Constitution, the Nice Charter remains a document that is merely politically (and not legally) binding on EU member states. Moreover, even that symbolic importance is questionable, because, first of all, 'shall respect' is a significantly weaker formulation than, for example, 'guarantee' or 'secure'. As such, it involves a considerably lighter commitment for states. Second, the Explanatory Note does not spell out the essence or scope of cultural diversity, which suggests a non-committal attitude to – or wariness of – its actual or potential implications.

It is also disappointing that the commentary on Article 22 provided by the EU Network of Independent Experts on Fundamental Rights should only stretch to little over two pages (Benoît-Rohmer 2006). Its brevity could not possibly do justice to such an expansive and expanding topic. Despite the fact that the substance of the Charter shall not reduce or restrict the level of human rights protection guaranteed *inter alia* by international law and other international agreements by which the EU or its member states are bound (Article 53; see also Article 52(3)), the commentary on Article 22 hardly engages with the treatment of relevant legal issues under international (human rights) treaties at all.

More pointedly, the commentary is, in effect, dismissive of the importance of European Convention on Human Rights (ECHR) jurisprudence dealing with cultural matters. It states, in a brief paragraph, that in the absence of any specific provision in the ECHR that is 'comparable to' Article 22 of the Charter, the relevant case law of the European Court of Human Rights is limited to Article 14, ECHR, which focuses on non-discrimination in the exercise of rights safeguarded by the Convention. It then dispenses with the relevant case law by cursorily mentioning three cases – without

---

16 Note from the Praesidium, Draft Charter of Fundamental Rights of the European Union – Text of the explanations relating to the complete text of the Charter as set out in CHARTE 4487/00 CONVENT 50, 11 October 2000, CHARTE 4473/00, p. 23. Explanations relating to the Charter of Fundamental Rights, as prepared under the authority of the Praesidium of the Convention which drafted the Charter (and since updated under the responsibility of the Praesidium of the European Convention, which drafted the European Constitution): see OJEC of 16 December 2004, C310/424 *et seq.*, and for Article 22 of the Charter, p. 439.

even giving their facts or indicating their doctrinal importance. It is regrettable, to say the least, that such short shrift should be given in such an influential document to an area of 'burgeoning' jurisprudential growth within the ECHR (Gilbert 2002). Cultural diversity can only be achieved when pluralism is safeguarded at societal level, meaning that groups are able to practise their distinctive cultures both in public and in private. The exercise of cultural rights therefore entails the right to lead particular lifestyles, participate in cultural life and assemble, associate and organize for cultural purposes (Donders 2002; McGonagle 2008). As such, cultural rights can be described as having a high level of valency and interdependence with other rights. For that reason, the absence in the ECHR of a specific provision comparable to Article 22 of the Charter is not a valid reason to downplay the importance of provisions and case law ostensibly dealing with other rights, but also having clear relevance for cultural rights.

The commentary makes an explicit link between cultural diversity and broadcasting. It describes the Television without Frontiers Directive as being the text that is probably the closest to Article 22 of the Charter because of the instrumentality of its quota system for European works for preserving cultural creation and therefore diversity. However, the present tense is used when stressing the importance of Article 8, Television without Frontiers Directive, for guaranteeing linguistic diversity, and the text (thereby) fails to mention that Article 8[17] was deleted by Directive 97/36/EC (although its essence has been subsumed into the reformulated Article 3, Television without Frontiers Directive).[18] All in all, because the analysis is so brief and broadbrush, its explanatory value is rather limited.

Cultural-cum-Commercial Objectives

It has been noted by the European Parliament that 'a majority of the quotas are filled by national works' (European Parliament 2005, 11–12). Although the Parliament considers this to be 'positive' in respect of the Directive generally, it finds that 'it is not sufficient for creating a European audiovisual space, which has yet to take shape' (see also Ward 2004). This would clearly suggest that Article 4 falls well short of the mark in respect of one of the (nominal) aims of the EU's audiovisual policy. This impression needs to be viewed in light of a couple of contextualizing – and perhaps ultimately mitigating – considerations. First, it has been noted that quotas relating to European content (as opposed to national content) did not exist in any of the member states prior to the adoption of the directive (Holmes 2004, 194–195). Furthermore,

---

17   Article 8 of Directive 89/552/EEC read: 'Where they consider it necessary for purposes of language policy, the Member States, whilst observing Community law, may as regards some or all programmes of television broadcasters under their jurisdiction, lay down more detailed or stricter rules in particular on the basis of language criteria'.

18   The operative sentence reads: 'La directive 89/552/CEE du 30 juin 1987 [*sic*] sur la télévision sans frontières est sans doute le texte le plus proche de l'article 22 dans la mesure où il prévoit un système de quotas d'oeuvres européennes afin de préserver la création, et donc la diversité culturelle, et où il permet aux Etats membres, dans son article 8, d'avoir des exigences plus strictes afin d'assurer la diversité linguistique', Benoît-Rohmer (2006), p. 199.

predominant reliance on national works can hardly be regarded as surprising. The appeal of the local – across a variety of programme genres and formats – has frequently been confirmed by audience research. This is largely explained by audiences' viewing preferences and their perceptions of the relevance of programming to their own experiences. Such a sense of experiential connectedness is often missing when it comes to audiovisual content produced in other member states that might not share obvious cultural affinities with the state of reception. It is interesting to note that concerns have been expressed that the protection of 'European works' could even have detrimental consequences for national works. More concretely, this involves the fear that 'the protection of "Community works" favours essentially the most powerful audiovisual industries within the EC (France, FRG, Italy, UK)' and that consequently, 'small countries with low audiovisual production should be authorized to fix, at least for a transitional period, safeguard clauses in favour of their national industry within the EC quotas' (EIM 1987, 11). It was proposed that such safeguard clauses 'could be fixed at 25 per cent of Community production' (EIM 1987).

The European content requirement would appear to be premised, in part, on a vision of the EU as a cultural area of at least approximate coherence. It has correctly been pointed out that the EU is not a 'culturally homogeneous area', and that some member states share greater cultural commonalities with some non–member states than with many other member states (De Witte 1995, 112). This is explained in some cases by the reality of geographical proximity, and in others by historical factors such as (former) political boundaries and (traditional) patterns of emigration and immigration. Nevertheless, the wording of Article 4 ignores the dynamics of cultural affinity and engagement with non–EU member states. Those dynamics are often more determinative of a given member state's cultural identity than its tenuous cultural relationship with other EU member states. This point is perhaps best illustrated with a concrete example. Whereas Ireland has few obvious and long standing cultural connections with, say, Greece or Malta, the importance of its relationship with the United States in defining its current-day cultural identity cannot be gainsaid.

The principal practical upshot of the observation set out in the previous paragraph is that the European content requirement neither recognizes nor accommodates cultural affinities with non–EU member states insofar as they are not covered by the provisions of Article 6. In this respect, at least, the protectionist essence of the European content requirement is exposed. The cultural relevance of non–member states is *prima facie* excluded.

The Contestability of European Identity

Benedict Anderson has famously defined/described a nation as 'an imagined political community' that is limited [by physical boundaries] and sovereign (Anderson 1991, 6). Anderson's description of a nation as 'imagined' places it very consciously in opposition to Ernest Gellner's characterization of a nation as an invention (Gellner 1974, 169). For Anderson, invention rhymes with 'fabrication' and 'falsity', whereas 'imagining' and 'creation' would actually be closer to the mark. He explains: 'In fact, all communities larger than primordial villages of face-to-face contact (and perhaps even these) are imagined. Communities are to be distinguished, not by their falsity/ genuineness, but by the style in which they are imagined' (Anderson 1991, 6).

But nations – and indeed other communities – can be imagined in different ways, including ways which are less contingent on geopolitical limitations. Cultural and national contours do not always match, after all. These imaginings can incorporate a diasporic dimension (Morley and Robins 1995), a term which itself comprises a high level of internal differentiation. Whether communities are imagined as nations, or in sub-, inter-, or extra-national terms, or whether groups are constituted on the basis of ideological or other affinities or objectives, an appropriate, formal framework is necessary to ensure the protection and promotion of their identities (Hjarvard 2003, 11).

There is, however, something more contrived about the European identity building project (McQuail 2005, 266). Indeed, the legitimacy of using Community cultural policy 'as a vehicle to promote European identity' is itself open to question (Craufurd Smith 2004b, 295). As the maxim 'unity in diversity' has become increasingly *de rigueur* in EU cultural policy, the project of promoting a so-called European identity has increasingly become a red herring. Its former appeal should be noted, at least for the historical record. In this respect, the aforementioned Hahn Report has some residual relevance. The following excerpt from the Report is perhaps its most quoted passage:

Information is a decisive, perhaps the most decisive factor in European unification ... It is essentially true that ... European unification will only be achieved if Europeans want it. Europeans will only want it if there is such a thing as a European identity. A European identity will only develop if Europeans are adequately informed. At present, information via the mass media is controlled at national level. The vast majority of journalists do not 'think European' because their reporting role is defined in national or regional terms. Hence the predominance of negative reporting. Therefore, if European unification is to be encouraged, Europe must penetrate the media'. (European Parliament 1982a, 8 (para. 3))

The Report goes on to rue the fact that the media are predominantly organized and operate along national (as opposed to European) axes. Basically, the Report pines for the creation of a viable public sphere at the European level,[19] but appears to mix up concerns about a democratic deficit in the EEC (as it was then known) and the complex but flawed notion of a distinct European identity. Kevin Robins has the measure of the challenges ahead when he writes about:

... the imperative to effect some kind of distancing from the national imagination and the national paradigm if we are to develop a European media policy that is sensitive to the new cultural diversity of the continent. In the 1990s, the European Commission struggled with the question of diversity within the framework of a policy primarily concerned with the need to create an expanded, pan-European market ('television without frontiers'). But diversity was seen in rather limited terms – in terms of the Europe of nation states and/or the Europe of the regions. The *imaginaire* remained essentially national. And it was an *imaginaire* that did not address – because it could not recognize – the actual complexity

19 For a comprehensive analysis of the relevance of EU media policy for the notion of a European-level public sphere, see generally Ward (2004).

and diversity of Europe. The national imagination stood in the way of moving cultural thinking and policy forward in order that it might accommodate the realities of the new Europe (Robins 2006a, 144).

Conclusion

The foregoing discussion has demonstrated the complexity, not only of the Television without Frontiers Directive edifice, but of the architectural principles employed in its construction. It rests on different legal foundations, fixes different objectives and uses different strategies for the attainment of those objectives. These factors give rise to tensions that can be both centrifugal and centripetal. Articles 4–6 illustrate the point nicely. The objectives of stimulating cultural creativity in the European audiovisual sector and of pursuing the philosophy of the internal market are not necessarily mutually exclusive: the economic dimension to cultural production is often inevitable. However, the additional rationales for Articles 4–6, *viz.* to protect the European Community, culturally and economically, from US hegemony in the audiovisual sector, introduces a new and complicating variable into the equation. Cultural objectives have thus become transmuted into primarily commercial objectives by the prioritization accorded to increasing the competitiveness of the European audiovisual industry.

Another erstwhile goal of the European audiovisual project – the creation of a European public sphere or sense of European consciousness – increasingly appears to have only residual relevance for policy-making at the EU level. It is unfortunate that this goal has often been equated with, and even eclipsed by, ill-conceived ambitions to use the audiovisual sector as a catalyst for the creation (or reinforcement) of a putative European identity. The European public sphere objective has not yet been articulated with sufficient clarity and thoroughness in legal or political texts, nor has it been pursued with sufficient vigour in relevant fora, to dislodge the current supremacy of economic logic in European audiovisual policy-making. Philip Schlesinger identifies and usefully synopsizes the underlying issues when he writes:

> Although economic competitiveness in the global market is of major importance, it cannot be equated with meeting all the needs of citizens for participation in the determination of political and cultural affairs. As part of rethinking media structures and regulatory regimes, we also need to consider their relations to cultural diversity and democracy without totally subordinating these considerations to the logic of the market. (Schlesinger 1996, 105)

All things considered, it is difficult not to endorse a conclusion tentatively put forward by Schlesinger: 'Perhaps, worrying about America has become an alibi for not thinking creatively enough about Europe' (Schlesinger 1996, 105). The faith placed in the vigour of the European audiovisual sector in the EC's Proposal for a directive to amend Directive 98/552/EEC, discussed above, proved very short-lived. The animating priorities of EU's audiovisual policy, whether cultural, commercial or democratic in their orientation, all tend to show signs of atrophy from having spent too long in the shade of fearfulness towards the United States. It is high time that they find their own place in the sun and be allowed to grow accordingly.

References

Anderson, B. (1991), *Imagined Communities: Reflections on the Origin and Spread of Nationalism*. Revised Edition. London and New York: Verso.

Benoît-Rohmer, F. (2006), 'Article 22 – Cultural, Religious and Linguistic Diversity', in EU Network of Independent Experts on Fundamental Rights, *The Commentary of the Charter of Fundamental Rights of the European Union*, 197–199.

Collins, R. (1993), 'The Screening of Jacques Tati: Broadcasting and Cultural Identity in the European Community', *Cardozo Arts & Ent. L.J.* 11, 361–385.

Collins, R. (1994), 'Unity in Diversity? The European Single Market in Broadcasting and the Audiovisual, 1982–1992', *Journal of Common Market Studies* 32(1), 89–102.

Council of Europe (1989), *European Convention on Transfrontier Television (1989), ETS No. 132, as amended by its Amending Protocol* (1998), *ETS No. 171*, which entered into force on 1 March 2002.

Craufurd Smith, R. (2004a), 'Community Intervention in the Cultural Field: Continuity or Change?', in Craufurd Smith, R. (ed.), *Culture and European Union Law*. Oxford: Oxford University Press, 19–78.

Craufurd Smith, R. (2004b), 'Article 151 EC and European Identity', in Craufurd Smith, R. (ed.), *Culture and European Union Law*. Oxford: Oxford University Press, 277–297.

Craufurd Smith, R. (1997), *Broadcasting Law and Fundamental Rights*. Oxford: Clarendon Press.

De Witte, B. (1995), 'The European Content Requirement in the EC Television Directive – Five Years After', in Barendt, E. et al. (eds.). *Yearbook of Media and Entertainment Law*, Vol. I. Oxford: Oxford University Press, 102–127.

Dolmans, M. (1995), 'Quotas without Content', *Ent. L.R.* 6(8), 329–333.

Donders, Y.M. (2002), *Towards a Right to Cultural Identity?* Antwerpen: Intersentia.

Dupagne, M. (1992), 'EC Policymaking: The Case of the "Television without Frontiers" Directive', *The International Communication Gazette* 49(1–2), 99–120.

Eide, A. (2001), 'The Use of Indicators in the Practice of the Committee on Economic, Social and Cultural Rights', in Eide et al. (eds.) (2001), *Economic, Social and Cultural Rights: A Textbook*. Second Revised Edition. Dordrecht: Martinus Nijhoff Publishers, 545–551.

European Commission (1983), Realities and tendencies in European television: perspectives and options, Interim Report, COM(83) 229 final, Brussels, 25 May 1983.

European Commission (1984), Television without Frontiers: Green Paper on the establishment of the Common Market for broadcasting, especially by satellite and cable, Communication from the Commission to the Council, COM(84) 300 final, Brussels, 14 June 1984.

European Commission (1986), Commission of the European Communities, Proposal for a Council Directive on the coordination of certain provisions laid down by law, regulation or administrative action in Member States concerning the pursuit of broadcasting activities, COM(86) 146 final/2, Brussels, 6 June 1986.

European Commission (1994), Strategy options to strengthen the European programme industry in the context of the audiovisual policy of the European Union (Green Paper), COM (94)96 final, Brussels, 6 June 1994.

European Commission (1995), Report on application of Directive 89/552/EEC and Proposal for a European Parliament and Council Directive amending Council Directive 89/552/EEC on the coordination of certain provisions laid down by law, regulation or administrative action in Member States concerning the pursuit of television broadcasting activities, COM (95)86 final, Brussels, 31 May 1995.

European Commission (1999), Suggested Guidelines for the monitoring of the implementation of Articles 4 and 5 of the 'Television without Frontiers' Directive, 11 June 1999. http://ec.europa.eu/avpolicy/docs/reg/tvwf/eu_works/controle45_en.pdf.

European Commission (2002), Fifth Communication from the Commission to the Council and the European Parliament on the application of Articles 4 and 5 of Directive 89/552/EEC 'Television without Frontiers', as amended by Directive 97/36/EC, for the period 1999–2000, COM(2002) 612 final, 8 November 2002.

European Commission (2004), Sixth Communication from the Commission to the Council and the European Parliament on the application of Articles 4 and 5 of Directive 89/552/EEC 'Television without Frontiers', as amended by Directive 97/36/EC, for the period 2001–2002, COM(2004) 524 final, 28 July 2004.

European Commission (2006), Seventh Communication from the Commission to the European Parliament, the Council, the European Economic and Social Committee and the Committee of the Regions on the application of Articles 4 and 5 of Directive 89/552/EEC 'Television without Frontiers', as amended by Directive 97/36/EC, for the period 2003–2004, COM(2006) 459 final, 14 August 2006.

European Institute for the Media (EIM) (1987), *Towards a European Common Market for Television: Contribution to the Debate*. Media Monograph No. 8. Manchester: EIM.

European Parliament (1982a), Report on radio and television in the European Community, Drawn up on behalf of the Committee on Youth, Culture, Education, Information and Sport ('The Hahn Report'), Rapporteur: W. Hahn, European Parliament Working Doc. 1-1013/81, 23 February 1982.

European Parliament (1982b), European Parliament Resolution on radio and television broadcasting in the European Community, adopted on 12 March 1982, as published in OJEC No C 87/110 of 5 April 1982.

European Parliament (1985a), Report on a framework for a European media policy based on the Commission's Green Paper on the establishment of the common market for broadcasting, especially by satellite and cable (COM(84) 300 final), drawn up on behalf of the Committee on Youth, Culture, Education, Information and Sport ('The Hahn Report (No. 2)'), Rapporteur: W. Hahn, European Parliament Working Documents, Series A, Doc. No. A2-75/85, 5 July 1985.

European Parliament (1985b), Report on the economic aspects of the common market for broadcasting (COM(84) 300 fin.), drawn up on behalf of the Committee on Economic and Monetary Affairs and Industrial Policy ('The De Vries Report'), Rapporteur: Gijs De Vries, European Parliament Working Documents, Series A,

Doc. No. A2-102/85, 30 September 1985.

European Parliament (1985c), Resolution on a framework for a European media policy based on the Commission's Green Paper on the establishment of the common market for broadcasting, especially by satellite and cable ('The Hahn Resolution (No. 2)'), Doc. A2-75/85, adopted on 10 October 1985, as published in the OJEC C 288/113 of 11 November 1985.

European Parliament (1985d), European Parliament Resolution on the economic aspects of the common market for broadcasting in the European Community, Doc. A2-102/85, adopted on 10 October 1985, as published in the OJEC C 288/119 of 11 November 1985.

European Parliament (1987), Report on the proposal from the European Commission of the European Communities to the Council (COM(86) 146 final – Doc. C 2-38/86) for a directive on the coordination of certain provisions laid down by law, regulation or administrative action in Member States concerning the pursuit of broadcasting activities, drawn up on behalf of the Committee on Legal Affairs and Citizens' Rights ('The Barzanti Report'), Rapporteur: Roberto Barzanti, European Parliament Session Documents, Series A, Doc. No. A 2-0246/87, 8 December 1987.

European Parliament (2005), Report on the application of Articles 4 and 5 of Directive 89/552/EEC (the 'TV without Frontiers' Directive), as amended by Directive 97/36/EC, for the period 2001–2002 (2004/2236(INI)) ('The Weber Report'), European Parliament Committee on Culture and Education, Rapporteur: Henri Weber, Doc. No. A6-0202/2005, 21 June 2005.

Geller, H. (1990), 'Mass communications policy: where we are and where we should be going', in Lichtenberg, J. (ed.), *Democracy and the Mass Media*. USA: Cambridge University Press, 290–330.

Gilbert, G. (2002), 'The Burgeoning Minority Rights Jurisprudence of the European Court of Human Rights', *Human Rights Quarterly* 24(3), 736–780.

Goldberg, D. et al. (1998), *EC Media Law and Policy*. London and New York: Longman.

Harrison, J. and Woods, L. (2001), 'Television Quotas: Protecting European Culture?', *Entertainment Law Review* 12(1), 5–14.

Hjarvard, S. (ed.) (2003), *Media in a Globalized Society*. Copenhagen: Museum Tusculanum Press/University of Copenhagen.

Holmes, J. (2004), 'European Community Law and the Cultural Aspects of Television', in R. Craufurd Smith (ed.), *Culture and European Union Law*. Oxford: Oxford University Press, 169–203.

Humphreys, P.J. (1996), *Mass Media and Media Policy in Western Europe*. Manchester: Manchester University Press.

Katsirea, I. (2003), 'Why the European Broadcasting Quota should be Abolished', *European Law Review* 28(2), 190–209.

Krebber, D. (2002), *Europeanisation of Regulatory Television Policy: The Decision-making Process of the Television without Frontiers Directives from 1989 & 1997*. Baden-Baden: Nomos Verlagsgesellschaft.

Lupinacci, T.M. (1991), 'The Pursuit of Television Broadcasting Activities in the European Community: Cultural Preservation or Economic Protectionism?', *Vand.*

J. Transnat'l L. 24, 113–154.

Machet, E. (1999), *A Decade of EU Broadcasting Regulation: The Directive 'Television without Frontiers'*. Düsseldorf: The European Institute for the Media.

McGonagle, T. and Van Loon, A. (2002), 'Jurisdiction over Broadcasters in Europe: Report on a Round-table Discussion', in Nikoltchev, S. (ed.) (2002), *IRIS Special: Jurisdiction over Broadcasters in Europe - Report on a Round-table Discussion & Selection of Background Materials*. Strasbourg: European Audiovisual Observatory, 1–21.

McGonagle, T. (2008, forthcoming), *Minority Rights and Freedom of Expression: A Dynamic Interface*. Ph.D. thesis, University of Amsterdam.

McQuail, D. (2005), *McQuail's Mass Communication Theory*. Fifth Edition. London: Sage.

Morley, D. and Robins, K. (1995), *Spaces of Identity: Global Media, Electronic Landscapes and Cultural Boundaries*. London: Routledge.

Nikoltchev, S. (ed.) (2002), *IRIS Special: Jurisdiction over Broadcasters in Europe – Report on a Round-table Discussion & Selection of Background Materials*. Strasbourg: European Audiovisual Observatory.

Price, M.E. (1995), *Television, The Public Sphere, and National Identity*. Oxford: Clarendon Press.

Robins, K. (2006), 'Transnational Media, Cultural Diversity and New Public Cultures' in Robins, K. et al., *The Challenge of Transcultural Diversities: Cultural Policy and Cultural Diversity*. Strasbourg: Council of Europe Publishing.

Schlesinger, P. (1996), 'Should We Worry about America?', in Van Hemel, A., Mommaas, H. and Smithuijsen, C. (eds) (1996), *Trading Culture: GATT, European Cultural Policies and the Transatlantic Market*. Amsterdam: Boekman Foundation, 96–110.

Steenbruggen, W. (2003), 'NL – Dutch Regulator Cannot Claim Jurisdiction over RTL4 and RTL5', *IRIS – Legal Observations of the European Audiovisual Observatory* 8, 12.

Treaty on European Union (1992), OJ C191/01, 29 July 1992 (Title II - Provisions Amending the Treaty Establishing the European Economic Community with a View to Establishing the European Community), Article G, para. 37; signed in Maastricht on 7 February 1992.

Wallace, R. and Goldberg, D. (1989a), 'Television Broadcasting: The Community's Response', *Common Market Law Review* 26, 717–728.

Wallace, R. and Goldberg, D. (1989b), 'The EEC Directive on Television Broadcasting', *Yearbook of European Law* 9, 175–196.

Ward, D. (2004), *The European Union Democratic Deficit and the Public Sphere: An Evaluation of EU Media Policy*. Amsterdam: IOS Press.

Chapter 10

Promises and Pitfalls of the European Copyright Law Harmonization Process

Maria Lillà Montagnani and Maurizio Borghi[1*]

This chapter explores the current level of harmonization in copyright and related rights law[2] that has developed within the context of the European Union (EU) and its attempt to establish a legal framework to foster growth in production and distribution of content. In surveying the Community directives constituting the current *aquis communautaire* together with an analysis of their implementation, emerging trends and pitfalls are outlined that raise doubts as to the consistency of the assumptions underlying the current copyright law policy of the EU.

The first part of the chapter discusses the process of harmonization leading to the current legal framework and stresses its discrepancies in order to ascertain whether the current level of protection creates value and increases the EU's competitiveness. The second part of the chapter addresses current European copyright law policy in respect of two relevant issues: first, the impact of such policy on the ways in which cultural goods are produced and distributed in the digital environment, and second, the emerging conflict between the proprietary regime that has been developed and the fundamental rights of freedom of expression.

Creating Value through Harmonizing Copyright within the EU

In the Final Report of 20 October 2003 on The Contribution of Copyright and Related Rights to the European Economy adopted by the Media Group Business of the Research and Development Centre (Media Group Business 2003), it is claimed that:

> The legal protection afforded by the relevant rights i.e. copyright and related rights allows for the development of a copyright industry that contributed more than €1.2 trillion (€1,200 billion) to the economy of the European Union, produced value added of €450

---

1 * Although this chapter is the result of mutual research and analysis and the authors share the views therein expressed, the first part is attributable to Maria Lillà Montagnani and the second part to Maurizio Borghi.

2 The term 'copyright law' herein encompasses both copyright and related rights unless otherwise specified and it refers to both civil law and common law jurisdictions. The distinction between author's right and copyright is thus made only when the different traditions are considered.

billion, and employed 5.2 million persons in 2000. The total gross value added, which measures wealth added to the economy, represented more than 5.3 % of the total value added for the 15 EU member states. (Media Group Business 2003, 1)

Although this estimate of the value of the copyright industries is based on data from 2000, it gives an idea of the progressive awareness of copyright as a key element of European economies, to the extent of requiring increasing attention from legal and policy points of view. The Report suggests that:

[T]he Commission and member states ... continue to ensure that EU copyright policies, member state laws, and international copyright agreements provide *adequate protection* of copyright and related intellectual property rights (*emphasis added*). New forms and formats of copyright material and the changing nature of information is not always recognized or fully addressed in existing legislation. The Commission and member states should continue to ensure that appropriate copyright enforcement mechanisms and processes are in place so that the Community benefits economically from these important industries and activities. (Media Group Business 2003, 10)

The reasoning underlying the report's conclusions is self-evident. Adequate legal protection is perceived to increase the productivity of the culture industries, which in turn strengthens the internal market and competitiveness of industry. The whole harmonization phenomenon is based around this concept of adequate legal protection as a means to increase production. What is lost in the concept of adequateness of protection is that it does not always mean stronger protection, while it may mean increased artificial scarcity whenever a loss of economic efficiency occurs due to the creation of unnecessary monopolies over non-rival resources such as cultural and information goods.

Before entering into details of the harmonization process, it is important to stress that the current copyright framework at the EU level derives from the EU's lack of direct legislative competence in this area. The absence of a Community wide copyright is primarily due to copyright harmonization being based on the EC Treaty provisions which enable the EU to coordinate member states' laws with regard to the freedom of goods and services throughout the internal market (Articles 45, 47(2) and 55). Therefore, as long as national copyright does not distort the internal market and limit distribution, it is a matter for member states' national laws with EU law restricted to what is necessary for the sole purpose of enforcing and developing the principles of the internal market against the territoriality of copyright and related rights.

Such tension between the exclusivity of national intellectual property laws and the economic interests promoting a common market is further amplified by the co-existence of different legal traditions across member states. While in continental Europe copyright statutes belong to the realm of civil law *droit d'auteur*, in the UK the common law system adopts a utilitarian approach to cultural expression (Goldstein 2001, 5–11). Furthermore, even within civil law countries different approaches to copyright coexist due to national laws being rooted in either monistic or dualistic theory (Salokannel and Strowel 2000). The harmonization of copyright which is deemed necessary to increase the competitiveness and value of the

European cultural industries cannot therefore have developed without consideration of the variety of cultural, historical, legal and social differences that have historically underpinned the member states' approach to the culture industries and copyright protection (Sterling 2003, 585–590).

Community Case Law Initiating the Legislative Harmonization Process

Prior to the start of a more formularized harmonization process the tension between copyright territoriality and the establishment of the internal market emerged in a number of cases dealt with by national and regional courts. The cases tended to confirm the predominance of the common market principles over exclusivity and territoriality in the field of copyright protection.

The mechanism balancing internal market principles over copyright territoriality is the judicial interpretation of Article 30 of the EC Treaty which justifies quantitative restrictions on import and exports of goods and equivalent measures (prohibited under Articles 28 and 29 of the EC Treaty) on the grounds, *inter alia*, of the protection of industrial and commercial property, under which intellectual property rights fall. Though permitted within the terms of the EC Treaty, such restrictions 'shall not, however, constitute a means of arbitrary discrimination or a disguised restriction on trade between member states' (EC Treaty, Article 30). Such a basis suggests that, whenever a conflict between free movement of goods and services and intellectual property rights arises, a 'qualified priority' should be given to the latter (Keeling 2003, 28).

In *Deutsche Grammophon* v. *Metro*[3] the former tried to prevent the resale in Germany of copyrighted musical recordings, which its French subsidiaries had marketed in France, by invoking the exclusivity of the distribution right that the company held as the producer. Such behaviour was deemed unlawful as it distorts the internal market. All subsequent tests elaborated by the European courts to solve this tension between territoriality of copyright and common market principles are already evident in this early decision. Firstly – and according to the 'qualified priority' given by Article 30 of the EC Treaty to industrial and commercial property – Community law can never affect the existence of intellectual property rights, rather, the exercise of EC law is limited to a narrow area where trade between member states is distorted. Secondly, restrictions to the *exercise* of intellectual property rights can only be imposed to prevent right holders' behaviours that is not consistent with the exclusive right which they have been granted. In other words, such restrictions should not impede right holders from commercially exploiting and morally protecting their works, rather, they should prevent them from expanding the boundaries of their rights outside their traditional scope through the adoption of behaviour falling outside the specific subject matter of the exclusive right. Finally, the right to control the distribution of copyrighted works exhausts with their first lawful commercialization as right holders cannot invoke their distribution rights to

---

3   *Deutsche Grammophon* v. *Metro* (78/70) [1971] ECR 487.

prevent third parties who have lawfully acquired the rights from further exploiting them.

Although Community exhaustion in copyright is the dominant mechanism in promoting the internal market, it still encounters a few limits: there are a few cases in which territoriality of copyright does not surrender to the internal market principles. A first limit to the free circulation of copyrighted products lies in the right holders having authorized the circulation of those goods. In *EMI Electrola* v. *Patricia Im-und Export*[4] the German copyright holder successfully prevented copyright recordings from being marketed in Denmark since this was occurring without his consent. In this case the Danish company argued it was entitled to distribute the copyrighted goods initially marketed in Germany on the grounds that, because of the differences in term of protection, copyright protection would have already expired in Denmark. However, the ECJ deemed that consent does not exist (therefore circulation can be prevented even within the common market) when a third party makes and distributes goods in a country where the right has lapsed. Hence, once the availability of copyrighted goods by third parties is exploited without the right holder's consent, the distribution right enables the latter to control any further transfer and to prevent those goods from further circulating.

A second limit to the internal market reasoning in favour of copyright territoriality was found in the nature of the works whose free circulation is sought. In *Coditel* v. *Ciné Vog Film*[5] the ECJ was required to rule whether a French company holding the copyright to a series of movies could prevent the retransmission of them by a cable company operating in Belgium that was retransmitting the French company's films from Germany without copyright permission. It emerges from this decision that films can be both material goods (when they are contained on discs and so on) or broadcast transmissions. In the case of material goods the distribution right is exhausted as soon as the products are marketed with the right holder's consent. In the case of broadcast transmissions of films the court's approach is rather different in view of the fact that television is a one-to-many medium, which is widely available, free to air to the public, and programmes can be infinitely repeated. In this respect, the right holder's transfer of the right to distribute a film does not imply that a single performance has exhausted it. What is at stake here are performances and not tangible goods: while it is outside the scope of copyright law controlling the circulation of copyrighted products marketed with the right holder's consent, it is within its scope to control a series of performances. The different nature of copyrighted works affected thus the ECJ reasoning on this point.

A third limit to the free circulation of copyrighted products can be derived from *Warner Bros and Metronome Video* v. *Christiansen*.[6] In this decision imports of video cassettes from Denmark that were initially sold in the UK with the right holder's consent were deemed to infringe the country's copyright law and therefore prohibited. The reason was that the cassettes were meant to be for rent in Denmark and, at the time the case took place; copyright holders had rental rights in Denmark

---

4   (341/87) [1980] ECR 79.
5   (62/79) [1980] ECR 881.
6   (158/86) [1988] ECR 2605.

but not in the UK. Because the cassettes were acquired in the UK, the company importing the tapes was not obliged to pay royalties on its rental activities. The ECJ held that despite the absence of rental rights under UK copyright law, the imports in Denmark were infringing the copyright holder's rental rights and should therefore cease.

It is evident from the cases above that the ECJ's rulings only partially overcame the tension between territoriality of copyright law and internal market principles because of the differences amongst national copyright statutes. Dissimilarities related to the scope of copyright, terms of duration, copyrightable works could – and only can – be addressed by either legislatively harmonizing member states' laws or introducing a unitary exclusive right (as was the case for trademark law). The path chosen by the EU has been that of legislative harmonization, the results of which are imperfect for several reasons including the impossibility of dealing with territoriality of intellectual property rights as well as the level of copyright protection that has been established.

The First Generation of EU Instruments

With the exception of the Satellite and Cable Directive, the first group of copyright directives are rooted in the Green Paper on Copyright and the Challenge of Technology, adopted by the European Commission (EC) in 1988 (EC 1988), and its follow-up published in the 1990s. The EC's starting point was the growing importance of copyright to industry and commerce. Amongst the reasons for growth the EC stressed that:

> [A] shift has continued in the economic activity of industrialized countries away from the production of goods having the character primarily of staple commodities and towards the production of goods to which considerable value has been added through the application of technology, skill and creativity (EC 1988, 1.2.2).

In parallel to recognizing industrial and commercial opportunities, the EC also raised the issue of the risks associated with infringements of copyright law and the need to protect the rights of authors from a range of novel methods to infringe copyright associated with technological innovation. In fact,

> [T]he very activities which offer the best hope for economic expansion, and are consequently the subject of considerable new investment, are those which are particularly exposed to losses through copying and accordingly have been seeking appropriate forms of protection, including suitably adapted copyright laws (EC 1988, 1.2.3).

The rapidly changing production and distribution environment, the EC proffered, required important structural changes to ensure the functioning of the internal market. To this end it suggested that there was a need to develop policies fostering competitiveness in the EU in relation to its trading partners as well as avoiding infringements outside of the EU of works produced within the EU zone. However, there was also recognition that the protection of economic interests should be balanced with the promotion of access to information and the pursuit of cultural goals (EC 1988, 1.1.1), though this was probably more a theoretical statement than a real objective.

In order to stimulate artistic and intellectual creativity and to maximize the benefits of growth in the culture industry for the internal market, the EC's policy initiative focused on a number of priority issues raised by the changing environment. These priority areas included piracy, home copying of sound and audiovisual material, distribution and rental rights for certain classes of works – in particular, sound and video recordings, protection of computer programs and databases and finally limits on the protection available to Community right holders in non-member states.

After extensive consultation with stakeholders, in 1990 the EC published a follow-up to the Green Paper addressing additional areas for possible intervention. New issues were raised such as the duration of protection, moral rights, reprography, resale right and broadcasting activities. Some issues were closely related to those already stressed in the Green Paper, such as broadcasters' rights in relation to the growing threat of piracy whilst others were novel such as resale rights which were later to be dealt with in 2001.

The majority of issues raised in the Green Paper and its consultation process were addressed in the directives belonging to the first generation of instruments adopted by the EC to harmonize copyright law, with the exception of moral rights that have not been dealt with as yet due to both the different approaches adopted in common and civil law jurisdictions, and the diversity existing within civil law jurisdictions (Salokannel and Strowel 2000). Other issues, such as home copying of sound and audiovisual material, have been partially considered in the second generation instruments which adopt a vertical approach to copyright law and are not focused on specific protection or rights as are the first generation directives. Finally, further topics such as piracy have been tackled at a parallel level through instruments dealing with whole range of the intellectual property rights such as the Directive 2004/48/EC of the European Parliament and of the Council of 29 April 2004 on the enforcement of intellectual property rights, which requires all member states to apply effective and proportionate remedies and penalties against those engaged in counterfeiting and piracy of goods protected under copyright, patent and trademark laws in order to create a level playing field for right holders in the EU.

The directives analyzed in the following section are characterized as belonging to the first generation of instruments and therefore they address specific aspects of copyright law. In 1991 and 1992 the first two directives, dealing with software protection and the rental and lending rights respectively, were adopted.[7] The following year two more directives were issued: the former on satellite and cable broadcasting, the latter on the term of protection.[8] Then, in 1996, a Directive partially

---

7　Council Directive (EEC) 91/250 on the legal protection of computer programs [1991] OJ L 122/42; Council Directive (EEC) 92/100 on rental right and lending right and on certain rights related to copyright in the field of intellectual property [1992] OJ L 346/61.

8　Council Directive (EEC) 93/83 on the coordination of certain rules concerning copyright and rights related to copyright applicable to satellite broadcasting and cable retransmission [1993] OJ L 248/15; Council Directive (EEC) 93/98 harmonizing the term of protection of copyright and certain related rights [1993] OJ L 290/9.

mirroring the software Directive was introduced covering database protection.[9] Member states were required to introduce two layers of protection for databases: copyright protection for creative databases (that is, software) and a *sui generis* right to protect the contents of databases resulting from substantial investment. Finally, the specific issue of resale rights that was raised in the Green Paper and the following consultation was resolved in 2001.

The Software Protection Directive

The first legislation harmonizing copyright law was Council Directive 91/250/ EEC of 14 May 1991 on the legal protection of computer programs.[10] There were large differences between some of the member states in the protection of computer programs due to the common and civil law approaches towards protection granted to computer programs. While the UK showed less concern in recognizing software as copyright subject matter, France – or more accurately continental Europe in general – were experiencing difficulty bringing together functional works, such as software and authors' artistic creations into the field of copyright protection. Furthermore, although forms of software were considered as copyrightable, the criterion for software to be granted protection differed across member states with the highest degree of protection in Germany (Tritton 2002, 326). However, since:

> The development of computer programs [was requiring] the investment of considerable human technical and financial resources while computer programs can be copied at a fraction of the cost needed to develop them independently [and]… computer programs [were] playing an increasingly important role in a broad range of industries and computer program technology can accordingly be considered as being of fundamental importance for the Community's industrial development ..…certain differences in the legal protection of computer programs offered by laws of the member states [were having] direct and negative effects on the functioning of the common market as regards computer programs and such differences could [have] well became greater as member states introduce[d] new legislation on this subject (Council Directive (EEC) 91/250 on the legal protection of computer programs [1991] OJ L 122/42, recitals 2–4).

The European Council required member states to place software protection into the category of *literary works*, within the meaning of Berne Convention Article 1(1), whenever original in the sense of being the result of the 'author's own intellectual creation'.[11] Although a definition of computer programs was not provided, a uniform criterion of protection was for the first time introduced – though limited to software – as a compromise between the utilitarian effort, skill, labour and judgement on the one hand, and the reflection of the author's personality (or mark of personality) on the other. The author's own intellectual creation, though not involving any particular

---

9   Directive (EC) 96/9 of 11 March 1996 on the legal protection of databases [1996] OJ L 77/20.
   10   [1991] OJ L 122/42.
   11   *Ibid.*, Article 1.

inventiveness or novelty, does require something more than a mere qualitative or quantitative investment: namely a personal and intellectual result.

Even on the topic of software authorship the EU institutions demonstrated a high degree of diplomacy by stating that authors should be the 'natural person' or the 'group of natural persons' creating the program or, where admitted by law, 'the legal person designated as the right holder by that legislation'.[12] The only exception is the employer's exclusive ownership whenever a computer program is created by an employee 'in the execution of his duties' or following the employer's 'instructions'.[13] This provision seeks to reconcile the personality right principle of authorship – typical of continental Europe – with the wider ownership principle of common law countries except for cases where computer programs have been created by employees, on which all member states agreed to grant the economic exploitation to software houses.

The Directive further proceeded to introduce harmonization on the scope of software protection by requiring member states to provide right holders with the exclusive rights of reproduction and alteration (including the right of authorizing translation, adaptation, and arrangement), and distribution. On the other hand, the exception regime was harmonized by introducing two exceptions to the exclusive rights: the former for lawful acquirers (or persons having the right to use the program) willing to make back-up copies; the latter for software programmers. Lawful acquirers are eligible to perform acts necessary to execute the intended purposes of the program (such as reproduction and when necessary for its use and even for correcting errors, modifications) and make back-up copies. Decompilation is also allowed for compatibility and interoperability purposes for programmers who have acquired the right to use the program and need to obtain the information not previously made available, and in relation to the parts of the original program which are necessary to achieve the purpose.

Criticism during the wide-ranging debate that followed the adoption of the Directive on computer program protection was raised from various perspectives. Firstly the ambiguity of the Directive's provisions did not provide for straightforward implementation of the provision by member states and it subsequently affected the harmonization of national legal frameworks to an extent that case law was relied upon to provide clarity due to the vagueness and ambiguity of some of the provisions (Derclaye 2000, 16). Secondly, the software Directive is still highly debated as to the uses allowed to lawful acquirers, independent programmers, and third parties in general (Ullrich and Lejenne 2006) due to the restrictions to derivative innovation in the software market that this piece of legislation is considered to impact upon (Esteve 2006, 280).

---

12   *Ibid.*, Article 2.
13   *Ibid.*, Article 2.

The Rental and Lending Right Directive

The second piece of legislation that evolved out of the Green Paper was the Council Directive 92/100/EEC of 19 November 1992 on rental and lending rights and on certain rights related to copyright in the field of intellectual property.[14] Although known as the 'rental and lending' Directive, it addressed three different problems: (1) harmonization of lending and rental rights whose differences constituted barriers to phonograms, CD-Roms, and films (basically works acquiring increasing rental value); (2) limiting the increase of piracy enabled by new technologies in the absence of legal protection and (3) making related right owners economically participate in the exploitation of the works that they contributed to through secondary remuneration.

The first goal was achieved by requiring member states to provide authors (of works in the meaning of Berne Convention Article 1(1)), performers, phonogram and film producers with the right to authorize both the rental and lending of original works and their copies. This could be done by introducing the above-mentioned rights as distinct from distribution rights and providing that, contrary to the distribution rights, their exercise does not exhaust them. In this context, member states are permitted to introduce an exception for public lending though, provided that authors (not related rights owners) of phonograms, films, and computer programs (not other copyright works) are remunerated.

The second objective was pursued through harmonizing the rights of fixation and reproduction, the broadcasting rights and the rights of distribution to the public. Because of the differences in national copyright law as to what constitutes piracy in a jurisdiction, the problem arose that an infringement of copyright in one member state did not represent a breach of copyright laws in another one where the same rights are not granted by law to copyright holders. In such a fragmented regulatory environment the problem of piracy was felt to compound these problems but also offer solutions because of the development of recording technologies enabling fixation, copying and reproduction of live performances, literal works, broadcasting and the like. Therefore, piracy and copying that infringed certain copyright was perceived to require a common definition, and this would be possible only in an environment where identical rights were granted to identical categories of stakeholders across the common market.

Finally, the third goal was considered accomplished by compelling member states to provide performers, phonogram and film producers with the right to fair compensation whenever the fixation of their works or the phonogram or film is distributed to the public. Furthermore, in case the rental right owners assign their right on phonograms, or originals or copies of a film to producers, they should be also entitled to fair remuneration for rental. However, nor the system of remuneration or the qualification of fair remuneration was dealt with in the Directive which devolved these areas so that they would be regulated by national legislators.

---

14 [1992] OJ L 346/61.

The Satellite and Cable Directive

The Council Directive 93/83/EC of 27 September 1993 on the coordination of certain rules concerning copyright and rights related to copyright applicable to satellite broadcasting and cable retransmission[15] shows a slightly different approach in comparison with the pieces of legislation previously adopted. This is largely due to the fact that it has evolved from a different source (the 1984 Green Paper instead of the 1985 one). In order to eliminate copyright related barriers to transfrontier broadcasting and radio services, the Directive introduced two legal instruments designated to facilitate the licensing of satellite broadcasters and cable retransmission of radio and television programming.

Firstly, member states were required to introduce a Community wide right of communication to the public by satellite under which the activity of broadcasting is protected only in the country of origin of the satellite up link. A satellite operator does not need to seek regulatory approval in the numerous member states for offering such service; it is entitled to transmit from the so-called country of origin without regulatory barriers from other member states and thereby benefiting from a streamlined licensing process across the common market. The so called 'injunction right' (Hugenholtz et al. 2006, 25), however, needs to be coordinated with Article 3 of the Information Society Directive[16] providing harmonization of any communication to the public by any means (wire and wireless), with the exclusion of public performances, recitations and display. Since Article 1(2) of the Information Society Directive leaves the provisions of the Satellite and Cable Directive intact, a tension arises between the Community wide dimension of the 'injunction right' and the territoriality of the communication and making available rights harmonized under the Information Society Directive.

Secondly, the Directive created a system of collective management for cable retransmission. Because of the fact that cable operators may not be capable of negotiating licences with all right holders (both copyright and related right owners) of programmes that have been already broadcast, the EU required broadcasting rights to be administered through collecting societies, regardless of the right owners having transmitted the right to them.[17] By doing so, cable retransmission was perceived to be more easily facilitated. However, Article 9 of the Satellite and Cable Directive did not establish a compulsory licensing regime since collective management is supposed to take place only when right owners (both copyright and related rights owners) have not transmitted their rights to broadcasting organizations to enable cable operators to clear the cable retransmission rights. When a broadcaster can be easily contacted by the cable operator the collecting society's activity is not needed and whenever

---

15   [1993] OJ L 248/15.

16   Directive (EC) 2001/29 of 22 May 2001 on the harmonization of certain aspects of copyright and related rights in the information society [2001] OJ L 167/10.

17   Council Directive (EEC) 93/83 on the coordination of certain rules concerning copyright and rights related to copyright applicable to satellite broadcasting and cable retransmission [1993] OJ L 248/15, Article 9(2).

the rights have not been transferred to the broadcaster the cable operator can always transmit the programme by requesting authorization from the collecting society.

The Term Directive

In the same year as the Satellite and Cable Directive was published the EU also adopted Council Directive 93/98/EEC of 19 October 1993 harmonizing the length of protection for copyrighted works and certain related rights.[18] Amongst the reasons that led to the adoption of the Term Directive was a court case coined the *Patricia* case,[19] where it emerged that differences in the periods of protection granted to copyrighted works in Germany and Denmark could have been used as barriers to trade especially when countries where copyright lasted seventy years *post mortem auctoris* (p.m.a.), like Germany, coexisted with countries where it lasted sixty years p.m.a., like Spain, and yet other member states had established a fifty-year period of protection. Drawing on internal market arguments, the EU required all member states to extend the term of protection of copyrighted works to seventy years p.m.a. and related rights to fifty years (from the date of the performance, from either the phonogram and film fixation or their first publication or communication, and from the first broadcast transmission respectively). This was stated for both works created after the introduction date of the Directive and works created before that date insofar they were protected at that date by at least one member state.

Coupled with the internal market logic further arguments to justify harmonization towards the top lied in the assumed personality right approach to copyright. However, the rise upwards was finally usurped by the legal impossibility of reducing established rights and the protection at that time enjoyed by right holders within the Community[20] and by the need for prompt harmonization. However, the Term Directive did not limit itself to standardizing the duration of the term of copyright and related rights; it also introduced provisions on certain specific subject matters, such as films, photographs, unpublished works, and critical and scientific publications. In this context, it is worth mentioning that raising member states' protection on photographs to the level afforded under German copyright law required the former to introduce seventy-year copyright protection for photographs satisfying the originality criteria in the sense of being the author's own intellectual creation.

Although the Term Directive appeared to be an arguably relevant step towards a more harmonized copyright regime, it opened several inconsistencies, such as the exclusion of works of applied art and typographical arrangements from the extension of the term protection, the regime of photographs not satisfying the originality requirement, and the duration for moral rights (Emilianides 2004, 539).

---

18 [1993] OJ L 290/9.
19 *EMI Electrola GmbH* v. *Patricia* (341/87) [1989] ECR 79.
20 *Ibid.*, recital 9.

The Database Protection Directive

Strong economic motives underpinned the adoption of Directive 96/9/EC of 11 March 1996 on the legal protection of databases by the European Parliament (EP) and Council.[21] The Database Directive, as was the case for the Term Directive, represents a step towards a more harmonized level of protection, though uniformity is sought on a specific subject matter perceived as highly relevant because of its economic value. In order to strengthen competitiveness in the internal market member states have been required to introduce a two-tier system for the protection of databases: by copyright as intellectual creations and by *sui generis* right (database right) to protect content in which a substantial investment has been made.

As for copyright protection, it partially mirrors the Software Protection Directive in regards to the protection criterion and ownership. Member states are required to grant copyright protection to databases constituting an 'author's own intellectual creation' 'by reason of the selection or arrangement of their content'.[22] Secondly, and similarly to ownership of software copyright, authors of databases can be either natural persons or a group of natural persons who created them or – where legislation of member states allows it – legal persons.

Although the rights that a copyright owner on a database possesses are almost as broad as in other subject matters, the harmonization intent led the EU to list the rights that member states must adopt. Namely: rights of reproduction, adaptation, distribution and communication to the public by any means. In this context lawful users are still granted exceptions such as reproduction of non-electronic databases for private purposes use for purposes of illustration for teaching or scientific research 'as long as the source is indicated and to the extent justified by the non-commercial purpose to be achieved'[23] and for public security or administrative or judicial procedure.

However, the real innovation introduced by the Database Directive is the introduction of a *sui generis* right on database content which required a 'qualitatively and/or quantitatively substantial investment' in either the 'obtaining', 'verification' or 'presentation' of content.[24] Such a right is independent of copyright on the original structure (selection or arrangement of content) so that databases fulfilling both protection criteria can be protected under both regimes. Member states are then required to provide developers of such databases with the right of preventing temporary or permanent extraction and re-utilization of the whole or any substantial part of the database. On the other hand, lawful users cannot be prevented by contract from extracting and re-utilizing insubstantial parts of the content of a database for whatsoever purpose. The lawful users right on a public database must be kept separate from the limited exceptions to the rights of database producers, which mirrors the exceptions adopted for copyright databases. Extraction and re-utilization of unsubstantial parts can then be allowed by member states in relation

---

21   [1996] OJ L 77/20.
22   *Ibid.*, Article 3.
23   *Ibid.*, Article 6(2).
24   *Ibid.*, Article 7(1).

to non-electronic databases for private purposes and more generally for teaching or scientific research as well as for reasons of public security and administrative or judicial procedure.

Unlike the copyright term of protection, database right protection expires fifteen years from the first of January of the year following the date of its completion. However, additional investments of any relevance can prolong the term for a further fifteen years so that the term of protection may became perpetual in regards databases which are constantly or regularly subject to significant updates, revision and integration.

The Resale Right Directive

Even though Directive 2001/84/EC of the EP and of the Council of 27 September 2001 on the resale right for the benefit of the author of an original work of art[25] is the most recent amongst the EU copyright directives, it is rooted in the EC's follow-up to the Green Paper on Copyright and the Challenge of Technology. The Directive stems from the necessity of harmonizing (and in certain cases introducing) the resale right which was adopted (though not strictly applied) in most of the continental European countries – with the exception of Austria and the Netherlands – but was not provided for in the common law member states.

The aim of the resale right is to enable artists who have already sold their works to partially participate, for the term of copyright, in any subsequent sale of their works with a percentage of the sale price. Although inalienable and un-waivable as is also the case with moral rights, the resale right is included in copyright because of its basically economic nature. Therefore, differences in members states' copyright laws with regard to categories of works to which the principle of resale right applies, persons entitled to receive royalties, rates applied, and the basis on which they are calculated, as well as transactions subject to payment, were deemed to have a negative and direct effect on the internal market in works of art. This was considered as distorting competition and treating artists unequally as remuneration depended on where their works were sold.

In order to eliminate these disparities, member states were firstly required to introduce or extend the resale rights to all acts of resale with the exception of sale effected directly between persons acting in their private capacity – without the participation of an art market professional – and sales between private individuals and museums; instead, it was the discretion of member states to apply the right to sales between art galleries and private individuals. Sales considered in the Directive involve a physical work and do not exceed the resale price of €10,000. Secondly, member states were required to identify both the persons obliged to pay royalties on sales falling into the above mentioned categories and those entitled to receive royalties. In the absence of any provision, the person paying the remuneration to the author is the party on whose behalf the sale is concluded, but others such as dealers or intermediaries can be designated to receive the payment. However the sole individuals entitled to remuneration remain the authors and, after their death,

---

25 [2001] *OJ L 272/32.*

this is passed down to their heirs. Finally, the rates to be followed are set out in detail and are fixed percentages of the sale prices depending on the price bands under which the price falls.

The Resale Right Directive is controversial in its underlying rationale since the internal market argument appears weak. In this area more than in others it is difficult to sustain the argument that it was adopted to foster the single market since most of sales take place on the London art market. Moreover, the logic that such a right was necessary to establish a common market may be flawed as the adoption of the resale rights has negative affects on the internal market by leading to the displacement of art works outside the EU (Tritton 2002, 374) where percentages on the sale price are the preserve of authors and their heirs.

Copyright in the Information Society

Directive 2001/29/EC of the EP and of the Council of 22 May 2001 on the harmonization of certain aspects of copyright and related rights in the information society[26] commences the phase of second generation directives, under which the approach towards harmonization appears more horizontal. This is reflected in the Information Society[27] and even more in the Enforcement[28] Directives: the former aiming at introducing provisions applicable to all copyright subject matters and right holders; the latter dealing with a whole of range of intellectual rights.

In particular, the Green Paper aimed to provide a harmonized and flexible framework for copyright and related rights in order to protect and stimulate the development and marketing of new products and services within the internal market. However, the Information Society Directive sought to introduce a higher level of protection for works in the digital environment. Because of the very nature of the Internet, ensuring that copyrighted products were not copied, transformed or exploited without the knowledge of the copyright holder and contrary to their interests was considered so difficult that increased harmonization of copyright protection in the digital environment was essential.

In the first place member states were required to harmonize the level of protection of traditional rights granted to copyright and related rights holders taking into account the challenges of a digital environment. This led to the introduction of two amendments to national statutes: (1) the express provision that the exhaustion principle does not apply in case of communication to the public and (2) the inclusion of a 'making available' right within the right of communication to the public. According to Article 3 of the Information Society Directive, then, copyright and related rights holders should be entitled by member states to:

---

26   [2001] OJ L 167/10

27   This Directive is sometimes referred to as the Copyright Directive, (EC) 2001/29 of 22 May 2001 on the harmonization of certain aspects of copyright and related rights in the information society [2001] OJ L 167/10.

28   Directive (EC) 2004/48 of 29 April 2004 on the enforcement of intellectual property rights [2004] OJ L 195/16.

[T]he exclusive right to authorise or prohibit any communication to the public of their works, by wire or wireless means, including the making available to the public of their works in such a way that members of the public may access them from a place and at a time individually chosen by them. The rights [of communication to the public and making available to the public] shall not be exhausted by any act of communication to the public or making available to the public as set out in this Article.

Article 3 implemented the corresponding provisions of the Treaty adopted by the World Intellectual Property Organisation (WIPO) in 1996 (Article 8 WTO, and Articles 10, 14 WPPT),[29] enriching the traditional notion of public (whose members are traditionally gathered in the same place at the same time) and including a more modern element: a public made of members accessing works uploaded via the Internet whenever and wherever they prefer. Furthermore, unlike the case of distribution of physical products, both rights mentioned in Article 3 are required not to be exhausted by any act of communication or making available. Therefore, online distribution of copyrighted works is not considered as a substitute to physical distribution, but more as a provision of a service to which the principle of exhaustion does not apply. Moreover, the principle of exhaustion does not even apply with regard to a tangible copy of a work or other subject matter made by a user of such services with the consent of the right holder.

Secondly, the Information Society Directive established protection for technological measures and rights management information whose provisions – adopted by the WIPO Treaties – are amongst the more debated rules ever implemented. With the requirement that member states provide adequate legal protection to technological measures, such as copy control technologies, it aims at preventing any circumvention of these measures, and at prohibiting activities preparatory to prospective circumvention in order to offer a secure framework for distributing copyrighted works. In relation to the prevention of prospective circumvention, Article 6 of the Information Society Directive states that:

Member states shall provide adequate legal protection against the manufacture, import, distribution, sale, rental, advertisement for sale or rental, or possession for commercial purposes of devices, products or components or the provision of services which:

a) Are promoted, advertised or marketed for the purpose of circumvention of, or

b) Have only a limited commercially significant purpose or use other than to circumvent, or

c) Are primarily designed, produced, adapted or performed for the purpose of enabling or facilitating the circumvention of, any effective technological measures.

---

29   WIPO Copyright Treaty, adopted in Geneva on 20 December 1996, http://www.wipo.int/treaties/en/ip/wct/, accessed 10 January 2008; WIPO Performances and Phonograms Treaty, adopted in Geneva on 20 December 1996, http://www.wipo.int/treaties/en/ip/wppt/trtdocs_wo034.html, accessed 10 January 2008.

The criticism of Article 6 was aimed at the copyright protection threshold it provided for, which increased the number of areas where copyright protection could be infringed. While in the tangible environment copyright is infringed when works are reproduced, communicated to the public or distributed without the right holders' consent in the digital world copyright infringement occurs when technological measures protecting copyrighted materials are circumvented regardless of the purpose of this circumvention. Moreover, copyright law is infringed by producing and marketing devices and technology enabling circumvention. Finally, the Information Society Directive designed an exception regime for online and offline works that are technologically protected. In this context, and according to the Directive's aim, the sole mandatory exception that member states are obliged to introduce is for:

> Temporary acts of reproduction ... which are transient or incidental, which are an integral and essential part of a technological process and whose sole purpose is to enable:
>
> a) transmission in a network between third parties by an intermediary, or
>
> b) lawful use of a work or other subject-matter to be made, and which have no independent economic significance, shall be exempted from the reproduction right provided for in Article 2.

As for the other exceptions, member states were left free to decide which of the twenty limitations to exclusive rights to reconfirm or introduce into national legislation. The most complex part of the Information Society Directive is the interface between exceptions to copyright (which traditionally are inherent components of any copyright regime) and technological measures capable of extending copyright protection well over its legal boundaries. In order to solve the conflict between provisions affording legal protection to technological measures on the one hand, and provisions providing exceptions on the other, the EU allowed a wide variety of approaches to be implemented by member states:

> Notwithstanding the legal protection provided [to technological measures], in the absence of voluntary measures taken by right holders, including agreements between right holders and other parties concerned, member states shall take *appropriate measures* to ensure that right holders make available to the beneficiaries of an exceptions provided for in national law. (Directive (EC) 2001/29 of 22 May 2001 on the harmonization of certain aspects of copyright and related rights in the information society [2001] OJ L 167/10, Article 6(4), emphasis added).

However, legislative actions implementing such appropriate measures are due to the absence of private agreements, for certain categories of exceptions, such as copying privileges for libraries, researchers, museums etc. They are optional for others, such as copies for private purposes and not even mentioned for the remaining categories of limitations. Thus, the way each member state implemented the appropriate measures (and even the voluntary measures) vary from country to country.

Again, as in the case of the exception regime, the aims of harmonization appear to be frustrated by the freedom of national legislators who encounter limitations only when technologically protected content are made available to the public on 'agreed contractual terms in such a way that members of the public may access them from a place and at a time individually chosen by them'.[30] Whenever works are accessible on demand and on contractual grounds (mainly mass contracts), member states are not allowed to take appropriate measures in favour of the exceptions beneficiaries.

Assessing the *Acquis Communautaire*: Does Stronger Protection Equal Greater Harmonization of Legislation?

The above analysis demonstrates a trend whereby the EU has proceeded to approximate distinct elements of copyright law in the first phase, and has implemented a more horizontal approach by considering a greater range of issues related to the Information Society in the second phase extending the number of areas falling under the directives. Legislative actions of both periods have led to inconsistencies and unsatisfactory results.

The 'piecemeal approach' (Hugenholtz et al. 2006, 16) initially adopted resulted in an 'impressive body of specialized rules that lacks, however, a measure of coherence' (Hugenholtz et al. 2006, 21). Inconsistencies in this framework need to be understood in relation to specific topics, such as subject matter and criteria for protection on the one hand, and economic rights on the other.

As to the former, the level of approximation is low. Member states have been required to harmonize no more than three categories of works, namely: computer programs, databases and photographs whenever they are original in the sense of works representing the author's own intellectual creations. Also, in relation to photographs, the criterion of protection is further detailed as the author's intellectual work that has to reflect the author's personality. Even though it is unquestionable that *droit d'auteur* and copyright approaches vary to the extent that they complicate the alignment of national laws, many topics, such as authorship and moral rights have never been touched by the harmonization process due to the impossibility of reaching a consensus between member states. Surprisingly, such a compromise has been reached on software and databases and as far as software and databases are concerned, subject matter, criteria for protection, ownership and rights granted are addressed in the related directives, which tend to stress the relevant economic interests at stake in those markets and the need for protection.

As to the latter (the economic rights), the situation appears more harmonized but remain controversial. According to EU legislation, the distribution of tangible copyrighted goods within the internal market is enabled by the adoption of the exhaustion principle, firstly adopted in case law and then incorporated into legislation. The same did not occur in relation to cross-border services or to online distribution of copyrighted material, even though these services are transfrontier in nature.

---

30 Directive (EC) 2001/29 of 22 May 2001 on the harmonization of certain aspects of copyright and related rights in the information society [2001] OJ L 167/10, Article 6(4).

Article 3 of the Information Society Directive has missed the opportunity to properly harmonize activities related to communication to the public and as well as failed to adequately regulate the making available right since it reaffirmed the Coditel ruling under which content related services offered across the EU require licenses from right holders of all member states. Article 3 of the Information Society Directive is unlikely to match the forward looking 'injection right' introduced under the Satellite and Cable Directive under which the communication right needs to be cleared in the up link country. The Satellite and Cable and the Information Society Directives deal with a similar phenomenon: communication to a public (in the broad notion of many members of the same public not physically and timely gathered together) of broadcasting and digital content respectively. In both cases the communication is transfrontier. However, while in the case of broadcasting broadcasters are granted a cross-border 'injunction right' (Hugenholtz et al. 2006, 25) enabling them to clear the communication rights in the country of origin in the case of the making available right its cross-border nature is not recognized and operators are required to clear this right in each member state. The difference in regulation can be traced to the many reasons standing against the adoption of an 'injection right' for cross-border provision of services and online content distribution (Hugenholtz et al. 2006, 28–29). Even through time the legal environment has not fully accepted the adoption of transfrontier communications and making available to the public rights. The EC appears to be aware of the problem of online distribution of content to the extent that it adopted a Recommendation on Online Music (EC 2005). The Recommendation seeks to overcome the territoriality nature of the making available right. However, this is not compulsory and member states retain wide discretion, hence:

> Licensing of online rights is often restricted by territory, and commercial users negotiate in each member state with each of the respective collective rights managers for each right that is included in the online exploitation (EC 2005, recital 7).

Since online music distribution is likely to create obstacles to the internal market for music, rather than taking advantages of the opportunities that the Internet offers, the EC suggests that:

> Commercial users need a licensing policy that corresponds to the ubiquity of the online environment and which is multi-territorial. It is therefore appropriate to provide for multi-territorial licensing in order to enhance greater legal certainty to commercial users in relation to their activity and to foster the development of legitimate online services, increasing, in turn, the revenue stream for right-holders (EC 2005, recital 8).

The Recommendation is illustrative of the EU's *modus procedendi*: despite the 'piecemeal approach' (Hugenholtz et al. 2006, 16), the corrective measures adopted seem to implement the same course of action that led to the fragmented framework and were incapable of overcoming the territorial nature of copyright law. The Recommendation, focusing on the specific issue of online distribution of musical works, does not seek a mechanism enabling the dissemination of creative production so to increase the creation of value.

Similarly controversial is the recent consultation launched by the EC on Copyright Levies in a Converging World (EC 2006a) in order to consult the member states on the private copying exception and the existing system of remuneration. Instead of taking the opportunity to rethink the current regime of economic rights and more specifically the feasibility of a new system in which statutory remuneration rights are introduced in addition or in replacement to exclusive rights so to spread the possible uses of creative works against fair remuneration, the EC seems to narrow down the question to the levies collected for private copying. The EC also apparently favours the adoption of Digital Rights Management systems so to definitively hinder (at least from a theoretical point of view) private reproduction, or subject them to a contract and a direct payment to the producer or other right holders. The approach does not take into account the introduction of statutory remuneration rights that would have the effect of not only enabling greater use of copyrighted works, but also benefiting authors and performers. The latter could receive a greater share of remuneration for use if they were administered through collecting societies rather than determined on the basis of individual contracts with publishers, producers and other intermediaries.

Moving to the second generation of directives, their results, specifically those deriving from the Information Society Directive, raise many doubts despite the horizontal approach adopted. If the goal pursued under the Information Society Directive was to align member states' laws in order to foster the internal market, legal instruments not harmonizing national rules that do not facilitate the free movement of goods or the freedom of services should then be removed (Hugenholtz 2000, 501–502). This questions the proper functioning of horizontal legal instruments (though queries can be extended to vertical legal instruments as well) whenever they fail to accomplish the objectives of promoting the internal market, but merely require member states to adopt stronger protection which generates obstacles to the free circulation of goods and services instead of lowering national barriers and reducing territorial fragmentation.

The latter argument leads us to the issue of overprotection of copyrighted works resulting from the process of harmonization. Copyright has been extended in relation to terms of protection, rights granted to right holders, subject matters, and limitations placed on the free use of copyrighted works. Overprotection is not always a matter of quantity but quality matters too: exclusive rights can offer more protection than remuneration rights. While it is understandable that in certain cases 'harmonization up' is caused by the necessity not to reduce rights already existing in certain member states (as in the case of terms of protection), since 'people are apt to complain very seriously – raising cries of destruction of property without compensation – if their rights are cut down' (Jacob 1997, 8), it is less clear for what reason the EU chose exclusive rights instead of remuneration rights for the digital environment, where the transfrontier nature of distribution generates transaction costs even higher than in the analogue world.

The current overprotective framework for copyright industries suggests that the harmonization process has far exceeded the minimum level of protection required at international level by the Berne and Rome Conventions for authors and related rights owners respectively. An upwards regulatory phenomenon has taken place altering, in more than one respect, the balance between public and private interests traditionally struck by copyright. The question arises as to whether harmonization was ever the sole goal of the whole process (Tritton 2002, 325). In more than one preamble the EU clearly states that more copyright protection is positive as it rewards authors and stimulates creativity: the more and stronger protection is the higher the level of production will be according to this logic. Such reasoning does not seem to take into account that creation and diffusion of original works is not only an economic matter and it is not simply grounded purely on market efficiency logic. The goal of increasing production and diffusion of content is not always achieved by providing new or stronger exclusive rights. This should be the case only when a real economic need is proved (Jacob 1997, 9). Therefore, if the prime goal of harmonization is providing incentives for the creation and diffusion of original content higher protection may not be the key instrument of success, but more closely aligned protection is required.

In the first part of this chapter we have outlined some of the inconsistencies and flaws in the *aquis communautaire* resulting from the harmonization that have been isolated in order to question whether the current legal framework increases the value of the European cultural industry. In the following part a broader assessment of the European legislator's policy underlying the harmonization process will be assessed to demonstrate a shift that has occurred in European copyright law towards a more economic-utilitarian approach. The unintended consequences of such a shift on information goods and the freedom of expression will be analyzed in turn.

Upwards Harmonization and the Paradigm Shift in European Copyright Law

An analysis of the current process of upwards harmonization in European copyright law can not only be assessed by looking at emerging trends in copyright policy, but it must also take into account the effects of such policy. Several commentators have argued that the trend in the directives constituting the *acquis communautaire*, particularly the Database and Information Society Directives, represents a remarkable shift from the traditional view of copyright as grounded in the author's personality right to an economic-utilitarian approach. This would signify a substantial move away from the long established continental European paradigm of *droit d'auteur* to a more Anglo-American model of copyright (Koelman 2004, 604).

In the paradigm of personality right the author's rights reflect the permanent bond between authors and their original creations, thereby configuring a strict hierarchy between author's rights *stricto sensu* (which include moral rights) and rights depending on these, namely related or neighbouring rights. In contrast the utilitarian view of copyright is fundamentally perceived as a temporary monopoly conceded to authors as reward for their efforts; a reward whose ultimate reason lies in the necessity of providing incentives to production that has beneficial effects on social welfare.

Economic arguments have strongly influenced all eight directives. This has no doubt been determined by the EU bodies' traditional role in dealing with problems of economic and market regulation. A review of recitals accompanying the directives reveals a huge recourse to arguments directly or indirectly connected to economic-utilitarian views, and only sporadic and largely insubstantial use of personality right rationales. Arguments put forward are, in many cases, that strong copyright protection is a means of promoting both individual interests and the interest of the 'society at large', thereby assuming that copyright as such is capable of pursuing a general welfare objective and a fair balance between all interests at stake.[31] A further kind of argument stems from the classical 'labour-reward' rationale, that is, the idea that property rights are granted to individuals in order to reward their investment in terms of labour, skill and judgement. Such a rationale underlies, for instance, the controversial *sui generis* right introduced by the Database Directive, where the intellectual property protection on these goods is conditional on the evidence of 'substantial investment'.[32] Again similar arguments were put forward in the Council Directive 87/54/EEC on legal protection of topographies of semiconductor products,[33] focusing on the economic disadvantage of the producers of a typical public good:

> [W]hereas the development of such topographies requires the investment of considerable resources, human, technical and financial, while topographies of such products can be copied at a fraction of the cost needed to develop them independently (Council Directive (EEC) 87/54 on the legal protection of topographies of semiconductor products [1987] OJ L 024/36, recital 3).

In sum copyright is essentially seen as a remedy for market failure, thus having primarily an economic *raison d'être*. Conversely, arguments echoing the personality right are only sporadically put forward and, apparently, only with the function of validating broadening protection. For instance, recital 5 of the Term Directive mentions the growth in 'average lifespan of the Community' to justify the extension of the term of protection to seventy years p.m.a. to 'to provide protection for the author and the first two generations of [their] descendants'. Subject to correction, this is the only occasion where the EC recalls the sacred bond between authors and their works, so recovering a personality right rationale. Concerns regarding market regulation in a broader sense – that is, the need to eliminate barriers and distortions to the internal market, competition and free movement of goods – are repeatedly mentioned and are constant themes in all eight directives. It suggests EU copyright harmonization has been largely, if not exclusively, driven by economic-utilitarian rationales.

This extensive use of utilitarian arguments in each stage of the harmonization process goes hand in hand with the progressive empowering of right holders. This

---

31 Council Directive (EEC) 93/98 harmonizing the term of protection of copyright and certain related rights [1993] OJ L 290/9, recital 10.

32 Directive (EC) 96/9 of 11 March 1996 on the legal protection of databases [1996] OJ L 77/20, Article 7.

33 Council Directive (EEC) 87/54 on the legal protection of topographies of semiconductor products [1987] OJ L 024/36.

policy combines the expansion of the private domain with the centrality of the economic perspectives in a property right approach to copyright. Under this paradigm extending the proprietary regime over information goods and granting stronger and broader property rights to information producers is the best way to foster production of these goods, both quantitatively and qualitatively (Koelman 2004, 606). According to this view, optimal efficiency in the marketplace of information products is achieved when effective property rights are conferred on their producers. It is difficult to say to what extent such a policy framework is the result of informed political choice or the effect of lobbying by interest groups. Commenting on the EP's approval of the Information Society Directive, Commissioner Frits Bolkenstein recalled the 'unprecedented lobbying onslaught' to which the Parliament was subjected, and regretted 'that some of the parties concerned strived to obtain nothing less than total victory, using sometimes highly emotive arguments, rather than seeking a balanced compromise between the various legitimate interests involved' (E-Policy News, March 2001).

This seems to have happened even though alternatives to strong proprietary rules were available, and possibly applicable, at least in the digital environment. Article 3, though not expressly prohibiting member states from implementing the making available right as a liability rule, does urge them to insert an exclusive right, that is, a property rule. Under a property rule, owners are entitled to exclude others from using copyrighted works without their consent (*ius excludendi alios*); whereas, under a liability rule, owners cannot prohibit use as they are only entitled to receive compensation for such uses. In short: a property rule secures both remuneration *and* control, while a liability rule secures only remuneration, leaving the question of control outside the right holder's powers (Elkin-Koren 2002, 106).

Historically, liability rules have been introduced in copyright laws whenever a new form of exploitation has emerged and this required a huge amount of licences to be lawfully undertaken. For instance, Article 11-*bis* of the Berne Convention was introduced in the Rome revision of 1928 in order to cope with radio broadcasting, and Article 13 was revised in 1948 (the Brussels revision) in order to enable the introduction of compulsory licensing regimes for sound recordings. In both articles, signatory states are left free 'to determine the conditions under which [the mentioned rights] may be exercised' providing that these conditions shall not be prejudicial to 'the right [of the author] to obtain equitable remuneration which, in the absence of agreement, shall be fixed by competent authority'.

Such exceptions to exclusive rights are justified not only to reduce transaction costs but also to maximize production and distribution of content on new media platforms and to benefit from the effects of exploiting new technologies. Therefore, by conferring to authors 'the exclusive right to authorize or prohibit any communication to the public of their works, by wire or wireless means, *including the making available to the public* of their works, in such a way that members of the public may *access* them from a place and at a time individually chosen by them',[34] the Information Society

---

34   Directive (EC) 2001/29 of 22 May 2001 on the harmonization of certain aspects of copyright and related rights in the information society [2001] OJ L 167/10, Article 3, emphasis added.

Directive takes a precise policy decision about online distribution through the new media of copyrighted content. Besides the doubts already mentioned as to whether Article 3 is consistent with the 'injunction right' introduced under the Satellite and Cable Directive, it may be further questioned whether, and to what extent, the policy underlying this provision is correct. One can ask, for instance, whether this approach is consistent with the goal of promoting efficiency and equality in the market place of information goods on the one hand, and with the aim of improving the cultural and scientific domain on the other.

Shortcoming of the Property Right Regime in Information Goods

Since the property right approach tends to focus on the mere incentive effect on private investments, it overlooks the overall outcome of this particular kind of copyright regime on the creative environment. This is even truer in a context like the Internet. In recent years, an increasing number of scholars have raised the issue of the future of a networked public sphere in a world characterized by the seemingly relentless privatization and commodification of information (Elkin-Koren and Netanel 2001).

According to a familiar assumption about the progress of knowledge, every generation builds upon the knowledge accumulated by previous generations, thereby standing on the shoulders of giants. Hence, incentives created for a specific generation of creatives, by granting them the right of excluding others from using the information they produce, turn into a hindrance for subsequent generations. The classic copyright paradigm resolved this dilemma by limiting temporally exclusive rights, and by mitigating the *ius excludendi* through a broad exceptions regime and a system of liability rules for certain uses. However, in the current networked information environment the conflict between first producer and second is no longer a clash between generations, but it almost tends to take place *within* the same generation, since every producer is at the same time user, and (at least to some extent) vice versa. The assessment of the EU copyright harmonization process thus is likely to confirm that 'As currently practised, harmonization tends to extend or create rights for investors or creators of information products, while subtracting existing rights from users' (Vaver 2002, 236). Moreover, in a system characterized by a decentralized flow of information like the Internet, conflict is not only between producers and users. Yochai Benkler has identified a threefold source of potential conflict in our current system:

- The division between commercial and non-commercial producers as the 'non-commercial sector' (universities and so on) become 'integral parts of the production of information on both large and small scale'.
- Secondly, the division within the commercial sector between those who rely on property rights and those who appropriate the benefit of their production in different ways, for instance through value created around the information itself (for example, enterprises commercializing open source software and related services).

- Thirdly, the division between those who produce and sell information goods and the property rights between individual authors and corporations. (Benkler 2001, 269–270

A strong proprietary regime benefits commercial producers at the expense of both non-commercial producers and producers not relying on property rights. Moreover, it favours commercial organizations that hold a large inventory of existing information over small-scale enterprises and individuals. A copyright regime that relies solely on exclusive rights therefore turns into a *non-neutral* regulatory system, engendering detrimental effects on market competition as well as on cultural diversity.

Rebalancing Copyright and Freedom of Expression

In a recent report containing recommendations for implementing the Information Society Directive into the copyright statutes of member states, Gasser and Enrst pinpoint a series of clusters (Gasser and Ernst 2006). First of all, concerns are expressed about the use of anti-circumvention provisions included in Article 6 in order to reinforce dominant market positions by preventing interoperability (Gasser and Ernst 2006, 6). At the same time, evidence emerges that a long range prohibition of circumventing behaviours – that is, a prohibition not strictly limited to situations where actual copyright infringements occur – have a negative impact on scientific research, innovation, and circulation of information in general.

This impact is not only due to the 'commercialization of culture' that a strong property right based copyright is deemed to foster. As Elkin-Koren points out 'copyright law has always facilitated the commercialization of culture by enabling right holders to circulate copies of their works for a fee. Yet, information was never turned into a perfect commodity, and the law allowed owners to control only a limited number of uses' (Elkin-Koren 2002, 83–84). The commodification of cultural goods is not novel, it is the level of *control* that right holders retain on the exploitation of these goods to be altered. In this perspective, it has been repeatedly stressed that there is a need to redraft an adequate exception regime in the EU copyright system to establish a legal framework flexible enough to account for the digital environment and the practices of peer production, distribution and sharing (Gasser and Ernst 2006, 10).

One of the most notable effects of the upwards harmonization process is the emerging potential conflict between copyright and freedom of expression and information. In common law countries rights of freedom of speech are often invoked as limits to excessive copyright protection, and they have been the grounds for many court decisions on fair use and fair dealing exceptions. A different tradition has evolved in continental Europe, where, according to the personality right approach, author's rights are instruments *par excellence* to exercise freedom of expression, thereby encompassing *ipso facto* a proper equilibrium between the authors and public prerogatives (Hugenholtz 2001, 350–351). Moreover, in the European legal tradition the right of freedom of expression as established in Article 10 of the European Convention on Human Rights is understood as governing a vertical relationship between citizens and the state, rather than a horizontal relationship between private subjects, like those occurring in the market place. For these reasons a potential conflict between copyright and freedom of expression has been recognized in recent European literature as well as in Community and member state case law and represent another element of the paradigm shift from the traditional *droit d'auteur* to a more utilitarian approach to copyright. Such emerging conflict is likely to affect the next steps of the harmonization process. As it has been recently pointed out in a study commissioned by the EC:

> The effectiveness, in economic and social terms, and credibility, in terms of democratic support, of any system of intellectual property depends largely on finding that legendary 'delicate balance' between the interests of right holders in maximising protection and the interests of users (i.e. the public at large) in having access to products of creativity and knowledge. (Hugenoltz et al. 2006, 202)

rIf the harmonization process represents a less than satisfactory 'balance', it is nonetheless true that awareness of the importance of actively defending access to information goods from proprietary tendencies and overprotection has improved.

Conclusion

The copyright harmonization process that the current *aquis communautaire* has created presents inconsistencies in relation to both the level of harmonization reached – or, more accurately, the adequateness of the level of protection established to increase the value of the European cultural industries – and the policy implemented – or, more accurately, the assumptions underlying this policy.

The first part of the chapter has shown that neither the first nor the second generation of instruments managed to establish a legal framework that increases the value of the cultural industry. While a strong and harmonized level of protection has been introduced in relation to works and rights regarded as core for certain markets (such as computer programs and databases or the making available right and the resale right); such compromise has not been achieved (or even sought) in regards to many other topics such as moral rights, collective rights management, orphan works and so on. Some of these are already under discussion; others will hopefully be dealt with in the next future.

The process has thus affected a fragmented framework where the combination of the piecemeal and vertical approaches has generated a coexistence of harmonized areas characterized from a strong level of protection with other areas entirely left to national regulation. The assessment of the upwards harmonization process raised two main considerations. Firstly, the territoriality of copyright has only partially been overcome, and there is a long way to go to establish a Community copyright regime. Secondly, the stronger protection established in certain areas (such as copyright in the information society or terms of protection) does not seem to take into account the way that new technologies can affect the production and distribution of creative works. As long as the law does not embrace innovative ways of creating and exploiting works and their new uses both internal and national markets will fail to fully exploit growth.

The shift in the stages of development of EU copyright law suggests a shift from a personality right paradigm to a more economic-utilitarian approach that has generated unintended consequences. This is particularly so in the progressive establishment of a proprietary regime in information goods because of the detrimental effects on market competition and cultural diversity. Similarly vital are the effects of this shift on freedom of expression which is likely to need active defence against the maximization of protection that the upward harmonization has generated.

In this respect, a new phase in the process of establishing a European copyright regime needs to be initiated. After fifteen years of upwards harmonization by means of directives, the moment may have arrived for amending some aspects of the proprietary shift in the *acquis communautaire*. This review process may be best pursued through soft law instruments, such as recommendations, guidelines, interpretative notes and best practice rather than through strong centralized legislative intervention. Such short-term objectives pursued through soft law could pave the way for real long term objectives leading to the adoption of a Community copyright regime that replaces the existing directives, pre-empting the national laws of the twenty-seven member states, and eventually providing a substantial rebalancing of rights among all the parties involved.

References

Benkler, Y. (2001), 'A Political Economy of the Public Domain: Markets in Information Goods Versus the Marketplace of Ideas' in Dreyfuss, R.C., et al. (eds) *Expanding the Boundaries of Intellectual Property.* Oxford: Oxford University Press, 267–292.

Benkler, Y. (2006), *The Wealth of Networks: How Social Production Transforms Markets and Freedom.* New Haven: Yale University Press.

Derclaye, E. (2000), 'Software Copyright Protection: Can Europe Learn from American Case Law?', *EIPR* 22(2), 56–68.

Elkin-Koren, N. (2002). 'It's All About Control: Rethinking Copyright in the New Information Landscape' in N. Elkin-Koren and N. Netanel (eds.) *The Commodification of Information.* The Hague: Kluwer, 76–106.

Elkin-Koren, N. and Netanel, N. (2002), *The Commodification of Information.* The Hague: Kluwer.

Emilianides, A.C. (2004), 'The Author Revived: Harmonisation without Justification', *EIPR* 26(12), 538–541.

E-Policy News (March 2001), available at http://ec.europa.eu/archives/ISPO/ecommerce/epolicy, accessed 10 January 2008.

Esteve, A. (2006), 'Patent Protection of Computer-Implemented Inventions Vis-à-Vis Open Source Software', *Journal of World Intellectual Property* 9(3), 276–300.

European Commission (1988), Green Paper on Copyright and the Challenge of Technology – Copyright Issues Requiring Immediate Action, COM(88) 172 final,

7 June 1988.

European Commission (2004), Working Paper on the review of the EC legal framework in the field of copyright and related rights, SEC(2004) 995, <http://ec.europa.eu/internal_market/copyright/docs/review/sec-2004-995_en.pdf>, accessed 10 January 2007.

European Commission (2005), Recommendation of 18 May 2005 on collective cross-border management of copyright and related rights for legitimate online music services, 2005/737/EC, OJ L 276, 54–57.

European Commission (2006a*), Stakeholder Consultation on Copyright Levies in a Converging World,* <http://ec.europa.eu/internal_market/copyright/docs/levy_reform/stakeholder_consultation_en.pdf>, accessed 10 January 2007.

European Commission (2006b), Study on the Economic and Technical Evolution of the Scientific Publication Markets in Europe, Final report, January 2006 <http://ec.europa.eu/research/science-society/pdf/scientific-publication-study_en.pdf>, accessed 10 January 2007.

European Research Council (2006), ERC Scientific Council Statement on Open Access, December 2006 <http://erc.europa.eu/pdf/open-access.pdf>, accessed 1 February 2006.

Gasser, U. and Ernst, S. (2006), 'EUCD Best Practice Guide: Implementing the EU Copyright Directive in the Digital Age', the Berkman Center for Internet & Society at Harvard Law School, Research Publication No. 2006-10, <http:cyber.law.harvard.edu/publications>, accessed 10 January 2007.

Goldstein, P. (2001), *International Copyright. Principles, Law, and Practice.* Oxford: Oxford University Press.

Hugenholtz, B. (2000), 'Why the Copyright Directive is Unimportant, and Possibly Invalid', *EIPR* 22(11), 499–505.

Hugenholtz, B. (2001), 'Copyright and Freedom of Expression in Europe' in Dreyfuss, R.C., Zimmerman, D.L. and First, H. (eds) *Expanding the Boundaries of Intellectual Property.* Oxford: Oxford University Press, 343–363.

Hugenholtz, B. et al. (2006), 'The Recasting of Copyright & Related Rights for the Knowledge' Economy, Final report <http://ec.europa.eu/internal_market/copyright/docs/studies/etd2005imd195recast_report_2006.pdf>, accessed 10 January 2007.

Jacob, R. (1997), 'Industrial Property – Industry's Enemy', *IPQ* 1, 3–15.

Keeling, D.T. (2003), *Intellectual Property Rights in EU Law.* Oxford: Oxford University Press.

Koelman, K.J. (2004), 'Copyright Law & Economics in the EU Copyright Directive: Is the Droit d'Auteur Passé?', *IIC* 6, 603–638.

Media Group Business Research and Development Centre for the European Commission (2003), 'The Contribution of Copyright and Related Rights to the European Economy', Final Report, 20 October 2003 <http://ec.europa.eu/internal_market/copyright/docs/studies/etd2002b53001e34_en.pdf>, accessed 9 January 2007.

Salokannel, M. and Strowel, A. (2000), 'Study Contract Concerning Moral Rights in the Context of the Exploitation of Works through Digital Technology Final Report', <http://ec.europa.eu/internal_market/copyright/docs/studies/etd1999b53000e28_

en.pdf>, accessed 9 January 2007.

Sterling, J.A.L. (2003), *World Copyright Law*. London: Sweet & Maxwell, second edition.

Tritton, G. (2002), *Intellectual Property in Europe*. London: Sweet & Maxwell, second edition.

Ullrich, H. and Lejenne, M. (eds) (2006), *Der internationale Softwarevertrag*. Heidelberg, Betriebs Berater.

Vaver, D. (2002), 'Copyright Developments in Europe: The Good, the Bad and the Harmonized' in Elkin-Koren, N. and Netanel, N., *The Commodification of Information*. The Hague: Kluwer, 223–237.

Chapter 11

The Culture Industries: From the Common Market to a Common Sense

Rostam J. Neuwirth

The culture industry is a concept describing a truly global phenomenon of universal relevance and applicability. The term not only encompasses a philosophical discourse about art and aesthetics or a critique of enlightenment associated most closely with the Frankfurt School and ideas of cultural freedom and creativity as force of emancipation in society, an anthropological vector of cultural identity or a legal category of cultural goods and services. The concept and the policy discourses based on an understanding of the role of the culture industry in society affects a myriad range of activities including the political and democratic organization of our societies and the future development of our economies and their underlying productive processes. This dual or multiple nature of the culture industry causes the persons engaged in the creation of cultural goods and services to adopt particular practices; the consequences of which often create difficult policy dilemmas for the institutions that are competent in their related fields. This has been so at the global level as well as at the member state and the European Union (EU) level. The sheer complexity of the numerous political, economic, cultural and technological aspects intrinsic to the culture industries earns them their characterization as a novel medium and a persuasive paradigm for the tasks and challenges of the present time as well as for the future.

In its first section, this chapter clarifies the terminology behind the concept culture industries by briefly elaborating on its origin and by following its subsequent developments to its entry into the realm of law. Based on these developments, it ultimately advocates the understanding of culture industries as a paradigm for the emergence of a novel sense of perception which integrates the various distinct senses into a novel, that is, common sense. The second section presents a short overview of the historical development of the legal schism between culture and trade at the international level. The third section follows the concept of culture industries in the process of integration leading to the establishment of the EU; a concept which equally displays a certain tension in the form of an apparent contradiction. Such tension is the source of a range of regulatory challenges that Europe faces today. By way of reference to past culture and trade conflicts related to the cultural industries, the nature of these regulatory challenges, in both the global and the European context, is more closely analyzed in three important stages of European integration. Before concluding, the fourth section takes the current constitutional debate about the future of Europe as an opportunity to tackle the regulatory challenges posed by the complex and multifaceted nature of the culture industries. Paradoxically, at the same time the culture industries, when understood as a mandate for greater coherence and consistency in policy making, not only create a variety of problems but can also provide a stimulus for the elaboration of a constructive method for their successful resolution.

Deriving from an analysis of the international legal order as well as three different stages of European integration, this chapter understands the culture industries as a critique of our fragmented regulatory approaches and as a reminder for the growing need of bringing concerns of culture and of industry (or trade) closer and even to foster a search for positive synergies between them. This, it is argued, can only be achieved on the basis of an optimum coherent legal order which ideally is one of a constitutional nature where apparently divergent interests and positions are balanced against each other and finally resolved in a mutually acceptable solution.

The Nature of the Cultural Industries: A Conceptual Clarification

Kulturindustrie (culture industry) was a term originally coined in 1947 by Adorno and Horkheimer (Adorno 1991). Since then it has undergone a variety of uses in a large number of different contexts (Neuwirth 2006a). Related concepts in use today are those of cultural industry and cultural industries and finally, as used in this book, culture industries. There exists also a plethora of synonyms such as copyrighted industries, sunshine industries, creative industries and so on. These synonyms all highlight the intense debate about technological innovation and progress as it affects the organization of our societies which suggests the advent of a major paradigm shift. From a technological perspective this paradigm shift began, or perhaps, accelerated with the invention of cinema towards the end of the nineteenth century, which continued the important changes the invention of the printing press had initiated almost 500 years before but also set hitherto static images into motion. This transition from static to dynamic perception Paul Nora has aptly termed 'acceleration of history' which he defined as a 'tremendous dilation of our very mode of historical perception, which, with the help of the media, has substituted for a memory entwined in the intimacy of a collective heritage the ephemeral film of current events' (Nora 1989).

The concept of the culture industry originally employed by the Frankfurt School was used to critically engage with the consequences of the emergence of new technologies and industrial means of mass production affecting not only the mass reproduction of a work of art but also their impact on our understanding of culture in close connection with the rise of capitalism as the predominant economic organization of societies across the world. However, the term has evolved within a policy framework and moved away from its basis in critical theory, though it has not fully escaped from the contradictions inherent in the concept and the role played by the culture industries in modern society.

From a philosophical and sociological context the term culture industry moved on to the areas of economics and political economy until it officially entered the realm of law with the entry into force of the Canada and United States Free Trade Agreement

(CUSFTA), of which Article 2012 defines the cultural industry as comprising the sectors of books and magazines, films and video recordings, musical recordings as well as radio-communications and broadcasting. This shift from culture industry to cultural industry appears to have stripped it from its negative meaning associated with Horkheimer and Adorno's critique of the enlightenment as a means for the deception of the masses through the emergence of mass culture. Later the concept became gradually transformed into its plural form of cultural industries as enshrined in Article 2107 of the North American Free Trade Agreement (NAFTA). Also at the international level the plural use of cultural industries has strongly established itself during the last years as formalized in the adoption of the Convention on the Protection and Promotion of the Diversity of Cultural Expressions (CDCE) which was adopted on 20 October 2005, and entered into force on 18 March 2007 (Article 4 (4) and (5) CDCE).

Thus the meaning of the original concept of the culture industry can be characterized as providing the basis for a critical analysis of the emergence of a new means of mass production, the emergence of new media and their impact on the economic and political processes governing society. The by and large synonymous concepts of cultural industry and cultural industries mainly define a set of cultural goods and services which form the media and which are of a dual, cultural and economic nature.

Last but not least, it is their dual nature which also makes the cultural industries a *pars pro toto* for the so called 'global culture and trade debate' within the framework of the broader trade linkage debate, which focuses on the question of how to reconcile trade values, such as the continuous process of trade liberalization using the principles of non-discrimination, with so called non-trade or trade-related values, such as culture, environmental protection, national security or human rights. This quality entails also governance questions of how to organize the relationship between the global and the local level or, more generally, between multilateralism and regionalism. Hence, the culture and trade debate entails many questions, such as how to further liberalize trade, especially in services, while still protecting and promoting the cultural diversity of societies, or how to regulate cultural goods and services and whether to treat them like ordinary goods or give them different treatment (cultural specificity) or exempt them from trade regimes altogether under mechanisms such as the cultural exemption clause. In a wider sense the trade and culture problem can also be characterized as the most comprehensive 'trade and ... problem' because it points out the principal problem of a lack of policy coherence at the international level based on a deficient institutional framework and the resulting duplication or clash of policy objectives formulated by different international actors. One good example for such clash is found in the work done by the World Trade Organization (WTO) on the one side and the many specialized agencies of the United Nations on the other.

From a holistic viewpoint covering the past century, the concept of culture industries has undergone significant changes in an even more significant number of different contexts. Today it has become well established at the global level in many distinct areas including international law and policy discourses. The concept's variety of uses and its utility indicates a major quality which consists mainly in its elasticity and cohesive nature which is largely due to its inherent dual character encompassing two apparently antagonistic concepts, such as the two areas of culture and industry or as it is better known today as culture, on the one hand, and trade one the other. Historically, the respective areas of culture and trade have been generally perceived as belonging to two distinct spheres and standing in a mutual relationship characterized by clash and conflict rather than harmony or mutual synergy. As a final point, the culture industries can be said to stand for the responsibility to not only mutually approach the cultural and the economic qualities intrinsic to various cultural goods and services or to reconcile trade and culture but also to consider their various constituent subcategories as an integrated whole. In other words, the culture industries are a constant reminder for the need of a defiance of a solely fragmented sensory perception in favour of an integrated or so-called 'common sense.'

A Brief Chronology of Global 'Culture and Trade' Conflicts

The division of culture and of trade into distinct spheres also marks the evolution of the regulatory approaches adopted at international level. Hence, much in line with our fragmented perception and reflected in the fragmentation of the then existing international legal order, the first half of the twentieth century saw only rudimentary regulatory approaches to various sectors that we nowadays classify as being relevant for the cultural industries. Early important examples are the Paris Convention for the Protection of Industrial Property (1883) and the Berne Convention for the Protection of Literary and Artistic Works (1886) which are separate but yet linked by covering, on the one hand, the industrial and, on the other hand, the cultural (or artistic) aspects of property. Not only were cultural and industrial aspects perceived as belonging to distinct spheres; equally, the positive and negative, or constructive and destructive potential inherent in the new means of mass communication were regulated in distinct international legal instruments, namely the Convention for Facilitating the International Circulation of Films of an Educational Character (1933) and the International Convention Concerning the Use of Broadcasting in the Cause of Peace (1936). While the first builds upon the trust in the educational potential of the media, the second fears their abuse and the possible incitement of aggressive behaviour. As in the case of the Paris and Berne Conventions, again two closely related issues were regulated in separate instruments.

This trend persisted after World War II with the entry into force of the General Agreement of Tariffs and Trade (GATT), which as the economic regulatory pillar of global affairs was itself, unlike the planned International Trade Organisation (ITO) separated from its political sister organization, the United Nations Organization (UNO). In concrete terms, Article IV GATT exempted cinematograph films from the strict requirements of the non-discrimination principle or national treatment based on the persisting belief in the separation of cultural and trade policies. Again twenty years later, the legal question arose what the implications of international trade in television programmes were and, particularly, whether television programmes would, like cinematograph films, be covered by the provisions of trade in goods.[1] This controversy itself anticipated further conflicts, such the *Canada Periodicals* case,[2] that arose from the separate regulation of trade in goods and trade in services following the negotiation of the General Agreement on Trade in Services (GATS) during the Uruguay Round where the question arose as well and – in the form of the controversy over the so called '*exception culturelle*' almost blocked the successful establishment of the WTO. But these examples are not exhaustive and the regulatory fragmentation persists in the latest of the so called 'culture and trade conflicts', that is, the controversy surrounding the adoption of the UNESCO Convention on the Protection and Promotion of the Diversity of Cultural Expressions (2005), which again was established outside and without due consideration by the competent economic organization (Neuwirth 2006b).

From these selected examples we can see here that our fragmented senses lead to fragmented institutional and regulatory approaches, which may impede our 'judgment' and in turn perpetuate the *status quo* and due to a lack of imagination prevent new ideas from being formulated. However, from the many issues that can be linked to the culture industries, ranging from media violence, via concerns about cultural sovereignty or identity, media pluralism, national security, to complex issues related to the rapid changes in the technological environment, such as intellectual property rights, digitalization and competition law related questions, such as vertical integration and other possibly anti competitive business practices, we can see the increasing necessity for a more integrated and coherent regulatory approach. This need can be well exemplified in the evolution of the European legal order from its origins in the Rome Treaty until the Treaty Establishing a Constitution for Europe.

The Process of European Integration

The First Stage: 1958–1974

During the first stage of European integration, cultural concerns were widely absent from the process of European integration, which primarily focused on economic considerations. Thus most Community measures affecting the cultural industries were economic in nature. Moreover, no explicit reference to the concept could be found and the main activities related to it were indirect or fragmented in a sense that they were strictly limited to one of their constituent sectors, such as the film, book or music industry. Examples of a few preliminary important developments are first the interpretation established by the European Court of Justice (ECJ) according to which cultural goods came under the rules of the common market like any other category of so called ordinary goods.[3] This ruling, it can be argued, paved the way

---

1   See, for example, General Agreement to Tariffs and Trade (1962).

2   *Canada – Certain Measures Concerning Periodicals* (Complaint by the United States) (13 June 1997), WTO Doc. WT/DS31/AB/R (Appellate Body Report).

3   See *Commission of the European Communities* v. *Italian Republic* (7-68) [1968] ECR 617 at para. 2, which contains the following statement: 'By goods, within the meaning of Article 9 of the EEC Treaty, there must be understood products which can be valued in money

for the later recognition of the dual, that is, economic and cultural nature of the cultural industries. A second important development concerned the adoption of several legislative measures affecting sectors belonging to the cultural industries in the context of the free movement of individuals and the freedom to provide services.[4] More concretely, these were measures targeting the film sector, as one of the central sectors pertaining to the culture industries of that time. With regard to the freedom of establishment and to provide services, these measures mainly pursued the objective of removing numerous restrictions affecting the right to take up and pursue activities in the film sector across the common market.

Restated briefly, the first stage covering the two decades following the entry into force of the Treaty of Rome in 1957 featured neither a direct reference to culture nor an explicit mention of the cultural industries. It also bears no evidence of any intention to consider the wider cultural implications of economic integration. Obviously, it was felt that, in accordance with the institutional division of labour between the Council of Europe and the European Economic Community, there was no need for a common consideration of culture and trade, as the two principal constituents of the cultural industries.

The Second Stage: 1975–1991

The second stage largely continued the trend of the previous period since, in the absence of an explicit legal competence in the cultural field, any positive engagement in the legal or policy fields by policy makers in the cultural sector was rare. If an initiative was taken that influenced the sector, it was either based on the residual powers clause of Article 235 (now 308) EC, used for issues which could not be foreseen by the drafters of the EU Treaty, or relied on intergovernmental cooperation outside the Community framework.[5] Still positive cultural activities in a strict sense were pursued within the framework of the Council of Europe. The absence of legal provisions in the Treaty of Rome required some creativity on behalf of the European

---

and which are capable, as such, of forming the subject of commercial transactions. The rules of the common market apply to articles possessing artistic or historic value subject only to the exceptions provided by the Treaty'.

4   See Council Directive 63/607/EEC of 15 October 1963 implementing in respect of the film industry the provisions of the General Programme for the abolition of restrictions on freedom to provide services, [1963] OJ P159/2661, November 2, 1963; Second Council Directive 1965/264/EEC of 13 May 1965 implementing in respect of the film industry the provisions of the General Programmes for the abolition of restrictions on freedom of establishment and freedom to provide services, [1965] OJ P85/1437, May 19, 1965; Council Directive 1968/369/EEC of 15 October 1968 concerning the attainment of freedom of establishment in respect of activities of self-employed persons in film distribution, [1968] OJ L260/22, October 22, 1968; and Council Directive 1970/451/EEC of 29 September 1970 concerning the attainment of freedom of establishment and freedom to provide services in respect of activities of self-employed persons in film production, [1970] OJ L57/1, March 12, 1970.

5   See, for example, European Commission (1977a) at 19; and Art. 2 of the Convention Setting up a European University Institute (1976).

Community, which led to an interesting distinction between the concepts 'culture' and the 'cultural sector.' The latter concept, which can also be equated with the cultural industries, was defined in a Communication entitled Community Action in the Cultural Sector, as the 'socioeconomic whole formed by persons and undertakings dedicated to the production and distribution of cultural goods and services' (European Commission 1977a). This marks an important distinction because the concept of culture has proven to be too elastic, too diverse and too inclusive as to become the subject of a legal definition acceptable to all. Moreover, it acknowledges that 'culture' cannot be created at will but at its best emerges spontaneously if the required conditions depending on the respective temporal and geographic setting are in place. Lacking competence in the cultural field, the European Community hence focused its actions on the economic conditions facilitating the creation of artistic works and cultural goods and services.

Due to the progress in the field of economic integration, an initiative began for greater political integration as set forth as an objective in the founding Treaties and backed by the European Parliament's direct election in 1979, which as a supplementary and important element during this stage brought about the principal recognition of the cultural dimension of European integration.[6] Thus, following progress in the economic and political field, the necessity for action in the cultural field literally became 'stronger' (European Commission 1982).[7] Equally, it was also during this period the concept 'culture industry' was introduced for the first time into an official document of the Community (European Commission 1987).

Thus, during the second stage, the cultural dimension of European integration had *de facto* received substantive recognition. *De iure*, however, the cultural dimension was still absent from primary sources of European Community law and was still lacking formal legal recognition. This absence started to become a real problem given that the ECJ was confronted with an increasing number of cases involving sectors which belonged to the cultural industries. The respective case law included the music, book and the audiovisual industries as well as the television and film sectors.[8] The cases presented before the Court had in common the problematic dual, that is, cultural and economic, nature of these cultural goods and services. In view of the principle of conferred powers and given that the EU Treaty legally recognized only the economic dimension of European integration at the expense of the cultural one, the Court was restricted in its scope due to the absence of appropriate provisions to deal with the particular and, most of all, dual nature of these industries and therefore also lacked the impartiality and other required tools to do justice to the complexity of the underlying problems. As a matter of fact the Court has only

---

6   See, for example, European Parliament (1974) and European Parliament (1982).

7   See also European Commission (1984); European Commission (1985) and European Commission (1986).

8   See, for example, joined cases *Musik-Vertrieb Membran GmbH et K-tel International* v. *GEMA - Gesellschaft für musikalische Aufführungs- und mechanische Vervielfältigungsrechte* (55/80 and 57/80) [1981] ECR 147; *Commission of the European Communities* v. *French Republic* (90/79) [1981] ECR 283; *Bond van Adverteerders and others* v. *The Netherlands State* (352/85) [1988] ECR 2085; and *Federación de Distribuidores Cinematográficos* v. *Estado Español et Unión de Productores de Cine y Televisión* (C-17/92) [1993] ECR I-2239.

reluctantly entered into arguments of underlying cultural considerations raised by the parties in different disputes and usually emphasized only the economic merits of the cases.[9] In concrete terms, this meant that the Court's task was restricted by a lack of an explicit legal mandate in the cultural sphere which is why the Court could not always render judgments that would live up to the required standards of legal predictability and legal certainty for the member states' governments to adopt the regulatory instruments implementing their respective cultural policies. This, however, appeared to be justifiable in light of the ongoing process of negative integration and need for the strengthening of the common market.

Nonetheless, as time passed and the common market gradually took shape the need for measures for positive integration grew as a result of the gradual vacuum created by the removal of barriers on the one hand and the parallel challenges created by the far reaching technical advances which moved cultural considerations closer into the sphere of economic integration on the other. Consequently, the cultural sector received greater attention and support from all the main institutions of the Community (European Parliament 1982). The active role by the EC and European Parliament in the cultural sphere in adopting several communications or reports in the cultural field was equally matched by the European Council by, for instance, adopting the Solemn Declaration in 1983, which explicitly called for 'closer cooperation in cultural matters.'[10] With such broad institutional consensus, it was only a matter of time until the cultural dimension of European integration would also receive formal legal recognition in sources of primary law, which eventually happened with the adoption of the Treaty of Maastricht in 1992.

The Third Stage: 1992–2005

The third stage, it is argued, began with the adoption of the Treaty of Maastricht, which by virtue of Articles 3 (1) lit. p [now q] and 128 [now 151] EC introduced a legal provision and other explicit references to cultural concerns as well as the Declaration on the Ratification of the Treaty Establishing a Constitution for Europe adopted in June 2005 following the negative referenda in France and the Netherlands (European Council 2005). The Declaration marks the turning point for the third stage, because it can be taken to represent the creation of an initiative towards a constitutional answer to the process of European integration. Before the constitutional issue developed, however, the third stage brought about not only the legal recognition of the cultural dimension in the context of the primary law governing European integration but also the insight that culture and trade, as the two main constituents of the cultural industries, could indeed not be separated (Fechner 1999). It is also interesting to highlight two particular features that underlie the way that the article on culture was drafted: firstly, Article 151 EC Treaty does not define culture, and secondly, it

---

9   See, for example, *Giuseppe Sacchi* (155-73) [1973] ECR 409 at para. 13; *Commission of the European Communities* v. *French Republic* (269/83) [1984] ECR 843 at paras. 8–9; and *Bond van Adverteerders and others* v. *The Netherlands State* (352/85) [1988] ECR 2085 at paras. 35 and 39.

10   Solemn Declaration on European Union, EC Bulletin 6-1983 at 24–29.

entrusts the Community with the apparently contradictory task to 'contribute to the flowering of the cultures of the Member States, while respecting their national and regional diversity and at the same time bringing the common cultural heritage to the fore'.

As the core of Article 151 EC Treaty, paragraph 4 contains the so called 'integration clause', which stipulates that Community institutions are obliged to 'take cultural aspects into account in its action under other provisions of this Treaty'. Furthering the integration clause, Article 87(3) lit. d. TEC declares, provided that certain conditions are met, compatible with the common market state aid regimes are acceptable in the terms of the EU Treaty to promote culture and heritage conservation. Similarly and deviating from the general rule of qualified majority voting in matters of common commercial policy, Article 133(6) EC Treaty requires the common accord of member states for the conclusion of international trade agreements if they relate *inter alia* to cultural and audiovisual services.

With regard to the integration of culture into other areas covered by the EU Treaty, even after a repeated reading, it is not entirely clear how the Community may successfully live up to this difficult task, especially in view of the strict exclusion of any harmonization of the laws and regulations in the cultural field as laid down in paragraph 5. A more holistic interpretation following the general rule of interpretation as laid down in Article 31(1) of the Vienna Convention on the Law of Treaties, according to which 'a treaty shall be interpreted in good faith in accordance with the ordinary meaning to be given to the terms of the treaty in their context and in the light of its object and purpose' alters the situation and the apparent contradiction vanishes in favour of a broader understanding of the duality. This duality prevents us from realizing that it is only in a common economic framework where individuality and the cultural diversity of our identities can flourish. In accordance with such broader understanding, the second important feature is that, by virtue of paragraph 4, Article 151 EC Treaty was formulated in by and large in a positive way, being designed as an integration clause instead of a cultural exception, as was opted for in the case of the NAFTA or as it was discussed at the same time in the dispute over the *exception culturelle* towards the end of the Uruguay Round establishing the WTO. The only remaining negative aspect is found in the explicit exclusion of any harmonization of the laws and regulations of the member states for that matter.

In view of today's growing complexity, a positive drafting style must be given preference over a negatively formulated exception because it theoretically gives rise to greater coherence in policy making since the Community institutions are required to consider cultural aspects in any other Community action. This means in principle that cultural aspects must not only receive due attention in the core economic areas enshrined in the EU Treaty but also in the context of other areas, such as education and the environment. In this context, the impossibility to harmonize the laws and the regulations of the member states, which was originally designed as a safeguard to growing fears of an intrusion of Community competences in the member states, however, may prove to be counterproductive in the long run.

This potential for greater coherence, however, was largely theoretical. Following the Maastricht Treaty, the Court continued to struggle in reconciling the forces behind the subtle tensions between culture and trade inherent in the cultural industries, which often make their appearance in the form of conflict situations between various cultural policy objectives and the provisions of the four freedoms guaranteeing the functioning of the internal market. For instance, in the *Free Record Shop* case, a case involving a book price fixing arrangement in the Netherlands, no mention of cultural considerations or a reference to the new Article on culture (Article 128) was made.[11] This is interesting since only three years later, the Court ruled in the *Echirolles* case that the application of national legislation requiring publishers to impose on booksellers fixed prices for the resale of books is not precluded by the Treaty.[12] Although the Court explicitly recognized the integration clause of Article 128(4) EU Treaty, its main concern was still with the potential negative effect of reinforcing the compartmentalization of markets on a national basis. Most of all, the Court erred in stating that Article 128(4) gives a 'definition of culture that is oriented primarily towards artistic and literary creation'.

A more positive sign from the Court came in the application of the cultural consideration clause in the context of a series of connected cases on state aid (Article 92(3) [now Article 87(3)] EU Treaty when the Court declared a French state subsidising the export of French books, the principal objective of which was to further 'the promotion of French culture throughout the world', as compatible with the common market.[13] Equally positive was a sign of the Court in the field of the audiovisual sector when the Court, by reference to former case law, expressly acknowledged that a 'cultural policy aimed at safeguarding the freedom of expression of the various components of a state, in particular those of a social, cultural, religious or philosophical nature, with a view to the exercise of that freedom in the press, on the radio or on television, may constitute an overriding requirement relating to the general interest which justifies a restriction on the freedom to provide services guaranteed by Article 59 of the EU Treaty'.[14] This case underscores the importance of competition rules for tackling of a great variety of cultural diversity problems, such as the risk of a decrease in the diversity of cultural content not only in book printing but also in the audiovisual media due to the potential dangers of anticompetitive practices or other negative effects linked to the growing concentration through vertical and/or horizontal integration in the industry.

During this period the Court, in spite of greater sensitivity to cultural issues, still failed to consider more closely cultural considerations connected to the economic specificities and peculiar dynamics of the cultural industries, in particular concerning their economics of production and distribution in light of their public goods

---

11   *Koninklijke Vereeniging ter Bevordering van de Belangen des Boekhandels* v. *Free Record Shop BV and Free Record Shop Holding NV* (C-39/96) [1997] ECR I-2303.

12   *Echirolles Distribution SA* v. *Association du Dauphiné and Others* (C-9/99) [2000] ECR I-8207.

13   *Société internationale de diffusion and d'édition (SIDE)* v. *Commission of the European Communities* (T-155/98) [2002] ECR II-1179; *French Republic* v. *Commission of the European Communities* (C-332/98) [2000] E.C.R. I-4833; and *Société Internationale de Diffusion et d'Edition (SIDE)* v. *Commission of the European Communities* (T-49/93) [1995] ECR II-2501.

14   *Commission of the European Communities* v. *Kingdom of Belgium* (C-11/95) [1996] ECR I-4115 at para. 55.

character and inherent cultural content. In the Court's defence there are arguments in favour of its role in maintaining stability and continuity in its case law especially during a time of repeated amendments to the EU Treaty provisions as well as the transition from the common to the internal market. Equally, it shows that the Court is only partially responsible since it is the member states' legislation and ancillary Community legislation which is also agreed in the co-decision process by member states' representatives that does not allow for broader and deeper consideration to be decided before the Court. Moreover, the member states' frameworks for cultural policy objectives is frequently organized in terms of national boundaries, which in economic terms poses the danger of the erosion of the objectives of the internal market or, indeed, the potential abuse of cultural policies for protectionist goals. In this light, again paragraph 5 of Article 151 EC Treaty must be regarded as problematic since the adoption of supranational legislation must not automatically lead to a threat to the diversity of national and regional cultures. Sometimes, an equal set of universal regulatory standards only creates the basis for different entities being different, such as the international principle of equality of states attributes – at least *de iure* – to small and big states the same number of votes. In the case to the contrary, the recent UNESCO Convention would mean a contradiction in terms. Any prohibition of harmonization as exemplified in paragraph 5 is also problematic in view of the preparation, coordination and cooperation in international fora as stipulated by paragraph 3, such as the practice in the context of the negotiations for the said UNECO Convention has shown.

The Court's relatively modest use of the Treaty provision on culture must also be seen in the context of the other institutions. The EC, as was shown, already put greater emphasis on the cultural dimension of Community action. The Council too has showed greater interest in culture and adopted several documents in line with the newly added provision on culture. For instance, it considered the implications of culture for the four freedoms,[15] the impact of state aid on the audiovisual industry and the problem of book price fixing systems.[16] In its cultural affairs capacity, the Council has also become increasingly aware of the close connections between culture and economics (European Council 1995). The Council also formulated ideas for better integrating cultural aspects into Community actions.[17] Other aspects of culture were discussed in the context of the emerging information society and of improving cooperation in the field of culture.[18]

Last but not least, the European Parliament has once more confirmed its past innovative role as an advocate and leading voice in the field of culture. On numerous occasions, it has raised awareness about a range of cultural issues, which hitherto

---

15   See European Council (2000) and European Council (2003).

16   European Council (2001a); Council Decision of 22 September 1997 on cross-border fixed book prices in European linguistic areas, [1997] OJ C305/2, October 7, 1997; European Council (1999); and European Council (2001b).

17   European Council (1997); Council Decision of 22 September 1997 regarding the future of European cultural action, [1997] OJ C305/1, October 7, 1997; and European Council (2003).

18   European Council (2002a); European Council (2002b); and European Council (2002c).

have not received satisfactory attention.[19] Most importantly, the European Parliament has confirmed its competence in the ongoing and complex process of convergence between the various media sectors especially in view of the rapid rise of digital technology. This acknowledgment might explain the preference of the concept of cultural industries over an individual sector specific approach, which in view of convergence appears not only justified but necessary. In this context, the most relevant action in the field of the cultural industries was the European Parliament's Resolution on Cultural Industries (European Parliament 2004a). This resolution mentions numerous issues which are directly related to the cultural industries, such as cultural identity, cultural diversity, a right to culture for all citizens and the safeguarding of democratic access to cultural products (Neuwirth 2004). The Resolution's non-exhaustive list of issues related to the cultural industries underscores the fact that there is practically no regulatory area which is not directly or indirectly affected by the cultural industries.

In sum, beginning with the adoption of the Maastricht Treaty in 1992, the third stage not only formally introduced the concept of culture into the primary sources of Community Law but also saw a constant rise in references to cultural aspects as well as an explicit recognition of the concept of cultural industries. Still the member states and the Community institutions often not only lack a good understanding of the underlying problems but also their interplay under the EU's framework which appears to lack a sufficient degree of coherence for a successful response to the complexity of the cultural industries' sectors and their intrinsic and subtle tensions between their economic and cultural characteristics.

The Culture Industries and the Quest for a Constitution for Europe

At length, the concept of culture industries, as understood in this chapter, denominates first and foremost a philosophical impulse for pondering on a new mode of perception of life and the world we live in. As such it bears the potential to function as a mirror reflecting our current state of being in the view of past developments and their potential for the realization of future aspirations.

From this comprehensive understanding of the concept of culture industries derives a great many regulatory challenges of which the complexity can only be fully tackled by way of a 'constitutional' approach, not only in Europe but also in a global context (Howse and Nicolaidis 2003). In a seemingly paradoxical process, this means that we must first ensure the correct legal treatment of the cultural industries as a source for the shaping of public opinion before a common sense can emerge on the basis of which a constitutional framework can be designed and implemented. This wisdom was already addressed in a European Parliament resolution more than twenty years ago, which stated that: 'adequate and expert information is essential to the development of *a sense of common responsibility and willingness* to take joint political action' (European Parliament 1982). Only with a constitution, as the primary or *Grundnorm* from which all secondary norms derive to form an order, the

---

19   See, for example, European Parliament (2004b) and European Parliament (2004c).

cultural industry's complex role and characteristics can receive adequate legal and regulatory treatment.

This challenge entails the safeguarding of the diversity of content and opinion (media pluralism) countering the negative implications of the latent trend of the cultural industries to vertically and horizontally integrate in order to minimize the inherent risks while maximizing profits. It also, however, entails a close surveillance of possible dangers inherent in the media, capable of distorting reports about the reality we are really exposed to. Also in a wider sense we must further enhance regulation as well as – where applicable – the deregulation of this category of cultural goods and services of which the principal characteristic is not only their dual, that is, economic and cultural nature but also their role as a dynamic industry (Lampel et al. 2000).

Further elements of this problematic include greater coherence between not only economic and cultural aspects of the cultural industries, but also flanking policies such as education as the *conditio sine qua non* for the safeguarding of public interest values. In total, it is greater policy coherence in combination with more long-term considerations and planning that is needed which already indicates the point where the thin line between the cultural industries and culture industries is encroached. The balance between the two poles is the difference between a regulatory state of an international treaty and a constitution.

Only the latter can actually constitute an order and, most of all, is capable of guaranteeing the inclusion of a wider set of conflicting information, whether expressed in views or interests. Only at the constitutional level, the fragmented perception of our environment can legally be resolved and integrated into a more holistic system. A constitution, providing the framework for the entirety of the institutions governing our multilevel societies is the only place where divergent concepts and views can be successfully reconciled. This applies to culture and trade as the two principal constituents of not only the cultural industries but also of human life which is constantly torn apart between the striving for *otium* (leisure) and *negotium* (work), or spiritual and material well being. Equally, a constitution is not only 'made for people of fundamentally differing views'[20] but is also supposed to be drafted by people of fundamentally differing views.

Seen through the prism of the culture industries, a more integrated and coherent approach also points out certain obvious failures in the present Treaty Establishing a Constitution for Europe. Among these flaws is first of all the voluntary withdrawal clause enshrined in Article I-60 CT. This clause clearly contradicts the letter of the law of the existing treaties which (with the exception of the Treaty Establishing the European Coal and Steel Community) were concluded for an infinite time. The clause also not only stands in stark contrast to the spirit of the founding treaties of the EU as laid down in their various Preambles[21] but also negates, first, the geopolitical fact of a limited space on the European continent.

---

20 *Roe et al.* v. *Wade* 410 U.S. 113 (1973).

21 See, for example, 'RESOLVED [...] to lay the foundations for institutions which will give direction to a destiny henceforward shared'; Preamble of the Treaty Establishing the European Coal and Steel Community (ECSC); 'DETERMINED to lay the foundations of

Moreover, a more constructive approach to the question of the sharing of powers in the EU in combination with the understanding of European integration as an ongoing process also requires a new interpretation of the principle of subsidiarity (Article I-11 (1) CT) as well as of the numerous clauses which exclude 'any harmonization of the laws and regulations of the Member States'. The principle of subsidiarity needs to be understood not as a unilinear principle reserving all areas which do not fall within the exclusive competence for the competence of the member states. In times where the only constant appears to be change itself, such clear cut distinctions have to be avoided. It is thus possible that an area which has once fallen within the exclusive competence of the Community to be referred back to the member states level.[22] Equally, certain issues, which are barred from any harmonization, may at times become necessary to be regulated at the Community level.[23] In this question, the residual powers clause of Article 308 EC Treaty or so called 'flexibility clause' of Article I-18 CT should not be prevented from being invoked. Equally, such a new understanding should be applied to the reform of the institutions of the EU, where in particular a broader perspective is required which will help to reinstall the institutional balance. In sum, it is advocated that the perception and reform of the EU as a complex entity requires a constitutional reform which simultaneously takes into account its constituent parts and the system as a whole.

Conclusion

Irrevocably, the culture industries underscore the need to focus and adapt our world view to the drastic changes that have taken place and that are currently underway at breakneck speed. In this task, the culture industries mark a persuasive concept in two ways. First, the culture industries include the vast repertory of experiences gained since the coining of the original concept 'culture industry' until its gradual transformation into 'cultural industries', as a legally recognized special category of cultural goods and services. This repertory of experiences as well as the present tendencies for these special categories of goods and services to converge allows for the speculation of their long-term future. This leads to the second feature of the culture industries, which applied to the legal realm especially in the European context, means that such an integrated mode of perception is best realized in the

---

an ever closer union among the peoples of Europe'; Preamble of the Treaty Establishing the European Community (EC Treaty); 'RECALLING the historic importance of the ending of the division of the European continent and the need to create firm bases for the construction of the future Europe'; 'Resolved to continue the process of creating an ever closer union among the peoples of Europe [...]'; Preamble and Art. 1 of the Treaty on European Union (EU Treaty).

22   Council Regulation (EC) No 1/2003 of December 2002 on the implementation of the rules on competition laid down in Articles 81 and 82 of the Treaty [2003] OJ L1, 4 January 2003.

23   Such considerations occurred in Austria in the aftermath of the judgment of the ECJ of July 7, 2005, concerning the conditions of access to university education: *Commission of the European Communities* v. *Republic of Austria* (147/03) [2005] ECR I-5969.

form of a constitutional approach to the reform of the European legal order and the governance of European affairs. Only a constitutional approach is in the position of coping with the complexity of today's social and economic structures through greater coherence and consistence in policy-making. In accordance with the culture industries' intrinsic quality of contradiction, a constitutional approach stands for a more holistic understanding of reality and the reconciliation of fundamental but only apparently antagonistic phenomena and concepts, such as culture and trade. In other words, only a constitutional approach ensures that all relevant and pertinent facts are collected and balanced against each other and is capable of bringing their potential complementarity to the fore.

In very brief terms, the culture industries first provide a powerful and ever more relevant critique of the media and residual categories of the cultural industries as the sources of our senses experienced as individuals being part of one or more collective polities. Second, they also indicate the gradual emergence of a novel, that is, so-called 'common sense' which can bring about a new mode of perception which, in turn, is capable of instituting new sources of imagination which subsequently may alter drastically our understanding and organization of our reality. This is exemplified by the beginning of European integration by way of the formulation of the objective of creating a common market in Europe which has – through the establishment of a common economic framework – allowed not only the creation of greater prosperity and security in Europe but also the diversity of our cultures and identities to be brought to the fore. Fifty years after the formation of the EU a constitutional debate in Europe invites us to seriously think about the realization of a 'common sense' in Europe, which may not only redefine our understanding of the foundations of our coexistence on the continent but also give greater sense or meaning to our life in an ever more complex and rapidly changing globalized world.

References

Adorno, T.W. (1991), *The Culture Industry*. London: Routledge.

Canada-United States Free-Trade Agreement, Ottawa, 22 December 1987 and 2 January 1988, and at Washington, DC and Palm Springs, 23 December 1987 and 2 January 1988. (1988) 27 ILM 281.

Convention on the Protection and Promotion of the Diversity of Cultural Expressions, adopted in Paris on 20 October 2005; available online at http://unesdoc.unesco. org/images/0014/001429/142919e.pdf, accessed 20 February 2007.

Convention setting up a European University Institute, [1976] OJ C29/1, 9 February 1976.

European Commission (1977a), Commission Communication to the Council, Community action in the cultural sector, EC Bulletin Supp. 6/77 at 5, pt. 3.

European Commission (1977b), Commission Report on the Establishment of a European Foundation, EC Bulletin Supp. 5/77 at 19.

European Commission (1982), Communication from the Commission to the Council and Parliament, *Stronger Community action in the cultural sector*, EC Bulletin

Supp. 6/82.

European Commission (1984), Communication de la Commission au Conseil, *Télévision sans frontières – livre vert sur l'établissement du marché commun de la radiodiffusion, notamment par satellite et par câble*, COM(84) 300 final, 14 June 1984.

European Commission (1985), *Communication de la Commission au Conseil sur l'action dans le domaine du livre*, COM(85) 681 final, 27 November 1985.

European Commission (1986), Communication by the Commission to the Council, *Action programme for the European audio-visual media products industry*, COM(86) 255 final, 12 May 1986.

European Commission (1987), Notes de réflexion de la Commission, *A fresh boost for culture in the European Community*, COM(87), 603 final, 14 December 1987.

European Council (1995), Council Resolution of 20 November 1995 on the promotion of statistics on culture and economic growth, [1995] OJ C327/1, 7 December 1995.

European Council (1997), Council Resolution of 20 January 1997 on the integration of cultural aspects into Community actions (97/C 36/04), [1997] OJ C36/4, 5 February 1997.

European Council (1999), Council Resolution of 8 February 1999 on fixed book prices in homogeneous cross-border linguistic areas, [1999] OJ C/42/3, 19 February 1999.

European Council (2000), Council Resolution of 19 December 2002 implementing the work plan on European cooperation in the field of culture: European added value and mobility of persons and circulation of works in the cultural sector, [2003] OJ C13/3, 18 January 2003.

European Council (2001a), Council Resolution of 12 February 2001 on national aid to the film and audiovisual industries, [2001] OJ C73/2, 6 March 2001.

European Council (2001b), Council Resolution of 12 February 2001 on the application of national fixed book-price systems, [2001] OJ C73/3, 6 March 2001.

European Council (2001c), Council Resolution of 17 December 1999 on the promotion of the free movement of persons working in the cultural sector, [2000] OJ C8/2, 12 January 2000.

European Council (2002a), Council Resolution of 21 January 2002 on culture and the knowledge society, [2002] OJ C32/1, 5 February 2002.

European Council (2002b), Council Resolution of 21 January 2002 on the role of culture in the development of the European Union, [2002] OJ C32/2, 5 February 2002.

European Council (2002c), Council Resolution of 5 June 2002 on a new work plan on European cooperation in the field of culture, [2002] OJ C162/3, 6 July 2002.

European Council (2003), Council Resolution of 26 May 2003 on the horizontal aspects of culture: increasing synergies with other sectors and Community actions and exchanging good practices in relation to the social and economic dimensions of culture, [2003] OJ C136/1, 11 June 2003.

European Council (2005), Declaration by the Heads of State or Government of the Member States of the European Union on the Ratification of the Treaty

Establishing a Constitution for Europe (European Council, 16 and 17 June 2005), SN 117/05, Brussels, 18 June 2005.

European Parliament (1974), European Parliament Resolution on the motion for a resolution submitted of the Liberal and Allies Group on measures to protect the European cultural heritage, [1974] OJ C62/5, 30 May 1974.

European Parliament (1982), European Parliament Resolution on radio and television broadcasting in the European Community, [1982] OJ C87/110, 5 April 1982.

European Parliament (2004a), European Parliament Resolution on Cultural Industries, [2004] OJ C76/459, 4 September 2003.

European Parliament (2004b), European Parliament resolution on the General Agreement on Trade in Services (GATS) within the WTO, including cultural diversity, [2004] OJ C61/289, 12 March 2003.

European Parliament (2004c), European Parliament Resolution on a Community Framework for Collective Management Societies in the Field of Copyright and Neighbouring Rights, [2004] OJ C92/425, 15 January 2004.

European Union. Treaty of European Union; available online at http://europa.eu.int/eur-lex/lex/en/treaties/index.htm, accessed 30 July 2006.

Fechner, F. (1999), 'Titel IX (=Titel XII neu) Kultur', Groeben, H and J. Thiesing and C.-D. Ehlermann, (eds), *Kommentar zum EU-/EG-Vertrag*, vol. 3, 5th ed. Baden-Baden: Nomos.

General Agreement to Tariffs and Trade (1962), Application of GATT to International Trade in Television Programmes – Report of the Working Party, L/1741 of 13 March 1962.

Howse, R. and Nicolaidis, K. (2003), 'Enhancing WTO Legitimacy: Constitutionalization or Global Subsidiarity?', *Governance* 16:73, 73–91.

Lampel, J. et al. (2000), 'Balancing Act: Learning from Organizing Practices in Cultural Industries', 11 *Organization Science* 263, 263–4.

Neuwirth, R.J. (2004), 'Culture and Trade? A European Way 'Towards an 'International Instrument on Cultural Diversity', (2004) *Italian Yearbook of International Law* 97(13), 119–121.

Neuwirth, R.J. (2006a), *The Cultural Industries in International Trade: Insights from the NAFTA, the WTO and the EU*. Hamburg, Dr. Kovač.

Neuwirth, R.J. (2006b), 'United in Divergency: A Commentary on the UNESCO Convention on the Protection and Promotion of the Diversity of Cultural Expressions', *Zeitschrift für ausländisches öffentliches Recht und Völkerrecht (ZaöRV)/Heidelberg Journal of International Law (HJIL)* 66, 819, 830, 861.

Nora, P. (1989), 'Between Memory and History: Les liuex de Mémoire'. *Representations* 26(7), 7–8.

North American Free Trade Agreement between the Government of Canada, the Government of Mexico and the Government of the United States, 17 December 1992, (1993) 32 ILM 605.

Solemn Declaration on European Union, EC Bulletin 6-1983.

Index

Tables are indicated by italic page numbers.